European Casebook on

Managing Industrial and Business-to-Business Marketing

The European Casebook Series on Management

Series Editor: Paul Stonham, EAP European School of Management, Oxford.

Competing Through Services: Strategy and Implementation, Vandermerwe / Lovelock with Taishoff, IMD

European Casebook on Business Ethics, Harvey / Van Luijk / Steinmann

European Casebook on Business Transactions and Human Resource Management, Hiltrop / Sparrow

European Casebook on Competing through Information Technology, Jelassi

European Casebook on Cooperative Strategies, Roos

European Casebook on Finance, Redhead / Stonham

European Casebook on Managing Industrial and Business-to-Business Marketing, Jenster, IMD

European Casebook on

Managing Industrial and Business-to-Business Marketing

Edited by

Per V. Jenster

Prentice Hall

New York   London   Toronto   Sydney   Tokyo   Singapore

First published 1994 by
Prentice Hall International (UK) Limited
Campus 400, Maylands Avenue
Hemel Hempstead
Hertfordshire, HP2 7EZ
A division of
Simon & Schuster International Group

IMD cases reprinted with kind permission of IMD International

Typeset in 10½/12pt Palatino and 11/13pt Times
by Hands Fotoset, Leicester

Printed and bound in Great Britain by
Redwood Books Ltd, Trowbridge, Wiltshire

Library of Congress Cataloging-in-Publication Data

LOC data is available from the publisher

British Library Cataloguing in Publication Data

A catalogue record for this book is available from
The British Library

ISBN 0-13-097148-0

1 2 3 4 5   98 97 96 95 94

Contents

Series Editorial

The idea of a series of European Case Books on Management arose from discussions during the annual case writing competition organized by the European Foundation for Management (EFMD) in Brussels. The case writing competition itself was set up to encourage the production of more case studies in management with a specifically European content, to meet the growing demand in European business schools and training programmes of corporations.

However, knowing that many European cases were being produced outside the context of the competition, it was decided to extend the search for cases more widely. The project was taken up by Prentice Hall International in 1991, who undertook to publish the series, and appointed a Series Editor to manage the academic aspects of the collection of volumes.

From the start-up of the project, the EAP European School of Management, a grande école of the Paris Chamber of Commerce and Industry, agreed to finance the costs of the Series Editor, and Prentice Hall International funded secretarial assistance. As well as its financial support, EAP is well positioned to supply an appropriate academic infrastructure to the editorial management of the series. From its headquarters in Paris, it maintains establishments in Berlin, Madrid and Oxford, and its masters' level students train in three countries. EAP is one of the leaders in European multicultural management education and, of course, a major user of case studies with a European focus in its courses.

Early market research showed a strong and largely unsatisfied demand for case studies in European management, at a time when interest in the completion of the Single European Market was at its height. Calls for case study writers and for volume editors met a good response, and the major fields of management were quickly covered as well as several important specialized areas not originally conceived of.

At the time of writing, 17 volumes of European case studies on management are either in production, in the process of being written, or being negotiated. These are: Accounting, Business Alliances, Business Ethics, Competing through Services, Co-operative Strategies, Entrepreneurship and New Ventures, Environmental Issues, Family Businesses, Finance, Human Resource Management, Industrial and Business-to-Business Management, Industrial Policy, Information Technology, International Business, International Market Entry and Development, Management in Eastern Europe, Organizational Behaviour, Production and Operations Management, Research and Technology Management, including, of course, the present volume.

The case studies are intended to draw on the main developments and changes in their respective fields of management in recent years, focusing on managerial issues in corporations trading in or with the European Union. Although the principal concentration is on the non-governmental sector, the experience of governments and governmental agencies is included in some of the volumes to the extent that they affect the corporate sector. In the light of the title of the series, cases dealing with European cross-border involvements have been given priority in inclusion, but material that relates to national experience or is conceptual or global in nature has been considered relevant if it satisfies the criteria for good cases.

A driving motive for developing the Series of European Case Books on Management has been the wish to encourage the production of cases with a specifically European dimension. Not only have the regulatory background, institutional framework and behavioural traits of cases developed in the American business schools like Harvard always been barriers to their use in European management education, but the developing European Union has emphasized aspects of corporate development and strategy completely ignored in most American cases. With the build-up of cross-border business activity in Europe has come difficulties in cultural adjustment. The growing legislation of the European Commission in its '1992 programme' has imposed constraints and given freedoms not known in an American context, in such fields as technology, patents, competition, take-overs and mergers, freedom of establishment and workers' rights. There was clearly a need for case studies which took account of the rapid changes occurring in the European Union and which analyzed corporations' responses to them. It is recognized in the kind of terminology which is now much more current in management thinking: 'European management', 'Euromanagers' and 'Pan-Europeanization' no longer raise eyebrows even if not everyone believes these are totally valid terms.

In selecting cases for their volumes, the editors and the Series Editor asked the leading question again and again – what is a good case? It was not sufficient to take the accepted Harvard view. Cases are critically important to teaching at the Harvard Business School and have been since they were first produced in 1910. For example, it was said that 'One must understand the fundamentals of course design, because each case must fit into the rubric of the course' (Benson Shapiro, 1986). Shapiro also said the case-writer should 'Ensure the case includes a balanced conflict'. Robert Davies, also of Harvard, wrote (1955) that 'There are two kinds of cases . . . the *issue case* in which the writer poses a particular problem and the reader prepares a recommendation designed to overcome the problem, and an *appraisal case* in which the writer describes a management decision already made and the reader evaluates this decision'. Generally, cases now being written in Europe are less rigid and constrained. They reflect the multifunctional and multicultural aspects of modern European business. They are pedagogical, but less tied to functional disciplines than the Harvard cases described by Shapiro, and this again is probably because the boundaries of the functional disciplines themselves, like marketing and finance, are becoming less distinct. Many of the 'good' points of Harvard case study teaching are nonetheless incorporated into European case writing: the emphasis on complex, real-life situations, the degree of interest aroused, the use of 'springboard cases', and the need for good reporting (Paul Lawrence, 1953).

The essentials of 'good' case writing in European management have been discussed extensively by the judges of the annual case writing competition organized by EFMD. They can be summarized as follows from the main points of a presentation by Robert Collins of IMD Lausanne at the annual conference workshop and prize-giving in Jouy-en-Josas, Paris, in September 1993.

Although writing case studies in management involves an element of opportunistic, investigative journalism, the pedagogical needs of students should be paramount. The case-writer should be objective; there is no place for personal opinion or advocacy – the case-writer or teacher is neither judge nor jury.

As far as the audience for cases is concerned, the case must be interesting. The setting or topic should be attractive and the case raise compelling issues. A decision-forcing case is more likely to turn students on that a descriptive or expository one – but the snag is that students do not generally like open-ended and vague cases. The case should be transferable – across faculty members, programmes and institutions.

In terms of product quality, the case should exceed audience expectations in terms of both performance and conformance. The length of a case is important – it should give optimal time for reading, for analysis, and the quality and quantity of data should be right. Assimilation is made easier when the case focuses on characters or issues, is structured, has internally consistent data, avoids jargon and is written in high-quality prose. It should be remembered that inexperienced students have a low tolerance of ambiguity and of data/information.

Writing a good case involves creating a favourable climate among all the stakeholders in a company. They will not assist if there is not confidence, discretion and co-operation. In a company there are archetypal executives who must all be managed, for example, the 'champion' may steer the case-writer through the company (but only when he is on hand); the 'guerilla' will appear to help, but snipe from out of sight; the 'security guard' will consider everything classified and not for discussion. The reality for a case-writer on site in a company is that not everyone will love you.

The teacher can maximize the benefits of a good case. Opportunities for customization and experimentation should always be sought – among different sets of participants, programmes and in-team teaching. A good teacher can exploit the richness of a case and the acuity of the participants.

Clearly, the case method is not the only pedagogical method of teaching management. Charles Croué of the Ecole Supérieure de Commerce de Tours believes it is the most revolutionary, because unlike teacher-centred or self-tutoring methods, it is an active and interactive method.

The method encourages students to organize their work, to exchange different points of view in complex discussions, to find compromise by negotiating, and to improve their skills at oral presentation. They learn to compare different solutions and to synthesize information and decisions. They can observe the relationships between different disciplines of management – like marketing and strategy, and understand the difference between theory and practice. In the case-study method they do all this in a situation of reality, solving a real management problem. All of these skills prepare students well for manager status.

The case method has three main distinguishing characteristics which set it aside from other teaching methods. It is *co-operative* – students work in groups, they exchange information, and it improves their communicative abilities. It is *dynamic* – students are stimulated from passivity to effort. And it is *democratic* – teachers and students have equal roles; there are no preset solutions, and ideas are freely exchanged.

Finally, the case method is well suited to the changing nature of management and business at the present time. The current environment is moving very quickly, case studies can 'catch' new events and issues as they happen (likewise, they may quickly date). They lend themselves well to performance measurement, as the managerial qualities of the students improve. The current wish for 'action-learning' is satisfied, and cases can be delivered using multiple media like videos and computers.

The present volume, by Per Jenster, is composed mainly of cases written by faculty at the International Institute for Management Development (IMD International) Lausanne, Switzerland. IMD is uniquely placed to generate case studies in European management; it is also strongly committed to do so.

IMD is at the centre of Europe. It was founded in 1989 with the merger of IMEDE in Lausanne and IMI in Geneva, both long-standing management training institutes. IMD's approach to executive development rests nowadays on four characteristics which it implements vigorously; internationality – executive development classes have participants from many countries; practical implementation – organizational learning is favoured over individual learning; a strong partnership with industry – more than 115 leading companies co-operate with IMD in programme design and research; and a flexible programme structure. Clearly, this environment, resource base, and focused direction is a favourable background to the generation of European-dimension case studies which are based firmly on co-operative research with industry and used extensively in IMD's executive programmes. IMD's success rate in the annual case-writing competition is only one indicator of the quality of the cases it produces.

This volume, *European Casebook on Managing Industrial and Business-to-Business Marketing*, is edited by Per Jenster of IMD International, Lausanne, and is the second volume in the European Case Book Series. As with volume one, all the cases are written by IMD faculty or faculty having close connections with IMD, and reflect the commitment and high quality of case writing at that institution.

Managing Industrial and Business-to-Business Marketing has assembled 22 cases on a topic that is appearing more and more in the management literature and has become an important element in the minds of corporate strategists. As businesses become more and more interlinked and competitive, industrial marketing, product management, pricing, promotion, distribution and marketing planning have become significant items in competitive advantage. Per Jenster has written and collected cases which analyze all the major aspects of industrial marketing across Europe from East to West. As well as organizing the cases into groups corresponding with these major aspects, he lists key issues and relevant topics to discuss in each group. This places the cases in their appropriate academic context, and also allows students to widen their discussion based on the cases. It is also interesting that Jenster has concluded his volume with cases which illuminate topics/issues in industrial marketing, like alliances and strategic customer relationships and technology licensing. The field is fast-moving and it is a mark of the achievement of this volume that it is able to capture these rapid developments with real-life cases.

Paul Stonham, Series Editor,
EAP European School of Management, Oxford

Preface

Most excellent business schools have for a long time prescribed to an action-oriented philosophy of management education. This philosophy argues that students of business must *do* in order to achieve proficiency, and that managers succeed or fall not so much because of what they know but what they do.

It is with this philosophy in mind and the experience of 20 years of management education that this book on the *management of industrial and business-to-business marketing*[1] has been developed. I believe that you will find this collection of 22 cases to be pedagogically sound, appealing to the class participants, stimulating to teach, and focusing on the essential problems of modern business-to-business marketing.

The cases are all based on in-depth field research and close collaboration with the managers and companies described. In addition, all the cases have been thoroughly tested and refined by experienced professors of IMD and other leading business schools in teaching situations with students and executives of many different nationalities.

This casebook can be used successfully in several different formats. Firstly, it can be used as a comprehensive case supplement to any of the industrial and business-to-business marketing texts available on the market. Secondly, it can be used in conjunction with a set of readings and articles on industrial marketing issues. Thirdly, it can be used as a stand-alone casebook to support the instructor's own cases and lectures, as a supplement to a management decision simulation game, or as a corollary to student group projects. Finally, the book may serve as the guiding document for in-company development of young business-to-business and industrial marketing managers.

---

1. *The terms industrial or business-to-business marketing are used interexchangably throughout this book.*

Preparing a Case

The preparation of a case used to examine a business situation is very different from skimming through a newspaper article or reading a book. In general, I recommend that a four step process is followed in the preparation process.

1. *The Overview.* Read quickly through the case. Try to highlight or note down the names of key decision makers, locations, dates and numbers.

2. *Deepen Your Understanding.* With the overview behind you, read the case thoroughly. Make sure you have a full comprehension of all the aspects of the case. Try to identify contradictions and paradoxes.

3. *The Analysis.* Now you are ready to undertake the analysis of the case. You must attempt to get the fullest understanding of the following three aspects:
   (a) Industry trends, customers and competitive dynamics.
   (b) Company analysis, including financial issues.
   (c) Strategic issues and options.

4. *Decisions and Actions.* After the analysis you should now be ready to consider the various alternatives. Place yourself in the role of the decision maker(s) and decide what you would do in this situation. What decision would you lean towards and what advantages and disadvantages are the consequences of your choice(s). Finally, consider how the implementation of your decision would have to proceed and what the reactions would be.

Along with the case, your professor may have assigned specific study questions which will help you focus in on specific issues. You certainly will have prepared answers to these questions, but do not consider those answers sufficient for what would constitute a proper preparation of the case.

The case method is a *student centred* approach to learning and involves a classroom situation where *students do most of the talking*. The role of your professor is mainly to ask questions, thus encouraging student interactions on ideas, analysis and recommendations. The professor will also ask you to justify your comments, clarify the logic of your recommendations, set priorities and go beyond the case and draw on your own experience of other cases and articles you may have read. As the discussion in class unfolds, do not hesitate to take a stand on an issue or even present a contrary perspective. High points will also be given to the student who is able to place case facts and issues in theoretical frameworks, in order for the class to develop more generally applicable heuristics in marketing.

The student participation is such a fundamental part of the education that if a class participant is not fully prepared, he or she is unlikely to benefit from the class session. The discussion in class is a unique opportunity to learn more about yourself, your colleagues and their experience or views and the decision making in organizations. However, your gain will very much depend on the effort you and your colleagues put forth. So be prepared!

Per V. Jenster

About the Authors

Francis Bidault French. Technology Management. Director of the M.B.A. Program. Doctorat d'Etat, Business Administration, University of Montpellier. Doctorat d'Etat Economics, M.Sc. Economics, University of Paris I. Diploma, Institut d'Etudes Politiques de Paris. Formerly head of Business Environment Department, Lyon Graduate School of Business. Extensive consulting experience. Research interests: How companies develop and exploit their technology base especially through licensing and strategic alliances.

Pierre Casse Belgian. Organizational Behavior. Doctorat de 3ème Cycle, University of Lille. Lic.Soc.Sc. University of Liège. Formerly Senior Staff Development Officer at the World Bank. Has worked as a consultant with national and international organizations in Africa, Asia, Europe and the U.S. Research interests: Leadership issues in European business, international negotiations, communication and the impact of cultural differences on business.

Thomas J. Cummings Management of Technology Research Fellow. Prior to IMD, Thomas was with the Technology Resources Group, a Cambridge, Massachusetts consulting firm. At IMD he conducted research and taught about the management of technological innovation with an emphasis on the cooperative strategies of new technology firms, and transfer of technology across industries and technical settings.

William A. Fischer American. Manufacturing Management. D.B.A. George Washington University. M.S. Industrial Management and B.S. Civil Engineering, Clarkson College of Technology. Dalton L. McMichael Sr. Professor of Business Administration, University of North Carolina. Work experience in technology management in both industry and government in the U.S., the People's Republic of China, the Far East and developing world. Research interests: International manufacturing and technology transfer.

Christopher Gale Professor of Business Administration A.B., M.B.A., D.B.A., Harvard University. Professor Gale has been involved in executive education and is amongst other co-author of *Cases in International Marketing*. He has also been Visiting Professor of Business Administration, IMEDE, Lausanne, Switzerland.

Michael Hayes Ph.D., University of Michigan, B.S., University of New Mexico. Professor of Marketing and Strategic Management and Director of Graduate Programs at the University of Colorado at Denver. Dr. Hayes has had extensive experience with GE in field sales, sales management and executive education. His current research interests include international sales management and management of the delivery of customer satisfaction.

Per V. Jenster is a faculty member of IMD, Lausanne, responsible for teaching and research in strategic management and marketing. Prior to joining IMD in 1989, he spent five years in the US as a strategy consultant and faculty member at the University of Virginia. He has published more than 35 cases, books and articles, and has further new books forthcoming. His industry experience includes senior management consulting in strategic management, marketing planning, competitive analysis and cost evaluation studies, and past clients include international organizations such as Alcoa, Westinghouse and IBM. Professor Jenster is a board member of several entrepreneurial organizations and serves on the Executive Board of the Journal of Strategic Change.

Vijay K. Jolly Indian. International Business Policy. Ph.D. in Business Economics, Harvard University. B.Tech. in Mechanical Engineering, I.I.T., New Delhi. Experience in industrial project evaluation with Citibank and the World Bank. Consulting experience with several technology-based firms. Research interests: Strategic management, international strategy formulation, new business creation and the commercialization of technology.

Juan F. Rada Chilean. Executive vice president DEC Europe and formerly Director General of IMD, Lausanne, 1990–91. Professor of Technology Management. Ph.D. University of London. Undergraduate studies, Catholic University of Chile. Director General of IMI-Geneva, 1986–89. Fellow, World Academy of Art and Science. Member of the Club of Rome. Consultant to governments, international organizations and companies. Research interests: Technology management, impact of advanced technologies on management and strategy.

Dominique V. Turpin French. International Strategy. Egon Zehnder Fellow of International Management. Ph.D. Sophia University, Japan. Dipl. ESSCA, France. Extensive experience in teaching and research both in Europe and Japan. Consultant to several consumer goods and industrial service companies. Research interests: Strategies of Japanese firms in and outside Japan.

Sandra Vandermerwe Irish. International Marketing and Services. D.B.A. Stellenbosch University. M.B.A., B.A. in Sociology, University of Cape Town. Formerly Professor of Marketing, Witwatersrand University, and Visiting Professor in Europe, U.S. and Canada. Working experience in sales and marketing management. Consultant to consumer, industrial and service companies. Research interests: Market-driven change, marketing strategies, transformations in services management.

Thomas E. Vollman American. Manufacturing Management. Ph.D., M.B.A., B.A. University of California, Los Angeles. Formerly on the faculties of Boston University School of Management, Indiana University, INSEAD, University of Rhode Island and Dartmouth College. Consultant to numerous companies on manufacturing systems, lecturer in executive programs throughout the world. Research interests: Manufacturing planning and control, performance measurement and restructuring.

Organization of the Cases

The 22 cases are organized into 10 groups as listed below. Under each group heading you will find a listing of some of the key issues covered directly or indirectly by the cases placed in the particular grouping. However, let me warn that the cases often span a number of different topics, just as real life marketing issues are rarely placed into clean and easy separable categories for discrete decision making. The complexity of managing industrial and business-to-business marketing is exactly rooted in the interactions between distinct problem sets, conflicting functional responsibilities, variations in international priorities, frictions between vendors and buyers, and role needs of various decision makers in the customer organizations.

Section 1 An Overview of Industrial and Business-to-Business Marketing

Relevant topics to discuss:
A. Differences between industrial and consumer marketing
B. Marketing analysis
C. Customers and industrial buying behavior
D. Marketing mix
E. Challenges in organizing and managing the process

Cases:
Toro: Industrial Flavors
The World Flavor Industry – An Overview

Section 2 Market Analysis – Analyzing the Battlefield

Relevant topics to discuss:
A   Business definition: What we make and sell, or . . .?

B.   Structuring business system analysis
C.   Organizing competitive analysis

Case:
West European Car Rental Industry

Section 3 Industrial Customer Segmentation and Customer Buying Behavior

Relevant topics to discuss:
A.   Why is segmentation important?
B.   Principles in industrial market segmentation
C.   Macro and micro segmentation
D.   Process
E.   Procedures
F.   Persons
G.   Purchasing and purchasing models
H.   Organizing and structuring the analysis

Cases:
Maillefer SA (A)
BP Nutrition/Hendrix Voeders B.V. (A)
Ciba-Geigy Allcomm

Section 4 Industrial Marketing Analysis and Intelligence

Relevant topics to discuss:
A.   Managing information
B.   Demand analysis
C.   Sales forecasting

Case:
Quest International

Section 5 Product Management

Relevant topics to discuss:
A.   Product planning
B.   Product life cycle
C.   Introduction of new products
D.   Managing the product line
E.   Rejuvenation of mature products

Case:
Iskra Power Tools

Section 6 Industrial Pricing Strategies

Relevant topics to discuss:
A.   Basic types of industrial pricing
B.   Organizing the pricing process
C.   Complex pricing situations
     1.   Forward pricing
     2.   Solution pricing
     3.   Commodity pricing

Case:
The Cochlear Bionic Ear

Section 7 Promoting and Advertising Industrial Products

Relevant topics to discuss:
A.   Branding and promoting industrial products
B.   Advertising principles
C.   Organizing industrial communications

Cases:
Leykam Mürztaler
Lussman-Shizuka

Section 8 Place/Promotion

Relevant topics to discuss:
A.   Sales force, agents and distributors
B.   Developing the channel structure
C.   Designing physical distribution
D.   Planning and controlling distribution
E.   Managing the conflicts

Cases:
Jac Jacobsen Industrier A/S
Grampro B.V.
Grasse Fragrances SA

Section 9 Industrial Marketing Planning

Relevant topics to discuss:
A.   The marketing plan
B.   Developing the marketing plan, the process
C.   Designing the planning system

Cases:
Lafitte Oil (A)
Van Moppes-IDP Limited (A)

Section 10 Topical Cases

Acknowledgements

Case research has become an integral part of modern management development in both universities, business schools and in-company training. Cases on issues of management are invaluable in exposing the inherent kinds of issues which organizations face, in forming an understanding of market behavior and strategic choices, and drawing experience-based generalizations about sound management practice. Good cases should thus enable the students the essential practice in analyzing and evaluating options and choices, as well as the trade-offs in the implementation.

As industry after industry undergoes radical change, however, timely cases are becoming more important (not to say that one cannot learn from classical examples). As with all research the skills, time and dedication to develop outstanding case material is still as scarce. I am therefore indebted to my IMD colleagues and their research associates whose efforts appear in this book, as well as to the executives in the companies who cooperated in making the material possible.

My colleagues at IMD and I would welcome any comments you might have about this book or the cases in it, or any specific errors or developments. My address is: IMD, P.O. Box 915, CH-1001 Lausanne, Switzerland.

Per V. Jenster

SECTION 1

An Overview of
Industrial Marketing

CASES

Toro: Industrial Flavors
The World Flavor Industry – An Overview

Toro: Industrial Flavors

*This case was prepared by Professor Per V. Jenster and Research
Assistant Bethann Kassman as a basis for class discussion rather than to
illustrate either effective or ineffective handling of a business situation.
This case was developed as part of an Institutional Project on the
Management of Internationalization, and conducted in collaboration
with the Industrial Development Authority of Ireland.*

On a crisp Fall morning in October 1990, Jan Emil Johannessen, strategic
planner for the Toro division of Rieber & Son, sat in his Bergen office looking
out at the fjord as he contemplated the analysis work on his desk. The firm's
decision to formally enter into the industrial sales of flavor products had been
a challenge to its traditional capabilities in consumer culinary products. In
August 1987, management had decided to follow up a 1985 entrepreneurial
effort to pursue international opportunities in the industrial flavors business
more rigorously (*refer to **Exhibits 1** and **2a** and **2b***). By early 1990, however,
they realized that the firm's organizational resources and competencies were
already being stretched to the limit. As Jan Emil Johannessen stood
reflecting on the European industrial flavor market, he had to acknowledge
that some tough decisions needed to be made regarding Rieber & Son's
future strategy in culinary products and the international industrial strategy
in particular.

Exhibit 1   *(Source: company records)*

Rieber & Søn A/S
Bergen 21.10.85

MEETING NOTES

Action Program – Marine Powders

Objectives:

Primary: To be the world's leading producer of natural marine powder products.

Secondary: Within marine powder, we will aim to have an assortment of products which cover the main needs of our customers.

We will aim always to be able to deliver products when needed.

We must be competitive with respect to price and quality of our products.

Budget:

	1986	1987	1988	1989
Turnover (NOK mn.*)	7.5	9.5	12.0	15.1
(actual sales)	*6.5*	*9.0*	*13.5*	*15.0*

* SF1.00 = NOK 4.50

Exhibit 2a   *(Source: company records)*

Rieber & Søn A/S
Bergen 26.8.88

STRATEGY – INDUSTRIAL PRODUCTS 1988–1994

Status

We have a solid point of departure in our own production of dried food products to a discerning market. This has forced us to develop a large degree of proprietary processes and semifinished products of high quality.

Wth this in mind, we have developed sale of NOK 20 mn., with a satisfactory/good profitability.

The selling process is largely characterized as technical sales to a target group consisting of the technical decision makers in flavor houses and other food producers.

Marine Products

Product/Markets:

- 2 fish powders (one high end, another somewhat lower in costs)
- Crab powder
- Lobster powder
- Crimp powder
- Oyster powder

Strategic position:

High quality of powders, with some brought forth with own proprietary processes based on natural raw materials. The emphasis is on long shelf life for these products.

Critical Success Factors!   Raw materials and replication of recipes of consistent nature.

Exhibit 2a *Continued*

Future Possibilities:

As of now, our customers have primarily been flavor houses. This has been a good fit with our pure taste systems, without formulated mix combinations, e.g., hydrolysate spices, starches. However, we assume that the food producers are demanding products with a high value added dimension.

Thus, we see a need for

- less expensive products, e.g., crimp products
- mixed raw materials (different levels of value added)
- developing other extract products in collaboration with universities
- possibly looking for acquisition candidates producing similar or complementary powder products.

Bouillon (Hydrolysate)
Sales 1987 – NOK 9 mn.
Budget 88 – NOK 12 mn.

Product/Markets
Internationally, we sell formulated bouillon, that is, hydrolysate with meat extract, spices, etc. Here, our main clients are in the U.K.

Although we do not have strong competitive advantages in pure hydrolysate, we have developed talent in formulating end products. Thus, we have been functioning as a flavor house, and are offering our products in formulated condition to our customers.

Strategic Perspective
We have strong talent in formulating products vis-à-vis end producers, based on our own experience in vacuum-based products.

Future Developments
We believe that further efforts in this area should follow the direction pursued in the U.K. This will be emphasized after the purchase of our British agent. Such opportunities may be pursued elsewhere.

Meats

Status
Our own developments in meat based product, particularly for use in micro ovens, are very encouraging. However, as of yet no international sales have been made, partly due to our cost disadvantage created by import restrictions.

Future Developments
Viewed in light of our effort in bouillon, we see certain possibilities which are being pursued.

Budgets
As per attachment.

Exhibit 2b

	Growth	87	88	89	90	91	92	93	94
FORECAST IN NKR									
Existing Marine powders	10%	9,2	12	14	16	18	20	22	24
Formulated Marine powders			1	3	5	7	8	10	12
Acquired mixes			12	13	14	15	16	17	18
Total Marine			*25*	*30*	*35*	*40*	*44*	*49*	*54*
Dried meats			3	6	9	12	15	18	21
Peas, lentils			1	2	3	4	4	4	4
Flavour blends	7%		200	214	228	245	262	280	300
Bouillon			9	12	17	22	27	32	37
Total			*238*	*264*	*292*	*323*	*352*	*383*	*416*

Company Background

Rieber & Son A/S

The history of Rieber & Son A/S began in 1817 when the Rieber family from the Kingdom of Wurtemberg set off from Amsterdam aboard the sailing vessel 'De Zee Ploeg'. Their destination was Philadelphia, but fate led them to Norway instead. During a terrible storm, their ship was wrecked off the Norwegian coast, but they were towed to safety into the harbor of the small town of Bergen.

In 1839, one of the sons of the Rieber Family, Paul Gottlieb, founded the company Rieber & Son A/S, which engaged in various activities, particularly in the building materials sector.

Building materials became the mainstay of the company for the following 100 years. By 1990, Rieber & Son A/S was a professionally managed Norwegian Group with a turnover of approximately NOK 3,200 million and 2,850 employees. The key business areas were food, packaging materials, road surfacing materials and building materials. *(Financial data is presented in Exhibit 3.)* The companies' activities ranged from industrial production to purely commercial operations. Each division had its own business concept and, likewise, separate strategies for reaching its objectives.

Over and above the ordinary advantages of group structure, such as management, availability of resources and systems common to all members of the group, there initially seemed to be few points of contact between the individual divisions within the company. Yet, the firm stressed that there

Exhibit 3 *Financial information on main areas*

(Figures in NOK mill.)	Food		Packaging Materials		Road/ Asphalt		Building Materials		Joint Costs/ Elimination		The Group	
	89	88	89	88	89	88	89	88	89	88	89	88
INCOME STATEMENT												
Net sales	697	657	691	645	654	551	1102	1032	−2	−15	3142	2870
Of which, exports etc., represent	51	49	331	320	24	29	243	163	−	−	649	561
Contribution from sales and other income	424	399	336	315	306	265	383	376	6	2	1455	1357
Operating costs	−152	−143	−86	−78	−80	−67	−132	−139	−10	3	−460	−424
Wages/social security costs	−135	−133	−166	−147	−154	−132	−170	−159	−35	36	−660	−607
Depreciations	−22	−27	−31	−29	−30	−28	−21	−18	−4	−4	−108	−106
	115	96	53	61	42	38	60	60	−43	−35	227	220
BALANCE SHEET												
Net operating capital[1]	38	63	68	57	9	−27	242	209	−142	−120	215	182
Capital assets	180	183	200	196	125	111	178	173	223	161	906	824
Net working capital	218	246	268	253	134	84	420	382	81	41	1121	1006
KEY FIGURES												
Yield ratio[2]	46%	37%	20%	25%	31%	33%	16%	19%	−	−	22%	24%
Turnover rate[3]	2.8	2.5	2.6	2.6	4.7	4.6	2.8	3.0	−	−	2.7	2.7
Profit margin[4]	17%	15%	8%	10%	7%	7%	6%	6%	−	−	8%	9%
AVERAGE NUMBER OF EMPLOYEES	578	573	735	701	524	517	884	884	79	78	2800	2753

1) Net operating capital
   Receivables plus stock less interest-free credits.
2) Yield ratio
   Operating result plus financial revenues in percent of average net working capital.
3) Turnover rate
   Net sales divided by average net working capital.
4) Profit margin
   Operating result plus financial revenues in percent of net sales.
   The average net working capital used in the calculation of the key figures appears as a weighted average of the consumption of capital throughout the whole year, and is thus not directly comparable with the above net working capital which is obtained from the balance sheet at 31 December.

was, in fact, commonality in financial management and, to a certain degree, corporate philosophy. Nevertheless, day-to-day synergies among the divisions were limited due to the highly diversified nature of the overall Group.

Strategy and Future Outlook

Rieber & Son's attention had been directed towards the domestic markets with 80% of the company's sales taking place in Norway. Overseas sales were made within defined niches and were mainly linked to the packaging sector and natural stone products. Rieber & Son had concentrated its efforts on growth within sectors often considered 'established areas'.

The company's strategy was twofold. On the one hand, it was working for a logical further development of all 10 divisions both nationally and internationally. This strategy included both the growth of the divisions own products, the acquisition of companies well suited to fit into existing divisions and the achievement of competitive advantage through strategic alliances. On the other hand, the firm was seeking further development by taking over various companies in areas where it could achieve a sounder strategic position through the takeover.

Toro

In 1948, Rieber & Son laid the foundation for its current food division, Toro Foods, by introducing Bouillon Cubes, rapidly followed by related dehydrated food products. By 1989, sales of Toro Foods had reached NOK 697 million *(refer to **Exhibit 3** for the division's financial results)*. Toro Foods was the most profitable of the 10 Rieber divisions.

With production concentrated in Norway, the firm was proud of its expanding plant outside Bergen, equipped with sophisticated technology for the production of dried products. Air and vacuum dehydration processes were used in internal production while raw materials processed by freeze, drum and spray drying techniques were acquired. By early 1990, annual production had exceeded 11,000 tons of dehydrated foods and ingredients for consumers, catering markets and other food producers.

The firm could proudly point to significant domestic success, despite the presence of large multinational producers, such as Nestlé (Maggi), CPC (Knorr), and Unilever (Lipton). The Toro brand brought the Rieber organization impressive market share results in the Norwegian culinary retail sector with the following products:

Soups	87%
Stews	95%
Sauces	86%
Casseroles	99%
Bouillons	75%

In catering, the firm held similarly strong positions with an overall estimated market share of 70%. *(Refer to **Exhibit 4** for details of the Toro Organization.)*

Introduction of Dehydrated Fish Soup

Historically, Toro was a major world player in the whale-extract market. The extract was dehydrated and used to add flavor to processed food products. When whaling declined during the 1950s and 1960s, Toro used the knowledge gained in the whaling industry and applied it to other food ingredients. Real success came in 1959 when Toro developed and launched dried soups in sachets. Four years later another breakthrough came when Toro produced dehydrated fish soups. Dehydration, the oldest form of conservation, was actually a fairly simple idea. Water, removed at the beginning of the process, was then added at the time of preparation, without losing any of the product's major nutritive value. The problem was to retain the finer flavors of the raw materials. It was this problem that Toro solved and marketed, initially to the Norwegian market, followed shortly by entry into the Scandinavian market.

Catering

The Toro Catering Division was created as a specialized organization responsible for developing the catering product range, and for sales and marketing in the Norwegian catering market. The division achieved total sales of NOK 102 million in 1989. Despite a decline in the total market, Toro's Catering Division enjoyed an increase in volume. The product line was expanded to include products produced in Toro's factory as well as products from several Norwegian and foreign suppliers of dried, canned, chilled and frozen foodstuffs.

Toro's Catering Division's strategy was to combine high quality with labor-saving properties for the user and advantageous prices. The products were specially developed for and adapted to use in catering establishments. The end users of these products included all types of catering establishments such as hotels, restaurants, transport companies and the armed forces. Distribution took place through wholesalers and ships' chandlers.

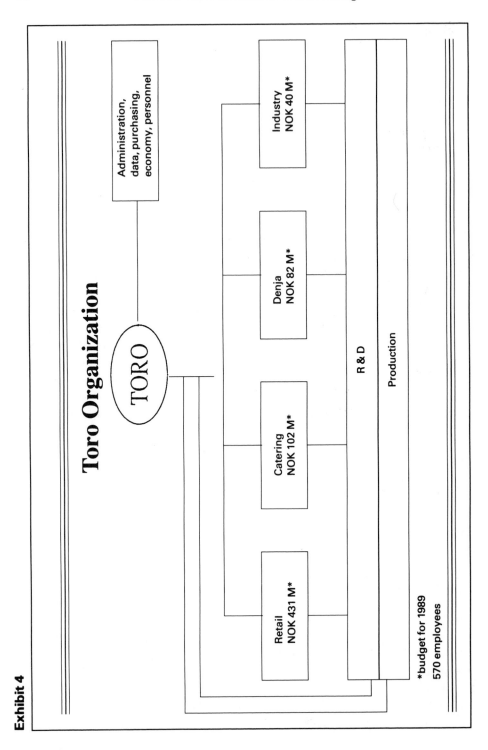

Exhibit 4

Expanding to Other Markets

Toro was the undisputed retail market leader in Norway with 90 per cent of the market in dehydrated foods comprising a wide range of products – soups, casseroles, stews, sauces, etc. The quality of these dehydrated foods was perceived to be very high. In addition, Toro had adapted its products to Norwegian tastes.

With the successful launch of its dehydrated fish soup in the 1960s, Toro decided early on to expand into the neighboring Scandinavian market. Through an informal process, the other four Nordic countries (Sweden, Finland, Denmark, Iceland) were targeted. Toro embarked on a niche strategy using distributors and local people to test the market, then tailor the product to the demands of the broader Scandinavian marketplace. Considerable money was spent, especially in Sweden as it was the largest and most attractive market, but the outcome was less successful than had been anticipated.

For 25 years, the market had been dominated by big three players: Unilever, Nestlé, and CPC. These players had the resources to stay in the market long enough to become profitable, had successfully covered the market for many years and had a product line similar to Toro's. Thus, Toro made the decision to retreat from the branded products' market in all the other Scandinavian countries except Iceland.[1] In both Sweden and Denmark, however, Toro's name had become recognized, a fact the firm used to its advantage by producing private label products for two of the largest chains in both countries. Toro sold through the Swedish Cooperative Society in Sweden under the Foodia name and in Denmark under the IRMA label. Toro's experience in the Nordic market did not discourage the company from trying to enter the wider European market with export of branded retail lines. The strategy was to develop unique products in Norway and exploit them with niche marketing on the Continent.

In the early 1970s, Toro had developed a range of seafood specialties through a specific process technology for producing tastier fish powder. These products were believed to be superior to those available in Europe. The strategy objective was to introduce the product into as many countries as possible in order to achieve volume through market penetration (in contrast to its first international effort where Toro targeted only the 'home market', Scandinavia). However, it soon became apparent that there were many issues which needed to be addressed in order to succeed in the Continental European markets.

First, Toro faced Unilever, Nestlé, and CPC, which together accounted for 80–85 per cent of the market share in dehydrated foods worldwide. These competitors commanded considerable resources and, through sheer volume, were able to bring economies of scale to their product development and market maintenance costs which Toro could not match. In other than fish soups, Toro was at a cost disadvantage because it imported raw ingredients for use in its products and then often exported the finished products to the same countries that the ingredients had come from. In addition to being unable to meet a vast set of packaging requirements, Toro received little support from distributors and agents, who were largely selected using the simplest criteria. This resulted in inconsistent marketing plans which varied from country to country and were insufficient to penetrate the Continental market.

Sales remained flat for 10–15 years while production problems increased due to packaging requirements and small order runs. By 1985 Toro had decided that the Continental niche was too small and required excessive effort for too little profit. It decided to stop selling to the retail market in most European countries, but to keep a presence in those countries where it had the best agents and the highest sales volume. Thus, Toro increased its marketing in Spain, the United Kingdom and the United States, while moving more into private label sales for specific stores in Continental Europe.

By 1986, Toro found at this point in time that the retail market for its products was declining in both absolute and relative terms. Private label sales were largely sold through cooperatives, which were also losing business. Therefore, Toro decided to discontinue its strategy of entering new retail markets in the dried and dehydrated product lines, and to confine its retail food sales primarily to the Norwegian market. Meanwhile, the company discovered an emerging market for expansion – wholesale flavors to the larger European community.

Dabbling in Industrial Ingredients

In the late 1980s, sales remained flat in the finished product sector but continued to rise in the raw materials market. Toro management looked at these results and realized that, over the years, the firm had developed a unique knowledge in the production of seafood and fish powders. Toro also had a strong research and development base in the process and product technology for dry foods, especially relating to taste. Management concluded, therefore, that Toro not only had a role as supplier of finished culinary products to major retailers, but it also had a viable role helping other producers with product formulation and process expertise. To larger firms,

Toro offered its special knowledge in fish products, and, to smaller companies, research and development support.

In addition, Norway suffered from a tariff burden on the shelf-ready products it exported to the EEC, so it made sense for Toro to sell its knowledge and raw materials to others. During a large strategy meeting in 1988, management decided to limit retail sales to the Nordic market and treat Europe as its industrial market. Having made this decision, Toro withdrew from the finished product sector so as not to compete directly with its potential industrial customers. It was felt that the product segment where Toro had an advantage over its competitors was in the development of natural savory products related to seafood. Consequently, this was the area that Toro targeted for expansion within the European industrial flavors market.

The strategy quickly became a challenge to the various functional disciplines within the organization, partly due to its broad scope. Over the next year and a half, as experience increased, the strategy narrowed down to focus on different distribution methods in various countries and on a more limited product range specifically geared to convenience foods, dried and frozen foods. Using advanced technology and a combination of available first-class raw materials, Toro produced a powder with high quality taste. Its R&D unit produced flavor systems which were sold to other culinary companies for use in their products. As demand increased, the majority of powders and granulates of various fish were exported either as semi-manufactured goods, such as stocks and sauces, or as raw material. By the end of 1989, 50% of industrial sales were direct sales to convenience food producers, with the remaining 50% to flavor houses and mixers.

Worldwide Flavor Industry

Because flavors and fragrances used similar materials and technology in production, most producers made both types of product customarily called the Flavors and Fragrances (F&F) industry. However, the market dynamics (i.e., driving forces for growth) and the bases for competition differed between the flavors and fragrances segments. Fragrances included combinations of natural and/or synthetic raw materials, whereas flavors tended to be less exotic and were usually based on something found in nature.

Growth and profitability of the flavors segment (retail and industrial) had to be viewed in the context of the F&F industry as a whole. Until the late 1970s, the world F&F industry was seen as an extraordinarily high performer. Industry profitability approximated 15% of sales in the mid- to late 1960s and 10% in the 1970s. Since that time, slower growth and increased competitive pressures had reduced profitability to about 6–7% industry-wide. For the past 10 years, real sales growth averaged 5–6% per year, reaching $5.8 billion in 1987. Because of widely fluctuating world currencies, especially the dollar, actual growth was difficult to estimate; however, expected growth was projected to be roughly 5% per year through 1992.

Valued at nearly $2.6 billion in 1987, flavors comprised nearly 45% of the total F&F market, with 15% of the total flavor market from savory flavors. Western Europe and the United States were the largest regional markets, together accounting for 63% of world flavor sales. Japan was the third major market. Consumption in the rest of the world was significantly lower. However, the USSR and the Far East were identified as having the greatest growth potential.

Industry Trends

In the 1960s, artificial flavors accounted for 75% of the market, while natural flavors accounted for 25%. These percentages were reversed by the late 1980s. Although natural flavors were more costly to develop and could not withstand all techniques of food processing, most of the major flavor houses oriented their development programs to meet the growing demand for natural flavors. As the costs of flavor ingredients continued to rise and product development became costly and complex, strategic acquisitions became an important means of company growth. Most of these acquisitions were made for market reasons: to gain a base in a particular regional market, to acquire a market niche, to allow for R&D expansion in an area, or to acquire a talented flavorist or a key food account.

Despite the high level of merger and acquisition activity, the world flavor industry remained highly fragmented. This was not expected to change, although Arthur D. Little, a management consulting firm, predicted that an acquisition slowdown would occur through the early 1990s. Continued success in the industry required an enhanced working relationship with customers in order to understand their changing needs better and thus be able to offer more applications research and technical service.

Companies in the F&F business spent significantly more on R&D than did most participants in their end-use markets. R&D spending varied by company size; the large multinationals spent 7–12 per cent of sales on R&D, while the smaller companies spent 2–5 per cent. Heavy investments in biotechnology focused on developing ways to produce better quality natural flavors at a lower cost. Major research was also conducted to develop more stable natural flavor systems to protect against the effects of processing, packaging, and ingredient interaction. High temperature short-time (HTST) food processing, retorting and microwave cooking, in particular, presented challenges and opportunities to the flavor houses. New techniques to further improve the stability and shelf-life of flavors was also being investigated.

In the industrial flavor segment of the market, the growth of processed foods as a percentage of total food consumption was expected to continue through the 1990s, with particularly strong growth in Northern Europe. An increase in sales of savory flavors was anticipated as well. Because of the high cost of research and development, product development would continue to be contracted out to flavor houses, mixers, and raw material suppliers. Overall, ingredients were seen as a profitable area of activity since they did not demand the heavy marketing expenditure required to promote food products to the retail trade. Furthermore, the considerable increase in demand for convenience foods was likely to continue to grow throughout the 1990s, creating new opportunities to expand the market.

Industrial Competitors

The largest producers of seafood products were the Japanese; however, industrial sales from Japanese companies were concentrated almost exclusively in the Far East. In Europe, competition was confined to a limited number of small niche players, primarily located in Norway and France. Of these companies, only one (Isnard Lyraz located in France) produced a high quality product similar to that produced by Toro.

Toro's major competitors in the retail sector (Maggi, CPC, Unilever) were not direct competitors with Toro in the industrial seafood powder area. Although there were areas where some competition existed (HVP and bouillons), by and large, these flavor houses as well as others were Toro customers who purchased and reprocessed Toro's products.

The top 15–20 participants in the F&F industry accounted for the majority of flavor sales; 14 of these companies had sales of $100 million or more *(refer to Exhibit 5)*. The remaining sales were dispersed among some 100 other major producers and nearly 1,000 smaller companies around the world. Thus, in spite of the concentration of sales at the top, fragmentation of the industry was not reduced, primarily because many of the hundreds of small flavor houses were not vulnerable to takeover and because many new companies had entered the business due to the low entry barriers.

Exhibit 5   (Sources: *Annual reports and Arthur D. Little Inc., estimates*)

Companies with 1987 Flavor and Fragrance Sales of $100 Million or More		
Company/Parent	Headquarters	1987 World Sales (MM$)
International Flavors & Fragrances (IFF)	United States	745
Quest International/Unilever	United Kingdom/Netherlands	635
Givaudan/Hoffman-La Roche	Switzerland	480
Takasago Perfumery	Japan	440
Haarman & Reimer/Bayer	West Germany	350
Firmenich	Switzerland	240
Dragoco Gerberding	Germany	350
Bush Boake Allen (BBA) Union Camp, U.S.	United Kingdom	140
Florasynth-Lautier	France	130
Fritzsche Dodge & Olcott/BASF	Germany	130
PFW Division/Hercules	United States	120
Universal Group/Universal Foods	United States	110
Roure	France	100
Hasagawa	Japan	100
Total		*3,870*

Note: In today's world monetary system of fluctuating currencies, all calculations in current U.S. dollars, or any other currency, are subject to considerable exchange rate distortions. Thus, the dollar sales for each of these companies do not necessarily reflect the company's true size or position relative to the other major players.

Buying Process

Flavor was one of the major differentiating factors among various brands within a food product category. Safety, nutrition, convenience and price were also important, but taste acceptance by the consumer was essential to the creation of brand loyalty. In spite of the importance of flavors to the food industry, food processors exerted considerable pressure on suppliers of food additives. These pressures included demand for natural ingredients, high quality but low cost products, and product diversity to meet the varied tastes of the increasingly sophisticated consumer.

Responding to buyer influence led to tremendous growth in new product introduction (according to Productscan/Marketing Intelligence Service, more than 8,000 new food products were introduced to the European markets in 1987). The trend towards an expanding product market was expected to continue. All of which required a corresponding development in the area of new flavor systems. Product obsolescence – caused by changes in consumer preferences, habits and lifestyles – also occurred at a higher rate in the industry. These factors, combined with the competitive pressures stemming from the food industry, forced flavor suppliers to increase their internal capabilities in product application, basic research and development, technical service, and marketing.

The eruption of more freedom in Eastern Europe and the Soviet Union foreshadowed economic opportunities comparable to the period of international business expansion in the 1950s and 1960s. The internationalization of tastes and increasing health concerns among consumers in all countries presupposed heavy investments in research to keep pace with innovation, or changing the focus to a compounder or blender. As the costs of producing innovative flavors increased, more producers looked to others in the industry for product development, technical expertise and market knowledge.

Many flavor houses predicted that the 1990s would bring a continuation of the flavoring fads of the 1980s – exotic flavorings, natural flavorings and easy to prepare foods. However, the area receiving the greatest interest was in natural flavorings and 'healthy' foods. Toro had a fairly large advantage in this area in that all its products were 100% natural, unlike the Japanese whose products were mixed with enhancers and additives. In essence, Toro's processing consisted of taking the frozen blocks of fish fillet, crushing and boiling them, drying and milling them. Although this process sounded simple on paper, its technology was quite advanced for the complex production of seafood.

Toro's Initial Efforts in Industrialization

Until 1986, Toro had grown through retail sales and finished products. The decision to enter the European industrial market required a change in sales, distribution and production. Staff that had been working with retail sales and technology was quickly shifted to serve the requirements of an industrial market. It soon became evident that the organization had difficulty with this transition. The staff was not trained to deal with the different requests from industrial customers; specific recipes had to be developed and sold, creating an impact on both R&D and sales; new country-specific regulatory requirements had to be incorporated into the product specifications; and production had to be adjusted to accommodate short runs. There were, however, a number of key strengths which Toro built upon as it entered this new environment. Backward integration (the processing of its own raw materials) continued to be handled by the processing department. The vertical integration allowed Toro to take raw ingredients, process them to specification, and produce a finished product for sale to the marketplace similar to the way it had done in the retail market. Its large, well-staffed research and development department was already familiar with developing a wide range of formulations, and Toro's presence in the retail market lent credibility to its entry into the industrial market.

Sales Department

Focusing on the industrial market required specific sales tasks and behavior which differed from those used in the retail market. Initially, Toro went in with its standard products, but discovered that the customer wanted tailored or specially developed products within short time frames. The salesmen were not prepared to deal with the technical issues raised by industrial clients and were unfamiliar with the amount of effort required to meet these demands, particularly by the research and development department. It was felt that a sales force with technical skills was needed. To meet this new demand, R&D staff were teamed with the sales staff. In addition, one technical sales manager was recruited from the factory and one was hired from the outside. This new staff and technical focus allowed for greater communication between the client and R&D at an earlier stage in the customer relationship, and eliminated basic misunderstandings as to availability of products and the time frames required for production. It raised, however, a different problem – taking research and development staff away from its other tasks. In-house education as well as attendance at seminars helped enhance the skills of both the sales staff and the R&D staff. In fact, one individual from research and development was moved into the sales department to enhance the technical understanding of this unit.

Export sales were split 50/50 – half on finished goods for the consumer and half on semifinished product and raw material. Rieber/Toro's biggest markets for selling fish powders were West Germany (25%), Benelux (20%), the USA (10%) and France (10%). Spain, as a large fish-eating nation, was on the verge of becoming a big market for the company, with sales running at 10% of total industrial turnover. The rest of the sales went to the Far East, Australia and Scandinavia. In Europe, the products were sold through agents; in the Nordic countries, the product was sold directly. In 1989, Rieber/Toro decided to apply a model of direct sales representation in the UK added an additional 10% of sales. An English staff of two salespeople and a technical person were obtained when a small distributor was purchased in an effort to gain a better understanding of the English customers' requirements. Small distributors were usually selected in the various countries, because they were more responsive to Toro's needs than were the larger distribution houses, which were perceived to be less loyal. As a common sales strategy, the largest producers and mixers were targeted priorities for both the agents and the sales force.

Large food producers buying directly from Toro accounted for 50% of sales. Selling directly enhanced Toro's ability to offer advice on usage and to provide blended products. Direct sales to flavor houses accounted for 30% of sales. The flavor houses made a living out of extracting taste from raw materials and selling it to the customer at a high markup. Also, the flavor houses had access to an international market which Toro neither knew nor understood. The remaining 20% of sales were to mixers who serviced smaller companies and other industries, such as those in meat-based products *(refer to **Exhibit 6**)*.

Research and Development

With a budget equivalent to $2.4 million invested each year (representing 2.6% of total turnover), the company was proud of its applied developmental work. The R&D department was responsible for dealing with a customer's technical questions as well as formulating new products and controlling existing ones. With 45 staff members working in its development laboratories and pilot plant, the company was continually testing new methods and ways of handling ingredients.

An industrial market focus, however, strained the R&D department's resources. Used to having one to two years' lead time to develop products for the company to sell, the department's position had reversed – it now had to produce products to demand as well as develop new products. As the company focused its emphasis more on the industrial component, staff who had been working in the retail area were moved to the industrial area. Most of these people needed time and education in order to understand the new business focus as well as to deal with the new regulatory requirements demanded by the various countries in which Toro was now selling. Ensuring quality also needed additional resources to comply with the changing requirements of data and documentation. But, perhaps the biggest change was that, as orders came in, products had to be tailor made, reformulated and produced under very tight time lines to meet customer demand. This situation created a lot of internal pressure.

To deal with these new demands, R&D focused on building up its staff

Exhibit 6

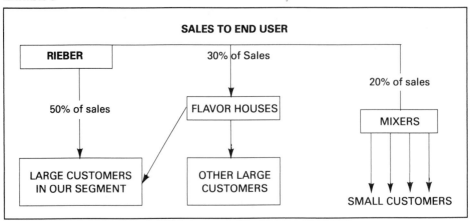

to deal professionally with individual customers. Technical staff were assigned to travel with the sales staff and to communicate directly with clients. By being on the scene, the technical staff were able to lay out the product requirements and to identify problem areas early in the process. Within the company itself, increased communication with all departments, but particularly with sales and manufacturing, was emphasized.

Being located so far from the market made it imperative that Toro do everything possible to facilitate communication and product delivery. This strategy required a large investment in new equipment, as well as in personnel training and continually helping the staff to adapt. There were, however, some economies of scale which surfaced. Some recipes were able to be used across borders and, in some cases, industrial projects provided the testing ground for retail products. The research and development department had faced the challenge of being responsive to the developmental needs of the industrial environment well. Nevertheless, continuing the effort to maintain a strong research focus was of some concern to the department manager.

Production

Production problems centered around the difficulties created by small runs as opposed to the larger runs common for products in the retail market. This change affected scheduling and equipment as well as the process used. R&D staff were often needed in the factory to provide hands-on expertise during small trial runs. The short timetables requested by customers exacerbated the issues. To meet these new production requirements, specific small batch, dedicated equipment was purchased. R&D staff continued to be involved in production runs, particularly pilot runs which focused on developing products. The buying department found alternative sources for shellfish in order to have the necessary resources on hand for production to meet client demand. Although communication among the various departments had improved, the increased interaction among the departments involved in production required having constant communication about, and evaluation of, the problem areas.

A New Way of Working

The development of flavorings and natural additives for the international food market forced many changes in the day-to-day operations and the overall aspects of the business. The need for technical and production staff to be located closer to the clients – especially those smaller companies located in Europe – was acknowledged. A strategy was developed which included acquisition of a network of smaller companies already in the industrial market in Continental Europe. Distribution networks were expanded and staff requirements in R&D, Export, and Manufacturing were under constant review. Contacts with flavor houses and agents were expanded. This intense evaluation involving the entire Toro division was geared to speed up and facilitate entry into the industrial market.

With over 40 years of retail marketing and a strong presence in the Norwegian market, Toro had consistently relied on its technical formulation and product expertise. The changing retail environment and the opening of international borders implied that Toro would have to use those strengths to face the many challenges which lay ahead. Jan Emil Johannessen was optimistic that Toro would meet the challenges and succeed in its new industrial environment.

Notes

1. In Iceland, a market equivalent in size to the city of Bergen, Toro was able to maintain the dominate position.

The World Flavor Industry: An Overview

This case was prepared by Research Associate David Hover, under the supervision of Professor Per V. Jenster, as a basis for class discussion rather than to illustrate either effective or ineffective handling of a business situation.

The term 'flavors', when applied to a variety of chemical products, added taste and aroma to processed foods and beverages. Flavors were usually classified as either 'natural', 'nature identical' or 'artificial', depending on the production method used. A flavor was classified as natural when it was extracted from animal or vegetable products by some physical process – including the normal kitchen activities of cooking, heating, boiling, etc. Flavors produced through fermentation were also generally considered natural flavors. Nature identical flavors, or enzymology, consisted of synthesized substances but ones that occurred naturally in food. Artificial flavors were substances derived from any source which did not occur naturally in food.

Traditionally, the manufacturers of flavors, known as flavor houses, had also supplied fragrances (for perfumes, personal hygiene products, soaps, detergents, etc.) because both flavors and fragrances were extracted from raw materials using the same fractionation and distillation processes. However, the changing market and technology were eroding many of the synergies between the two segments. Not only was the demand for flavors increasing as the food processing industry became more competitive, but the food industry also demanded more sophisticated flavors, ones able to withstand rigorous food processing procedures, and able to meet government and consumer standards. These market conditions made creating suitable flavors much more difficult and technologically demanding than creating fragrances. As one executive noted:

Everyone knows what green peas taste like – coming up with the exact same flavor is challenging. However, with fragrances you can be more creative.

At the same time, the market for fragrances had become static and, in the case of designer perfumes, was actually declining.

The impact of the market changes was felt in the performance figures of the industry. Until the late 1970s, the world flavors and fragrances (F&F) industry had shown consistently strong results. Industry profitability had been approximately 15% of sales in the mid to late 1960s, and 10% in the 1970s. In the 1980s, however, slower growth and increased competitive pressures had reduced profitability to about 6–7% industry-wide, and real sales growth had averaged 5–6% per year, reaching an estimated $6.7 billion in 1990. Projections into the 1990s estimated growth rates to remain in the 5% range. Flavors comprised nearly 45% of the total F&F market and were valued at approximately $3.1 billion in 1990. Western Europe and the United States were the largest regional markets, together accounting for 63% of world flavor sales. Japan was the third major market. Consumption in the rest of the world was significantly lower. However, Eastern Europe and the Far East were identified as having significant growth potential.

In the flavor segment of the market, the growth of processed foods as a percentage of total food consumption was expected to drive up demand through the 1990s. An increase in sales of savory flavors (25% of the total flavors market) was anticipated as well. Because of the high cost of research and development, the food processing companies were increasingly contracting product development out to flavor houses, seasoning houses, and ingredient suppliers, thus further strengthening demand. The considerable increase in demand for convenience foods was also likely to continue growing throughout the 1990s, creating new opportunities for market expansion.

Other developments had also influenced the industry in the late 1980s, including changing customer profiles, an evolving competitive environment and more sophisticated end-consumers. Together, these factors that were acting on the industry were forcing flavor houses to reevaluate the way they did business.

Importance of Flavors

Although the flavor component usually represented only a small fraction of the total cost of a food product, its benefit to the final product was very large. Price, image, nutrition, convenience and texture were also important, but the consumer's satisfaction with taste was essential to the creation of brand loyalty. Food processors placed considerable pressure on flavor houses to deliver consistent, high quality flavors at a low cost.

Major research was also conducted to develop more efficient delivery systems. The natural and nature identical flavors favored by the producers were difficult to protect from degradation in processing, packaging, and reactions with other ingredients. High temperature short-time (HTST) food processing, retorting and microwave cooking, in particular, were harsh environments for delicate flavors. Price premiums paid for the natural products, but they also increased demands for efficient delivery systems. New techniques to enhance stability and shelf life were also important. Leading edge technologies such as micro encapsulation were expensive to develop and tailor to different types of applications. The high capital outlays required for many of the new high-tech processes could only be recovered by having very large subsequent markets, which were frequently only possible through a global presence.

End product consumers were also changing their demands. Natural healthy foods, low cholesterol, low fat, low sodium, high fiber, and low sugar were increasingly in demand and able to command a price premium. As the population in most of the developed world aged, tastes became more sophisticated. Rising interest in tea-flavored drinks was one of the manifestations of this development. Convenience (largely related to the microwave) was also a major interest of consumers, despite their increasing demand for natural ingredients. Furthermore, the flavor houses had to work with the packaging companies, so that the combination of ingredients, flavors and packages would have the flavor, texture, browning ability (appearance) and shelf life demanded by the consumer. Each of these trends placed heavy demands on the R&D activities of the flavor houses.

Labelling and Regulation

The distinctions between natural, nature identical and artificial flavors were frequently subtle, and no firm international standards existed. For example, flavors which were non-declarable (nothing had to be mentioned on the label) in some countries could require labelling or even be prohibited in other countries. There were also few international standards on acceptable ingredients. Until recently, German brewers, for example, were unable to use any additives in beer. Other countries were much less restrictive in potential ingredients. Individual product requirements forced flavor houses to reconfigure their product lines for some countries. With the exception of some EC regulations coinciding with the realization of the European common market in 1992, industry experts did not anticipate comprehensive coordination of national food regulations.

Emphasis on natural products by end-consumers was having its own impact on product rationalization. In response to the changing market and regulatory trends, most major flavor houses had reoriented their development programs to focus on natural flavors. Natural flavors, however, were more technologically demanding. Artificial and nature identical flavors generally cost less to manufacture and were better able to withstand the modern food processing techniques such as ultra high temperature (UHT) and industrial scale microwaving which degraded many natural flavors. Despite the advantages of artificial flavors, they were increasingly shunned by the market, so that the market share of artificial flavors fell from 75% in the 1960s to 25% by the late 1980s.

Competitors

In 1990, International Flavors and Fragrances (IFF) was the largest flavor house with 12% of the worldwide market. Quest was a close second with 11% market share. *(Refer to **Exhibit 1**.)* The market share of the two companies, however, differed from market to market. Quest was the market leader in a number of smaller European countries, while IFF's market leadership was primarily a result of its dominant position in the US. In other countries – notably Japan and Germany – neither IFF nor Quest had significant market shares.

In the F&F industry overall, 14 companies had sales of $100 million or more. The remaining sales were dispersed among some 100 other major producers and nearly 1,000 smaller companies around the world. Most of the smaller companies were very specialized and closely held. New companies were constantly entering the market. It was relatively easy to be a niche player with a specialized product or an individual producer (especially in fragrances). As new product development became more costly and complex, strategic acquisitions had become an important means of company growth in the flavor industry. Acquisitions were also made for other reasons: accessing a base in a particular regional market, acquiring a market niche, expanding R&D in a particular field, or retaining a talented flavorist or a key food account.

Despite the high level of merger and acquisition activity, the world flavor industry (and the F&F industry in general) remained highly fragmented in the early 1990s, and this situation was not expected to change. The management consulting firm Arthur D. Little even predicted a

Exhibit 1   *Top 15 flavor houses by flavor sales (market share in parentheses)*
(Source: Quest International)

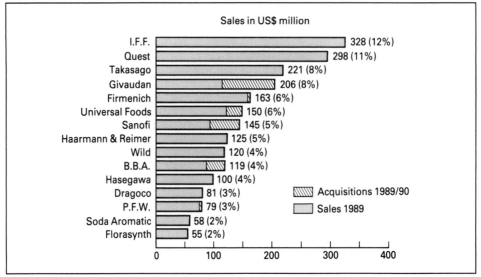

slowdown in the rate of acquisitions during the first part of the decade. Continued success in the industry required an enhanced working relationship with customers; mergers and acquisitions were one way for flavor houses to obtain the necessary range of products and knowledge to meet customers' demands.

Customers

Competitive strategies and changes in the flavor industry were partly in response to the fast pace of change in the food processing industry, the primary flavor market. Concentration and globalization, frequently through mergers and acquisitions, were the dominating trends as food processors tried to enhance their competitive position. The search for global products, and the associated economies of scale, was motivated by such factors as the emergence of free trade areas like the European Community and the US-Canadian Free Trade Association, and an increased interest in ethnic foods. In Europe, the industry was responding more slowly to the market trends than in Japan or the US, but the more aggressive European producers had already begun to establish a Europeanwide (and occasionally global) base of operations.

One result of the new industrial order was more competition. In the past, regional political and physical boundaries had sheltered many companies from outside competition. The gradual erosion of many of these barriers had allowed companies to expand into new markets more efficiently. Similar to the situation in the flavor industry, meeting the new competitive challenge frequently meant making acquisitions for additional market share, national presence, or product range extension. Many of these acquisitions, however, also increased debt loads, which put pressure on the companies to allocate funds away from such 'investment' areas as R&D. Because of cutbacks in R&D by many food processors seeking greater cost efficiency, the flavor houses were spending significantly more on R&D than their customers. R&D spending varied by company size: the large flavor houses spent 7–12% of sales on R&D, while the smaller companies spent 2–5%.

Global branding had an impact on the food processing industry. Food product companies, interested in reducing costs, continuously searched for product concepts that could be applied trans-culturally. Some products were more suitable to global branding and marketing than others, although David Stout, the head of Unilever's economics department, claimed 'there is no such thing as an edible Walkman'. Many beverages, snacks, fast foods and some dairy products were relatively easy to sell across national borders. Despite sharing the same product concept, the product inside the can or package was frequently modified (sometimes substantially) from country to country to satisfy local tastes, cooking habits, and/or cultural norms.

The structural changes in the food industry had led to increasing polarization between the very large multiproduct companies (Kraft, itself a division of Philip Morris, CPC International, Nestlé, BSN) and the small, highly specialized niche players. The large multinationals strove to enlarge their market shares while the remaining niche players specialized more. Medium-sized companies, in order to survive, were forced to either expand or specialize. When food processing companies became international, they wanted their flavor suppliers to accompany them.

Providing international service to their customers was not easy for the flavor houses. Because of the extensive resources needed, it was important to identify which customers were going to be successful in the 1990s and the decades beyond. With only limited resources, they could not pursue every option with each customer. It was potentially disastrous for a flavor house to spend limited resources working hard to maintain extensive relations with a customer unable to compete in the long term. Consolidation in the food processing industry also reduced the number of potential alternative customers, thus further increasing the risk associated with a failing customer.

Declining numbers of customers, besides increasing the proportion of business associated with one customer, changed the nature of the sales relationship. Fewer salespeople were needed, but a higher level of expertise and interaction was required. Sales personnel had to interact with managers and technicians at many levels and functional areas – including R&D, production, operations, purchasing and marketing. These interactions had to be managed carefully: each area had different interests, needs and concerns which had to be addressed if the relationship were to work effectively. Being effective also depended on completely understanding the customer's business needs. It was no longer sufficient to just sell a product; the supplier also had to know how the product integrated with the rest of the customer's operation.

Flavor Industry Developments

In the latter part of the 1980s, a number of notable trends were becoming apparent in the flavor industry which had long-term implications for industry players. These trends included more emphasis on flavor systems, high rates of new product introduction and the breakdown of traditional distinctions among competitors in the different segments.

Total Food Systems

As food processing companies concentrated internal activities on marketing, they were increasingly interested in flavor houses that were able to offer solutions to particular problems rather than merely provide individual flavors. The development of low-fat, low-calorie ice cream was a typical example of the kind of service food processors wanted from their suppliers. Removing fat from ice cream was not difficult technically. However, the fat was the basis for both the taste and the 'mouth feel' of the product. To create the same sensation that the customer experienced when eating ice cream – but without the fat – meant developing a complete system comprised of flavors, food ingredients and additives. Companies that had previously operated only as suppliers of specific products – like emulsifiers, colors, or preservatives – were discovering that customers who lacked the ability to develop flavor systems on their own wanted more than just the basic product.

A total food system combined various products (flavors, food ingredients and additives) to create an end product with certain desired flavor texture and appearance qualities. Food ingredients that replaced bulk or assisted in product enhancement were a fundamental part of many systems, although the actual costs of the flavor or ingredients was frequently only 5%

of the final end-consumer product price. There were few flavor houses with the necessary expertise or production facilities, yet they had to begin adding food ingredients and additives (such as fats, fat substitutes, emulsifiers, preservatives, etc.) to their product range.

In 1990, however, only six flavor houses were serious players in food ingredients. Together, they held only 34% of the market; however, their share – worth $1,029 billion – was growing quickly (an increase of 42% from 1989), primarily through acquisitions. *(Refer to **Exhibit 2**.)* Many in the industry believed the best way to gain the necessary expertise in ingredients was through acquisitions. Quest and other industry players were convinced that the ability to offer complete systems was becoming a definite prerequisite to remaining a worldwide competitor.

Previously, food ingredients had been produced by specialty chemical companies. Just as flavor houses had begun to invest in food ingredients, food ingredient manufacturers had started investing in flavors. Many chemical companies had found that food ingredients were a natural outgrowth of their specialty chemicals operations. Grindsted, and Gist Brocades had made investments with varying levels of success in the area of flavors.[1] It was becoming apparent that the successful flavor houses and food ingredient companies would be those that could provide global one-stop services or particular niche products.

Product Innovation
Redoubled efforts to reach new consumers had caused a significant jump in the number of new food product introductions. According to Productscan/

Exhibit 2   *Food ingredient sales of flavor houses: sales and market shares* (Source: *Quest International*)

Food Ingredient Sales (in US$ million)	1989	% share	Including '89/90 acquisitions	% share
Sanofi	412	14	414	14
Haarman & Reimer	–	0	231	8
Quest	98	3	158	5
Universal Foods	67	2	83	3
P.F.W.	75	3	75	3
Takasago	68	2	68	2
Subtotal	720	24	1,029	34
Others	2,280	76	1,971	66
Total	3,000	100	3,000	100

* Acquisition effect: 43%

Marketing Intelligence Service, more than 8,000 new food products were introduced in European markets in 1987. The trend towards expanding product offerings was expected to continue and would, in turn, increase the demand for new flavors and flavor systems. Many flavor houses predicted that the 1990s would bring a continuation of the flavoring fads of the 1980s – exotic flavorings, natural flavorings and easy to prepare foods. However, the area receiving the greatest interest was in natural flavorings and 'healthy' foods. Product obsolescence due to changes in consumer preferences, habits and lifestyles was also occurring faster than before. Together, combined with the competitive pressures stemming from the food industry, these factors were forcing flavor suppliers to improve their customer services in product application, research and development, technical assistance, and marketing.

Extended Product Lines

The blurring of distinctions among different fields in the industry was also having a major impact on the competitive structure of the food industry, thus creating an excellent opportunity for flavor houses. Companies were expanding existing product lines by utilizing either existing technological expertise in a particular area (such as chocolate or tea) or a successful brand image (such as Mars Bars or Lipton). The occurrence of blurring industry definitions was especially marked in the area of soft drinks. Companies from many previously unrelated fields were becoming interested in obtaining a share of the market. For example, the 'healthy-athletic' trend in parts of North America, Japan, and Northern Europe had prompted pharmaceutical companies to develop nutritional and 'sport' drinks as alternatives to traditional soft drinks. Also, because soft drinks – like Coca-Cola – were increasingly being marketed as an alternative to coffee for a morning beverage, coffee producers likewise tried to develop iced coffee as an alternative to soft drinks for consumption throughout the day. *(Refer to Exhibit 3.)*

Note

1. Biotechnology was another industry which was encroaching on the flavor houses. While flavor houses had spent considerable sums in developing the technology themselves, companies with a biotechnology background were still at an advantage in applying the technology to the production of natural flavors. (Most regulations treated flavors that were made through enzymology or fermentation as natural as long as the flavor met the other requirements.)

Exhibit 3 *Example of sources of new entries from other industries (Source: Quest International)*

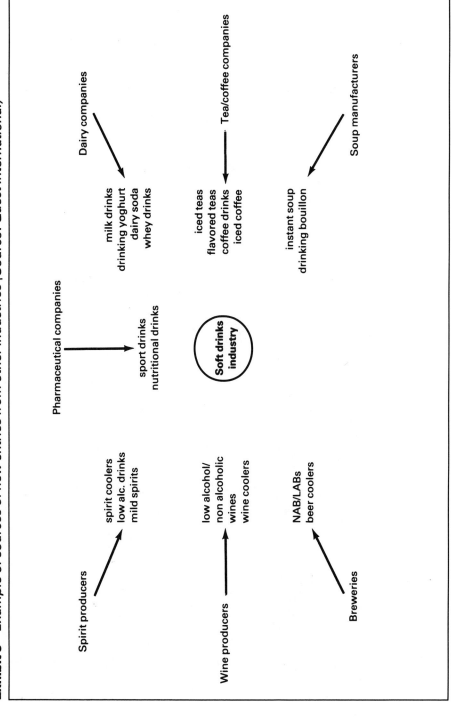

SECTION 2

Market Analysis:
Analyzing the Battlefield

CASE

West European Car Rental Industry

The West European Car Rental Industry

*This case was prepared by Manuel F. Colcombet, IMD MBA Research
Assistant, and Professor Per Jenster as a basis for class discussion rather
than to illustrate either effective or ineffective handling of a business
situation. It is based on industry sources and the work of: Laurent
Bachmann, Regina Erz, Gustavo Fernandez Bonfante, Barbara Lauer, and
Manuel Ordas Ferndandez.*

By 1990 the revenue of the West European car rental industry[1] was expected
to reach £3,1 billion ($5 billion), 12 per cent more than the previous year
(*Refer to **Exhibit 1***). The year 1989 had been an exciting one for the major
players in the business. Hertz, the largest worldwide car rental company, had
dramatically ensured its presence in the UK by reaching exclusivity
agreements with British Rail (representation at 2,500 stations) and with
British Airways through their BABS reservation system. Avis, the second
largest worldwide operator, showed a 31 per cent increase in pretax profits
for its European car rental network. Budget, the third worldwide operator,
had increased its European fleet by 38 per cent over a 12-month period.
Europcar, by merging with Interrent in January 1989, had become the largest
European operator with an overall 13 per cent market share.

Market Segments

There were two dimensions of customer usage patterns which industry
executives viewed as important market segments: 'usage scope' and 'usage
purpose'.

Exhibit 1   *Market size (Sources: Budget, ECATRA, industry estimates)*

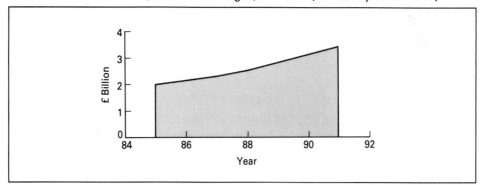

Usage Scope

The first dimension referred to the location where the car was booked and where it would be used. 'Local usage' was when the car was booked and used in the same city; 'incoming' rental was when the booking was made in a different city. Industry operators realized that serving incoming customers required a different infrastructure and commercial approach than what was needed to serve local customers.

One manager explained:

> For the 'incoming' customers, the most important sites of car rental outlets were airports, where more than 30% of European car hires were generated. Travellers also required outlets at major railway stations and hotels. Stations were expected to increase in importance with the expansion of high speed rail lines and the completion of the Channel Tunnel projected for 1993. The supra-local customers were eager to be able to book the car in their home country and even pay for the service with their own currency. These customers were keen to avoid anything going wrong in a city that they might not know well; therefore, they would choose the operator that instilled the most confidence from among the ones they managed to contact.

> Local renters looked for convenience and price. These customers knew the place, managed the environment, and were aware of the other means of transportation that could substitute for car rental such as taxis and public transportation. Finding a telephone book was nearly all they needed to price shop, check proximity and the opening time of outlets.

Usage Purpose

The second dimension was divided into the following categories: business, car replacement and repair, and tourism. The relevance of each segment varied among countries and seasons, but the business segment was the most important with 50% of the overall market value, 30% for replacement and local traffic, and tourism 20%.

The demand for rental cars for business purposes was higher on work days, especially Mondays to Thursdays, and throughout the year from September to June. The industry viewed business people as emphasizing the following factors: reliability, convenience, image and status. They expected to have no hassles, speedy delivery, easy check-ins and rapid check-outs. To attract this segment, car operators constantly made efforts to improve their service standards. As part of this program, they issued personal cards such as Budget's 'Rapid Action', and Hertz's 'Number One Card' (7 million in circulation). Avis had established a self-imposed standard maximum check-in-to-rent time of five minutes. At certain airport locations like London's Heathrow where customers had to go elsewhere to collect their vehicles, this was obviously not always possible. In an effort to increase convenience, Hertz had experimented with 'Travel-pilot', an in-car electronic vehicle navigation system.

Industry sources stated that, in selecting a car rental company, half of the business people were restricted to using the operator that had a corporate account relationship with the employer. Additionally, these sources mentioned that secretaries would make all the travel arrangements in one out of five occasions.

Tourism and leisure was a particularly active segment in summer. Tourists welcomed reliability and convenience; however, if the consumer were young, price mattered more. In the UK, 60% of those under 34 years of age shopped around for a 'better deal', but only 40% of those over 45 years old bothered to do so. In choosing a car rental company, customers preferred those which offered all inclusive rates, eliminating surprises on tax and mileage expenses.

The car replacement segment was particularly active at the beginning of every week, as Monday was the day people most often took their car in for repair. In some countries, like Germany, this segment was important because insurance companies were compelled to offer a replacement for cars damaged in an accident. In recent years, this segment was declining because there were fewer car accidents, and car insurance companies were attempting to reduce costs by compensating people who did not rent a replacement. In the early 1970s, consumers who were replacing cars that were out of order or hiring an extra car for short-term usage represented 60% of the German car rental business; in the late 1980s this figure was approximately 40%.

In selecting a car rental company, the garage owner exerted some influence, particularly if his garage offered a replacement service. This service tended to be 'free' or included in the repair bill.

Main Geographical Markets

More than 70% of the West European car rental revenue was generated in six countries, the biggest market being West Germany, followed by the UK, France, Italy, Sweden and the Netherlands. (*Refer to Exhibit 2.*) Prices tended to vary across borders, according to the following index (UK=100):

Netherlands	135
Sweden	131
Italy	123
France	110
UK	100
Germany	97

Usage also varied. In Britain, customers typically rented a car for four days (versus an average of three days on the Continent), predominantly for private use. In Northern France and in Germany, business and replacement were the main segments with one-way rentals constituting 30% and 23%, respectively, of all rentals; these were the highest in Europe. In the Mediterranean area, foreign visitors (both tourists and business people) were the main client groups, representing over 40% of the market; the average driven rental distances covered were the largest in Europe.

Exhibit 2   *1989 revenue by country (*Sources: *Budget, ECATRA, industry estimates)*

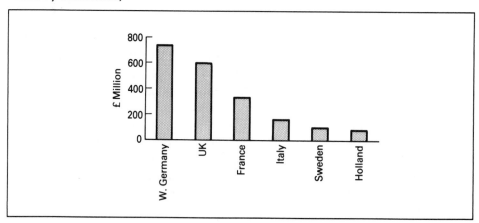

Industry operators also studied differences in consumer attitudes across countries. For example, for Germans the car's characteristics such as model, luxury, maintenance, and cleanliness were important in addition to the speed of service. British customers were viewed as price shoppers; their interests also focused on convenient locations (pick-up points) and all inclusive rates. The French generally viewed the industry with scepticism and, therefore, preferred all inclusive rates (as opposed to base rates plus additional charges for distance, insurance, tax, etc.). Payment mode, one-way rentals and having a selection of models to select from were also considered relevant in the French market.

There were also notable differences according to gender. In Europe, France had the highest rate of cars being rented by women, with 24% of the market. In the UK, even though women represented only 6% of the rental market, they were believed to play an important role in the purchasing decision; for example, it was found that women made half the enquiries about car rental in the leisure market.

Market Outlook

Industry observers expected the market to continue growing by 10–13% over the next three to five years, up from a 7% growth rate in previous years, due to these factors:

- General growth of the overall economy (based on a moderately strong increase of 4% for GNP). Improved business conditions would generate more business travel; increased income would expand the leisure industry, and growing car ownership would also increase replacement rentals because of more trips and breakdowns.

- The '1992' phenomenon was also seen as a factor which would stimulate rental due to the ease by which . . . could cross borders in a single market.

- The '1992' phenomenon was also seen as a factor which would stimulate rental, because cross-border trade would be easier in a single market.

- Car rental executives also saw business opportunities coming from industry consolidations. A range of factors was contributing to more growth – such as better reservation systems, better services, different pricing, new products such as cabriolet cars. Industry

members resisted disclosing the financial results due to the new
products. But, one Central European operator increased business
by 10% just from luxury cars and evening hire. Another area where
operators were seeking new opportunities was in car ownership
replacement.

One Budget executive reached the following conclusions after an extensive
analysis of the UK market:

> For town or country dwellers, car rental is also an efficient alternative to
> owning a second car which might be idle most of the time but still incurring
> tax, insurance and maintenance costs. With many car rental companies
> able to deliver a car to the doorstep, the rental alternative offers good
> value and convenience. An Escort, for instance, could be rented for
> 134 days a year, including delivery and collection, within a 15-mile radius
> of an office at the same cost as owning it. If the second car is actually
> used less than 134 days a year, renting as needed offers significant
> savings.

Several industry experts based their outlook on comparisons with the US
market. They expected that the single market would result in a narrowing
of differences between Europe and North America. Cross border differences
in car taxation and car rental taxation were expected to disappear. One-way
cross border rentals would not be restricted. Air transportation was
going to be deregulated, thus providing additional opportunities for car
rental firms.

Alan Cathcart, chairman and chief executive of Avis Europe, clearly
expected greater prosperity from a unified Europe:

> The USA is an excellent precursor of what 1992 could lead to in Europe.
> Consider the following statistics: less than 5% of the European drivers has ever
> rented a car, compared to 10–20% of US adults. Further, there are only 1.5
> rental vehicles per 1000 Europeans, compared to 5.5 for every 1000
> Americans.

Others felt, however, that the US market would not necessarily be
replicated in Europe. The differences in distances, lifestyle and the
European transportation system were sufficient reasons to explain this
point of view (i.e., in Europe only 30% of the car rental business was
generated at airports, compared to 70% in North America). *(Refer to
Exhibits 3 and 4 for key country indicators and size of the private and rental
car fleets.)*

Exhibit 3   *Country indicators: population, number of cars and rental cars*
(Sources: *Eurostat, ECATRA, industry estimates)*

Country	Population (Millions)	Cars (Millions)	Rental Cars (Thousands)
Belgium	9.9	3.6	7
Denmark	5.1	1.6	5
France	55.9	22.5	90
Germany (West)	61.5	29.2	80
Greece	10.0	1.4	12
Ireland	3.5	0.8	10
Italy	57.5	23.5	45
Luxemburg	0.4	0.2	2
Netherlands	14.8	5.3	17
Portugal	10.3	1.4	23
United Kingdom	57.2	21.3	140
Spain	38.9	10.5	30
TOTAL EEC	325.0	121.2	461
Austria	7.6	2.8	3
Sweden	8.5	3.5	23
Switzerland	6.5	2.7	9
USA	247.0	140.0	1380

Exhibit 4   *Per capita country indicators: income, number of cars and rental cars* (Sources: *Eurostat, ECATRA, industry estimates)*

Country	Gdp per capita (*)	Cars per 100 pers.	Rental Cars per 1000 p.
Belgium	16	36	0.7
Denmark	17	31	1.0
France	17	40	1.6
Germany (West)	18	47	1.3
Greece	9	14	1.2
Ireland	10	21	2.9
Italy	16	41	0.8
Luxemburg	19	40	5.0
Netherlands	16	36	1.1
Portugal	9	14	2.2
United Kingdom	17	37	2.4
Spain	12	27	0.8
Total EEC	16	37	1.4
Austria	16	37	0.4
Sweden	19	41	2.7
Switzerland	21	42	1.4
USA	25	57	5.6

(*) Gross domestic product per capita at current prices and purchasing power parities.

Industry Structure

Even though global competitors dominated the market, there was no clear market leader. Large local markets with regional differences in preferences, rental patterns, taxation, historic development and low barriers to entry were seen as key reasons for significant market fragmentation. Traditionally, firms had entered the car rental business as a sideline to auto retail or gas station operations, where the overhead costs could be kept to a minimum through operational synergies. Garages handling car repairs were an excellent example of the local company that competed within the replacement segment. The garage owner could keep a few cars on hand which he then rented out to a customer having repairs made.

Another reason for fragmentation was that national borders prevented the global competitors from fully exploiting their relative size. Economies of scale through volume discounts on car purchases and insurance were not always possible because of frontiers. In addition, country regulations significantly increased the cost of cross border rentals because the car had to be returned to the country of origin at the company's or the consumer's expense.

Some local operators (licensees) had franchise agreements whereby they could use the brand name of global players. This arrangement benefited both parties. The licensees enjoyed the benefit of using a recognized name, won access to computer reservation systems and to international clients. As the licensees supplied themselves with outlets and vehicles, these agreements enabled the licensor to extend its presence with little capital expenditure and to benefit immediately from a 3–4% fee on gross licensee sales. Additionally, the licensor enjoyed the strategic advantage of penetrating an area that might not have been accessible to him. Another way of extending coverage without too much increase in fixed costs was by establishing agencies, that is, independently-owned firms that operated the outlets, received a commission, but did not own the hired cars.

The existing market structure was far from static. A growing number of mergers as well as many new entrants indicated that this industry was undergoing significant changes. The previously mentioned Europcar–Interrent merger was only one example of the industry's restructuring. Increased concentration was also occurring as local firms joined global companies or departed from the industry. In 1989 alone, almost 1,000 companies (12 per cent) left the industry (i.e., discontinued the business or were absorbed). The primary reason appeared to be the fight for market share by the international companies. In an effort to increase their business base, these firms tried hard to enter new regions and to approach new customer sub-segments. Using the US as a comparable single market, major companies clearly expected gaining from 1992. The top four companies in the US had an 80 per cent market share versus only 43 per cent in Europe. With this comparison in mind, an industry marketing director asserted that the 'big four' would command 70–75 per cent of the European market by the year 2000. Yet, Europe still faced new entrants coming from the US: Eurodollar, Alamo, and Thrifty were looking for a stake in the market before the consolidation process ended. All three companies had entered the market through partnerships or franchising, and had competed in the US on a price platform. Some operators feared that Japanese car rental companies, backed by the powerful vehicle manufacturers of that country, would also try to enter the market.

Sales and Marketing

The industry used a wide range of channels to maximize the speed and availability with which customers could book their services, including travel agents, corporate accounts arrangements and dedicated sales people. Travel agents accounted for 20 per cent of the bookings. In return for their selling services, travel agents and tour operators received a commission, ranging from 5 per cent to 25 per cent. The highest fee corresponded to the sale of a full rate car rental package.

CRS Systems

Travel agents would either call the car rental company or use their computer reservation system (CRS). When receiving a telephone reservation, the larger car rental companies immediately booked the reservation on their in-house CRS. These CRS systems were continuously developed and improved. Avis asserted that its World-Wide Wizard system enabled the company to offer improved service, because customers could 'check out' (rent a car) in just two minutes, and 'check in' (return it) in only one minute.

When a travel agent reserved directly on a CRS, it was generally through an 'outside' system, to which the car rental firms did not have direct access. However, changes were taking place for some industry participants. Budget was proud to claim that it was the first international car rental company to sign up with both the Amadeus and Galileo airline reservation systems. These two systems, Amadeus and Galileo, founded by the major airlines, were backed by groups of European carriers.

Commenting on the effects of CRS systems, Robin Gauldie, editor of *Travel Trade Gazette*, stated:

> There is no doubt that these systems will become vital to the survival of the
> travel agent in the complex environment of post-1992 Europe. They will give
> agents an enhanced sales tool, will speed up their reaction time to fare changes
> and, importantly, in view of the threat of increased paperwork, provide them
> with a vastly more powerful back office facility, as well as faster and more
> comprehensive reservation facilities. Agents who adopt the new technology
> are likely to become increasingly hostile to principals who are not themselves
> accessible through CRS, a move which will have profound implications for tour
> operators, hoteliers and other travel service providers.

Robin Gauldie's forecast implied that small car rental operators would
encounter an increasingly tough environment, as these systems would not be
able to carry more than 20 car rental companies.

The range of alliances was extending beyond the airlines and travel
intermediaries. Railways were willing to provide selling services to the car
rental industry and, on some occasions, signed agreements providing
exclusivity. Examples included a contract between the SNCF in France and
Avis, and between British Rail and Hertz. In another type of arrangement,
the car and hotel CRS CONFIRM had a development agreement with
Budget as an equity partner along with Hilton, Marriott and AMR.

Corporate Accounts

Industry sources estimated that corporate accounts represented nearly one-
fifth of the car rental industry. In some countries, such as France, Germany
and Italy, this segment represented nearly 30 per cent of all car rentals. To
obtain these agreements, car rental companies offered discounts between 10
per cent and 40 per cent. In France, where a price war was raging for
corporate accounts, these discounts reached 30 per cent in 1990. In return,
the car rental companies received first choice on all rentals and thus were
ensured a non-seasonal captive market. These corporate accounts, in
addition to favouring the market share of a particular operator, could
increase the size of the rental market by providing a corporate fleet.

Gentlemen's Agreements

Industry operators often maintained informal agreements with automobile
mechanics and hotel receptionists, who served as sales intermediaries by

referring clients. These intermediaries could receive a commission of 10 per cent, or even 20 per cent, for a full rate sale. Regarding this type of sale, global companies did not show any sizeable advantage over local companies.

'Walk-in' and Telephone Sales

Direct contact between the car rental company and the consumer, where telephone reservations were made by the customer directly, accounted for more than half of total sales. To attract the customer's attention, firms relied on good advertisements in telephone books and on billboard postings in multiple urban locations.

In this area, local operators had the same advantages as global players, especially when there were synergies with existing businesses, such as when garages rented replacement cars to customers having repairs done. The major companies were slowly gaining market share by offering affiliated garages repair and maintenance work on the operator's fleet, as well as a commission of 10 per cent for referring clients.

Pricing

Car rental rates varied by country, city, season, day of the week, rental length and mileage requirement. Prices were also affected by the booking mechanism and the predelivery booking period, creating complex pricing schedules which even employees found difficult to manage and apply. The extra cost options and insurance charges made pricing even more complicated. *(Refer to **Exhibits 5** and **6** for a typical tariff structure for one company in one country.)* Pricing had little relation to operating costs, in part because the cost related to a particular hire was difficult to allocate, and because pricing was a tool used to attract different segments and increase the utilization of the rental fleet.

The pricing policies of the various competitors in the industry were also designed to change when possible, as much as the 'market will bear'. As in other service industries, one way to support this marketing policy was by rewarding the employees when clients chose higher margin products from the firm's portfolio, i.e., upgrading, ordering additional options, or selecting a more luxurious car. For example, customers perceived that rental rates corresponded to the prices for different new car models, even though the operator's costs did not correlate proportionally. A customer might also walk into an outlet in a hurry and with no advance booking, and be willing to take

Exhibit 5

Price List for International Customers

BUDGET 1990 rent a car				BUDGET 1990 rent a car
	Unlimited mileage tariff, per day			Unlimited mileage tariff
	1-3days	4-6 days	7 days and more	Friday 12oo to Monday 9oo
	Special offer - Not discountable			
OPEL Corsa	142.-	108.-	96.-	182.-
VW Golf OPEL Kadett	195.-	152.-	136.-	213.-
OPEL Kadett Stationw.	196.-	157.-	137.-	215.-
OPEL Kadett, Autom.	210.-	161.-	147.-	223.-
OPEL Vectra TOYOTA Corolla Wagon 4x4	227.-	182.-	167.-	247.-
OPEL Vectra Autom.	205.-	205.-	180.-	285.-
OPEL Omega	268.-	207.-	181.-	310.-
OPEL Omega Stationw.	323.-	250.-	225.-	385.-
VW Microbus ISUZU Bus	375.-	315.-	275.-	400.-
BMW 316i OPEL Vectra 4x4	379.-	316.-	285.-	430.-
MERCEDES 190 E Autom. BMW 525 i Autom. (sunroof)	281.-	230.-	199.-	550.-
MERCEDES 230 E Autom. A/C	512.-	440.-	385.-	590.-
MERCEDES 300 SE Autom. A/C	583.-	496.-	436.-	670.-

Source: Company Price List 1990

Exhibit 6

Price List for Local Customers

BUDGET rent a car	Local tariff	1990		BUDGET rent a car	
	Unlimited mileage, per day 1-3 days 4-6 days 7 days and more			Week-end tariff 2 days 3 days	
	Special tariff				
OEPL Corsa	71.-	54.-	47.-	119.-	156.-
VW Golf OPEL Kadett	91.-	73.-	63.-	146.-	188.-
OPEL Kadett Stationw.	94.-	74.-	65.-	147.-	190.-
OPEL Kadett Autom.	96.-	76.-	66.-	157.-	203.-
OPEL Vectra TOYOTA Corolla Wagon 4x4	115.-	89.-	81.-	175.-	224.-
OPEL Vectra Autom.	124.-	97.-	87.-	188.-	244.-
OPEL Omega	136.-	112.-	97.-	207.-	270.-
OPEL Omega Stationw.	182.-	147.-	133.-	259.-	339.-
VW Microbus ISUZU Bus	195.-	159.-	142.-	302.-	392.-
BMW 316i OPEL Vectra 4x4	184.-	146.-	132.-	278.-	359.-
MERCEDES 190 E Autom. BMW 525 i Autom. (sunroof)	233.-	188.-	170.-	336.-	435.-
MERCEDES 230 E Autom. A/C	290.-	236.-	214.-	419.-	541.-
MERCEDES 300 SE Autom. A/C	361.-	293.-	267.-	499.-	651.-

Source: Company Price List 1990

a more expensive model, even if initially attracted to that outlet by ads claiming a special offer. (The simplified pricing example outlined below provides an illustration.)

	Regular	Contract*	Weekday	Weekend
Business	100	80	100	100
Tourist	100	70	100	60

* Corporate account contracts were arranged through the head office. Tourist contracts were booked in advance.

Prices also varied significantly amongst the European countries, although they were always much higher than those in the US *(refer to Exhibit 7)*. Tax differences explained only a small part of the difference *(refer to Exhibit 8)*.

Other Marketing Tools

Creating brand awareness through advertising was considered important to attract the supra-local traveller. It was estimated that global companies spent around 2% of sales on advertising. Achieving the right spending balance posed continued problems, as advertising was not uniformly recognized as an order winner. One industry observer commented that Budget Switzerland had difficulties in 1987 and was subsequently sold, largely because of its belief that it could win increased sales through heavy advertising and promotion.

In addition to pricing discounts, most large companies were willing to spend more than 5% of sales on various promotional activities. The main objectives were to:

● Maintain an information flow about the company's products to the market, that is, point of sales offerings, brochures, maps, etc.

Exhibit 7 *USA–Europe rate comparison (*Source: AVIS Supervalue weekly rates at April 90 exchange rates)

Region	Subcompact	Compact
Germany	440	580
UK	430	575
Spain	335	415
New York	290	315
Florida	160	180

Note: Prices in US dollars including taxes, unlimited mileage and insurance

Exhibit 8 *Value Added Tax by country (*Sources: *Hertz, ECATRA)*

Country	On short term car rental (%)	On car purchase (%)	On car insurance (%)
Belgium	25	25 to 33	(*)
Denmark	22	22	–
France	25 to 28	25	–
Germany	14	14	7
Greece	16	6	(*)
Ireland	10	25	NIL
Italy	19 to 38	19 to 38	12.5
Luxemburg	12	12	12
Netherlands	20	18.5	(*)
Portugal	17	17	–
UK	15	15 to 25	NIL
Spain	12	33	NIL
Austria	20	32	10
Sweden	23.5	–	–
Switzerland	NIL	6.2	–
USA	6 to 12	6 to 12	–

Note: This list does not include import duties and other special taxes on vehicle.
(*) The value added tax is replaced by a specific tax.

- Meet clients' expectations and attract the repeat client segment by offering free gadgets, better service, etc. Some operators also launched so-called 'internal promotions', such as training programs for personnel.

Outlet Management

Outlet management involved the ongoing management of the rental outlets, including activities such as 'checking out', 'checking in', invoicing, car cleaning, and staffing. Selection of the site and the people were considered the key factors because of their promotional impact. The main outlet costs (totaling 35% of revenues) were maintaining properties (offices and garages) in key locations, and supporting a trained staff with long working hours (e.g., Avis's location in Amsterdam Airport employed over 120 people).

Airport administrations, aware of their control at key locations and having only limited space, charged car rental firms a premium of 10% of their sales for an outlet on the premises. Some companies, in an attempt to avoid this charge, established outlets just outside the airports and relied on a shuttle service to transport their customers (e.g., Heathrow) with resulting delays.

Major companies carried an extensive network of outlets in order to meet the needs of the supra-local traveller and to fully capitalize on their established brand names (e.g., Hertz had more then 150 locations in Germany). In addition, these companies regarded increased distribution as a way to gain market share. To help reduce investments and swap fixed costs for variable costs, they relied on subcontracting in less critical locations. In contrast, local firms minimized outlet costs through synergies with other lines of business such as car sales or repairs.

Car Control

Ensuring that a given car was in the right place at the right time was considered critical for the large firms in order to obtain high utilization rates. This was not easy, considering the amount of one-way travelling, the need to wash and service the cars, and the industry's practice of not penalizing clients who did not respect their reservations.

All international companies made extensive use of information technology to optimize car utilization. By considering booked reservations and historical sales figures, they determined the mix and number of cars at any given outlet. When adding the expenses of redistribution of vehicles and staff needed, 10% of revenues were typically spent performing this operation. In smaller firms, this activity was either limited or unnecessary.

Fleet Management

Fleet management represented up to 30% of revenues. It involved the purchase of the vehicles, maintenance and repair of the fleet, as well as insurance and, eventually, resale. The large rental companies were important customers for the vehicle manufacturers. An estimated 4–7% of all new cars were purchased by the car rental industry. In addition, car rental represented an important test opportunity for potential new car buyers. The large volume of cars purchased resulted in significantly reduced prices for the car rental companies. The importance of these firms as customers had led to acquisitions by the car companies. For example, Avis was partially owned by General Motors, Europcar by VW, Hertz by Ford and Volvo.

New cars were purchased and resold every 6 to 12 months by the large companies. Market conditions within the new car and resale market tended to move together. Thus, if the resale market were soft, the new car market would also be soft, offsetting any arbitrage risk for the rental companies.

Repair and maintenance costs tended to be minimal for the larger companies, because their cars were generally sold within the normal warranty period. In addition, the companies tended to contract insurance only for damages to third parties, thereby self-insuring their own fleet. Local rental companies tended to keep their car fleet longer, thus reducing their acquisition costs, but increasing maintenance and resale expenses.

Main Competitors

The industry could be divided into three groups of competitors: the 'big four', the other international firms, and the local operators.

The 'Big Four'

This group consisted of Avis, Hertz, Budget and Europcar. The first three had started operating in the US and now enjoyed market leadership positions in that country; Europcar was, as its name suggests, European and owned by major European car manufacturers. The 'Big Four' could be called Pan European in the sense that they were present in all West European countries. Their market share, size and structure differed somewhat *(as indicated in Exhibit 9)*. In some countries (West Germany, France, the Netherlands, Spain, and the UK), their presence was diluted by the existence of hundreds of competitors. In other countries like Sweden and Italy where competition was concentrated, the 'Big Four' managed to control well over half the market. *(Refer to Exhibits 10a and 10b.)*

Exhibit 9 *Profile of major competitors in Western Europe (Sources: company brochures, company directories, press releases, industry literature and estimates)*

	Avis	Budget	Europcar	Hertz
Market share (%)	12	7	13	11
Fleet (000 cars)	80	35	75	70
Outlets	1700	1200	1850	1600(*)
Airport market share (%)	25	10	20	25

(*) Plus 3300 railway representations

Exhibit 10a *Market share and number of competitors by country*

| | Market share | | Number of competitors |
	Big Four (%)	Others (%)	
Germany	46	54	* * *
UK	39	61	* * *
France	46	54	* * *
Italy	67	33	*
Sweden	60	40	*
Netherlands	34	66	* *

Notes on number of competitors: (orders of magnitude)
*   Italy, Sweden: a hundred
**   Netherlands: around 3 hundred
***   Germany: a thousand
      UK & France: more than a thousand

Exhibit 10b *Market share of major competitors by country (*Sources: *Budget, ECATRA, industry estimates)*

	Avis (%)	Budget (%)	Europcar (%)	Hertz (%)
Germany	10	9	19	8
UK	9	8	12	10
France	14	4	15	13
Italy	27	5	15	20
Sweden	10	13	19	18
Netherlands	10	9	6	9
West Europe	12	7	13	11

In the most rewarding segment, 'the walk-in customer', the major companies enjoyed large shares (approximately 80%), but the percentage was even higher in the commercial traveller segment. Such high shares were the result of efforts made by this group of competitors to cater to these customers at every airport and to capitalize on the selling power of their international network. Industry observers named Hertz as the most successful in following this strategy, with nearly two-thirds of their turnover generated at airports. Hertz was supposed to be closely followed by Avis, then Europcar and, finally, Budget where less than one-third of the turnover was generated at airports (*refer to* **Exhibit 10b**).

For all these companies, the segments reached and the strategies being used varied from country to country. As a result, price positioning also varied. Observers perceived that Avis was situated at premium price points followed by Hertz and Europcar, with Budget having the lowest prices among this group (*refer to **Exhibit 11***).

Avis Europe

In 1988 this company became public and independent of its parent, Avis US. By the end of 1989, however, it returned under parent control of Avis Inc., Lease International S.A., and General Motors. Throughout the period of independence, Avis Europe had continued to use Avis's reservations and marketing network.

Avis Europe's 1989 annual report revealed that its short-term rental operations had increased profits by 31% despite an 8% price drop and only 19% increase in revenue. Employee morale was high (70% owned company shares). The company was known for its slogan '*We try harder*' and enjoyed an 'international', 'upmarket' and 'good service' reputation.

Exhibit 11 *Examples of car rental prices in £ (all prices valid on March 31, 1988 (VAT included); one day's rental of a category A car, 200 km and CDW)* (Source: *BEUC, car rental price survey, 1989*)

	Avis	Budget	Europcar[1]	Interrent[1]	Hertz	Local *	Local **	Local ***
B	98.41	86.93	98.41	91.53	99.56	75.76		
DK	106.74		83.77	82.26	108.74	73.74		
D	89.55	67.33	83.61	83.55	89.09	72.78		
GR	54.03	49.77	49.77	50.98	69.50	44.71		
E	63.57	60.56	64.98	61.13	63.77			
F	111.19	106.06	111.71	105.64	111.15	87.74	99.61	84.17***
IRL	96.93		85.55		101.06**	38.76	34.23	
I	134.72		147.41	135.08	137.14	134.06	100.38	130.37
L	87.68		86.62	56.81	105.86			
NL	96.63		94.11	85.21	98.17			
P	43.13	41.83	42.45	51.18	43.00	33.92	37.71	41.08
GB	92.57		84.82					
A	113.63	93.10	100.87	101.09	83.75	91.92	79.86	
CH	114.57	105.04	111.39	95.56	112.57			
YU	50.34		43.11	52.01	59.80			

1   Europcar and Interrent have merged
*   Locally owned firms
** Becomes 115.26 when driver is under 23 years of age (CDW more than doubles)
*** PAI included as well

Though already enjoying a dense location network with more than 1,700 outlets, industry observers were expecting Avis to 'buy more market share'. The goal was: 'to grow ahead of hungry opposition' and at the same time meet its objectives of being present in all communities of over 50,000 inhabitants. It was felt that one of the key issues for Avis was to rethink its international pricing policies.

Hertz Europe

Hertz was the largest worldwide car rental company, with about half of its fleet in the US. Represented in 120 countries, Hertz had a network of around 400,000 vehicles in 4,700 locations. Its major strength was the control of the airport market and the consequent share of visitors to Europe, particularly those coming from North America.

The ownership of Hertz had continued to change. In 1987 the Ford Motor Company took control of Hertz. By 1989, Ford had sold 26% of its stake to Volvo North American Corporation and 5% to Commerzbank. The Hertz management team owned 20%, with Ford's remaining share amounting to 29%.

In the industry, it was believed that Hertz was performing well and was consolidating its presence in the European market. Hertz's West European network consisted of around 1,600 locations of which 350 were served on a contract basis or operated on a reduced schedule (i.e., seasonal outlets open for holiday periods, reduced hour outlets for low traffic airports). Hertz had also made an effort to be present at railway stations, in addition to its traditional airport locations. Hertz obtained 3,300 representations resulting from its agreements with British Rail and the Swiss rail system. Hertz was permanently installed at 140 airports, but was also present at another 210 airports, some of which largely served private aviation.

With Hertz's caption, *'Number one'*, it held a market perception of being 'big', 'American', and 'upmarket'. One industry observer commented that Hertz's management was faced with an organization which risked becoming bureaucratic because of its size. On the other hand, it was credited with excellent media advertisement and positioning.

Europcar/Interrent

On January 1, 1989, Europcar, a French operator with an international network, and Interrent, also international but mostly German, merged to create the largest European network. By the end of 1989, the combined organization had more than 1,800 locations in Western Europe. The merged company was then controlled by Wagons-Lits and by Volkswagen, a German car manufacturer.

The intent of the merger was to build strength through:

- An extensive coverage and a clear leadership position in the major European markets: Germany, the UK and France;
- The alliances built by Europcar with 'National Car Rental' in the Americas and the Pacific, 'Tilden Rent a Car' in Canada, 'Nippon Rent a Car' in Japan and the Pacific;
- Their established name and reputation;
- Synergies from operations.

An industry observer noted that the integration of the two operations was slow to come, because of cultural differences, differing goals of the shareholders, and different management and operating systems. Another asserted that the companies would have been stronger if they had remained separate.

> Merged operations will mean reduced desk occupancy at the airports, and half the offerings on the CRS screens of travel agents and airline personnel. Also there is the risk of redundant personnel and that subcontractors will migrate to the competition. Remember what happened to Hertz when it restructured its German operations in the mid-'70s; Interrent and Eutopcar profited from that opportunity.

Because much work still had to be done to complete the merger, Europcar's results were quoted as being poor, and the fruits of the merger were yet to be seen.

Budget

Budget was the most recently funded company of the big four (Los Angeles, 1958). In October 1988 Ford Motor company financed a management buyout of the company. By 1989, its worldwide operations served 3,400 locations with 200,000 cars. The European network consisted of 1,200 locations, with a majority held by licensees and their agents. Budget made extensive use of franchising. The result was that the company was less homogeneous than its major competitors in most areas – from marketing practices to operating performance. One example of this heterogeneous approach was the situation at the Madrid Airport. In contrast to all the other major European airports, Barajas Budget only offered a 'pick-up' service from the airport. Budget's franchising policy, however, provided a network of highly motivated entrepreneurial companies, such as Sixt/Budget in Germany. This strategy had resulted in a growth of 38 per cent over recent years.

Every country had to adhere to the overall strategy of providing '*Good value for the money*'. Hence, Budget was well regarded, especially in the leisure segment of the market. Some felt, however, that it relied too much on this particular segment. Yet, Budget claimed that it was getting the highest operating performances in the industry with utilization rates above 70 per cent, in contrast to the industry average of 60 per cent. In general, Budget used less media advertisement than its competitors, but this savings was compensated by more discounts and promotion (internal and external).

Other International Firms

A series of other companies were trying to establish themselves as pan-European, or even international. In pursuing that objective, they joined forces with other European or North American players.

Thrifty, regarded as number five in the US and clearly competing on price, had moved into the UK, France, Greece, Belgium, Spain, Portugal, Italy, Ireland and Scandinavia. In Germany, it had reached an agreement with **PROcar**. But, industry observers considered that, after achieving this network, Thrifty had become somewhat 'stretched' and 'coverage was very thin'.

Dollar, another US operator, had been able to merge with **Swan** (UK) and also signed convenient licensing and franchising agreements on the Continent. The resulting network operated 11,000 cars in UK and 4,000 on the Continent.

Another kind of alliance was 'reciprocal marketing and representation agreements' which, for example, had been achieved between **General** (Florida) and **Kenning** (UK).

Industry observers pointed to **Ansa International** as the most successful medium-sized company operating in more than 50 countries worldwide. Its shareholders were 40 per cent American, 40 per cent EC, 10 per cent Swiss, and 10 per cent Pacific based.

Local Companies

The overwhelming majority of these companies were small independent concerns operating at a regional or purely local level. For these firms, renting cars was generally an ancillary activity to vehicle repair and sales. Not generally 'geared up' for the businessman, these local operators received most of their turnover from accident replacement rentals and had suffered from the contraction of this market. Their relative inflexibility, the debilitating effects of insurance companies' cost-cutting on the industry and increasing competition from the multinational rental leaders also contributed to the continuous rationalization process which had occurred. Nevertheless, some of them benefited from the major players' appetite and sold their telephone numbers and client accounts for healthy amounts. Thus, the local company's client would be referred to the major one. Still others continued the operation as a strong contributor to the profitability of their main business.

Note

1. Short-term car rental in Europe, excluding Warsaw Pact countries, and excluding commercial vehicles.

SECTION 3

Industrial
Customer Segmentation
and Customer Buying Behavior

CASES

Maillefer SA (A)
BP Nutrition/Hendrix Voeders B.V. (A)
Ciba-Geigy Allcomm

Maillefer SA (A)

This case was prepared by Owen Dempsey, Research Associate, under the direction of Professor Robert S. Collins as a basis for class discussion rather than to illustrate either effective or ineffective handling of an administrative situation.

It was March 1980, the end of one challenge and the beginning of another for Jacques Bonjour. A party celebrating the end of the intensive Program for Executive Development at IMEDE in Lausanne, Switzerland, was still in progress, but Bonjour's mind was already considering the difficult task ahead of him. He had just accepted a new position as Marketing Manager for the MP Group (pipe machinery) of Maillefer SA, a leading Swiss manufacturer of equipment for the extrusion of plastic.

Although Maillefer had been for many years a major competitor in the cable machinery market, efforts over the past five years to extend this success into the pipe machinery market had not achieved very satisfactory results. As their new Marketing Manager, Bonjour was to be responsible for formulating a new strategy for the MP Group in the pipe machinery market. Specifically, his goal was to increase MP Group revenues from Sfrs. 3.5 million to over Sfrs. 7.5 million, while directing activities towards products and markets where Maillefer could compete profitably.

As Jacques Bonjour left the IMEDE party, he thought back over Maillefer's history, how the MP Group came to exist in the first place, and what steps he should take in order to achieve the goals that had been established for the MP Group.

Company Background

In 1900, Monsieur Charles L. Maillefer established a workshop in the old mill at Romainmôtier, a Swiss village in the hills near the French border.

Maillefer S.A., a privately-held Swiss company, originally manufactured machine-tool equipment for the forming, milling and grinding of metal. In 1925, M. Maillefer and his two sons began to manufacture cable-making machines which wound multiple strands of wire into a single-braided or twisted cable for mechanical or electrical use. Other machines were developed to coat or sheathe the completed cables with one or more layers of insulation, machines which formed the basis of Maillefer's current business.

With Europe at war, plastics became a widely-used replacement for rubber. In 1941, Maillefer S.A. produced its first extrusion machine. This marked the beginning of what was to become a specialty: the manufacture of machines for the cable-making and plastics industries. In 1964, a new assembly workshop was built at Ecublens, ten minutes from Lausanne, and by 1972 all manufacturing, technical and administrative functions were consolidated there. A subsidiary was established in the United States to manufacture and market throughout North America.

Maillefer specialized in sophisticated extruders and line equipment which originally were sold exclusively to the cable machinery market. Maillefer cable machinery extruded a variety of plastic materials to coat or insulate wires and cables. Mallefer's lines were known the world over for being able to extrude products which met the exacting specifications of suppliers to the electronics and telecommunications industries. As Monsieur Maillefer said,

> The performance level attained by Maillefer equipment is the result of painstaking research, innovative engineering and diligent attention to detail: the hallmarks of a company which, at all levels, is conscious of its role in the futhering of technological progress.

The high quality of the company's machines was measured by the dimensional precision (diameter and thickness), material homogeneity and surface quality of the extruded product, and the ease with which product specifications could be attained and maintained on line. Customers demanded precision in order to meet strict performance requirements (microelectronic wiring, life-sustaining surgical tubing) and/or to reduce the material cost of products manufactured in high volume (coaxial cable, water conduit). Such results were achieved by means of precise control of temperature, pressure and rate of flow at the extruder head. The geometries of the extruder screw and barrel were custom-designed for each group of plastics. The optimal geometry was then chosen to match a given customer's application. Maillefer extruders had always been known for their ability to process a wider range of thermoplastics than those of other manufacturers. Line equipment which handled the extruded product was adapted as well.

By 1980, Maillefer was employing 450 people and was averaging sales of 140 extruders annually, 80 of these as part of complete lines. Revenues were approximately Sfrs. 80 million of which 90% was export sales.

However, the cyclical nature of the cable industry made specialization risky. Management wished to diversify operations, which had led them as early as 1969 to investigate the market for pipe extrusion machinery, the idea being to adapt their extrusion technology from cable machinery and to generate new sales.

The MP Group

The MP Group was first set up in 1970 as an independent subsidiary which would market equipment to manufacturers of extruded pipe. Since pipe and cable both required extrusion equipment which was similar in design and function, it was presumed that Maillefer could anticipate additional sales of extrusion machines, and even complete lines, by transferring their extrusion technology from one market to the other. Before long, it became apparent to MP's commercial staff and Maillefer's technical people that a subsidiary relationship was impractical, thus in 1975 MP was brought in-house as a small, informally structured group. As one manager in Ecublens put it:

> The main idea in starting MP was to have a broad diversification, beginning with the pipe market segment, then eventually going on to include a range of extruder equipment for additional segments

In fact, however, the undertaking had proven to be more complex.

Jacques Bonjour, meanwhile, had been working from 1966 to 1979 as an engineer in the German-speaking part of Switzerland, as well as abroad. Then, in the autumn of 1979, he entered IMEDE's Program for Executive Development. It was at this time that he learned about the interesting and exciting challenge at Maillefer S.A. as Marketing Manager for the MP Group. After discussions with Maillefer's management, Bonjour accepted the appointment and moved into his new office in March 1980. He could have no illusions about the task ahead of him for it had been clearly spelled out in a policy memo issued before his arrival:

> General Management has decided not only to keep the MP Group, but to develop it, finding realizable diversification and seeking new growth. This decision has been made despite the fact that sales for the first part of 1980 are weak, 25% below the objective.

In 1980 the MP group was staffed by only six people. In addition to Bonjour,

Franz Jermann handled sales, assisted by one other person. Three additional people provided technical support. As the organization chart in *Exhibit 1* illustrates, MP relied upon the corporate organization for most services. In 1979, MP accounted for sales of 20 installations totaling Sfr. 3.5 million, all for plastic pipe. All the engineering and manufacturing was being done at the main facility in Ecublens.

The Extrusion Process

Extrusion is the process of shaping (metal or plastic) by forcing through a die.*

In plastic extrusion, the raw material first had to be transformed from a solid to a molten state. As shown in *Exhibit 2* an extrusion machine consisted of a hopper, barrel/screw assembly and extruder head. The hopper fed solid plastic pellets into the barrel where they were heated to melting point by a combination of controlled heating and cooling elements as well as by the mechanical energy produced by screw rotation. The screw moved the plastic towards the extruder head while mixing it thoroughly. The head then delivered a controlled flow of uniform, molten plastic of the desired consistency. The shape of the head varied depending on the task, such as coating a wire or forming a pipe.

As shown in *Exhibit 3*, an extruder operated as the main component of an extrusion line. To extrude pipe, plasticized material was pumped out in a steady flow by the extruder screw. While molten, it passed through the extruder head and vacuum calibration trough which formed the desired size and shape of pipe. The hot plastic cooled and set as it moved through one or more cooling troughs. A motorized haul-off provided the drive mechanism for the line.

The speed at which the haul-off drew the pipe away from the extruder head had to be precisely synchronized with the rate at which the rotating screw fed material into the system. Flexible pipe was then fed to a coiler where it was wound on large spools while rigid pipe was cut to the proper length and stacked on a dump table. Another option was the application of an identifying stripe or code on line. Alternatively, two or more extruders could be integrated into a single line in order to perform layering of several plastics in a single pass.

A critical component of plastic extrusion equipment was the extruder screw. The screw performed several functions. In addition to transporting

---

* *Webster's Ninth New Collegiate Dictionary.*

Exhibit 1 *Organization chart*

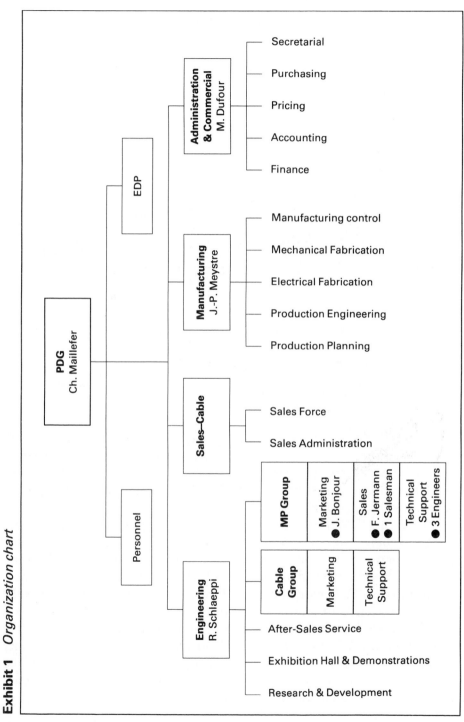

Exhibit 2 *Maillefer's BM screw (*Source: *Maillefer Technical Report,* The BM Extruders: A new generation)

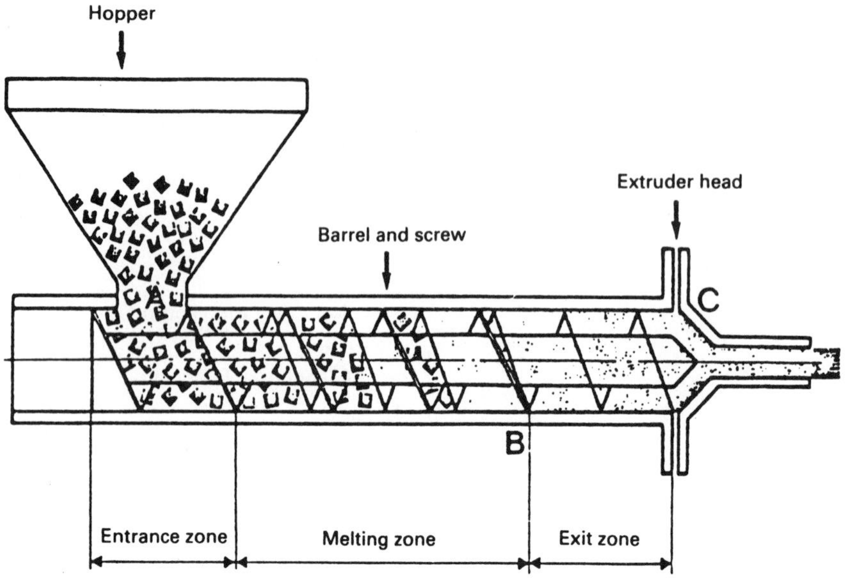

Ever since Archimedes, the screw has been used for the transportation of materials, but it is immediately obvious that a simple conveying screw is inadequate for extrusion, which demands not only displacement of the material but also heating, mixing, and pressurizing. The transformation must be progressive, to avoid deterioration of the substance being processed.

material through the barrel where heating, mixing and pressurizing occurred, the plastic being processed had to be transformed steadily in order to maintain homogeneity, a precise temperature, and a continuous flow to the extruder head. Screw design was one of Maillefer's recognized strengths in research and engineering.

Maillefer's 'BM Screw' was a patented design which made up the core of all the company's extrusion machines. The BM Screw revolutionized the industry when it was announced in 1960. Maillefer used a double-spiral design which effectively divided the barrel into three zones: entrance, melting and exit. Only molten plastic of the proper consistency could reach the extruder head. Advantages of the BM Screw were its ability to control temperature precisely in the barrel as well as at the extruder head. Even at a high output rate, the BM Screw was able to maintain material homogeneity and allow for rapid changes in materials or colors without shutting down the line. Screw and barrel geometries were custom-designed to accommodate the individual characteristics of each family of plastics and their respective processing rates.

Exhibit 3 *A pipe extrusion line, 1980*

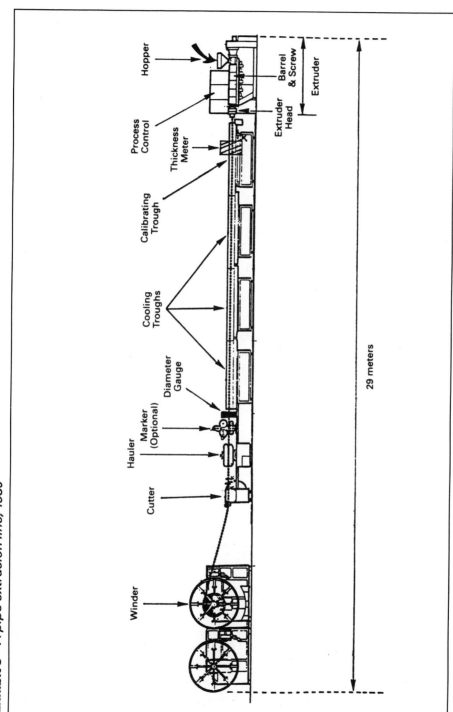

At this time, extruders were chosen to match the processing task at hand. Small extruders processed limited amounts of polymer while the largest extruders were capable of handling high volumes. *Exhibit 4* presents a breakdown, by screw-diameter size and number of units, of extruder machinery installed annually in Western Europe during the period 1977–1979. Screw-diameters ranged from 25mm to over 180mm and correlated with the raw material processing capacity (in Kg/Hr) of a given extruder.

Two variables were critical in determining how closely extruded pipe met specifications. The first was the consistancy of the rate of draw by the haul-off. This had to be synchronized with the rate at which the extruder screw fed material into the system. Deviations in speed resulted in varying wall thicknesses which reduced the strength of the pipe. Secondly, the vacuum pressure maintained at the extruder head had to be constant in order to ensure uniformity in pipe diameter. Any variation in diameter increased the amount of scrap, thereby reducing efficiency and raising the costs of production.

Exhibit 4 *Extruder machinery installed annually in Western Europe, 1977–79, by screw diameter size (*Source: The Extrusion Machinery Market in Europe, *Frost & Sullivan, 1979)*

Extruder Screw Size (mm)	Units Installed/Year	Millions Swiss Frs/Year	Share of Units (%)	Share of Swiss Frs (%)
30–60	1,350	95	30	18
60–75	1,045	89	23	17
75–100	903	104	20	20
100–140	800	132	18	26
140–180	300	59	7	12
180 and over	102	37	2	7
Total	4,500	516	100	100

Process Control System

A real-time process control system contained the hardware and software required to monitor production. Sensors monitored barrel and screw temperature, head temperature and pressure, screw rotation speed and rate of draw by the haul-off. Other sensors measured the thickness and diameter of the extrusion. The data were fed to the process control unit which was able to perform adjustments and maintain tolerances during operation.

Process control was a major part of the total cost of a line *(see Exhibit 5)* and played a central role in meeting the increasingly strict product specifications being demanded by pipe manufacturers.

Exhibit 5 *Pipe extrusion line components*

	'000 SFr.	% Total Price
Extruder		
BM–80 Extruder	120	27
Extruder Motor and Drive	* 55	12
Control Cabinet and Extruder Control	* 25	6
Total	200	45
Line		
Line Process Control	* 50	11
Extruder Head and Tooling	20	5
Calibrating Trough	30	7
Cooling Troughs	35	8
Hauler	35	8
Cutter	20	5
Winder	50	11
Total	240	55
Total Extruder and Line Components	440	100

Note: Example assumes a BM–80 extruder with standard line components.
* marks electronic and process control components;
Percentage could be even higher for specialized lines.

The Extrusion Machinery Industry in Europe

As shown in *Exhibits 6* and *7* approximately 4,500 extruders per year were installed in European plants during the period 1977–1979. This represented an annual investment of Sfr. 516 million. (By comparison, an estimated 1,400 extruders were installed annually in the USA during the same period.) Note that the Sfr. 516 million figure refers only to extruders and related control equipment. Additional line equipment offered significant additional sales potential. It was estimated that the extruder represented 30–50% of the price for a complete extrusion line, depending on the type, and that half of all extruders were sold as part of a complete line.

The extrusion market consisted of seven major segments *(see Exhibit 7)*: manufacturing machinery to produce plastic film, sheet, pipe and profiles, machinery to coat wire or cable, machinery to laminate paper or synthetics,

Exhibit 6 *Extrusion machinery installed annually in Western Europe by country* (Source: The Extrusion Machinery Market in Europe, Frost & Sullivan, 1979)

	Actual 1977–1979	Forecast 1980–1984	Forecast 1985–1989
West Germany	107.6	134.2	180.5
France	78.1	99.6	132.5
Italy	116.0	148.2	185.0
United Kingdom	65.4	83.9	114.0
Belgium/Luxemburg	15.7	19.4	24.7
Netherlands	20.8	25.8	31.5
Denmark	7.6	9.3	11.1
Ireland	3.8	5.0	6.9
Total EEC	415.0	525.4	686.2
Switzerland	10.3	12.5	15.4
Austria	11.9	14.6	18.3
Spain	39.2	53.5	71.0
Sweden	14.6	19.0	24.7
Norway	9.5	11.9	14.8
Finland	3.6	4.2	5.3
Portugal	3.8	4.8	8.0
Greece	6.5	8.8	13.3
Turkey	1.6	2.4	3.2
Total Non-EEC	101.0	131.7	174.0
Total Europe	516.0	657.1	860.2

Exhibit 7 *Extrusion machinery installed annually in Western Europe by application* (Source: The Extrusion Machinery Market in Europe, Frost & Sullivan, 1979)

	Actual 1979		Forecast: 1980–1984		Forecast: 1985–1989	
	Mio SFr.	Units	Mio SFr.	Units	Mio SFr.	Units
Film Machinery	130.7	1,141	171.1	1,494	229.1	2,001
Sheet Machinery	63.9	557	87.4	763	123.1	1,075
Pipe Machinery	118.1	1,031	147.5	1,288	188.5	1,646
Wire & Cable	59.2	516	67.2	587	79.3	692
Coating & Laminating	45.3	395	53.8	470	65.7	574
Profile Extrusion	26.0	226	33.9	296	45.6	398
Compounding/Recycling	52.6	459	71.4	623	98.0	856
Other Extrusion	20.2	175	24.8	216	30.9	269
Total Western Europe	516.0	4,500	657.1	5,737	860.2	7,511

Note: Market size (SFr.) counts extruders only in Europe. Counting line equipment and other export markets, Maillefer estimated that the numbers above represented 25% of their available market potential in cable and 33% in pipe.
Units calculated as the market size divided by weighted average extruder price of SFr. 114,455 (Exhibit 4).

and machinery to perform compounding (preparing polymer or recycling plastic)*.

The market was expected to grow at an average annual rate of 5% during the 1980s. This was down considerably from an average annual rate in excess of 10% experienced during the 1970s. The highest individual growth was predicted for compounding equipment and sheet extruders (8%), the lowest in wire and cable machinery (4%). Pipe extrusion equipment was predicted to grow at 6.3%.

Due to the recession, forecasts for extruder installations in 1980 had been revised down to 3,500 units. Maillefer competed in two segments: extruders for wire/cable and pipe.

Pipe Extrusion Machinery Market

In 1980, pipe extrusion machinery was the second largest market in the extrusion machinery industry, accounting for sales of approximately 1,000 machines in 1979, worth Sfr. 118.1 million. Downstream equipment accounted for an additional Sfr. 135 million in sales.

There were two main classes for thermoplastics used as raw material for pipe extrusion.

The 'Commodity' plastics, which were relatively inexpensive, were used in large tonnages. Five commodity plastics accounted for two-thirds of the total consumption in Europe, these were PVC (hard and soft), low density polyethylene (LDPE), high density polyethylene (HDPE), polystyrene (PS) and polypropylene (PP).

The 'Engineering' plastics, which were more expensive, were used in smaller tonnages. However, they also had certain special properties – such as higher load-bearing qualities or resistance to flammability. The principal engineering plastics were polyamide (PA) and fluorated plastics.

Plastic pipe was extruded in innumerable forms and used in as many different ways. Around one million metric tons of polymer were processed into plastic pipe in Europe each year. Sizes ranged from tiny 1mm-diameter precision tubing to water conduit as large as 1,400mm in diameter. Industry analysts classified pipe into three main categories: small pipe 1–50mm, medium pipe 50–225mm and large pipe 225–600mm plus.

Ideally, the scale of downstream equipment would also be standardized into comparable classifications, line equipment would match extruder size, material processing volume and speed, etc.

---

* *Extrusion blow molding was an additional market which could possibly offer some opportunity but has not been considered for the purposes of this case.*

From a design viewpoint, however, it made sense to establish break points around which to standardize scale, rather than maintain a continuous range of sizes for haulers, cooling troughs, etc. Pipe extrusion production lines were much longer than other extrusion lines as there were many downstream components which had to be integrated. Integration was especially critical in developing markets where precise tolerances were required.

Hard PVC accounted for the bulk of processed tonnage. It was used for the large water mains, simple conduit and sewerage mains required by the building and construction trades.

At the beginning of 1980, hard PVC still remained the most suitable and competitive material in the large tonnage range (225mm plus). But new applications were starting to emerge, especially outside the construction business, where other materials were proving to be more suitable. HDPE was being used more and more frequently for pipe in the medium-size range, such as high pressure gas or water pipe. At the same time, PA, an expensive engineering plastic, was being used with excellent results for pipe in the small-diameter range, the 'precision pipe' needed for automotive and industrial purposes. Flexible medical tubing, requiring precise dimensions for use in expensive, sophisticated equipment such as dialysis machines, was increasingly being made with soft PVC.

Buyers

In addition to in-house operations, the buyers were custom or contract processors. In-house extrusions were made by manufacturers for use in their own products, as long as there was sufficient volume to justify the large investment in equipment and skilled personnel. The custom processor performed contract work for smaller organizations and/or specialized in applications requiring the precision of expensive engineering plastics. The equipment selected was based on the prerequisites of their customers, the end users who then used the extruded pipe for a variety of purposes: construction, public works, precision products, etc.

Applications for Plastic Pipe

Sewerage and Water Conduit, a commodity item available in standard sizes, was used for piping water into residential and commercial neighborhoods. Conduit for water mains started at 400mm diameter and ranged up to the

Table 1   Dimensional Tolerances and Processing Speeds for Four Classes of Pipe

Description	Raw Material	Raw Mat. Price Sfr/Kg	Outside Dia. mm	Tol. mm	Thick-ness mm	Tol. mm	Line Speed M/Min
Water Conduit (250–1400mm range)	uPVC	1.90	250	±2.5	10	+3.0	5
Pressurized Water & Gas (30–250mm range)	HDPE	2.50	10–32	±0.3	2.0	+0.4	30–60
			110	±2.3	22.8	+2.5	
			250	±1.0	10.0	+1.2	10
Precision Automotive (5–25mm range)	PA	12–15	6–11	± .05	1.0	+ .03	
			12–18	± .075	1.2	+ .055	
			19–22	± .1	1.4	+ .04	60
Medical Tubing (1–10mm range)	sPVC	3.50	1.8	± .05	.5	+ .025	300
	PUR		4.0	± .05	.5	+ .025	
	or FEP		9.0	± .05	1.2	+ .03	250

Key: PA, polyamide (nylon); HDPE, high density polyethylene; sPVC, soft PVC; uPVC, unplasticized PVC (hard PVC); PUR, polyurethane; FEP (and others), fluorated plastics.

1400mm diameter size used in special public works projects. Conduit in smaller diameters (in the 250–400mm range) was used to link individual residences to water mains as well as for sewerage, storm runoff and drainage.

Hard PVC was the material most used for conduit. It was inexpensive, yet also had characteristics which provided strength and excellent resistance to the elements. However, the raw material, which came in powdered form, was difficult to process because of its hardness. To alleviate the problem, manufacturers had developed twin screw machines.

Large extruders, which had the capacity to process the large volume of material required, had to be used. That meant the line operated very slowly since no more than 5 meters of pipe could be extruded per minute.

In these large applications, the emphasis was on the efficient use of raw material. A significant amount of raw material could be saved by reducing diameter and thickness within given tolerances. In addition, scrap losses could be reduced by minimizing the amount of production which was not within these tolerances. Line equipment had to be large enough to handle such bulky pipe. In fact, for conduit over 400mm in diameter, the sheer size of cooling troughs, haulers and cutters began to outweigh the extruder in engineering, design and manufacturing emphasis.

Pressure Pipe was used in buildings, laboratories and industrial machinery for the distribution of water or gas under high pressure. Reliability was the end-user's primary concern, because a break (e.g. circulating cooling water to a diesel engine) could result in machinery shut-down, fire or danger to workers. The material used could be low, medium or high-density polyethylene which had superior characteristics for flexibility and strength. The characteristics made up for the higher price of these materials as compared with that of uPVC. Pressure pipe was of medium diameter (32–225mm) and was produced on single screw extruders at relatively low speeds (10 to 30m/min). Even over 225mm, HDPE pressure pipe could be used as a substitute for PVC.

The volume of material used for medium-diameter pipe was less than for PVC conduit, but the amount was still significant. Small variations in dimensional tolerance affected material usage; therefore, precise control over production parameters could produce savings. Reduction by 0.1mm of the average thickness for a tube 32mm in diameter and 2mm thick (assume production for 3,000 hours at 12m/min) would save 16,000kg.

Careful, even mixing by the screw of the material as it moved rapidly through the barrel, was essential to ensure a homogeneous result. If it were not homogeneous, the finished pipe would not perform reliably under pressure.

Medical Pipe was used by hospitals and surgeons providing care to patients. Uses included intravenous feeding lines, blood delivery, catheters and air or food tubes. During use, the plastic remained in contact with the patient's skin or internal membranes. Often, the lines also served life-supporting functions. Pipe which was thinner than specification or which varied in diameter could burst under use. Pipe with a rough or brittle surface texture was more prone to rejection by the body or could cause infection. Reinsertion of feeding or blood tubes was traumatic for the patient. As a result, users of medical pipe demanded rigorous specifications, not only for size and shape, but for composition and surface texture as well.

Medical pipe was of small diameter (1–10mm), produced at high speed (up to 300m/min) but had to meet strict specifications for inside diameter, outside diameter and wall thickness (*see Table 1*). The most frequently-used materials were soft PVC, fluorated plastics and PUR with diameters usually of 2–4mm. In production, a consistent output within the specifications had to be maintained for hours of continuous operation. Specifications for material uniformity and surface quality of the extruded pipe made production at a high rate difficult to achieve. However, a high level of productivity was necessary for an extrusion line producing very small-diameter pipe to be economically feasible.

The amount of raw material processed on medical pipe lines tended to be low, making reduction of raw material consumption a secondary consideration. Nevertheless, economy was possible, depending on how carefully the extrusion line was operated and the level of control maintained. A reduction by 0.02mm of the thickness of a tube 4mm in diameter and 0.5mm thick (assume production for 2,000 hours at 120m/min) would save over 11,000Kg.

Competition

There were 92 manufacturers of extruders in Western Europe in 1980, but only a dozen leaders in the field with strong international reputations. In several cases, they were part of large manufacturing concerns which built other machinery for the plastics industry in addition to extruders. Others, privately-owned and moderate in size like Maillefer, concentrated exclusively on the manufacture of plastic extruders and related line equipment. Some of the producers specialized in supplying one or two extrusion processes, while others would cover the whole range of processes. The trend seemed to be towards specialization in extrusion processes (cable, sheet, etc.), in materials (PVC, HDPE, etc.), and in applications. Other factors differentiating manufacturers' equipment included the ease with which such operations as start-up, shut-down and material changes could be effected, the control over the process during operation, and the level at which both the extrusion line and process controls were automated.

Seventy-eight (78) of Europe's manufacturers were located in the four largest countries (Germany, U.K., France and Italy). The thirty-two (32) manufacturers located in Italy were mostly small firms which mainly produced simple low-cost machines, bought by local processors supplying the building and construction trades. There were also 15 firms in the United Kingdom and 7 in France which provided some competition. However, in assessing Maillefer's competitive position, Bonjour directed his attention to the leaders among Germany's 24 extruder manufacturers. He believed it was essential to maintain a performance level as well as a reputation for quality which would equal or surpass German manufacturers in the marketplace. The principal 'top-of-the-line' competitors were Reifenhauser, Krauss Maffei and Battenfeld.

Reifenhauser immediately stood out as one of the leading companies specializing in extrusion machinery. In 1979 they had 1,100 employees and sales valued at Sfr. 83.2 million. An estimated 35% of this figure was in extruders, the rest auxiliary line equipment. As one of the oldest established producers, Reifenhauser supplied extrusion process equipment from small cable and pipe machines to larger extruders for pipe, film, compounding, etc., concentrating on the higher quality, higher priced, end of the market. They also were already well-established in a broad-based international market.

In 1979, Reifenhauser produced 288 machines, one-quarter of which were twin screw machines for processing hard PVC. The rest were single screw machines in the screw-diameter range of 30–150mm which directly competed with Maillefer's product line. And, Reifenhauser's prices were, on average, lower than Maillefer's.

Krauss Maffei was part of Fredrich Flick Industrieverwaltung, Germany's 30th largest industrial enterprise and a multi-product giant among machinery manufacturers. As part of the Plastics Machinery Division, Krausss Maffei accounted for extrusion machinery sales of Sfr. 27.4 million, an estimated 40% of this amount in extruders. In addition to single screw extruders and complete lines, they had developed twin screw extruders capable of handling PVC powder in high volume, and they also manufactured a three screw 'planetary' extruder.

In 1979, Krauss Maffei produced 120 machines, 20% of these being twin screw machines for hard PVC. Their smaller single screw machines were used to extrude pipe and profiles while larger machines were also used for compounding and sheet extrusion. Prices were comparable to Reifenhauser's.

Battenfeld was part of Schloemann-Siemag, well-known for their heavy industrial equipment used in steel milling and manufacturing. Although Battenfeld was primarily producing injection molding machinery, they had recently moved into extruders suitable for all pipe applications and lines. Battenfeld's sales in 1979 totaled Sfr. 357 million, 20% (equaling Sfr. 71.4 million) in extruders and line equipment. Bonjour estimated that 30% of this figure represented extruders, the rest line equipment. Battenfeld's resources for technical and commercial support were extensive: in addition to 2300 employees, they were able to draw on the experience of Gloenco, a British extruder manufacturer they had acquired in 1978, as well as various other holdings in plastics engineering and downstream line equipment.

Battenfeld manufactured and installed 132 extruders in 1979. 65% were single screw machines in the screw-diameter range of 45–120mm, the rest larger single screw and twin screw machines. Battenfeld's single screw extruders performed well processing LDPE, HDPE and PP in small and medium diameters at high speed. Larger single screw machines (120 and 150mm) were used to produce pressure and non-pressure pipe in HDPE and soft PVC up to 600mm diameter. *Exhibit 8* compares the products and prices among these competitors and Maillefer.

Exhibit 8 *Product and price comparison*

Manufacturer	Extruder Model	Screw Diameter (mm)	Output (Kg/Hr)	Price (Swiss Francs)	Extruder Height (mm)	Materials Processed	Applications
Maillefer	1. BM-30	30	12-25	57,700	1,000	1) PVC,PE,PP, PUR,PA,FEP	Pipe, Cable
	2. BM-45	45	35-60	80,100			
	3. BM-60	60	70-150	125,400			
	4. BM-80	80	190-250	200,000		2) PVC,PE,PP, PUR	
	5. BM-120	120	235-550	242,900			
	6. BM-150	150	370-760	288,100			
	BD-84	84×2	300-400		1,000	uPVC	Pipe, Compounding
(Twin Screw)	BD-112	112×2	700-800				
Reifenhauser	1. ST30	30	10-15	46,200	1,050	uPVC,PE,PP,PA,F	Pipe, Cable, Film
	2. RT121	50	70-100	62,500	450 or 1,000		
	3. RT281	70	120-200	83,100	650 or 1,150		General Extrusion, Film
	4. RT801	90	240-320	120,000	750 or 1,150	PE,PP,PUR,PA PA	
	5. RT1651	120	450-800	188,900	750 or 1,150		
	6. RT1801	150	600-1000	224,800	1,150		
	BT70	70×2	80-150		1,150	uPVC	Pipe, Profile, Compounding
	BT100	100×2	300-450				
	BT130	130×2	450-700				
(Twin Screw)	BT150	150×2	500-1100				
Krauss Maffei	1. EC138	35	10-14	43,300	1,000	PE,PP,PA	Pipe, Profile
	2. EC200	50	30-50	60,900			
	3. KME60	60	90-150	80,300		PE,PP,PA PUR,PS	Pipe, Profile, Sheet, Compounding
	4. KME90	90	240-320	121,200			
	5. KME120	125	500-600	187,000			
	KMD90	90×2	300-400		1,000	uPVC	Pipe, Profile
(Twin Screw)	KMD120	120×2	500-700				
Battenfeld	2. Uni-45	45	45-80	68,100	1,160	uPVC,PE,PP,PS	Pipe, Profile, Sheet, Film, Compounding
	3. Uni-60	60	50-220	92,300			
	4. Uni-90	90	250-350	135,600			
	5. Uni-120	120	200-700	201,600			
	6. Uni-150	150	250-950	239,200			
	Exi-90	90×2	160-600		1,160	uPVC	Pipe, Profile, Compounding
	Exi-130	130×2	700-1600				
(Twin Screw)	Exi-160	160×2	1200-2400				

1,2,3,4,5,6 designate comparable machines.
1) basically soft PVC.
2) filled PVC for cable (fillers like chalk).

Market Trends

Traditionally, small local processors had supplied most of the simple, low-cost plastic pipe; i.e. large-diameter conduit as well as medium-diameter general purpose piping such as garden hose. Technological requirements for the design of extruders and line equipment were straightforward, which meant that the delivery of equipment was rapid and the availability of spare parts was relatively assured. Reliable delivery and service influenced the decision to place an order. Manufacturers of extruders for this segment of the market were widely spread, especially in the countries of southern Europe where this equipment was most important. Where advanced extrusion techniques were required, specialization amongst extruder manufacturers was becoming a significant trend in the market. As a result of the economic decline of the late seventies, many manufacturers in Germany, France and England were concentrating their efforts on lines with specific applications and with material where they had unique skills. In this way, they hoped to carve out a special niche and achieve growth by gaining a reputation in a field of expertise.

In order to do this, machines had to be specialized as different raw materials varied with respect to their physical, chemical and thermal properties. Thus hard PVC tended to be processed on twin screw extruders which could process this dense powder more uniformly. In fact, the ability to process hard PVC had become a mark of technical distinction among manufacturers supplying the medium and large-diameter segments. Likewise, auxiliary line equipment, such as winders, markers or specialized attachments, had to be adapted to the specific dimensions and characteristics of the various extruded products.

The relative trade-off which customers made between cost and performance varied, depending on the application. One group produced generic products such as garden hose or construction conduit which sold for a low price. Because they processed large tonnages, high output and reduced scrap were the leading criteria in selecting an extrusion line. Another group made precision extrusions to be part of high value-added medical and industrial products. They were more concerned with an extruder's ability to provide a rigid tolerance for diameter and wall thickness. This tolerance also had to be maintained through long production runs without needing subsequent off-line inspection procedures.

Regardless of the application, adherence to strict tolerances resulted in reduction in material usage and waste which meant an increased yield per kilogram of raw material. This had always been important on lines which processed large tonnage, but now even on low-volume precision lines, processors were realizing that small improvements in the control of the extrusion process could reduce costs. More and more frequently, precision pipe processors were expecting higher productivity as well as precision through better control of production parameters and less manual intervention. Due to escalating raw material and labor costs, automation of the production process (e.g. computerized process control) and of the line (e.g. automatic winders) began to increase. However, with the plastic extrusion industry continuously changing, processors wanted flexibility as well. One plastics processor summed up his needs:

> We need the possibility to manufacture with a high degree of reproducibility, products which meet more stringent standards, at higher production rates, with less manual intervention, less nominal material consumption and less scrap. In terms of flexibility, the equipment must potentially be able to process a variety of raw plastic materials as new applications are developed.

MP Product Lines

In 1980, Maillefer's cable and pipe extrusion lines were based on their BM extruders. Their reputation was unsurpassed in the cable field where the emphasis had always been on machines of reasonable output which could also maintain strict tolerances, as well as on custom-designed line components which could add specialities such as color-coded striping. In order to develop MP's products further, the screw and barrel geometries were re-engineered for pipe plastics. New line components were also designed, particularly the extruder heads for pipe and the vacuum calibration trough. Other components, such as cooling troughs, haulers, winders and hoppers, were common to both cable and pipe extrusion lines.

Production tolerance was not achieved by any one component alone but by the synchronized operation of the entire line. Sensors continually monitored barrel temperature, calibrating vacuum and haul-off speed. Diameter and thickness were checked for accuracy and parameters were automatically adjusted to maintain output within specification. Buyers had become used to requesting customized line machinery. A laboratory simulator called the EXMATE enabled Maillefer to analyze the influence of different screw and barrel geometries on extrusion results. From such analyses, special designs were developed for specific families of plastics and their applications. Maillefer's extruders were among the most sophisticated in screw geometry, temperature and process control; they were also the most expensive, measured on the simple basis of price-performance (Sfr/Average Kg/Hr processed).

Maillefer's extruders were single screw machines which processed LDP, HDPE, PP, PA and soft PVC. Engineering plastics used in pipe and cable (PA, PUR and fluorated plastics) could also be processed on Maillefer single screw machines. Unplasticized PVC usually was processed on a double screw extruder. Unlike Maillefer's cable business, MP had neither a dominant characteristic nor an established reputation in the marketplace. Most of the extrusion lines sold had been for pressurized water and gas pipe of LDPE and HDPE in diameters of 50 to 225mm. Lines for HDPE pipe up to 400mm had also been produced, but they had required some adaptation of the larger cooling troughs and haul-off. A double screw machine for processing hard PVC was being developed with one or two prototypes, which also used the larger line equipment, already installed.

In the small pipe market, MP had sold lines for extrusion of pipe as low as 50mm. Drip irrigation was one application where MP had been particularly successful. Drip irrigation systems supplied water to crops using small-diameter, flexible HDPE pipe fitted with tiny drippers. Drippers delivered a controlled amount of water directly to the base of each plant. In addition to meeting specifications for diameter and thickness, the drippers had to be inserted at precise intervals along the pipe. MP had developed a piece of line equipment which could do this at the rate of one every second. Customers were satisfied and new inquiries were being received. A new automatic winder had also been introduced which met with immediate approval as it was capable of operating at the high speeds required by precision lines. In addition, automatic changing of the take-up reels reduced manual intervention and thus saved on personnel.

Delivery and Price

From order placement through installation, Maillefer's delivery lead time for a complete extrusion line averaged 10–12 months. After an agreement was signed, as much as two months could be spent confirming technical specifications. When the customer did not know or could not decide on a particular specification, the process was further slowed down. Then 4–5 months would elapse waiting for the ordering and delivery of parts. After that, 3–4 months usually were required for manufacturing and assembly. Testing came next and that, at least, proceeded rapidly. Testing lasted two days for simple lines and a week or two for lines which required multiple trials of materials and/or output samples for customer approval.

MP technicians and engineers helped customers to select the most appropriate system, put it into operation and train personnel to run it.

Customers were able to work before and after the sale with production lines at Maillefer's Exhibition Hall. In this 2,000 square-meter facility built in 1978, complete extrusion lines were available for test runs and instruction. Cable and pipe extrusion lines shared both fabrication and assembly at the facilities in Ecublens. Manufacturing occupied 5,000 square meters in the modern, one-story, steel-framed building next to headquarters.

A recent management meeting had reviewed the questions of delivery and price. Catalog prices of both extruders and lines averaged 15% above other top-of-the-line competitors. In some cases, prices were as much as 25–30% higher. Bonjour made the following recommendation:

> Our cable machines are among the best in the world, and we've also had some success with pipe, but the competition on cost and delivery is more stiff in the pipe market. It's inevitable that in certain applications, there are limits to what the customer will pay. Although I don't want to negotiate on price with a customer in order to win a contract, I do need enough flexibility to establish a price level which will attract potential customers.

He summarized the issue in a memo which presented two pricing scenarios *(see **Exhibit 9**)* which MP could adopt. At current price levels a 'status quo' was forecast; i.e. twenty machines in 1981 with sales of Sfr. 3.75 million. The alternative analyzed the effect of a price level 24% lower than current catalog. If the number of extruder and line sales could be proportionally increased, the result would benefit sales without damaging profits.

Exhibit 9   *Pricing analysis (in thousands of Swiss francs)*

	Status Quo Scenario	Bottom Line Scenario
Extruder Sales	2,663	4,210
Line Equipment	1,090	1,869
Total	3,753	6,079
Less:		
Manufacturing and Overhead	3,170	5,458
Profit before Tax	583	621

Status Quo:	20 extruder sales, 10 as part of a complete line. 1980 catalog prices.
Bottom Line:	40 extruder sales, 20 as part of a complete line. Prices 24% below 1980 catalog.

Exhibit 9 *Continued*

| | Extruder Size (Screw Diameter) | | | | |
	45mm	60mm	80mm	120mm	Total
Status Quo					
Extruders Alone	2	3	4	1	10
Extruders with Line	1	4	4	1	10
	3	7	8	2	20
Bottom Line					
Extruders Alone	3	7	8	2	20
Extruders with Line	3	7	8	2	20
	6	14	16	4	40

The Options facing MP

All of the options possible for the MP Group were being weighed in
Bonjour's mind. Sales needed to be increased, therefore a decision on pricing
was necessary. However, there was also the issue of positioning to be
considered. Lines for medium pipe had provided the bulk of MP's sales and
new sales could still be found in this market. Activities were also underway
in both large and small-diameter applications. The time would come when
the customers, as well as Maillefer's management, would expect him to
define MP's place in the market. And that time seemed to be rapidly
approaching.

BP Nutrition/Hendrix Voeders B.V. (A): The Consultancy Support System

This case was prepared by Professors Juan Rada and Per Jenster, and Research Fellow Thomas Cummings as a basis for class discussion rather than to illustrate either effective or ineffective handling of a business situation. The support of BP and contributions from Frans Van Es, BP Nutrition, are gratefully acknowledged.

This is not about a one-time stroke achievement; it is about trust, relationships and responsibilities that carry on over time.

Frans Van Es

Frans Van Es, manager of information systems for BP Nutrition, looked away from the road for a moment to peer across the windswept Dutch countryside. He was thinking of how he would describe his feelings to a visitor about receiving the BP 'STAR' 1990 award for the most innovative use of information technology in the company.

I felt honoured to present the Consultancy Support System project on behalf of BP Nutrition and Hendrix Voeders of the Netherlands. We believe that the computer and communications systems are important to the overall success of the project. But, our achievements must be seen in the context of the Hendrix Voeders organization and its business philosophy, for these factors have much to do with our success. Hendrix has remained dedicated to staying close to the farmer, even in difficult years when such behaviour was considered unprofitable.

But, as the market has undergone rapid change, the behavior and philosophy of a former family-run firm are being increasingly questioned. The most recent questions come from our shareholders; they ask, 'How can such a traditional firm generate a satisfactory return to our international shareholders?'

From the information systems management perspective, I translate these questions into: What are the distinctive competences of the firm? How should we support our competences and business functions using information systems? Can information systems make us more competitive so that we can achieve acceptable rates of return in the future?

History of BP Nutrition/Hendrix Voeders B.V.

Hendrix Feed was founded in the late 1920s to serve the small independent farmers of the Netherlands. By 1991 Hendrix was one of the main operating companies in BP Nutrition, with a yearly production of 1.2 million tonnes of feed, and 700 employees.

BP Nutrition

BP Nutrition was the fourth largest business of the BP Group after BP Exploration and Production, Oil Refining & Marketing, and Chemicals. The company was made up of some 120 companies that had been assembled and built in the nutrition sector in 20 countries over a period of 15 years. *(Refer to Exhibits 1a and 1b.)* During this time, the company had evolved to cover most aspects of the animal food chain, from breeding to the final consumer product. By 1991, BPN comprised dozens of typically small companies, operating at a local level, close to the market and close to their consumers. During a conference, a BP executive expressed the strategy in the following humoristic manner: 'By the year 2000, if BP's strategy is successful, we will be feeding you, your car and your dog.' An explicit aspect of the marketing strategy was to avoid using the BP name or the green BP shield on packages. As stated in the company brochure: '. . . even if we didn't produce a particular meat product, it's quite possible we either bred it or fed it.'

BP acquired the Hendrix Group in 1979, following its earlier acquisitions of Cooper Nutrition Products in the UK and its majority stake in Trouw International. From the initial acquisition, steps were taken to keep Hendrix autonomous from the BP structure. It was not until 1989, after several more acquisitions, that BPN established its worldwide headquarters in Antwerp, Belgium, close to Hendrix's headquarters in Boxmeer, the Netherlands.

Exhibit 1a

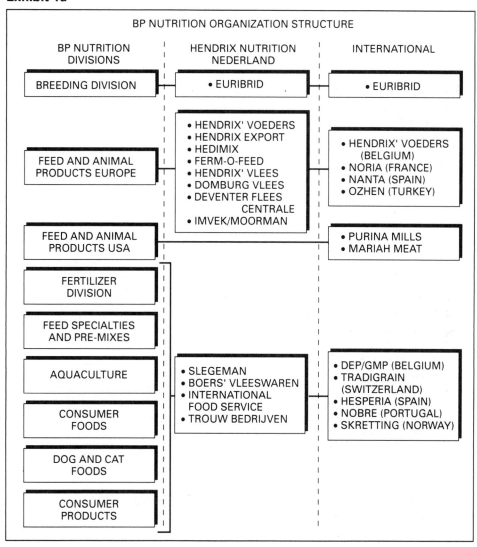

BP NUTRITION ORGANIZATION STRUCTURE

BP NUTRITION DIVISIONS	HENDRIX NUTRITION NEDERLAND	INTERNATIONAL
BREEDING DIVISION	• EURIBRID	• EURIBRID
FEED AND ANIMAL PRODUCTS EUROPE	• HENDRIX' VOEDERS • HENDRIX EXPORT • HEDIMIX • FERM-O-FEED • HENDRIX' VLEES • DOMBURG VLEES • DEVENTER FLEES CENTRALE • IMVEK/MOORMAN	• HENDRIX' VOEDERS (BELGIUM) • NORIA (FRANCE) • NANTA (SPAIN) • OZHEN (TURKEY)
FEED AND ANIMAL PRODUCTS USA		• PURINA MILLS • MARIAH MEAT
FERTILIZER DIVISION		
FEED SPECIALTIES AND PRE-MIXES		
AQUACULTURE	• SLEGEMAN • BOERS' VLEESWAREN • INTERNATIONAL FOOD SERVICE • TROUW BEDRIJVEN	• DEP/GMP (BELGIUM) • TRADIGRAIN (SWITZERLAND) • HESPERIA (SPAIN) • NOBRE (PORTUGAL) • SKRETTING (NORWAY)
CONSUMER FOODS		
DOG AND CAT FOODS		
CONSUMER PRODUCTS		

Hendrix Voeders B.V.

Hendrix had roughly an 8% total market share of the Dutch compound feed market in 1990, producing nearly 1.2 million tons of feed per year. As such, it was the largest private feed supplier in the Netherlands, competing with large cooperative feed producers and a large number of smaller millers (6% of the total market share). Most companies competed on price, and none of the major players had consultancy support.

Exhibit 1b

BP Nutrition Operating Companies

Operating Company	Location	Function
BP Nutrition	Antwerp, Belgium	Headquarters
Hendrix Voeders B.V.	Boxmeer, Netherlands	Animal Feeds
Nanta S.A.	Madrid, Spain	Animal Feeds
Noria/UFAC	Cergy Pontoise, France	Animal Feeds
Purina Mills	St. Louis, MO, USA	Animal Feeds
Consumer Products Division	London, UK	Packaged Goods
EuriBrid International	Boxmeer, Netherlands	Genetics
Consumer Food Group	Boxmeer, Netherlands	Consumer Food
Tradigrain S.A.	Geneva, Switzerland	Grain Trading
Trouw Int'l B.V.	Boxmeer, Netherlands	Fish Farming

BP Nutrition Milestones

1975 BP acquired Cooper Nutrition Products Ltd (later to become BP) Nutrition (UK) Ltd – from the Wellcome Foundation
1975 Acquired majority interest in Trouw International
1979 Hendrix Group acquired, including Euribrid and Stegeman
1981 Skretting acquired
1981 Euribrid acquired Hybrid Turkeys in Canada
1982 Hendrix acquired Nanta in Spain
1984 Hendrix acquired UFAC Noria in France
1986 BPN acquired Purina Mills, the largest feed producer in the US
1986 Moore-Clark acquired
1987 Suralim, Trouw International's Chilean fish feed operation, established
1988 Aquastar shrimp farming set up in Thailand
1989 BBN worldwide headquarters established in Antwerp

By 1991, Hendrix's feed production segments mirrored the breakdown of the total feed produced in the Netherlands:

Breakdown of Total Animal Feed Production by Key Segments
Percent and Tonnage Produced in the Netherlands by Hendrix

Animal Type	Netherlands Production (percent/tons)	BP Hendrix Production (percent/tons)	BP Hendrix Market Share (percent)
Swine	45.5 (7,280,000)	50 (600,000)	8.2
Beef	20.0 (3,200,000)	15 (180,000)	5.6
Poultry	34.5 (5,520,000)	35 (420,000)	7.6
Total	100 (16,000,000)	100 (1,200,000)	7.5

For BP Nutrition, the general term 'feed' business was somewhat misleading. Over the last 15 years, BP researchers, focusing on different business segments, had developed feed products for different species, specific animal life cycles, performance levels and nutritional needs. Hendrix had supplied feeds to four farm sectors: pigs (breeder sows and piglets), feeder cattle and milk cows, sheep, and chickens (laying hens and broilers).

BP Hendrix built the company on its reputation as a business that was willing to meet the animal's nutritional needs through each phase of its life. Over time, fulfilling this objective meant shifting from serving as a bulk feed supplier to providing a complete service to the farmer. For example, during an animal's early growth phases, BP Hendrix could provide most of its essential supplies – feed, milk replacers, vitamin and mineral mixes. It would even supply new livestock. At the other end of the cycle, BP Hendrix offered to arrange for the slaughter and sale of the animals, and further processing of the meat products. BPN's slaughterhouses and meat cutleries completed the cycle by handling this processing and providing direct outlets for the various animal products.

In discussing the company with a visitor, several Hendrix managers expressed the need to retain Hendrix's pioneering spirit with its 'Dutch thriftiness'. Many wondered whether the BP culture was slowly changing the nature of the company. One manager expressed it in this way:

> The Hendrix Company had a tradition of being open-minded to new ideas. People would say, 'If you believe in it, you prove it by trying it.' People became enormously committed to new ideas. If an idea failed, the innovator needn't worry about reprimands or loss of job security. Some of us feel this is different from the BP culture. Today, if top management were skeptical about an idea, it would probably have to be proven 100% before being accepted.

The Hendrix Way of Competing

Historically, the feed industry in the Netherlands was controlled by very large farm cooperatives that focused largely on high output animal production. Feed was viewed as an input to the farm cooperative's primary business. Hendrix Voeders was established to develop, from the very start, high quality feeds that would provide an alternative to the cooperatives. The company's initial market segment was the independent small farm producers, whose survival depended on producing higher quality animals and achieving higher performance targets than the customers of the cooperatives.

There were three key objectives governing the Hendrix strategy:

1. Provide customers with the highest quality, highest yielding feed products in the industry.

2. Develop the closest possible relationship with the independent farmers of the Netherlands by linking feed and animal growth to timely and effective consulting services.

3. By implementing (1) and (2), obtain the highest quality usage and industry premiums for feed and feed-related products and services.

These objectives were achieved in the following ways:

1. Provide customers with the highest quality, highest yielding feed products in the industry

The scale of Hendrix's R&D for a company of its size was impressive. Together with BP's Ralston Purina Research Center, BP Nutrition developed a portfolio of 1,500 feed products to cover the specific nutritional requirements of cattle, sheep, pigs and chickens. To this end, Hendrix's farmers received the direct economic benefits of the company's focused and precise animal feeding regimes. Hendrix had taken great pains to refine the measurement of animal development, monitoring for disease and genetic deficiencies, and control of the animals' environment. As one researcher explained:

> Twenty years ago, it took 2.8 kilos of Hendrix feed to add one kilo to the live weight of a chicken. Today, the same breed of chicken gains one kilo when fed 1.8 kilos of feed. For the farmer, this 36% increase in feeding efficiency translates directly to improved farm revenues. Thus, Hendrix has been able to charge a premium for improved feed efficiencies. Growth gains of 5–10% in pork and poultry are now possible through the use of enzyme products that improve animal feed efficiencies.

The Hendrix Corporate Philosophy statement reflected the company's aim to achieve its quality goals:

> The aim of Hendrix Voeders is to ensure that the farmers who want to assure themselves of a promising future can do so. The package that Hendrix Voeders offers farmers is therefore geared to enable its customers to make a good profit by means of a sound technical approach. Hendrix Voeders devotes constant attention to quality in the widest sense and focuses on: nutrition, animal end products, and care for the environment and the welfare of animals.

2. Develop the closest possible relationship with the independent farmers of the Netherlands by linking feed and animal growth to timely and effective consulting services

When Hendrix was founded, its research and development department was established to provide high quality advisory services and technical information to farmers. But, without a close relationship to the farmers, this information was of little use. Over time, the company built up a cadre of more than 100 technical consultants whose mission was to get as close to the farmer as possible. In this way, Hendrix believed it could serve as a link between the daily routine and requirements of farmers, and the increasing demands of consumers and government. As Frans Van Es pointed out to a visitor:

> If you look at our organization chart, there is one part which is rather different from other commercial organizations. This is the independent consultancy function that is separate from our sales force. Of course, there are other sales organizations that also use specialists in their pre- and after-sales but, in our case, the consultant has no direct sales task, he is responsible for the technical results at the farm. This group of nearly 150 professional employees, specialized according to type of animal, have to prove every day, year after year, the success of our formula. 'This story is not about a one-time stroke, it is about trust, relationships and responsibility in a complex environment.'
> *(Refer to Exhibit 2, Hendrix Voeders Organization Chart.)*

3. By implementing (1) and (2), obtain the highest quality usage and industry premiums for feed and feed-related products and services

By providing high quality feed and feed products, in combination with strong technical consulting, Hendrix was able to charge a 10–15% price premium for its products. Embedded at the core of this combination was a long-time company ethos: 'If the farmer is doing well, we'll do well.' To justify this premium, a farmer had to realize benefits. This statement, however obvious, implied that research knowledge about the effects of various feeding and shelter combinations had to get transferred back to the farmer in a timely manner. As a result, a farmer would use a given product more efficiently because the feed system had been built on expert knowledge and strong personal relationships.

Yet, by mid-1987 Hendrix was faced with a number of dilemmas: the farmers wanted more information; the technical consultants demanded faster processing of raw data and questions; and the farmers and consultants became demoralized as they spent more and more time on administration. Despite Hendrix's consultancy support to farmers, competitive pressures continued to squeeze the entire industry. As competitors also started to

Exhibit 2   *The Hendrix Organization: independent feed consultants (separate from the sales force)*

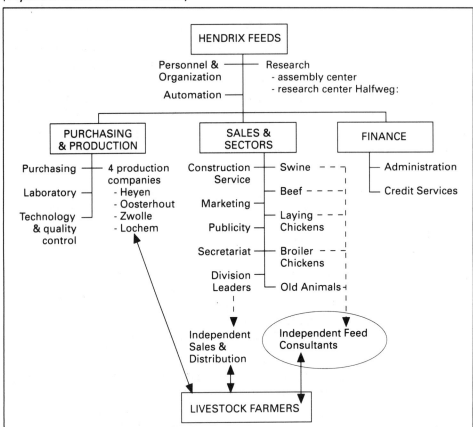

provide consultants on a limited scale, few farm accounts could be taken for granted. As Bertus Ensing, an experienced Hendrix consultant in the Pig Sector, clarified:

> If there were a disease problem in a section of a farm, it took six days for our farm consultants, using pen and paper, to report to a field office and, finally, to headquarters. Then, it took up to seven days to route the information to the proper in-house expert and several more days before the expert's recommendations were fed back to the consultant. Farmers were thus receiving information 30 days later.

The Dutch government had imposed an additional challenge for Hendrix. The coalition Dutch government passed legislation known as ATV, to stabilize mounting unemployment in the country. The new law forced employers such as Hendrix to decrease the work week from 40 to 35 hours. Thus, Hendrix had to reduce the workload of its consultants. At the same time, the company felt it had to maintain or increase its level of consulting support to the farmers. Yet, top management would not accept a 10% increase in the number of consultants. Frans Van Es summed up the dilemma, 'These critical events forced us to rethink our organization and market strategy.'

At that moment, Frans Van Es saw the potential for information technology. Computing and telecommunications had the potential for maintaining and improving the company's traditional strength as an information provider and, at the same time, would help overcome the mounting market pressures, earning pressures and legislative barriers.

Over the last few years, Hendrix's competitors had been quick to copy Hendrix's technical consulting system. Frans Van Es knew that to lock out the other feed providers, Hendrix's information technology solution would have to be both more efficient and more effective.

The Consultancy Support System

The Objectives of the Consultancy Support system

The objectives of the system had been to achieve quantity and quality improvements by recasting the consultant–farmer relationship in the information technology environment.

In the past, calculating simple feed to weight ratios – to monitor animal growth – had been done in a rather haphazard and unstructured way and, because of the workload involved for each consultant, paperwork was often neglected. Consultants were encouraged to give farmers the latest nutrition data about their operations and provide expert advice to prove the quality of Hendrix feed. But, the clerical duties and paperwork proved time-consuming. Some even believed that the less qualified consultants were being rewarded for being good bookkeepers, while the skilled farm advisors were getting bogged down in administration and frustrated by the turnaround time of the information system.

The Foundations of the Consultancy Support System

Frans Van Es noted:

> You have to remember that Hendrix had a history as a very innovative company in a rather static environment. We had a good approach to innovation in the company. Try something out, give people room, but keep it small. From this formula you get high motivation, and the people who develop the idea

become its primary salesmen. Payoff and investment in the innovation come later – after the scale of an innovation has been ramped up.

In the case of the Consultancy Support System, it began in the early 1980s when we developed a computerized prototype, the 'sow management system' for our Pig Sector. We were not trying to be rocket scientists. We were trying to fulfill the ethos of the company: 'If the farmer does well, Hendrix does well.'

The sow management system was straightforward. A typical sow farm had about 80 sows – 80 mother pigs at different stages of pregnancy. Each sow produced 18–24 piglets per litter (1,440–1,920 piglets in process during each growth cycle). The goal of the system was to achieve a 4–5% improvement in yield per sow per year, or one more piglet for every two sows. A key aspect of producing a good litter was to closely monitor the progress of the sow – and then make micro adjustments in the sow's nutrients, medicine, and growth environment (e.g., lighting, temperature and space). We set up the first sow monitoring databases on a personal computer running on a CPM operating system. Each sow was individually numbered so that its consumption and weight could be tracked daily. People in the business didn't believe the farmers would want such a system. They said that the farmers weren't sophisticated enough – one guy said they had the wrong kind of hands for the keyboard! Of course, this was nonsense. By the time the system was fully implemented, each sow farm was getting 1–2 piglets more per sow per year – four times our initial expectations. We sold over 1,000 sow monitoring systems.

But more important, it was a turning point for Hendrix. We had happy farmers, happy consultants, and systems developers who discovered that information technologies could be used for competitive advantage. When the results were monitored in real-time, our consultants had proof that our feed was of a higher quality than our competitors and that it would add value for the farmer. It was real. After that, we began to develop the consultancy support system.

By 1990 Hendrix had run 140 consultants through a training course to teach the farmers how to use the menu-driven system. The size of their hands proved not to be a problem, yet one on-site systems engineer admitted, 'Typing skills did become the bottleneck!' A standard set and a special set of applications were developed for each laptop system, and applications were segmented according to the animal product groups of a consultant's farm customers.

*The following describes aspects of the Consultancy Support System including: reports and planning, communications, the central database, developmental issues, prototyping, training and implementation, and security. **Exhibit 3** shows the general configuration of the system.*

Exhibit 3 *Consultancy Support System*

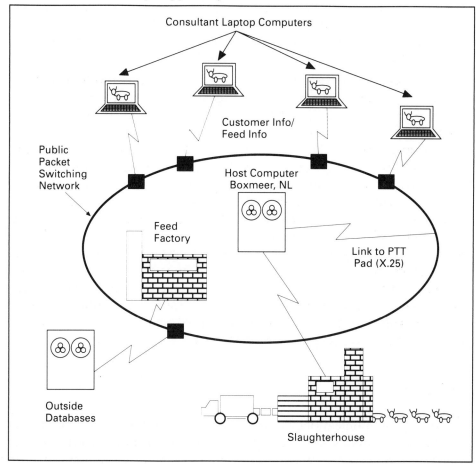

Reports and Planning

At the core of the system were the customer files. As Van Es noted, 'Maintaining customer files was a great deal more than keeping address records. We needed to know animal performance details so that our consultants could make timely recommendations to existing customers and identify segment information that could be used to target customers.'

At the lowest level, fields were set up to track simple facts – age and number of animals, competitor feed suppliers, expiring feed contract dates, etc. Van Es explained:

> Every consultant had his own style of reporting, varying from stenographic messages to literary prose. Imagine 140 daily reports sent, not always on time,

to the head office. Signals had to be sorted and fed back to the field. Reactions to those signals were almost always too late, and our ability to combine data and compare information was almost nonexistent. The result: if we wished to provide timely and relevant information, the reporting cycle had to be cut down from two full weeks to one or two days.

At the next level, a part of the database was set up for the consultant to track his own advice, review the results, and seek support from the home office. 'This was an important breakthrough,' noted Van Es. 'By recording his recommendations to a farmer, the consultant had the advantage of being in a position to clarify and show the value of his advice over time, thus building a strong consistent exchange between the consultants and the farmers.'

The consultancy system standardized the most common messages – changes in farm status, herd size, disease alerts, etc. – through a coding system and set up a selective address scheme to get the right messages to the right people within the company. The work of the consultant was systematically divided within the consultancy system between compulsory and non-compulsory items, depending on the animal sector and the experience of the consultant. For most of the consultants, showing the quality of their advice to the farmer became a routine but critical aspect of the work schedule. Whatever information the consultant had entered on the database could be analyzed or directly fed back to the farmer.

Communications

Developing communications between mobile consultants, the head office, and outside databases became a key factor for ensuring success of the project. There were several hurdles to overcome. Low-cost effective communications links were just emerging from the Dutch PTT, and it was difficult to communicate with the mobile targets as they were changing sites several times daily. The transactions per consultant would be small, so there was no need to acquire a massive private network. Public packet switching networks provided the solution, although the Dutch PTT was hard pressed to provide the needed capabilities. As one system developer noted, 'We thought that linking laptop computers to a host computer via the public switch was a common problem. We immediately discovered that we were pushing the laptop manufacturer, who at that time had never fitted a modem into a laptop PC, and we were pushing the Dutch PTT whose regulations prohibited the use of non-approved modems. In the end, we were delivering modems and specifications to both the PTT and the computer supplier.'

In the initial development, it was more important to build in flexibility rather than try to save on communications costs. The consultants had to be able to send messages to the head office whenever and from wherever necessary. In the past, consultants had been frustrated at not being able to contact key staff, and the staff, in turn, when they were available, were buried in telephone calls.

Prior to the addition of external databases on the Consultancy Support System, some customers were faster and better informed about market and external changes than the consultants. Hendrix knew that this would eventually erode the position of their consultants as experts in the field. A feature of the system was the ability to download information from external databases and send it to the consultants the moment it became available.

The Central Database

Hendrix's farm consultants had a long history of tracking their customers' results. However, only a small amount of the total data was used, and there was very little real-time comparison of results. This was a problem both for Hendrix management and for the customers. Management sought timely reports to understand the shifts and trends in the customer base. Yet, management tended to become buried in unanalyzed facts, and thus often relied on rumours circulating through a farm segment while waiting for the processed results. As Frans Van Es pointed out:

> We always stressed our individual approach to customer needs. But, as appealing as that sounded, the individual approach had to be built on an ability to know, understand, and notice things faster than our competitors and, hopefully, our customers. Otherwise, we would not continue to add value to our products.

The key words for developing the central database were: standardization, normalization, and defining entities and attributes. As these words imply, there was a need to build a common language and set of tools that could be used in a consistent and familiar way. If one consultant was using 'high protein' to mean one thing and another consultant was using the same term for an entirely different purpose, then the database would turn into a jumble of meanings and contexts.

These ideas did eventually become familiar to Hendrix consultants, but in 1985 it was a different story. Bertus Ensing, a consultant in the Pig Sector at that time, described the initial approach:

> Our first job was to produce daily and weekly reports. The database was segmented into general and technical information. General information was

of the administrative and commercial sort – name of the owner, details of the farm (e.g., size, financing), details of the farm's facilities, links to distributors, etc. The technical information database contained fields that allowed for detailed tracking of livestock statistics, feeding patterns, and environmental conditions.

Using the pre-set menus and coding system, a consultant would record financial and technical information on a daily and weekly basis. There were several built-in incentives for using the system, two worth noting. First, consultants wanted to be prepared to show their customers the results of their last recommendations, and second, consultants received a daily travel allowance that was refunded when their consulting visit reports were completed and sent to headquarters. We made sure that quick report submissions were rewarded by fast repayment.

Once the information was sent in to the central database, messages were routed according to specific codes, and aggregated analysis could be carried out for market research and technical advisory services. Frans Van Es stressed the value of having real-time technical information:

> In the past, much of the farm culture ran on rumours: low productivity was attributed to everything from mysterious diseases to the cycles of the moon. Rumours that were attributed to a specific feed might even cause a farmer to radically change his feeding patterns. Today, the technical analysts at Hendrix often see disease and poor productivity patterns emerging before the farmers do, and they have the ability to carry out quality tests and then issue warnings within hours of detection. Fact-based analysis went a long way toward shutting down the rumour mill. In addition, the database now allows for comparative and longitudinal analysis along nearly 1,000 variables.

Consultant Training

One of the most difficult aspects of implementing the Consultancy Support System was training the consultants. In the end, nearly half of the initial $2 million investment was consumed by this training activity. Frans Van Es emphasized the criticality of training during the implementation phase of the project:

> System definition and development is seen, in many cases, as the only crucial phase of a project. This may be a reason why so many promising systems fail – not enough attention is given to training.

Naturally, the younger users were very optimistic, whereas the experienced consultants behaved more cautiously. The goal was to train 100% of the consulting force so that everyone would use the system.

There were several methods of training the consultants: in groups, by do-it-yourself methods, train the trainer, and, when necessary, individual tutoring. Frans Van Es felt that a measure of success had occurred when, after several months into the project, he overheard one of the more reluctant consultants tell a colleague: 'If I leave my home to go to a customer and realize I've left my laptop, I turn around and go back. I can't make my rounds without it anymore.'

Benefits of the Consultancy Support System

The consultancy support system – readily adopted by Hendrix consultants – provided two major benefits in particular.

First, the system saved time. In the past, if Hendrix had a production error, a nutritional problem or improper raw material mixes, it would take weeks and even months before a problem was discovered, investigated, and resolved. With the consultancy support system linked to the company's central databases, most problems could be detected and confronted immediately. Where analysis was required, results were achieved within a few days. The time factor was especially critical when a virus or other epidemic was discovered. Within hours, a contaminated herd or feed could be isolated and quarantined. In the Netherlands, where pig farm density is the highest per square km in the world, such information had the potential to save millions. (*Exhibit 3* *describes the chain of activity covered in the consultancy support system.*)

The second major benefit was that it brought the Hendrix organization in direct real-time contact with its end users – the feed customers. Hendrix was able, not only to reinforce its relationships with its distributors, but to provide direct value-added services to the farmer.

Future Issues for BP Nutrition/Hendrix Voeders B.V.

Hendrix was known by its long-time managers as a company that was open to new ideas. 'If you believe in it, you try it and prove it,' one consultant noted. This goal led to enormous personal commitment to prove new ideas. Several managers said that even if the Consultancy Support System had failed, they would have gained the wholehearted commitment and understanding of top management. As Hendrix began to blend into the BP culture, many openly wondered if top management would, in the future, take similar risks.

Frans Van Es believed that there were several aspects and critical questions to resolve during the next stage of BP Nutrition's business and information systems development strategy. He and his colleagues shared a concern for the following issues:

- What would be the future relationship between BP corporate information systems and the applications developers in various other companies like Hendrix Voeders? BP corporate information systems provided strong technical knowledge to the company, but the operating companies paid a price for this knowledge. For instance, if one company was not on the top of the corporate priority list, key projects tended to be put off or shelved.

- Hendrix Voeders' business was built to support the small Dutch farmer, whose outlook was expressed in the following way by one consultant, 'Our farm has earned a lot this year, so we'll save for next year when times are lean.' This cyclical perspective was seen as an ingrained dynamic of the farming business. As part of the BP portfolio, Hendrix Voeders seemed to be moving away from the farmer's perspective and narrowing its corporate objectives. Some executives believed that this change was due to the BP corporate dynamic that sought to meet quarterly targets. BP Nutrition's information systems people wondered about the role of information systems in supporting this change. Currently, it was seen both as a way to support the farmer and as a way to report to corporate headquarters, but this balance could change.

- Competitors were starting to copy the Consultancy Support System. Being followers, they did not share Hendrix's first mover advantages; however, they posed a considerable threat. Maintaining an advantage would require, at the very least, ongoing systems development – a difficult issue for top management.

- One way to enhance the Consultancy Support System would be to start developing expert systems and knowledge-based systems for financial and technical analysis. Hendrix's management had not yet shown the marginal benefits of developing such a system.

Frans Van Es, sitting in his Boxmeer office, leaned back in the chair and quipped, 'There is an old Dutch saying, "to get where you want to go, you've got to be able to trust the bridges in the dark". If we are to support BP Nutrition and Hendrix's strategy through the use of information systems, we've still got a lot of bridges to cross.'

Ciba-Geigy Allcomm (B): Making Internal Services Market Driven
Setting Sail

This case was prepared by Professor Sandra Vandermerwe and Dr. Marika Taishoff, as a basis for class discussion rather than to illustrate either effective or ineffective handling of a business situation.

Any firm would have been thrilled at getting the new Ciba visual identity campaign, to publicize worldwide the change in the corporation's name from Ciba-Geigy to Ciba. *(Refer to **Exhibit 1** for the old and new logos.)* But none more so than Allcomm. 'Who would have thought,' Jurg Chresta declared on that early morning in September 1992, 'that we would have had to fight so hard for a job – from the one customer we once held captive?' It was a warm, Indian summer day, and the sun shone brightly into his office. He took his jacket off, rolled up his sleeves, and turned to Fred Wagner, recently appointed as head of Finance and Administration. The two were preparing for a Management Committee meeting later that day.

Wagner, who had spent over 10 years in Ciba-Geigy's legal department before coming to Allcomm in July 1992, looked at Chresta thoughtfully before responding, then said, 'You mean to tell me that you actually worked harder for this account than for the Amnesty International deal?' Chresta laughed and then went on to explain:

> Are you kidding? Winning Amnesty was like falling off a log compared to getting the Ciba deal. Maybe I'm exaggerating a little. But seriously, Fred, you've got no idea how we had to fight for that deal. The 'experimental group' moved right in and convinced Amnesty that we had what it took to make their campaign work. But, with Ciba we had to get around the politics as well and that was a completely different story. Let me tell you, the new guy in charge

Exhibit 1

at corporate didn't even want to speak to us at the beginning. In fact, he told me, 'If I want to change Ciba-Geigy's communications, I can't use anyone who's worked for us in the past.'

'How did you get around that attitude?' Wagner asked, now thoroughly intrigued.

'I had to get some help from the top,' Chresta replied, 'and we got the business unit managers involved. They ended up persuading Basel that we were the best people for the job. And we are, I can assure you.'

True to its word, Ciba-Geigy had financially supported the fledgling group during its first full year and a half of independence. It had guaranteed that Allcomm would have the same amount of turnover, SF 20.5 million, as in 1990. The volume of Ciba-Geigy business – which was mostly routine and small jobs – did, in fact, drop due to the chemical company's own restructuring plans and cost cutting program. This shortfall, however, was covered by Ciba-Geigy's turnover guarantee provision.

Chresta was proud of Allcomm's accomplishments in the just under two years of its existence. The Ciba logo deal was proof enough that dramatic strides had been made in the firm's customer satisfying capabilities. The Swiss advertising campaign for Amnesty International, the non-governmental worldwide humanitarian organization, together with new deals from a Swiss fashion company, Feldpausch, which operated in the German part of the country, and the Swiss brewery Warteck, was testimony to the fact that headway had also been made in the larger outside market. 'And right now,'

Chresta went on, 'we're all waiting anxiously to see if we got the auto account. Now that will be a big coup.' He checked his watch. It was 10:45. 'We had better get going; we don't want to be late for your first management meeting.' He rose, leading the way. 'So you see, Fred, we're OK . . . and if we continue moving at this pace, we might even strike it rich!'

They walked up a flight of stairs and along a series of spotless corridors. The offices were immaculate, all identically modern to the point of being spartan. Then they passed through the area which belonged to the 'experimental group'. Drawings, sketches and *papier mâché* models, which changed almost every day, lined the corridors. Each of the six offices was different. Some offices had wood floors, some had concrete; some were painted in colourful patterns, some had stark black and white tiles. Layout models were strewn on the floors; others were suspended from the ceilings.

'They are really something different,' Wagner remarked with amusement, noting also all the crumpled wads of paper which spilled out of the bins, onto the floors and into the hallways. 'Yeah,' Chresta said, 'they certainly are.' Finally, the two men reached the conference room and entered.

Allcomm After Two Years

The other six committee members were already present. Allcomm was now composed of eight divisions, having added, at the beginning of 1992, a new one called 'Marketing Communication' to handle market research as well as a unique, technologically based, expert market intelligence system. These divisions fell under either one of the two operating areas, Advertising or Business Communications. *(Refer to **Exhibit 2** for the structure.)*

Chresta opened the discussion by announcing that the Ciba visual identity campaign had been won. There was spontaneous applause. Then one of the members asked, 'Don't tell me the "chaos group" actually got into Basel?' 'No,' Chresta answered with a grin. 'As a matter of fact, we oldtimers were the ones who did it. And I'm pleased to say that the "chaos group", as you call them, has just won the Amnesty International campaign.' More applause.

Chresta had created the 'experimental group' in February 1992. He had personally gone looking for people who were more innovative and less tradition-bound. He found six individuals with these traits: three – including a lawyer – came from outside agencies; of the remaining three, one was a talented artist, one a secretary, and the sixth was a former communications unit misfit who had been looking for something else to do. All of these group

Exhibit 2

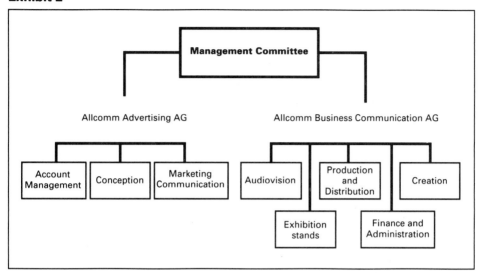

members shared the characteristics he had been looking for: they were excellent team players, and did anything and everything necessary – working days, nights and weekends – to get the customer's job done. They were also willing to take risks. 'I want you to be a self-managed team,' Chresta had told them. 'Show the world that you can get the business and satisfy our market. No one will interfere with you if you deliver the goods.'

Within seven months, they had signed up Amnesty International, the Feldpausch Fashion House, Warteck Beer and several other smaller projects. Now, they were waiting with baited breath for the outcome of the Swiss car dealership campaign. They were convinced that their chances of winning it were rather good. Chresta had encouraged them to try to transfer the learning from one account to another. In this way, he hoped that they could build 'economies of know-how' as well as cut the costs of material development. In this instance, an idea for a multi-media project they had originally developed for Swatch was taken up and adapted for the Swiss car dealership. The underlying concept was new to Allcomm and the trade. It involved a promotional program for retailers which allowed them, via interactive systems technologies, instant access to constantly updated information stored on digitalized systems.

The 'experimental' – or 'chaos' group as everyone at Allcomm and at Ciba referred to it – had actually chosen its own name – 'Allcomm 2', which was emblazoned on all its brochures and promotional material. The group had initially opted for the name 'A2', but Chresta had vetoed that idea. On two other occasions, Chresta had had to step in and interfere: he had banned bringing mountain bikes and dogs into the office, and had halted the distribution of the group's prospectus – because their humorous version of the corporate organigram offended many of the other Allcomm employees and the board of Ciba-Geigy.

Chresta remarked that some of his employees liked to complain that they were not given the same freedom as members of the 'experimental group'. But, he would always retort, 'No one ever told you couldn't be like them.'

Courting the Customer

By September 1992, Allcomm had approximately 3,800 customers. Of these, 10% were non-Ciba-Geigy clients who contributed about 15% to the total turnover. Some of these outside clients were Ciba-Geigy competitors in non-strategic product/markets. Approximately 90% of all customers selected just a few bits and pieces of the 450 different Allcomm services offered. The remaining 10% had bought a complete communications strategy.

Chresta had begun reducing the number of accounts to be serviced by Ciba-Geigy. He had found that many customers were not only too expensive to maintain, but that they could not provide the kind of long-term relationship he was now pursuing. Many of Ciba's longstanding customers simply used its services for convenience sake. Chresta decided that this kind of business must be discontinued.

> If you ask people around here how many customers we have, they'll say 3,800. And they say that 380 people outside of Ciba deal with us. But, they forget that almost all of these customers just do an ad here, and a leaflet there, with us. Our real challenge is to have fewer customers doing more things with us and make them more profitable.

The Advertising department segmented its market into Health & Nutrition, Agriculture, Industrial, Environment, and Public/Not-for-Profit. As for Business Communications, Chresta's aim was to provide a full communications offering – from strategic planning through to execution – and so he targeted companies that needed more than one kind of communication service. He was less concerned about the industries in which these firms operated than about Allcomm's ability to fulfill their requirements. The potential market in Switzerland totalled 200 businesses, essentially industrial corporations in need of business-to-business communications. Chresta also figured that there were 50 companies worth targeting in some of the other major geographic markets: France, Germany, Spain, the Benelux and Scandinavia (primarily Sweden and Denmark). Here, he used the same potential customer criteria as he did for Swiss firms.

Chresta believed that the relationship between Allcomm and its customers needed to begin early on, so that their marketing strategies could be developed together and then seen through from the inception of the campaign to implementation. The Ciba campaign was a prototype of the kind of setup now being sought: putting people together with customers, working with them from the beginning until the very end. This arrangement, Chresta reckoned, put Allcomm in the driver's seat and kept competitors out.

One of the dilemmas still facing Chresta was deciding which services to offer, which to eliminate, and what new ones to introduce. As criteria, he considered whether or not a service was necessary for having an innovative communications strategy and could be profitably executed. For instance, a new, expert system-based market research service had been added. The service was able to assess how well a given advertising campaign was likely to do under a variety of market conditions. A number of consumer firms used this service, which Chresta believed would in turn create an entrée for providing still more services to such firms. While he agreed that – from a consulting standpoint – Allcomm should offer everything, he knew that – from a production standpoint – this was not always possible. Allcomm had to cut down on services and buy them from others who could do them more efficiently.

Another factor to be considered was that customers increasingly were demanding the globalization of services. It seemed that Allcomm had no option but to begin building a global network to meet such needs. One of Allcomm's Swiss health customers, for instance, was expanding in the US and asked Allcomm to be its agent there. Anticipating this trend, Chresta had already entered into two cooperative arrangements in Brussels and two in New York. He had also arranged partnering agreements with suppliers in Switzerland to ensure that Allcomm would have capacity when needed.

Organizing to Work with the Customer

In the two years of its existence, the number of people at Allcomm had remained relatively constant at 140. The personnel turnover of about 12% was considered normal in the communications field. Most of that turnover was amongst the younger staff members, some of whom went on to form their own businesses. For example, two individuals – after their initial training with Allcomm – successfully opened a graphic design office in the United States, which was reported to be doing well.

Just over 40% of the employees now dealt directly with customers, thus fulfilling Chresta's objective of maximizing exposure to customers as an opportunity to cement relationships. This rule applied as much to the administrative as to the frontline people. For example, some administrative staff who had never given customers any thought were now involved in the account management process. The account manager, for instance, had to make certain that customers understood all the details of the contract prior to signing, and that each fine print clause of the billing and payment agreements was clear and acceptable to them.

Chresta was equally adamant that all employees, no matter what their job, be involved in quality measures to ensure that the customer's expectations could be managed and met. What customers expected was discussed in detail before finalizing an order. The briefing sessions he had with employees were thorough, so that both time and energy would not be wasted later. The agreed-upon terms were then defined in writing. Although, at present, this process could only take place with large clients, Chresta intended to follow the same procedure with all customers before long.

Chresta admitted that he felt it was vitally important to spend time, and have a mutual dialogue and discussion with customers:

> Before, whenever staff had to deal with a customer, the mood was either one of indifference, or confrontation. You never discussed needs. Now, we recognize that the business we're really in is a people business. And, that means we've got to get our customers to talk to us; we have to find ways for them to feel that they can discuss their needs and objectives with us. They've got to trust us. And that takes not only talent, but time.

Relationships had to be built where they had never before existed. They also had to be maintained. There was one case that Chresta particularly liked to recount about a longstanding Ciba client. The account was the standard kind, with print campaigns run at specified and predetermined times of the year. The relationship had endured for years, and there was little reason to believe that it could ever be jeopardized. Then, when it was time to receive the next order, it never came: the client had decided to do business elsewhere. Over the next three booking periods, Allcomm phoned and made a bid for the order, but each time Allcomm's bid was refused. Then Chresta recommended that the account manager and his team visit the client and talk. They learned that the client had indeed been very happy with Allcomm, but there was a particular freelance designer from a competing agency that the client wanted to use. Allcomm immediately arranged to hire the designer for the job. The account was saved. Chresta said: 'We just have to learn to be flexible, and do whatever's necessary to make customers happy, even if it includes using a competing agency. We don't have to do everything ourselves: as long as we are calling the shots.'

Teaming at Allcomm

Chresta tried to strike a balance between two seemingly contradictory imperatives. He wanted to instill in his people an entrepreneurial spirit so that they would take risks and push their creative talents but, at the same time – as he frequently reminded them – they had to make a profit. 'It was like a pendulum swing,' Chresta remarked. 'On the one hand, we have to make money as quickly as possible while, on the other, we have to cultivate long-term customer relationships.' Looking for ways to achieve economies of know-how, he tried to motivate staff to build on previous ideas, to work and learn so that they could execute projects more creatively, more quickly and productively. Teaming was a way to achieve this goal.

Chresta's approach to teaming was to get people together from different specializations and turn them loose on a project. He had taken this approach with the experimental group, and that was the model he wanted others to emulate. As he saw it, there was no other option: first of all, he believed that teaming was the most appropriate way to sell communication strategies and, secondly, he was convinced that it was the only way to motivate his people – whose energy, creativity, and abilities to blend their skills was ultimately, in fact, Allcomm's only real product.

It was Chresta's practice to personally interview all candidates in the process of being hired. A person's ability to be a team player was rarely apparent on the first interview. It would usually require a second round, on 'neutral' territory such as a restaurant. Even after that, Chresta had learned that it was safer to have candidates work for a while on a freelance basis with the team before signing them up permanently.

For Chresta, it was clear that everyone on a team would, at one time or another, have to be a leader: such was the nature of teaming in a know-how oriented environment. He therefore embarked on a series of 'team building and leadership' courses at Allcomm, which he insisted everyone attend. The skills and know-how taught in these courses resulted in the development of a new program for 7,000 Ciba managers.

From the very beginning, Chresta had decided to drop all hierarchical titles. Instead of being identified by rank, people were designated by the activities they performed. The martial labels – director, vice director, assistant vice director, and so on – which had little meaning to anyone outside the company, were replaced by professional differentiators like photographer, graphic designer, market analyst, account manager, etc. Chresta believed that customers were not interested in formal titles: what they wanted to know was what the person could do for them. There was a limit, however, as to how far this attitude toward titles could be taken; Chresta himself liked to joke, 'Otherwise, window cleaners might end up being known as "clear view managers"!'

Many of the oldtimers at Allcomm had difficulty with this policy, especially those who had been waiting years and years for promotions, and suddenly found that titles – no longer significant – were being dropped. Chresta explained that the traditional, formal titles had been more an internal than an external motivational tool. They got in the way of effectively designing and negotiating business communication strategy packages. In any case, he argued, team contact would have to be made at numerous levels within the potential client company. Hierarchical designations had little relevance in such meetings, he insisted, and were even known to obstruct their efficacy.

Chresta worked to get the teams identified and recognized, even though he knew that this approach radically differed from the typical Swiss culture where emphasis was on the individual. But, he firmly believed that everything had to be done to make the team, rather than any single person, the hero. He had different teams working separately on the same project, so as to instill a sense of competition and boost profitability. All team achievements were publicized in-house as a form of public recognition. If a team did well, its members were given a spontaneous reward. He fervently believed that money motivated people only up to a point. Some employees, for instance, were more enthused by the possibility of travelling to faraway places than by an extra financial incentive. And, in order to keep employees interested and motivated, he went to great pains to understand what individuals valued and to find ways to gear the incentives accordingly.

Employee and Customer Satisfaction Surveys

Both an employee and a customer survey had been completed during 1992. The same outside professional firm, together with Ciba-Geigy's Corporate Planning Function, had been retained to do both surveys. The employee survey was based on a questionnaire which had been sent out during the spring holidays; it was returned within 14 days by 80% of the employees. The customer survey was a combination of standardized, written responses and qualitative interviews. The first part had been sent to 95 customers, both within Ciba-Geigy and outside. Thirty-five customers responded. Sixteen face-to-face interviews were also conducted, with ten Ciba-Geigy customers and six external customers. *(Refer to **Exhibit 3** for results of the employee survey.)*

While the sample for the customer survey was small, Allcomm did seem to be on the right track. Chresta was particularly proud of these responses, which came out of semantic differentials:

> Allcomm comes close to being the ideal communications company. (78%)
>
> I would recommend Allcomm to other businesses. (90%)

Some of the reasons given by the 22% of the customers who felt that Allcomm still had to improve included:

> Allcomm should do more publicity: the company is not well enough known. (30%)
>
> Allcomm should try to improve its innovative and creative potential. (35%)
>
> The firm should try to focus on certain products and services, not be so widespread. (40%)
>
> Allcomm is a reliable company, but too traditional. (50%)
>
> Allcomm is not emotional, not flippant enough. (50%)
>
> There's still too much of a Ciba-Geigy culture at Allcomm. (60%)

Chresta considered the experimental group a great success. He intended to extend the way they operated to the entire Advertising Group, thereby diffusing still further the unique culture they had created. The result would mean that close to 20% of all Allcomm employees would be working according to a more market-driven mentality. But, because they had been great at getting business and 'lousy' at administration and finance, he decided to strengthen that part of the group's infrastructure in his plan. What Chresta wanted to avoid, though, was changing the whole organization simultaneously.

> That would cause instability. I want people to feel secure, not afraid and uncertain. The object is to build a culture of continuous improvement, not to cause chaos. I want people to come to expect change and accept it as a perfectly natural feature of their lives.

Measuring, Motivating and Rewarding Staff

Allcomm no longer had to call in the Assessment Board for promotional approval as it had done in the past. It now designed and applied its own measuring rods, which were both quantitative and qualitative. The former

Exhibit 3

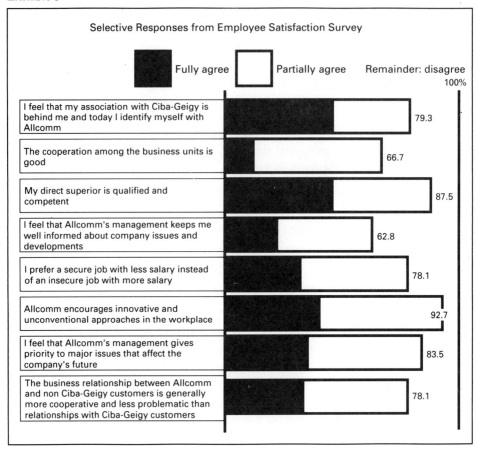

Selective Responses from Employee Satisfaction Survey

■ Fully agree   □ Partially agree   Remainder: disagree
100%

I feel that my association with Ciba-Geigy is behind me and today I identify myself with Allcomm	79.3
The cooperation among the business units is good	66.7
My direct superior is qualified and competent	87.5
I feel that Allcomm's management keeps me well informed about company issues and developments	62.8
I prefer a secure job with less salary instead of an insecure job with more salary	78.1
Allcomm encourages innovative and unconventional approaches in the workplace	92.7
I feel that Allcomm's management gives priority to major issues that affect the company's future	83.5
The business relationship between Allcomm and non Ciba-Geigy customers is generally more cooperative and less problematic than relationships with Ciba-Geigy customers	78.1

was based on whether bottom line forecasts had been satisfactorily met. This was new for many employees, who were now directly responsible for managing their part of the business. The latter – qualitative performance measures – were jointly designed for the upcoming twelve month period by the individual together with his/her coach. At the end of that period, both parties would try to reach a mutual agreement as to how well the employee performed, where improvement was needed, and how to achieve it. From time to time, lead customers participated in the agency review sessions that had been set up to gauge how well the account was being handled. For Chresta, this was a way of giving customers a voice in the individual performance assessments.

Chresta felt that there was much to do in terms of designing the right kind of performance system. But, at this stage of Allcomm's existence, using performance measuring rods as coaxing and controlling instruments was important only up to a point. Survival was the predominate word at Allcomm at this time. Chresta could see its effects everywhere: most of the lights in the Allcomm building, for instance, were typically on till 8 or 9 pm, while those at the Ciba building across the road were almost all off by 4, and definitely so by 5. As well, two thirds of his employees had purchased shares in Allcomm. At SF500 each, the gesture was mostly symbolic, but it did say something. What mattered was that they all showed up at the board meetings, and made their opinions as owners and members of the company – as well as employees – heard, and taken seriously. 'It's rather like Israel,' he mused. 'We have an urgent sense of mutual survival which is caused by having a collective understanding that we're living in a hostile environment. Under these circumstances, people automatically work together and work harder.'

Costing and Pricing Services

'Overall, then,' Chresta concluded the meeting, 'I think that we have made headway in some very choppy seas. Fred, since this is your first meeting, perhaps you would like to give us the benefit of some of your impressions.' Chresta looked at Wagner expectantly and found him eager and ready to respond. Wagner picked up a pen and began to scribble some figures on the white board. *(Refer to Exhibit 4.)*

> I must say I'm impressed. For instance, we had a total turnover of SF20.2 million in 1991 and just over 15% came from the external 10% of the client base. So, though our business with Ciba was worth 17.5 million in 1991, we only had to use part of the guarantee.
>
> In addition, we achieved this laden with overhead costs. These costs – SF2 million in all – are not transparent. Twenty percent I can trace, the rest is a mess. My instinct tells me, though, that many of them are unnecessary. And, those we do need we can probably find more cheaply outside.

Sounds of concern came from the group, but Wagner went on.

> The whole question of costs is incredibly complex. The truth is that we don't understand any of them or how they should be allocated. But, we must get them straight so we can ascertain once and for all which services, and customers, are profitable and which aren't.

'You're right about that,' Chresta said:

> We know what a person costs by the hour, but we don't know what an hour of machine use costs. We know what a piece of cardboard costs, but we don't

Exhibit 4

Income:	
Operating Turnover	20,233,485
Non-operating income	1,324,344
Total:	21,557,829
Expenses:	
Salaries & Wages	14,324,294
Other, including taxes	7,194,829
Total:	21,519,123
Profit:	38,706

know what a person's experience should be costed at. A lot of the costs are hidden, they simply can't be tracked and traced, and it's difficult, if at all possible, to decide with any degree of accuracy what goes where.

Customers have different ideas about the way they want to pay. Some want to work on an agency commission system, others have a global amount available and they want to achieve something with it – without spending one cent more. And still others want to work on an hourly fee basis. What it all boils down to is that, if we want to be truly customer oriented, we have to devise a financial system that lets us work with all these requests and understand our true profitability.

At this point, Chresta restlessly sprang up:

We also have to be concerned about our capacity. As we grow, we are going to have to look for alliances and for freelancers to fill the gaps. I'm in the process of talking to one or two competitors about the possibility of their coming in on some of our work. If we want to give our customers communications solutions, we've got to pull in all the talent we can muster.

Murmurs arose from the group. 'Isn't that unusual, Jurg?' Fred remarked. Chresta smiled. 'This is an unusual company, Fred . . .'

SECTION 4

Industrial Marketing Analysis and Intelligence

CASE

Quest International

Quest International: Industrial Market Research

This case was prepared by Research Associate David Hover, under the supervision of Professor Per V. Jenster, as a basis for class discussion rather than to illustrate either effective or ineffective handling of a business situation.

Jan de Rooij, the director of the flavor center at Quest International, contemplated the early retirement request that Hans Dieperink, the director of market research and strategic development, had placed on his desk. Jan was not surprised by the request as he had known Hans was approaching retirement age, but he had been counting on a couple of more years before having to face up to finding a replacement. Hans was a one-man phenomenon and would be missed. Yet, his departure opened up the opportunity to reevaluate the company's approach to market research. In the competitive worldwide industrial flavors business, market knowledge was an important asset, but was Quest going about it in the right way? The industry was changing and missteps were increasingly dangerous. 'What we know, we know well,' noted Jan. 'But I still feel vulnerable. What really scares me is that we don't know what we don't know.'

Quest International, a division of Unilever, developed and manufactured flavors, fragrances and, recently, food ingredients for end-consumer product companies throughout the world. Traditionally strong in both flavors and fragrances, Quest management believed that food flavors and ingredients were going to become increasingly important as the market for processed foods became more international and competitive.

World Flavor Industry[1]

The term 'flavors', when applied to a variety of chemical products, added taste and aroma to processed foods and beverages. Flavors were usually classified as either 'natural', 'nature identical' or 'artificial', depending on the production method used. A flavor was classified as natural when it was extracted from animal or vegetable products by some physical process – including the normal kitchen activities of cooking, heating, boiling, etc. Flavors produced through fermentation were also generally considered natural flavors. Nature identical flavors, or enzymology, consisted of synthesized substances but ones that occurred naturally in food. Artificial flavors were substances derived from any source which did not occur naturally in food.

Traditionally, the manufacturers of flavors, known as flavor houses, had also supplied fragrances (for perfumes, personal hygiene products, soaps, detergents, etc.) because both flavors and fragrances were extracted from raw materials using the same fractionation and distillation processes. However, the changing market and technology were eroding many of the synergies between the two segments. Not only was the demand for flavors increasing as the food processing industry became more competitive, but the food industry also demanded more sophisticated flavors, ones able to withstand rigorous food processing procedures, and able to meet government and consumer standards. These market conditions made creating suitable flavors much more difficult and technologically demanding than creating fragrances. As one executive noted, 'Everyone knows what green peas taste like – coming up with the exact same flavor is challenging. However, with fragrances you can be more creative.' At the same time, the market for fragrances had become stagnant.

The impact of the market changes was felt in the performance figures of the industry. *(Refer to **Exhibits 1, 2 and 3** for an overview of the competitors and market forces.)* Until the late 1970s, the world flavors and fragrances (F&F) industry had shown consistently strong results. Industry profitability had been approximately 15% of sales in the mid to late 1960s, and 10% in the 1970s. In the 1980s, however, slower growth and increased competitive pressures had reduced profitability to about 6–7% industry-wide, and real sales growth had averaged 5–6% per year, reaching an estimated $6.7 billion in 1990. Projections into the 1990s estimated that growth rates would remain in the 5% range. Flavors comprised nearly 45% of the total F&F market and were valued at approximately $3.1 billion in 1990. Western Europe and the United States were the largest regional markets, together accounting for 63% of world flavor sales. Japan was the third major market. Consumption

Exhibit 1   *Top 15 flavor houses by flavor sales (market share in parentheses)*
(Source: *Quest International)*

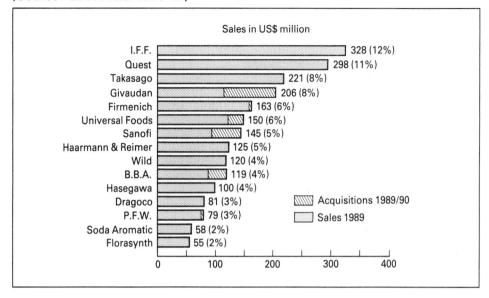

Exhibit 2   *Food ingredient sales of flavor houses: sales and market shares*
(Source: *Quest International)*

Food Ingredient Sales (in US$ million)	1989	% share	Including '89/90 acquisitions	% share
Sanofi	412	14	414	14
Haarman & Reimer	–	0	231	8
Quest	98	3	158	5
Universal Foods	67	2	83	3
P.F.W.	75	3	75	3
Takasago	68	2	68	2
Subtotal	720	24	1,029	34*
Others	2,280	76	1,971	66
Total	3,000	100	3,000	100

* Acquisition effect: 43%

in the rest of the world was significantly lower. However, Eastern Europe and the Far East were identified as having significant growth potential.

Exhibit 3 *Example of sources of new entries from other industries (Source: Quest International)*

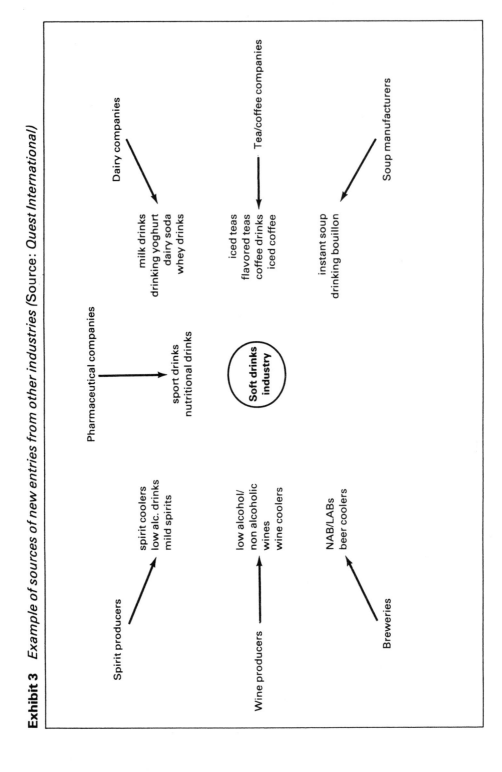

Quest International

Quest International was formed in 1986 when Naarden International was purchased by Unilever and merged with Unilever's existing flavors division, PPF International. Since the merger, approximately seven other companies had been purchased and incorporated into Quest's operations, including Biocon Biochemicals (Ireland) and Sheffield Products (US), both manufacturers of natural food ingredients. These later mergers were intended to increase Quest's knowledge or expertise in specific fields such as biotechnology and improve its ability to offer complete food systems. Financially, Quest had grown quickly during the late 1980s. In 1989, the division reported a turnover of $702 million. *(Refer to **Table 1** for a summary of the division's performance.)*

Table 1   Quest International Financial Data (in $mn)

	1988	1989
Sales	$625	$702
R&D Expense	39	48
Capital Expense	31	38
Operating Profit	71	72

Quest's parent company, the British/Dutch end-consumer and industrial products giant, Unilever, was one of the world's largest companies with 1989 sales in excess of $34 billion. Unilever owned such famous brands as Lipton tea, Ragu sauces, Iglo frozen foods, Lux soap, and Elizabeth Arden cosmetics. Besides Quest, Unilever had a number of other industrial product divisions including Lever Industrial (detergents and cleaning supplies), and National Starch and Chemicals (adhesives and starches). Unilever's industrial divisions operated relatively autonomously. They were not guaranteed in-company business and were required to find external markets for their products. Conversely, divisions such as Quest were able to conduct business with competitors of Unilever's end-consumer products groups.

The Marketing Organization

Quest had three main business areas: flavors, fragrances, and food ingredients. Because the flavors and food ingredients units often had similar clients, they were merged in 1990. The process experienced some difficulties initially, but management was confident the synergies would soon become apparent. The flavor center (as the flavor and food ingredients unit was called) was organized into five nodes each reporting to the director, Jan de Rooij. *(Refer to **Exhibit 4**.)* Operational contact with clients (although not sales) was through the four individual business development groups: beverages, savory, tobacco, and confectionery/ bakery and dairy. Each area was directed by a Business Development Manager (BDM), assisted by a marketing and technical contingent which varied in size depending on the nature of the particular product group. Savories, for example, had the largest technical support staff (12 people) with 4 in marketing. Beverages had 9 technical staff and 5 in marketing.

Each BDM team was responsible for servicing the clients' needs in terms of marketing, product support, product development, and applications for the specific product area. The BDM team, however, did not handle the actual sales. The BDMs worked closely with the marketing research group when gathering information and interpreting market signals. For managers at Quest, the market was the fundamental driving force of the company.

Exhibit 4 *Quest International: flavor center organization*
(Source: *Quest International)*

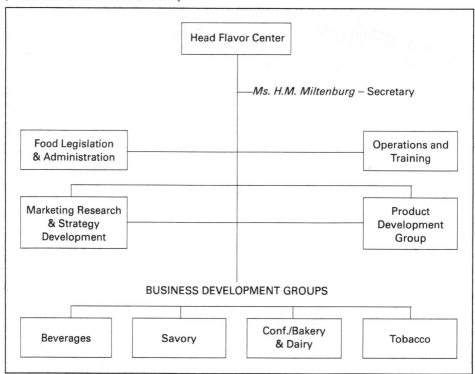

Sales Process

Sales at Quest, and at Unilever in general, were the responsibility of individual country salesforces for most products. The beverages and tobacco areas were notable exceptions. Beverages had been recently reorganized as a single unit for all of Europe in anticipation of the unified market. As tobacco organizations were small in number and globally oriented, they did not need diversified sales support.

Sales were generated in two ways: 1) clients issued a detailed description (called a brief) of the concept they wanted and selected the best proposal made by the competing flavor houses; or 2) flavor houses submitted unsolicited proposals giving details of new product ideas or of features to enhance the flavors already being purchased by the client. Clients would look for a variety of features in the briefs submitted – including the quality of the flavor, the price of the raw materials, suitability to processing techniques, etc.

Clients occasionally changed suppliers either to find lower prices or to reduce their dependence on a particular supplier. Quest had difficulty systematically identifying potential switchers and, generally, did not consider the opportunities attractive. Instead, the firm favored building strong relationships with existing clients and seeking out new clients only when new product opportunities were evident.

Quest had three types of clients – large international, large national and medium-sized national – each requiring different types of services. Customers with multinational operations needed special services, including global service coordination, which Quest provided from its host countries. Although contradictory for the country-based sales organization, the internationalization of some major clients was inescapable. The new demands on coordination meant that Quest units which had previously not worked closely together had to team up. National clients were served through the country-based Business Industry Managers (BIMs).

To permit the necessary flow between product areas, client demands and R&D, Quest had adopted a matrix organization. Client interaction was active primarily at the BIM and BDM levels. When the BDM groups were unable to manage a specific client need, they went to the product development group – also located at the Naarden flavor center. The project coordinators in Product Development focussed on special topics (there were eight in 1991) such as flavor delivery systems, natural flavors and process flavors (flavors produced during cooking). When project coordinators required special technical knowledge (for example, expertise in physical chemistry), they contacted the Research and Development group. Clients would demand that certain products be developed, or research and development could develop new products with applications in the market.

Additionally, for Quest, the different product areas occasionally overlapped. *(Refer to **Exhibit 5**.)*

Market Research Function

Knowledge of market conditions was considered important in all of Quest's activities. Some data on market conditions came from the salesforce, although the marketing research group provided the most significant contribution. The director of market research, Hans Dieperink, who was requesting early retirement, described his unit's function.

> There are three layers of the market research support function in an industrial marketing company: market research, marketing research and business strategy development. Market research looks specifically at the end product level and covers areas such as the market size, segments, growth rates, maturity, level of captured or tied demand, price levels, trends, and so on. Marketing research provides management with the information necessary to analyze the company on its strengths and weaknesses. Things like market share, client relations, the image the company has among competitors and clients, the technology capability of competitors, product lines, and so on. Business strategy development involves analyzing the total business approach of the company which includes everything from technology to financial status to profitability.

Exhibit 5 *Quest International: product market organization (*Source: *Quest International)*

Market	Units	Flavor Center		R & D	
		Business Dev. Groups	Prod Dev. Groups	Disciplines	
Customers →		→ Savory Sweet NAB Tobacco	→ PCs	→	
Trends	Opportunities	Objectives	Targets	Projects	Products/ Know-how

People at Quest believed that all three of these fields had to be adequately covered for the company to remain an industry pacesetter. Hans Dieperink discussed the importance of complete market research.

> Your current competitive position is a function of past strengths and weaknesses. If you want to develop your competitive position in a particular segment, you have to look at all of this relevant information, not just the advantages of your new products. It also involves looking at the technology, prospects for the segment, competitors and the clients. In our group, we have work in all of these areas.

Funding of Market Research

Conducting market research was not free. The market research department at Quest had a budget of G 600,000[2] provided by the division. Financing the function through the division was preferable to having the operational units pay for the services they received. Management felt units would be reluctant to use the services of market research if they had to pay for it out of their budgets. Under the existing system any unit could request assistance from the market research group. Mr. Romkes, the BDM for savory, added, 'Marketing research should know which requests are important to look at and support.' Recently, however, market research had received an influx of requests from the food ingredients managers. Market research was hesitant to accept these requests because of budget limitations and a staff shortage.

The market research budget allowed the purchase of a wide range of information sources both regularly and as necessary to complete individual reports. Data was also collected in-house from press clippings, brokerage reports, annual reports, etc. Quest maintained a large database on clients, competitors and markets. Some of the information was regularly circulated to management. Gathering the information from such a broad range of sources required a well-trained documentation staff with good industry knowledge.

Organization

Quest's Market Research and R&D group operated as central functions. Conversely, the sales and marketing units were decentralized in order to encourage maximum authority, accountability and responsibility. Some Quest managers wanted market research to be more decentralized, even as far down as the salesforce level. Others argued that this would be difficult or even inappropriate operationally. Not only would it be more expensive as various efforts would have to be duplicated, but the salesforce would need to be retrained in information collection. The nature of Quest's client base was thought to be a critical issue. Hans Dieperink explained:

> We have a relatively complicated and diverse client base, which means we have to do more market research. If you look at our largest competitor, for example, it doesn't have a large market research department. There are two reasons why: 1) it has strategically concentrated on retaining only the largest clients and 2) it has a very competent and highly experienced salesforce with a high retention rate.

> Most of IFF's clients are market leaders. The company doesn't need to do extensive market research because its clients are the market and its salesforce is excellent! If we were willing to spend that kind of money on getting the best of the best, we would probably be able to reduce the efforts of the central market research group. That's not how we have organized ourselves, though, and for us a centralized market research group is critical to the competitiveness of the firm.

Role in Strategy Formulation and Product Development

The market research group actively participated in strategic formulation. Quest had designated three strategic areas of concentration: beverages, savories, and dairy. In 1989, Quest completed a series of studies on the beverages and savories areas which, together with the company's good market position, gave the market research functions the ability to 'freewheel' in those fields for a couple of years and concentrate its energies elsewhere. It was apparent that Quest had only a limited market knowledge of the dairy industry and, consequently, the company made a substantial investment to explore that market. Quest relied on market research to provide justification for new product development and to act as an initiator of potential new product demands in the marketplace. Occasionally, Quest scientists developed new technologies which were not immediately accepted by clients. In this situation, managers looked to market research findings to determine whether or not a new product was too early and the market was not yet ready. If so, a new product might be kept in the product portfolio for release when market conditions improved.

Market research also exposed gaps in the portfolio. For example, if market research indicated a strong end-consumer interest in a fat-free beef flavoring for frying oils, management would consider the desirability of starting a development project to create a suitable product.

Role in Defining Markets

A recent internal report at Quest outlined the differences between 'tied' and 'untied' markets. Tied markets were for products such as Coca-Cola where the product was jealously guarded by the manufacturer and flavor houses were only able to sell raw materials. Untied markets were where manufacturers frequently relied on outside suppliers to handle everything from flavor development to supplying the prepared ingredients. Untied markets were considered more lucrative in terms of future business for Quest.

Periodically, market research reported on competitive trends. Management used the reports in analyzing Quest's performance, in developing strategic plans and in reporting to the board of directors. One such report had dealt exclusively with the effect of the recent spate of acquisitions in the industry and the motivation for them. The report explained in detail the impact of the acquisitions on relative market shares and new entrants in flavors by food ingredient companies, and vice versa.

The information was important because of the wide diversity of national market characteristics even within Europe. For example, Quest was relatively weak in beverages in Germany but also did not see the market as particularly interesting because of the high level of competition there. The UK, where there were a large number of smaller competitors, offered a number of opportunities.

Hans Dieperink commented on the degree of market research necessary:

> To determine how much marketing research you must do, you have to decide what phase you are in and what kind of company you are. Some of our competitors do almost no market research. For example, IFF does almost none. It was traditionally a fragrance company. Fragrances are more marketing driven and the technology is much more mature. Because of that and IFF's market position, market research is not so important. For us that isn't the case.

> We need market research to provide information on market size and the level of innovation to local sales management. They have to make choices and the information helps the decision-making process, how you want to compete, what markets you want to be in, and so on. We have to find out what our clients are looking for and then tell managers so they can make a decision as to where to focus our energies. Should we stay in the snack market?, for example. How do you guide management in setting the right marketing mix?

> Each market segment has something different going on and we have to ask ourselves what will be our role there. For example, we are already in the North American meat flavor market, but with the US-Canadian Free Trade Agreement the whole market will change.

Quest always began segment studies by looking at the market and Quest's position within the market. Then the company's strengths and weaknesses were evaluated as were profitability and technology contribution. When the particular market study was complete, a picture of that segment was available. S. Romkes noted:

> That's the time for a decision – do you want to do something in the market or do you want to leave it as it is? Once you decide that, you can determine your research programs, product development, and so on. Maybe we don't want to go into that market, but we don't know that until we have the market research.

Hans Dieperink added, 'Our task is solving the problems of uncertainty for the business managers.'

Not everyone at Quest agreed with the value placed on market research at Quest. Robert Sinke argued:

> We spent months putting reports together that had tremendous amounts of detail but, when you look at what we do with it, it is relatively limited. By working in Europe this last year, I can tell what the market is doing. My question is, do we really need all the market research we are doing?

Role in Market and Client Selection

Determining how and why a client should be approached in the first place was important, and many people at Quest saw this as the primary function of market research. According to Jan de Rooij:

> Previously, we chased everything that moved everywhere. We have a wide range of flavor products and were able to do that, but it probably wasn't the most efficient approach. Now, we are in almost all markets but they aren't always served the way they should be.

Quest did not have the resources to pursue every potential client, given the large number of candidates. Pursuing clients was expensive and the cost of failure high. The role of market research here was twofold: discovering 1) the potential of a client in terms of demand for flavors and food ingredients and 2) the ability of the client to succeed in the marketplace.

The units had a considerable amount of demand for information on various subjects. Filtering the demands was a constant struggle and some strategy was needed. Generally, however, the qualifying need was identifying the requirements of primary clients. As Mr. Romkes explained:

> We need guidance about what is going on in the market. Although very often

> I feel market research is looking too much at the past and not enough into the future. We need to be at the frontier of development. Our clients are anticipating market developments and we have to do that even more.

> My major requirement from market research is identifying, for each major client, what his needs are for the next few years. Where is he going?, for instance. If he is building a new factory, what will the factory be producing? You have to know from market research that this segment will be really important for your client in the future.

Clients were evaluated based on their prospective volume of business and the likelihood of getting the contract. The sources of information used to analyze clients were diverse. Frequently, the starting point for analyzing sales was the annual reports or press releases of the clients, or industry newsletters. Quest researchers also looked at market share figures either as published or, if public information were not available, through extrapolating from competitors' shares, factory size or any other method of estimating a potential client's output. The information was supplemented with any internal data available at Quest. By comparing the various figures, Quest was able to generate at least a rough approximation of how much a company was producing. From Quest's knowledge of flavor technology, it could then estimate a company's potential demand for flavors. If the purchases were estimated to be large enough, Quest would explore the relationships between the potential clients and their current suppliers.

Using the salesforce as a conduit for information, Quest evaluated the strength of a potential client's relationship with its existing suppliers. If the situation seemed to be conducive for Quest, either because of weak links with existing suppliers or interest in the potential for new sources, Quest would add the company to its target list. The process of evaluating potential clients was complex – just as challenging as the rest of market research.

Role in Sales Support

Market research findings were often an effective sales tool. Quest frequently found that it had better market knowledge than some of its clients. In fact, one manager noted, 'Sometimes we know more about a client's product offerings worldwide than he does.' Increasingly, as the food processing companies focussed more on marketing, they looked to the flavor houses to provide input on what was happening in their markets, what new products were being introduced and what trends were influencing the market. Occasionally, the clients were unaware of fast-breaking product developments and welcomed Quest's suggestions for new products. Quest placed a lot of emphasis on tracking new product launches throughout the world. Most of the time, however, the clients were informed about market trends, but nevertheless appreciated Quest's interest and understanding of their business. Managers at Quest believed that this awareness was an important part of their sales effort.

The new product introduction and market condition information that Quest shared with its clients was not, however, expressly charged to the client. It was assumed that the costs of providing the services would be recovered through the higher margins Quest was able to command. Not all of the managers at Quest believed this expectation was realistic. Robert Sinke, assistant to the director, commented, 'The clients are getting a lot of very expensive information from us free. It would be interesting to see at what price they value the information. We conducted the market research for internal purposes as well, but that doesn't prevent us from charging clients for it when we turn the information over to them.'

Market research, of course, also assisted sales in obtaining existing contracts from competitors. For example, after completing a study on strawberry flavorings in the dairy industry in Europe, Quest approached the client of one of its competitors. Quest asked the manufacturer, 'Do you know your competitor is saving money by using one flavor all across Europe. Why aren't you also doing it? You have a different profile in each country and that is adding to your costs.' When Quest then offered a flavor profile which could be used by the client all over Europe with only a little modification, it won the contract. Entering existing markets, however, was difficult and not a priority. Clients demanded that the new supplier match the existing flavor and offer lower prices or better service. The complex character of flavors was difficult (and very expensive) to match, and there were better opportunities for Quest in new product introductions.

———

Hans Dieperink, the director of market research and strategy development had been at Quest since 1975. 'Yes,' thought Jan de Rooij, 'his early retirement in February would stimulate a reevaluation of market research at Quest and the kind of person we want to replace him.' Quest traditionally had brought people up through the ranks and abhorred bringing outsiders into the company. The belief was that the detailed and complex nature of the flavors business required having people with a long history of experience.

When asked to comment on his departure, Hans Dieperink reflected, 'People tend to think that anybody can do this job and that's not true. Handling and getting the information is important; this job needs someone who can always get information and interpret it. You don't build up market knowledge quickly.'

Notes

1.   Please refer to 'The World Flavor Industry: An Overview', p. 22 for further information.
2.   In 1989, Dutch guilders (G) = $300,000.

SECTION 5

Product Management

CASE

Iskra Power Tools

Iskra Power Tools

This case was prepared by Research Associate Robert C. Howard, under the direction of Professors William A. Fischer, and Per V. Jenster, as a basis for class discussion rather than to illustrate either effective or ineffective handling of a business situation. This case is part of IMD's instutional research program on Managing Internationalization.

As he walked through his factory one frigid winter morning in January 1991, Miro Krek, General Manager of Iskra Industrija za Elektricna Orodja in Kranj, Yugoslavia, commented to his visitors, 'There are certain things we need to do in aligning our marketing and manufacturing. As you walk through here, you can see that our efficiency could easily be improved by 10–15%. For example, we could put in longer lines and plan larger volume runs to get better efficiency. At the same time, we are considering concentrating our manufacturing on certain parts such as motors.' Placing his hand on his chest, he said with considerable emotion, 'Motors are at the heart of any power tool – we need to manufacture them!'

For Iskra's management, the situation in Yugoslavia was tumultuous. Krek explained, 'Over the last three months, Yugoslavia has undergone incredible political change towards adapting a Western style market economy. As this change has touched all aspects of our society, so it has forced us to rethink our entire power tool business. The question for me is, "Should we try to become a major player in the West and East European power tool markets or, should we only focus on a few select markets or customers? Then, too, what would be the consequences for the Iskra organization?"'

Soon after the government approved several free enterprise laws in Yugoslavia in January 1989, revolutions occurred in many of the neighboring countries in Eastern Europe. Prior to those events, Iskra had concentrated its sales primarily on Western power tool markets, where the management believed their competitive advantages were low labor costs and, to a lesser

extent, a few niche products. In fact, until January 1991, these two
dimensions had formed the basis of Krek's plans for leading the Iskra Power
Tool Division into the 1990s. Now, however, with Europe's political
landscape in upheaval, new markets were emerging, and old advantages
were threatened. Consequently, it was necessary to review the interrelated
issues of manufacturing and marketing power tools.

As Krek saw it, there were at least three options available for Iskra
Power Tools. First, continue to capitalize on Yugoslavia's low labor costs
and compete on price in Western markets. Alternatively, Iskra could build
on the two major successes that it had enjoyed, and manufacture and market
a select few power tools in Western niche markets. Third, the management
of Iskra Power Tools could try to build on Yugoslavia's tradition as a
commercial link between East and West, and develop the power tool markets
of Eastern Europe.

Along with the above, Miro also had the continuing worry of how to
preserve Iskra's domestic position at a time when the firm was under direct
attack from a Black & Decker assembly operation in Yugoslavia. With less
than two weeks to prepare for his final presentation to senior management
of the Iskra Group, Krek knew a full review of the options for the 1990s was
necessary.

The Iskra Group of Companies

The Iskra Group of Companies was founded in Ljubjana in 1961 through the
merger of four major electrical companies in Slovenia, Yugoslavia's
northernmost republic. The group based its name on the oldest of these
companies – Iskra – which also meant 'spark' in Slovenian, and symbolized
the electronic nature of the group's products. By 1991, Iskra had become the
leading electronic and electrical manufacturer in Yugoslavia, manufacturing
and marketing a broad range of products through 14 domestic subsidiaries
and 18 foreign offices. Moreover, in Slovenia, Iskra was home to roughly
25,000 employees, making the Iskra Group of Companies the largest
Slovenian employer.

Iskra Power Tools

Although the Iskra Group was founded in 1961, the origins of some of its
companies could be traced to the end of World War II or earlier. What
became Iskra Power Tools, for example, had begun as a textile company in

Kranj during the 1930s when Czechoslovakian textile manufacturers moved their operations to Northern Yugoslavia to take advantage of the low-cost labor force. During World War II, the Nazis gained control of Yugoslavia and transformed the textile facility into a military factory for aircraft engine parts; in the process, they transferred substantial metal working and engineering skills into the Iskra factories.

Throughout the post war era, the mechanical expertise brought to Iskra by the Germans grew increasingly intertwined with electronics, supported by the expertise in Iskra's electronics companies. Until the early 1950s, Iskra's employees had channeled that expertise into industrial and consumer products for rebuilding the Yugoslavian infrastructure and meeting the needs of the domestic market, respectively. Included among the group's industrial products were electric power meters, transformers, capacitors, and electric motors. In the consumer area, typical products included automotive electronics such as starters, alternators and voltage regulators, and household appliances such as vacuum cleaners, toasters, and power tools.

In time, the Kranj production facility became too constrained to continue manufacturing the entire Iskra product offering, and several products were transferred to other sites in the area. Power tool production, however, along with kilowatt meters and telecommunications switching equipment remained in Kranj. *(See **Exhibit 1** for the Iskra Power Tools organization chart.)*

Iskra Commerce

As was typical in many centrally-planned economies, the production and distribution of Iskra Group's products were partitioned into separate responsibilities. While the factories concentrated on production, a separate sales organization, Iskra Commerce, was founded in 1961 to handle the marketing and distribution responsibilities of the organization. Originally, Iskra Commerce had served as a central commercial organization, conducting all purchasing and selling for the Iskra Group of Companies – both inside and outside Yugoslavia. In the early 1970s, following marked growth in size and responsibility, Iskra's domestic companies began to purchase and sell directly in Yugoslavia. However, Iskra Commerce retained responsibility for foreign commercial intercourse.

In foreign markets, Iskra Commerce continued purchasing and selling for all companies within the Iskra Group until the late 1980s. Thereafter, Iskra's foreign companies, like the ones in Yugoslavia, began to establish direct commercial links with suppliers and buyers. Mitja Taucher, former

Exhibit 1 *Iskra Power Tools organization chart (Source: company records)*

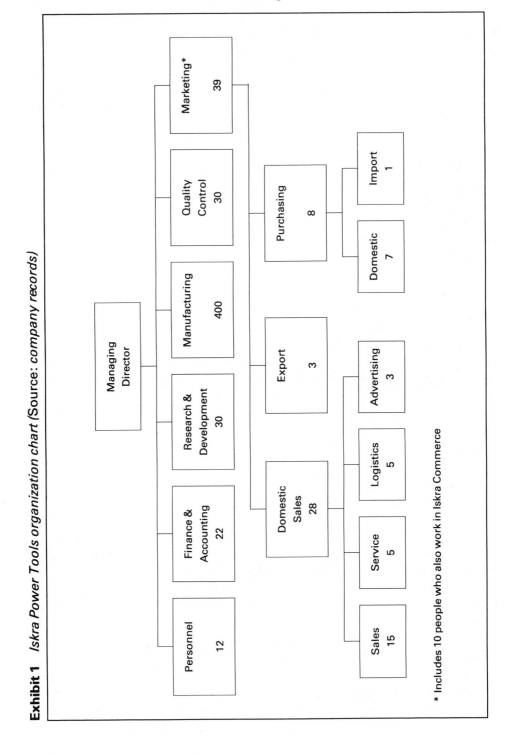

* Includes 10 people who also work in Iskra Commerce

Senior Advisor of Iskra Commerce, recalled the organization's mission: 'When Yugoslavia had strong regulations regarding imports, it made a lot of sense to channel all the group's purchases and sales through one organization; the group was stronger as a whole than as individual companies. Now, however, with the changes in Yugoslavia concerning imports and the strength of our individual companies, it makes sense for Iskra Commerce to serve in a different capacity.'

The Power Tool Industry

Generally speaking, power tools included any tool containing a motor that was capable of being guided and supported manually by an operator. Thus, power tools played an intermediary role between traditional hand tools and sophisticated machine tools. Typical products in the power tool family included the household drill, circular saw, jigsaw, router, angle grinder, hedge trimmer, chain saw and less familiar and more specialized products such as nut runners and impact wrenches used in assembly line manufacture. The wide availability of electrical energy and the relatively low cost of electric tools facilitated their use in small workshops, the building and construction industries, and in households.

Analysts and participants classified the industry into two broad segments according to end usage: professional and hobby. In the professional category, users worked in industries such as assembly-line manufacture, foundries, shipbuilding, and woodworking. The building and construction trade, on the other hand, covered both user segments; that is, tools dedicated to the professional builder as well as tools designed for the home enthusiast or do-it-yourself (DIY) market. Worldwide, power tool purchase behavior varied as a function of labor costs and disposable income. Generally, the professional power tool sector was most developed in high labor cost countries; the DIY market tended to be more pronounced in countries with higher personal disposable incomes.

In 1989, the worldwide electric power tool industry was valued at just over DM10 billion[1], with sales concentrated in three major markets: North America, 28%; Europe, 47%; and the Far East, 18%. Although the industry had grown an average of 3% per annum on a worldwide basis since 1980, market growth rates varied considerably among individual countries *(as indicated in **Table 1**)*. Within Europe, where the industrial segment had traditionally dominated, Germany, France, Great Britain and Italy represented 75% of the region's sales *(as summarized in **Table 2**)*.

Table 1   % Growth of European Power Tool Markets in 1989 and 1990

Country	% Growth 1989	Country	% Growth 1990
Portugal	20	Greece	35
Spain	18	Germany	18
Italy	15	Portugal	18
Greece	15	Italy	12
Finland	12	Netherlands	10
Austria	12	Sweden	10
Sweden	10	Ireland	8
Great Britain	8	Belgium	6
Germany	8	Spain	6
France	8	Austria	4
Belgium	8	Denmark	3
Switzerland	8	Switzerland	3
Netherlands	5	France	0
Ireland	5	Great Britain	0
Denmark	−5	Norway	0
Norway	−5	Finland	−3
Source: Databank 1989		*Source*: Bosch 1990	

Table 2   1989 Unit Sales in Europe's Four Largest Markets

Country	Thousands of Pieces	% European Sales
Germany	7,000	28
France	5,000	20
Great Britain	4,300	17
Italy	2,500	10
Other Countries	6,200	25
Total	25,000	100

Source: Bosch

Segments and Channels

Professional tools were traditionally bought in hardware stores, from wholesalers, large tool specialists or from a manufacturer's or distributor's direct sales force. Quality products suited to specific tasks, durability, and after-sales service were viewed as important buying criteria. In addition, some manufacturers of high-end tools viewed education and problem-solving as part of the sales effort, with trained sales people needed to meet the technical requirements of the user.

In the hobby segment, customers bought from wholesalers, hardware stores, department stores, home centers, mail order houses, and hyper-markets. In this segment, manufacturers considered image, product quality, and price as important purchase factors. Also in this segment, competition was becoming increasingly like that of other consumer products, namely, brand name and packaging were gaining in importance relative to other product features. At the low end of the market, products were designed to meet an expected lifetime use of 25 hours. At the high end, on the other hand, which tended to enlarge as the market matured, there was more emphasis on durability and ergonomic characteristics, similar to professional products.

In Europe, a shift in purchasing patterns had led to a shift in the distribution of power tools. In the professional sector, direct sales had begun to play a more significant role in the distribution process, particularly in the more mature and structured markets. And, in the consumer segment, the volume of tools sold through mass merchandisers was growing at the expense of conventional tool sellers. In short, increased specialization in power tool usage, combined with a proliferation of applications, was leading manufacturers to establish more direct links to professional users and more visible links to the DIY segment. The volume of power tools sold through any one of these channels varied as a function of country. Generally speaking, the markets in Northern Europe were more mature and more structured than those in the Mediterranean countries. Likewise, mass merchandisers and direct sales played a more significant role in the North than in the South. (***Table 3*** *contains comparative data on power tools sold through different channels in Germany vs Italy.*)

Table 3 % of Country Sales by Distribution Channel – 1990

Channel/Country	DIY Segment	
	Germany	Italy
Wholesalers	5	25
Hardware Stores	55	45
Department Stores (Mass Merchandisers)	15	11
Home Centers	21	–
Others (Cash & Carry, Mail Order)	4	19
	Professional Segment	
Direct	10	–
Hardware	50	55
Wholesalers	40	25
Large Tool Specialists (Mass Merchandisers)	–	20

Source: Black & Decker, Iskra Company Records

Manufacturing

Power tools embodied a range of technologies including a motor shaft around which copper wire was wound to form an armature, gears, plastic or metal housing, switches and cables. In conjunction with a trend in production specialization in the post war era, power tool manufacturers relied heavily on subcontractors to produce many of these components. Generally speaking, the major competitors only made components that were central to the performance of the final product, such as the motor. The following bill of material summarizes the key elements in a typical power tool.

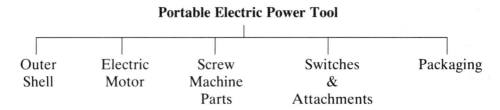

Portable Electric Power Tool

| Outer Shell | Electric Motor | Screw Machine Parts | Switches & Attachments | Packaging |

Typically, power tools were mass produced, although the extent of mechanization varied with the volume of production, nature of the product, and the efficiency of the individual manufacturer. According to one industry analyst, purchased materials accounted for 50% of a power tool firm's manufacturing costs, machining 15%, diecasting/molding 9%, motor winding and assembly 12%, and final assembly 14%.

Trends

By the late 1980s, a number of trends began to influence the level and nature of competition in the worldwide power tool industry. Among these were a growing preference for battery-powered tools, globalization of the industry, and the opening up of Eastern Europe.

Battery-Powered Tools
During the 1980s, battery-powered (also known as cordless) tools benefited significantly from advances in technology. Because of their low energy storage, initial battery-driven products were limited to the smaller jobs of the DIY market. However, the combination of superior power storage and lighter materials that were developed during the 1980s permitted battery-operated tools to be used in more demanding applications, thus facilitating their penetration of the professional market. At the end of the 1980s,

cordless tools represented 20% of all power tool production worldwide and, like many products using electronics, the Japanese were particularly adept at developing cordless power tools. During the 1990s, advances in materials science and battery technology were expected to increase both the usage life between recharges and the number of applications cordless tools could handle.

Globalization

Throughout the 1980s, the electric power tool industry became increasingly globalized, enabling larger players to have an operational flexibility unavailable to smaller companies. By decreasing a firm's reliance on a single market, multinational power tool companies were able to leverage their positions worldwide. That is, firms with manufacturing as well as sales in many markets were able to exploit uncertainties in exchange rates, competitive moves, or government policies far better than their smaller rivals.

Eastern Europe and the USSR

During 1989, communist dictatorships across Eastern Europe were replaced by a variety of governments which, in general, expressed their commitment to develop market economies. Analysts believed that these developments would influence the power tool business in two ways. First, these newly-opened markets and their power tool manufacturers were expected to be the targets of firms already established in the West. Secondly, once the legal issues surrounding privatization became clear, the surviving power tool manufacturers in Eastern Europe could begin to restructure their own operations, and market their products at home and abroad.

Competition

In 1989, there were approximately 75 power tool manufacturers worldwide. Generally speaking, these competitors could be grouped into two categories: large multinationals and, primarily, domestic manufacturers. Typically, the large players offered a full range of power tools to both the professional and the DIY segments, as well as a complete line of accessories such as drill bits, saw blades, battery packs and after-sales service. Smaller power tool manufacturers, on the other hand, tended to concentrate production on a limited line of tools, augmented by OEM products to one or a few segments of the market. Although these small firms lacked the product offering of their larger rivals, they were well known and respected for their expertise in their chosen fields.

Black & Decker

Black & Decker was the largest power tool maker in the world. With manufacturing plants in 10 countries and sales in nearly 100, the company reported 1989 power tool sales of $1,077 million. With approximately 25% of the total market, Black & Decker commanded a worldwide share more than twice that of its next biggest rival. Like most of its competitors, the company segmented the industry into professional and DIY sectors; between the two, Black & Decker derived two-thirds of its revenue from consumers and one-third from professional users.

In addition to its sheer size, Black & Decker enjoyed a number of competitive advantages. New product introduction, for example, was a high priority; the company launched 77 products in 1989 alone and, in the same year, new and redesigned products accounted for 25% of revenues. By 1991, the company expected new entries to represent more than half its sales.

In Europe, where Black & Decker pioneered the introduction of products to the DIY segment, its name was virtually synonymous with power tools. In Britain, for example, it was not uncommon for DIY remodelers to 'Black & Decker' their homes. And, in France, individuals 'plugged in' to the social scene were said to be *'très Black & Decker'*.

One company spokesman attributed his company's success to proper market segmentation and a restructuring that had begun in the mid-1980s. Thus, when the market for power tools as a whole was growing at a rate of only 5–6%, Black & Decker achieved 11% growth in 1989, twice the rate of the markets served, due in part to its concentrated focus on accessories and cordless products. Although the latter grew 30% in 1989, Black & Decker's successful identification of the trend toward cordless products allowed its sales in this segment to grow by 70%, reaching $100 million in 1989.

From the mid-1980s onward, the management of Black & Decker devoted significant attention to 'globalizing' its worldwide operations and, by the beginning of the 1990s, design centers, manufacturing plants, and marketing programs were adept at making and selling products to a worldwide market. As early as 1978, Black & Decker had undertaken the standardization of its motors and armature shafts, and it had, over the years, consistently pursued manufacturing approaches that combined product variety with volume output such as: dedicated lines and facilities for specific items (focused factories and group technology); flexible manufacturing systems (FMS)[2], just-in-time manufacturing (JIT)[3], and significant vertical integration of the fabrication and assembly process. In addition, Black & Decker achieved substantial cost savings through global purchasing programs and saved millions of dollars by restructuring its manufacturing facilities. In one facility, for example, the company standardized production around a limited number of motors. In another case, the company consolidated production of drills from five different plants to two.

To strengthen its presence in Eastern Europe, Black & Decker had recently established an assembly operation via a joint venture in Kranj. Although the company owned only 49 per cent, its proximity to Iskra was seen as a serious challenge to the latter's position in Yugoslavia. And, in May 1989 in Czechoslovakia, Black & Decker entered into a joint venture to produce DIY tools and lawnmowers for the Czechoslovakian and West European markets. Once the joint venture reached full capacity, planned for the start of 1990, Black & Decker intended to cease production at its French and Italian facilities, and rely on its new Eastern European manufacturing platform.

Makita

Based in Japan, the Makita Electric Works had entered the power tool market in the 1950s. In the mid-'70s and the 1980s, Makita established itself in a number of foreign markets by emphasizing its price competitiveness. At one point in the mid-'70s, for example, Makita products were selling at price levels that were 20–30 per cent lower than the industry average. Nonetheless, by the beginning of the 1990s, Makita had established a solid reputation for quality and after-sales service, supported by a 3-day repair policy. And, through engaging a large number of distribution outlets in target markets to promote and service its products, Makita had climbed to number two in the industry by 1991.

In contrast to Black & Decker, Makita concentrated only on the professional segment of the market, with a broad range of tools for professionals. The company attributed its success in overseas markets to superior after-sales service and a close working relationship with well-informed retailers who kept in touch with consumers regarding the latest in product development. Beginning with two factories in Japan in the mid-'70s, Makita had decided to globalize its operations during the 1980s, establishing factory operations in the US, Canada, and Brazil.

In Europe, Makita's 1989 sales increased by 15 per cent and, in the same year, a company spokesman stated that Makita intended to become the largest power tool supplier in the region. In a step towards fulfilling that vision and meeting the company's expressed goal of supplying 25% of European sales with locally manufactured products, Makita began constructing a new power tool plant in the UK in March 1990. Scheduled to begin operating in early 1991, the plant would initially make cordless and percussion drills, angle grinders and circular saws for the professional sector. Ultimately, however, the plant was to produce only electric motors.

As of January 1991, Makita had not begun to compete in any of Iskra's markets.

Robert Bosch
Robert Bosch was the third largest power tool producer in the world and had manufacturing plants in Germany, the USA, Brazil, and Switzerland. Like Black & Decker, Bosch produced a variety of power tools for both the professional and the DIY segments, buying the portable tool division of Stanley Tools in the US in 1979. The company was particularly strong in Europe where it distributed through all channels. In 1990, despite an unfavorable trend in the $/DM exchange rate, Bosch's sales increased 14% to over DM2.2 billion.

Following the unification of East and West Germany, Bosch management announced plans for a joint venture with VEB Elektrowerkzeuge Sebnitz to assemble power tools in Dresden (formerly East Germany) to be distributed through the latter's network of 1,400 hardware outlets. By the end of 1990, the Sebnitz facility was a fully-owned subsidiary and earmarked for DM50 million in investment, initially for producing one-handed angle grinders and small drills. In the longer term, the management of Bosch planned to concentrate all export production in Sebnitz.

Skil
Skil was a major manufacturer of power tools based in the US, where the company was originally known as a professional tool supplier. More recently, however, Skil had concentrated on developing tools that fulfilled needs somewhere between the professional and consumer levels. In Europe, Skil had positioned itself in the Nordic markets as a professional tool company. It approached the rest of Europe, on the other hand, in the DIY market with a strong price emphasis, and was particularly strong in Germany and France.

Niche Players
Aside from the larger multinational power tool companies, there was a host of successful, albeit smaller, players in Europe which pursued niche strategies. In Germany, for example, Festo and ELU were well known for their fine-crafted woodworking tools, especially circular saws. Likewise, Kango, a British company, was renowned for its percussion drills. Generally speaking, niche players in the European power tool business charged premium prices and earned the majority of their sales in their home markets. *(See **Exhibits 2** and **3**, respectively, for a summary of Iskra's competition according to category, and a competitor positioning diagram prepared by a team of Iskra management.)*

Exhibit 2 *Iskra's main competitors in Europe (*Source: *company records)*

Competitor	Location of Corporate Headquarters	Specialist (S) or Generalist (G)	Perceived Successful by Iskra
AEG	D	G	
Black & Decker	US	G	+
Bosch	D	G	+
Casals	E	G	
ELU	D	S, woodworking tools, esp. circular saws	
Fein	D	S, metal working tools, esp. drills, and angle grinders	
Festo	D	S, same as ELU	+
Hilti	D	S, drills	+
Hitachi	J	G	
Impex	D	S, drills	
Kango	UK	S, percussion drills	
Kress	D	G	
Makita	J	G	
Metabo	D	G	
Peugeot	F	G	
Rockwell	US	G	
Rupes	I	S, table saws	
Ryobi	J	G	+
Skil	US, NL	G	
Stayer	I	G	+
Wegoma	D	S, same as ELU	

Notes:
D = Germany
E = Spain
UK = United Kingdom
I = Italy

USA = United States
J = Japan
F = France
NL = Netherlands

Exhibit 3 *Competitor positioning diagram*

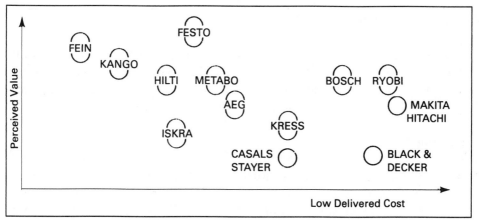

Iskra Power Tools' Competitive Position

Market Development

From its beginning in the early 1950s, the Iskra Power Tool division concentrated its sales in the Yugoslavian market. Ventures into Western Europe did not begin until the 1960s when the management sought to expand its product offering, consisting primarily of electric drills, based on the company's expertise in small electric motors. The cornerstone of this expansion strategy was exchange programs with other power tool manufacturers.

In 1966, Iskra entered into a cooperation agreement with Perles, a small power tool manufacturer in Switzerland. In exchange for Perles' angle grinders sold under the Iskra name in Yugoslavia, Perles received Iskra's drills which it distributed through its own network under the Perles label. In 1971, Iskra management sought to build on the Perles name and distribution network by acquiring the Swiss-based manufacturer. Mitja Taucher commented that, in the early 1970s, Iskra management realized they would have difficulties with an unknown name in Europe and, thus, decided to acquire Perles. 'Perles is still in existence mostly for its name, not its manufacturing capacity, which is small,' recalled Mitja. He added, 'It was a good name across Europe for large angle grinders and some drills.'

Bolstered by its first co-marketing arrangement with Perles, in 1972 the management of Iskra entered into an agreement with Skil Europe. In exchange for Iskra's small drills, sold under Skil's name through its European distribution network, Skil supplied Iskra with percussion drills, belt sanders and circular saws, sold in Yugoslavia under the Iskra name.

Eastern European Ventures

Following the first of a series of oil crises that began in 1973, it was difficult for Iskra to continue its expansion plans into Western markets. As an alternative, the management of Iskra Power Tools began to strengthen business ties with its socialist neighbors in Eastern Europe.

Czechoslovakia

Iskra's Eastern European experience began in 1978 with Naradi, a power tool manufacturer, and with Merkuria, a trading company, both based in Czechoslovakia. Due to a lack of convertible currency in Czechoslovakia, Iskra devised a three-way trading agreement: Perles shipped drills from

Switzerland to Naradi, which marketed the products under the Naradi name, and to Merkuria, which sold products under the Iskra name. In turn, both Czech firms delivered products to Iskra; the process was completed when Iskra sent its power tools to Perles in Switzerland. Although Iskra achieved nearly a 10 per cent market share through these two agreements in Czechoslovakia, its success was not without problems.

One executive stated that the weak point in the process was the power tools from Czechoslovakia; tools made by Naradi did not measure up to the quality standards demanded by Yugoslavian consumers. Moreover, after a few years, Naradi's products were out-of-date in comparison to competitors' offerings. Finally, because of the difficulties posed by the lack of real distribution channels or a service network in Czechoslovakia, Iskra management terminated the agreement in 1988.

Poland

Iskra had also participated in a cooperative arrangement to exchange power tools with Celma, a Polish power tool manufacturer. Like the agreement with Naradi in Czechoslovakia, Iskra marketed Celma's products under the Iskra name in Yugoslavia. However, Celma's products were of such low quality that Iskra soon found itself inundated with repair requests. Consequently, the management of Iskra devised a new agreement for close cooperation on specialty tools such as shears, steel cutters and die grinders.

USSR

More recently, Iskra Power Tools had tried manufacturing in the USSR. After five years of negotiating with the Institute for Power Tools in Moscow, in 1984, the first 100 power tools were brought to Yugoslavia. Unfortunately, due to the length of the negotiating period, the products were out-of-date on arrival. Like the previous efforts in Czechoslovakia and Poland, Iskra brought its Russian efforts to a halt.

Refocus on Western Europe

Like many firms that manufactured in and exported from Yugoslavia, Iskra earned a certain level of income from the domestic market. Although that income was not guaranteed, limited competition in the Yugoslavian power tool market had almost always provided Iskra with a source of funding to manufacture tools sold outside the country. By the beginning of the 1980s, however, the management of Iskra Power Tools grew concerned about becoming too dependent on the domestic market. Moreover, when it combined the uncertainties of the domestic market with its unsuccessful ventures in Eastern Europe, the management concluded it was time to resume strengthening ties with Western power tool producers.

Iskra as OEM Supplier

ELU
In 1980, Iskra signed a cooperation agreement with ELU, a German manufacturer of woodworking tools. Despite Iskra's successful development and initial manufacture of a small circular saw for sale under the ELU label, the management of ELU cancelled the agreement after two years. According to Branko Suhadolnik, Export Manager for Iskra Power Tools, Iskra was simply unable to supply the quantity of saws specified in the contract because of delays in starting production.

Kango
Iskra also began manufacturing for Kango, a UK company specializing in drills. In exchange for Kango's rotary hammer, sold under the Iskra name in Yugoslavia, Iskra provided Kango with circular saws sold under the Kango name in the UK.

Iskra as Volume OEM

Skil
In the mid-1980s, Iskra management expanded its cooperation with Skil. In addition to supplying Skil with a small drill, Iskra provided a small angle grinder, a circular saw, and orbital sander. These items were sold under the Skil name in support of Skil's low price strategy. In November 1990, the management of Iskra approached Skil to discuss strengthening their partnership still further. However, as of January 1991, no additional cooperation had been agreed to.

Ryobi
In 1990, Miro Krek and Branko Suhadolnik began negotiating a joint venture agreement with Ryobi from Japan. Suhadolnik explained that Ryobi was considering Yugoslavia as an entry point into the European Economic Community and wanted to capitalize on Yugoslavia's comparative advantage in labor costs. In return for supplying angle grinders to Ryobi, Iskra was to market Ryobi's battery-operated power tools in Yugoslavia. Although the

management of Ryobi was impressed with Iskra's products, they said that the manufacturing costs were too high; in order to meet Ryobi's terms, Iskra had to invest in more equipment. Shortly thereafter, the management of Ryobi decided to postpone further dealings in Eastern Europe until the political environment stabilized.

Bosch

In its most recent effort to supply a foreign manufacturer, Iskra approached Bosch concerning a router that complemented Bosch's offering. This deal, too, nearly succeeded, but was contingent on Iskra's dissolving its independent sales network in Germany and elsewhere. Because Bosch was not willing to purchase what Iskra management believed was the required volume necessary to compensate for the loss of its sales network, Iskra declined the offer.

In summary, the management of Iskra had made several attempts over the years to increase its attractiveness to foreign firms. With Skil, a generalist in the power tool industry, Iskra's competitive advantage was being a low-cost supplier; with ELU, Kango and Bosch, on the other hand, Iskra's success was based on the high perceived value of a niche product. With Ryobi, price competitiveness and market presence in Eastern Europe were important.

Iskra's Products and Channels

At the beginning of 1991, Iskra marketed a range of 200 products; 10 of these were obtained from other manufacturers via exchange agreements, while the balance were designed and produced by Iskra alone. Roughly speaking, accessories accounted for 20% of Iskra Power Tools' turnover, while drills and angle grinders accounted for approximately 50% and 30%, respectively, of tool sales. Outside, Yugoslavia, Iskra distributed its own products under the Perles name, almost exclusively through specialist hardware outlets in both the DIY and professional segments. In addition, Iskra Commerce marketed Iskra's power tools through its own offices. Although the influence of the latter was declining, Suhadolnik commented that, until the late 1980s, Iskra Commerce's foreign companies often made policies to survive for the short term, with little attention to the long term. For example, in those markets where the two organizations overlapped, prices sometimes differed between Iskra Power Tools and Iskra Commerce for the same products. More recently, he added, Iskra management had succeeded in changing this policy but, Suhadolnik commented, 'To change something with a life of its own is not so easy.'

In Yugoslavia, where Iskra had a market share of 50% in 1989, the company sold its power tools through Iskra Commerce with its own network of shops in each republic. However, the company had a significantly larger market share in Serbia than in Slovenia or Croatia. According to Branko, natives of the latter two provinces, because of their proximity to Italy and Austria, were not only better informed as to Western power tool alternatives, but could more easily access these alternative products. Power tools were also sold through the Iskra Power Tools sales organization, and directly from the factory in Kranj.

Design

In 1990, the design group at Iskra consisted of six people, all working primarily with pencil and paper. By contrast, their Western counterparts worked with computer aided design (CAD) systems. Despite the lack of modern design equipment, the Iskra design team possessed strong artistic talents and lacked the engineering bias of Western designers. In describing the evolution of the relationship between design and manufacturing at Iskra, one manager commented that, until the early 1980s, there was a 'We draw, you make' attitude. A few years thereafter, employees in the two functions began taking a more interdisciplinary approach to designing and making Iskra's power tools. Designers, for example, began asking those in manufacturing about the costs associated with individual parts; those in manufacturing, on the other hand, asked designers for new technological solutions. 'Yet,' recalled one designer, 'new solutions were not possible because they required too much investment in new technology.'

As of January 1991, there were two ways of concentrating on new product development at Iskra Power Tools. One was via direct cooperation with manufacturing on existing product lines, a process which tended to focus on minor changes and had been practiced for at least 15 years. The second pertained to new products and was primarily concerned with shortening product development time, through interdisciplinary teams, to a level comparable to Iskra's competition.

Not unlike the design-manufacturing relationship, the interaction between design and marketing was based on a philosophy of 'We design, you sell'. Beginning in the mid-1980s, however, this relationship also began to change as collaboration with Iskra's partners – Skil and Perles – on new designs began to increase, and greater and earlier cooperation between the two functions began to evolve.

Iskra was receptive to ideas from the marketplace, communicated to the design team via Iskra's customers and foreign distributors. In 1988, for example, Iskra formed a multidisciplinary team to determine which products had to be produced in the subsequent five years, at what price and what quantity. In the export market, ideas were solicited from Iskra's agents and distributors via an annual conference. As for feedback from end users, Iskra conducted market research for both its professional and its DIY customers, albeit only in Yugoslavia. *(See **Table 4** for design information at Iskra Power Tools.)*

Table 4 Information on Iskra Power Tools' Design Function

Year	1982	1983	1984	1985	1986	1987	1988	1989	1990
No. designers	5	5	5	5	5	3	6	6	5
Average age	40	41	42	42	43	35	37	40	41
Years of experience (absolute)	38	43	48	49	54	20	26	28	33
Reconstructed products	6				7				3
Modifications	148				208				190
Commercial variants	717				1,802				827
New products	0	1	3	1	2	1	0	1	0

Note: A reconstructed product was one which had been developed and produced, but corrected for flaws. A modification, on the other hand, corresponded to a product with an incremental innovation such as a new spindle, a different type of handle or an additional speed. As the name implied, commercial variants were simply the number of variations possible for Iskra's products, needed to meet the different demands of Iskra's many markets and customers.
Source: Company Records

Manufacturing

Despite Iskra's product offering of 200 power tools, most were variations of a common manufacturing mix of 10–15 models, all made in one factory using traditional batch production. Depending on the model, the array of products was manufactured on a monthly, quarterly, or annual basis. For example, Iskra had 70 variations of its drill, which was produced throughout the year in the same way as its angle grinders and circular saws. On the other hand, smaller volume products such as sanders and routers were made only on a quarterly basis.

Planning

At Iskra, batch sizes and sequencing were developed by a central planning department located in the Kranj factory. Typically, the planning department estimated the year's production and adjusted their forecast quarterly. In addition, three planners prioritized the work at each factory work-station, based on the assembly plan which, in turn, was based on delivery promises. Prior to final assembly, the manufacturing department received figures for specific markets and attached the correct labels to the final package.

Differences between the batches produced and the amounts needed for assembly at any point in time (due to lead time varations) were stored in inventories until needed. In other words, purchasing of components and product fabrication at Iskra were always begun before the ultimate destination of a power tool was known, thereby limiting the ability to use dedicated machining in the first and last stages of the production process. From 1987–1989, Iskra Power Tools' inventory turnovers averaged 4.4, with the biggest inventories occurring at the beginning of the assembly process. By comparison, one manager estimated that Bosch's inventory turnover was in the range of 5–10 per year.

Milan Bavec, Manufacturing Manager, believed that parts inventories were too high because of difficulties in linking purchasing more closely to assembly. As an example, he explained that, on August 1, he might begin a series of 3,000 sanders, for which he ordered parts three months in advance. However, he said, when some parts took six months to arrive, one simply had to maintain the necessary inventory. All parts, he continued, were moved in and out of inventory. That is, whether Iskra produced or purchased its parts, all parts were stored in a warehouse until the full range was available to make a particular product. As an aside, Igor Poljsak, Financial & Accounting Department Manager, mentioned that the constant shifting of parts between Iskra's many buildings added 10–15% to production costs. Then, too, at 40–50% per year to borrow money, he estimated that the interest on working capital was 10–12%. Within manufacturing, some believed that if the individual market demands could be better coordinated with the manufacturing function, inventories could be reduced and more dedicated assembly implemented, thereby raising productivity.

Productivity

In terms of performance, productivity at Iskra Power Tools was somewhere between that of Eastern and Western power tool makers, with direct labor estimated at 10–12% of the cost of goods sold. *(See **Table 5** for productivity figures, **Table 6** for a breakdown of the manufacturing costs associated with a typical product, and **Exhibits 4** and **5** for the Iskra income statement and balance sheets, respectively.)*

Table 5 Productivity Figures for Selected Power Tool Firms

Company of Location	No. Workers	Output (units/year)
Iskra	550	600,000
Bulgarian	5,000	40,000
Czechoslavakian	2,000	150,000
Western Firm	250	600,000

Source: Company Records

Table 6 Breakdown of Manufacturing Costs for Angle Grinders (%)

Purchased Materials	65.1
Machining & Diecasting & Molding	15.9
Motor Assembly	9.1
Final Assembly	9.9
Total	100.0

Source: Assembly Records

In discussing productivity, the management of Iskra acknowledged that labor costs were a serious burden and that the company probably had three times as many people as necessary. 'And,' commented one executive, 'indirect costs are always too high, and we think that we have extremely high indirect costs for our production volume. For example, we have data indicating that Skil, with approximately the same number of people as Iskra, produces nearly one million pieces. Kress employs 400–500 people and produces around one million pieces. We have around 550 people, recently reduced from 760 without any strikes; however, I don't believe that will hold if we try to reduce further.'

In addition to too many employees, Iskra's productivity was influenced by significant differences in production. Specifically, work was performed both in batch and in sequence, and, because all parts (except motors) were continually moved in and out of physical inventory, the flow of goods through the factory was complicated. *(See **Exhibit 6** for the flowpath of a typical item.)* On the third floor of the factory, where a dedicated motor assembly line was located, the situation was even more chaotic; there was little apparent continuity among workstations and, although the production machinery was only about 10 years old, the manufacturing process appeared much older. Lastly, the final assembly of tools was like a rabbit warren, with lots of discontinuities. As an example, newly-finished goods often sat for several days waiting for complementary parts, such as chuck-keys, which had become stocked out.

Exhibit 4 *Income statement for Iskra Power Tools*
(Source: *company records*)

Fiscal Year Ending December 31 ($US '000)	1986	1987	1988	1989	1990
Sales Revenue					
Domestic	25,362.9	4,842.5	18,196.4	20,658.6	24,886.9
Exports	7,559.2	12,311.6	11,882.3	10,204.6	12,815.1
Others	1,932.5	1,852.7	486.0	406.2	548.5
Total Sales	*34,854.6*	*39,006.8*	*30,564.7*	*31,269.4*	*38,250.5*
Cost of Sales	18,753.8	27,596.4	22,948.2	23,676.4	27,425.9
Gross Income	16,100.8	11,410.4	7,616.5	7,593.0	10,824.6
Selling and Administrative Expenses	10,065.4	8,226.5	5,032.3	5,191.8	6,020.4
Operating Income	*6,035.4*	*3,183.9*	*2,594.2*	*2,401.2*	*4,804.2*
Other Income:					
Interest	58.3	3.3	36.6	14,928.1	797.5
Sundry Income	1,049.6	269.3	152.8	406.2	2,320.8
Total Other Income	*1,107.9*	*272.6*	*189.4*	*15,334.3*	*3,118.3*
Other Expenses:					
Interest	3,611.4	907.9	1,753.9	12,201.8	4,558.6
Sundry Expenses	1,380.5	583.0	482.5	13,664.8	4,781.7
Total Other Expenses	*4,991.9*	*1,490.9*	*2,236.4*	*25,866.6*	*9,340.3*
Obligatory Contributions to Community Funds	1,090.7	1,521.9	507.6		
Net Income (Loss)	*1,060.7*	*443.7*	*29.6*	*(8,131.1)*	*(1,417.8)*
Allocation of Net Income (Loss):					
Business Fund	140.6				
Reserve Fund	269.7	292.8	26.6		
Collective Consumption Fund	557.2	128.6			
Joint Venture Partners	93.2	22.3	3.0		
Depreciation	1,109.7	1,402.7	1,269.9	1,470.2	2,591.5
Net Income	1,060.7	443.7	29.6	(8,131.1)	(1,417.8)
Cash Generation	2,170.4	1,846.4	1,299.5	(6,660.9)	1,173.7

Exhibit 5 *Iskra balance sheets* (Source: *company records*)

Fiscal Year Ending December 31	1986	1987	1988	1989	1990
Current Assets:					
Bank Balances and Cash	68.2	71.9	13.7	29.0	24.3
Bills and Trade Receivables	6,068.1	6,815.3	4,954.3	5,791.2	10.257.3
Prepayments and other Receivables	1,734.9	1,497.4	4,931.1	520.8	137.3
Current Portion of Long-term Receivables	29.1	1.8	0.5	408.6	184.1

Exhibit 5 *Continued*

Fiscal Year Ending December 31	1986	1987	1988	1989	1990
Inventories:					
Raw Materials	4,104.0	3,506.8	2,289.7	856.8	3,367.0
Work-in-Progress	1,538.8	1,367.4	957.8	245.9	1,148.0
Finished Products	1,367.9	1,211.4	640.9	802.2	1,750.0
Subtotal	7,010.7	6,085.6	3,888.4	1,904.9	6,265.0
Total Current Assets	*14,911.0*	*14,472.0*	*13,788.0*	*8,654.5*	*16,868.0*
Long-term Receivables	106.3	67.8	56.6	2,503.3	3,500.0
Investments	1,187.9	1,324.7	1,289.1	34.1	
Deposits for Capital Expenditure	147.4	16.9	201.8	28.9	998.4
Fixed Assets:					
Land and Building	1,635.0	1,343.1	1,199.8	1,453.9	2,611.6
Equipment	12,571.4	12,804.9	11,697.2	17,554.8	32,520.9
Deferred Expenditure	0.2	15.8	14.0	188.0	
Construction in Progress	241.3	24.9	70.5	107.5	191.9
Total Gross Fixed Assets	*14,447.9*	*14,188.7*	*12,981.5*	*19,304.2*	*35,324.5*
Less: Accumulated					
Depreciation	7,238.1	7,495.2	7,542.2	12,363.5	25,093.6
Net Fixed Assets	7,209.8	6,693.5	5,439.3	6,940.7	10,230.9
Intangible Assets			125.9		
Net Assets Allocated to Funds					
Reserve Fund	501.7	338.6	94.1	69.6	137.4
Collective Consumption Fund	1,328.1	847.3	466.1	169.6	380.6
Other Funds	43.9	21.4	9.6	21.3	168.5
Subtotal	1,873.7	1,207.3	569.8	260.5	686.5
Total Assets	**25,436.1**	**23,782.2**	**21,470.5**	**21,089.8**	**35,987.9**

Fiscal Year Ending December 31 Liabilities and Funds	1986	1987	1988	1989	1990
Current Liabilities:					
Bills and Trade Payables	2,859.0	2,945.6	2,581.5	7,656.1	4,282.7
Payables for Fixed Assets	2.6	6.5	1.3		
Customers Deposits and Other					
Current Liabilities	4,231.5	2,648.2	2,689.5	0.9	3,836.9
Short-term Loans	3,224.9	5,381.4	5,981.1	4,325.3	7,188.4
Current Portion of Long-term					
Loans	1,503.3	889.5	511.1	502.7	263.2
Amounts Due to Reserve and Collective					
Consumption Funds	91.2	309.3	17.3		
Deferred Sales	2,158.8	1,355.9	1,111.5	172.1	4,207.3
Total Current Liabilities	*14,071.3*	*13,536.4*	*12,893.3*	*12,657.1*	*19,778.5*
Long-term Loans	3,024.2	3,362.5	3,345.4	2,788.3	5,001.0
Joint Venture Partner Investments:					
Domestic Partners	107.9	17.8	22.1	0.7	
Foreign JV Partners					
Business Funds	6,476.4	5,668.0	4,659.5	5,368.9	10,541.4

Exhibit 5 *Continued*

Fiscal Year Ending December 31	1986	1987	1988	1989	1990
Other Funds:					
Reserve Fund	501.7	338.6	94.1	160.2	137.4
Collective Consumption Fund	1,236.9	847.2	448.8	69.6	380.6
Other Funds	17.7	11.7	7.3	35.2	149.0
Subtotal	1,756.3	1,197.5	550.2	265.0	667.0
Total Liabilities and Funds	**25,436.1**	**23,782.2**	**21,470.5**	**21,080.0**	**35,987.9**

Exhibit 6 *Flowpath for power tool gear manufacturing (*Source: *company records)*

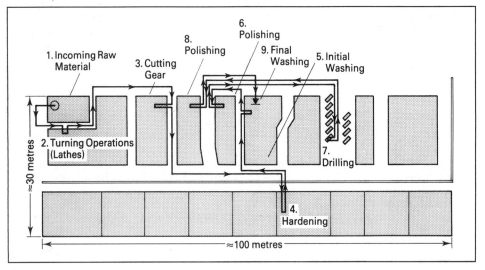

Quality

The management of Iskra Power Tools was well aware that it needed to establish, improve and maintain quality in products and processes. In fact, the manager responsible for quality had organized statistical process control (SPC) procedures within the factory but, to date, had had only mixed success. Specifically, the level of quality was nowhere near that required to move to a production process – like JIT which could significantly reduce work-in-process inventories.

As of early 1991, incoming goods continued to be checked on arrival, according to prearranged contractual standards, using a standard acceptance sampling (Acceptable Quality Level – AQL) system. In fact, acceptance sampling was done at final production and final assembly, as well as with incoming items. In all cases, quality control (QC) was based on the first five pieces in a batch, followed by statistical sampling.

For the future, the quality manager hoped to integrate a quality attitude throughout the company. As part of the process, management had prepared a book containing quality standards, based on the International Standards Organization (ISO) 9000 series set of standards.[4] As of January 1991, management had not had much success implementing quality improvement. To do so, management believed, would require reshaping the attitudes of Iskra's workers.

The Production Workers

Iskra Power Tools' production process was characterized by low employee involvement, poor changeover performance between different models, and relatively poor maintenance performance. The assembly line workers were analyzed using modern time and methods analysis (Work Factor), and the analysis used to allocate labor staffing. However, since assembly was performed on a paced line, it was not possible for the employees to work faster. Thus, no pay incentives existed for higher output and workers were paid as a group. On occasion, quality bonuses were paid within the factory, despite the fact that some of the production being 'rewarded' was not actually perfect.

Jakob Sink, Quality Assurance Manager, commented on the difficulties met in transforming the mindset of Iskra employees. 'It is a new idea to send back a QC approval form within a few weeks. "Why not do it in a couple of months?" is still very much the attitude of those working in production.' Then, too, Sink added, workers were concerned that identifying poor quality could cause either himself or a co-worker to be fired. Also, he mentioned that some employees might resist altering manufacturing processes, discussed by management in an attempt to deal with high variety manufacturing in a more efficient format. In defense of the workforce, Sink said that incoming materials played a key role in the quality problem and that, although Iskra controlled what it bought, it sometimes cost as much to control incoming materials as to produce a finished product.

The Supply Situation

Given that all major players in the power tool industry relied on suppliers for major components, it was not surprising that Iskra was also involved in such relationships. However, in Iskra's case, there was widespread agreement among the management team that the supply relationships were a competitive disadvantage. In fact, some thought that Iskra's manufacturing costs were 20–25% more expensive than for Bosch, for example, because of the supply situation. Then too, the company faced the added complication that one of its major suppliers was based in Serbia, a republic with which political tensions had been growing.

Within Yugoslavia, the manufacturing director distinguished suppliers according to raw materials or finished components such as gears and cables. He commented that, aside from having a lower quality, raw materials were also more expensive in Yugoslavia than in Western Europe. Furthermore, there were few finished component suppliers to choose from in Yugoslavia, and those that did exist did not possess a high quality standard. To use domestic components, Iskra would have to take what was available from several firms and remachine those components before assembling its power tools. In other words, the absence of quality suppliers and subcontractors added yet another step to Iskra's manufacturing.

As one remedy, Iskra forged close working relationships with its local suppliers. Generally speaking, these suppliers were able to respond to major design changes without any real problem, but efforts to upgrade the quality of the finished components had been unsuccessful. Despite the close relationships, it was highly unlikely that Iskra could put SPC into a supplier facility. According to Milan Bavec, 'SPC is still too new, and even though we've held seminars, run films and the like, our results are still poor. At present, the real problem is getting the suppliers to comply with Iskra's own quality checklists. And that will take at least another two to three years.'

Foreign Suppliers
Another manager pointed out that an obvious remedy to the problems encountered with domestic suppliers was to source from foreign firms. In general, sourcing at Iskra began after Iskra Power Tools had identified a potential supplier and negotiated the contract. Iskra Commerce then handled the commercial issues, such as invoicing and foreign exchange, for which it charged a fee of 4–6%. In addition, Iskra Power Tools paid an import duty of 4–5% on all items which it re-exported. For items sold on the domestic market, however, the import tax was 45%.

Another sourcing disadvantage for Iskra was customs delays. Typically, it took the company up to one month to obtain import clearance. To counter such delays, Iskra was obliged to order large stocks in advance. Additional factors that complicated Iskra's sourcing arrangements were premium prices because of small order volumes, payment problems due to foreign exchange availability, and the problem of Yugoslavia's external political image.

To summarize the above, one Iskra executive prepared a business system depicting the company's contribution to added value. For a customer paying a price of 100 (without VAT), distribution accounted for 50%, while parts, fabrication and assembly represented the balance (*as summarized below*).

The Iskra Business System

Parts	Fabrication	Assembly	Distribution	Customer
32.5	8.0	9.5	50.0	100.0

----------------------------->VALUE ADDED-------------------------->

Source: Company Records

Formulating a Strategy

In formulating Iskra's future strategy, Branko Suhadolnik believed the company should concentrate on less mature and less structured markets such as France and Italy. He reinforced his point by stating that the only way to succeed in these markets was to establish the Perles brand name and structure the distribution. Revamped manufacturing facilities, Branko added, would play a primary role in associating the company's image with quality products. Although he also supported the idea of serving as an OEM, he favored serving the niche players, provided Iskra could overcome what he believed was the company's inability to supply a requested volume of product at a competitive price.

On the other hand, Miro Krek believed the company's future lay in concentrating on becoming an OEM supplier to high volume producers, not trading under the Perles brand or worrying about distribution. As an OEM supplier, Krek felt that Iskra's inability to attract outside cooperation was due to a lack of price competitiveness, quality, and supply reliability. Consequently, special attention should be devoted to developing its price competitiveness and strengthening its ties with volume players such as Skil.

Then, too, a third group of Iskra executives believed that now was the time to attack Eastern Europe and the USSR. Specifically, these executives believed that Western suitors saw Iskra as a possible entryway into the Soviet Union.

Western Markets with Perles Branding

Based on the company's experiences through January 1991, Branko Suhadolnik felt that any activity in Western Europe required a concentrated focus on France, the second biggest market in Europe. Branko emphasized that with more than 8% growth in 1989 and five million power tools sold, France represented 20% of the total European market and warranted further attention.

He went on to say that in France, there was no strong national producer of power tools. Secondly, the market was not nearly as developed as in Germany or the Netherlands and, therefore, customers bought more on price, less on quality and tradition. Third, the distribution channels in France were not well defined. 'Then too,' he added, 'we believe the Latin way of life in France is closer to our way of life than the Germans, who are more formal and direct.'

Like France, Suhadolnik also stressed the need for Iskra to target the Italian market. 'Italy has a small power tool producer, but most of its production is exported; almost 60%. In value, almost 70% of the Italian market is imported. Bosch is number one, and Black & Decker number two with its own production through Star, a local company. Moreover, all the Japanese and other companies are minor, the market is close to Yugoslavia and, therefore, transport costs are low. Finally, Yugoslavia and Italy have a clearing agreement that allows unlimited import and export.' One of Suhadolnik's colleagues added that the clearing agreement was one reason why Iskra entered the Italian market in the first place; Italy was the cheapest source of raw materials for cables, switches, plastic, and blades – almost half of Iskra Power Tools' raw materials.

In developing a strategy for the Italian market, Suhadolnik proposed to concentrate on that half of the professional segment which catered to specialty repair shops. 'In Italy,' one manager commented, 'where the first thing for an Italian man is his car, there are an abundance of repair shops to service those cars.' The manager then referred to a market research survey stating that Italy had about 100,000 known repair shops of all kinds; the unknown number was anyone's guess. The study also mentioned a trend in these shops toward building maintenance. 'That's why,' the manager concluded, 'we believe Iskra can reach a 3% market share in Italy within two years, up from our present 1.3–1.5% share of market.'

Western Markets as Volume OEM

It was no secret that one of Iskra's competitive advantages in foreign markets was low price. In Germany, for example, Metabo sold one of its drills for DM299, AEG sold a comparable drill for DM199, and Iskra, under the Perles name, sold its drill for DM139. A number of Iskra managers believed that a low price should be vigorously pursued. In their opinion, bolstered by favorable comments from foreign power tool manufacturers, Iskra's products possessed good value for money. Therefore, one executive added, he saw no reason why Iskra could not continue to use its low labor cost advantage and underprice the competition.

Western Markets as Niche OEM

During one meeting, Suhadolnik emphasized that Iskra was simply too small and had too few resources to offer a full range of products the way Bosch did. On the contrary, he added, Iskra should concentrate on angle grinders and drills, beginning with a new focus on R&D and production. In other words, focus on those products that represent Iskra's distinctive competence, beginning with design, followed by component sourcing and new manufacturing technology. Taucher added, 'Our output is 600,000 pieces per year. All our large European competitors are in the order of 1.5 to 2 million pieces per year. That is probably the threshold; we are much too small to compete on their terms. We are too small and we don't have a name like Bosch or AEG. That's the problem and, to be a niche manufacturer, you still need the name. We are not a Formula 1, but a Yugo on which we have put a Maserati label.'

Eastern Europe

In Eastern Europe, Iskra management knew about power tool manufacturers in Poland, the DDR, Bulgaria, Czechoslovakia, and the Soviet Union. In three of these countries – Poland, Czechoslovakia, and the Soviet Union – Iskra had had some experience. In general, Suhadolnik explained that all these markets were virtually untapped and thus presented a tremendous opportunity for Iskra. Nonetheless, with the exception of the DDR, which was now part of Germany and where the one power tool manufacturer had been purchased by Bosch, none of the remaining countries could pay hard currency for Iskra's products. Therefore, Iskra was required to sell its products via counterpurchase agreements as it had done with Naradi in Czechoslovakia. Despite these countries' hard currency shortages, an executive pointed out that some of Iskra's competitors had not been discouraged from taking a further look at these markets. In particular, both Bosch and Black & Decker had planned to start manufacturing in the Soviet Union and were actively looking for personnel to run these facilities and market their products.

Notes

1.   In 1989, average exchange rates were 1 ECU = DM2.02, and US$1 = DM1.88.
2.   Flexible manufacturing systems consisted of sophisticated computer driven lines, with relatively independent routing and intelligent machining centers.
3.   JIT referred to the Japanese-inspired approach to manufacturing which had originated with the philosophy of continuous improvement, superior quality, low changeover costs, and greatly reduced work-in-process inventories.
4.   ISO 9000 was a technical standard that required the establishment of a complete system for monitoring quality standards.

SECTION 6

Industrial Pricing Strategies

CASE

The Cochlear Bionic Ear

The Cochlear Bionic Ear: Creating a High-Tech Market

This case was prepared by Professor Sandra Vandermerwe and Research Fellow Marika Taishoff as a basis for class discussion rather than to illustrate either effective or ineffective handling of a business situation.

'It's mystifying,' he muttered, gazing out at the bright June light across the Rhine to Germany, which was just visible from the Basel-based European headquarters. 'Our system works better than any other surgical procedure. We have a failure rate of 1%. No other kind of surgery offers that sort of result. Why aren't we selling more?' By June 1990 Mike Hirshorn, CEO Worldwide, was getting increasingly concerned about the drop in sales of the Cochlear hearing implant device.

He had been with the Australian company since its inception, and had experienced all the ups and downs of getting regulatory approval and carving out an entirely new market. As one of the original members of the project team, Mike had helped take the ear implant invention of a university professor and transform it into a commercially viable product for the profoundly deaf.

'Look,' he declared, 'we've managed to get rid of 3M, our biggest competitor. But still we've only succeeded in selling 3,500 units worldwide. Do you realize there are another 50,000 adults out there, if not more, who need us? Yet we can't seem to break through!'

After a brief silence Brigette Berg, CEO for Europe, responded, 'Maybe we just have to face the fact that the market is smaller than we think. The only place we're still growing is in Europe, and that's only because new countries are finally beginning to include us in their health coverage schemes.' Brigette had set up the Basel office in 1987 to market and distribute the Cochlear hearing system, the most technologically advanced in the world.

She went on. 'Maybe we should stop worrying about volumes. After all, we've got 90% of the market in the US and 60% in Europe and the best product in the world. Why shouldn't the market be prepared to pay more for it? It makes more sense to me to consider raising the price.' She looked across at Dennis Wheeler, her American counterpart, for a reaction.

'Perhaps in Europe, where most countries just fix quotas and aren't that price sensitive,' Dennis said quickly. 'But then we'll risk losing the 25% of the US market which depends on government support. In my opinion, if we want to stay ahead of the competition, we've got to bring down the price even if it means finding ways to cut back on spending.'

'We've got to be careful there, Dennis,' Mike replied. 'I would hate to hold back now. There's no way we can survive without opening up the market. Which means we must invest in marketing our implant better. At the moment, 95% of our potential customer base still doesn't even know we exist.'

Cochlear's Background and Financial Profile

In 1979, after ten years of researching the possibility of implanting hearing devices into the cochlea, or inner ear, Professor Graeme Clark, head of the Department of Otolaryngology at the University of Melbourne, Australia, looked for an industry partner to help further his project. The Australian government, seeking to encourage high-tech development, called for tenders from companies able to perform a market study and write a development cost plan for commercialization. Nucleus Limited, a local company specializing in cardiac pacemakers and diagnostic ultrasound imaging equipment, won the tender.

Nucleus quickly put together a project team to engineer the product's evolution. This entailed three tasks: development of the product itself, filing the necessary patents, and developing a strategy. By September 1982, they were ready to perform the first implant which proved to be a huge success. The following year Cochlear Pty Limited was formed in Sydney to handle the new innovation's research and development, manufacturing, and sales. The first US implant took place in 1983 and, in the following year, the subsidiary Cochlear Corporation was established outside Denver, Colorado.

Real momentum began two years later when the US Food and Drug Administration (FDA) gave its approval. Only when this had been granted would US health insurers provide coverage for the product and the surgical procedure necessary to implant it. Unit sales in the US increased from 409 in 1987 to 596 the following year, although they decreased to 553 in 1989.

In that same year, Cochlear produced and began clinical tests on the world's first inner ear implant for children.

Cochlear began to cultivate the European market in 1986, and in 1987 set up an office, Cochlear AG, in Basel, Switzerland. Although European countries did not have regulatory bodies such as the FDA for medical devices, the FDA's opinion was regularly adopted by the European medical authorities. By 1989, when the national health systems in certain countries began to reimburse patients in full or on a quota basis, the company's European position strengthened, with 198 units sold that year. This led to worldwide growth from 1988 to 1989 despite the decrease in US unit sales.

In an attempt to open up the Japanese market, a four-man operation called Nihon Cochlear was established in Tokyo in 1988; the company was the only player in that market. Clinical tests had been in progress since 1986 with 17 implants completed to date. However, FDA was not valid there and a governmental import license, which Cochlear was waiting for, had to be obtained. The Japanese trials cost $1.5 million. In order to get the import license, Cochlear had to provide implants free of charge.

The company reached financial breakeven for the first time in 1986. Beginning in 1987 profits improved steadily, and in 1988 Cochlear became a cash generating unit for the parent company. In 1987, R&D expenditure increased significantly while operating expenses decreased as a percentage of sales. During this time, the sales and promotion expenses remained constant at 80% of general and administration expenses. The worldwide promotion budget was steady at half a million dollars a year.

The cost of goods was maintained at a relatively low level in order to fund research and clinical support. Salesforce expenses were about 25% of the sales expense budget. The policy of allocating 15% of sales revenue to R&D was exceeded in 1989 due to the urgency of bringing out a new speech processor and a fall in anticipated sales volume. As a guideline, the company tried to spend 15% of its R&D budget on applications research for other developments. Any additional R&D expense had to be cleared by Nucleus, which insisted on a 20% return for all investments. *(Refer to **Exhibit 1** for unit sales and financial data.)*

On Deafness and Being Deaf

There were two categories of deaf people, about equal in size: 'postlingually' deaf (deaf as a result of illness, age or accident after having learned to hear) and 'pre-lingually' deaf (deaf at birth). This hearing-impaired market was comprised of the *profoundly deaf* and the *severely deaf*.

Exhibit 1   *Unit sales and financial data*

Unit Sales *(including clinical trials)*	1987	1988	1989
USA	409	596	553
Worldwide	574	798	839
Dollar Sales *(excluding upgrades)*			
Worldwide (in $ millions)	8.7	13.0	14.2
R & D (in $ millions)	1.1	2.3	3.2
General and administration expenses (in $ millions)	5.9	7.1	7.0
Promotion expenses	0.6	0.6	0.6
Cost of goods sold	constant	constant	constant

Severely deaf people could be helped, to a greater or lesser extent, by a hearing aid which amplified sound. Costing approximately 1,000 dollars, the customer bought this device after consulting a doctor or by going directly to a hearing aid retailer. These retailers, who were very commercialized, tended to regard Cochlear as a competitor and, therefore, a threat. Research showed that less than 20% of the people who needed a hearing aid actually bought one and, of those who did, only 50% used it. The rest put it in a bottom drawer either because it 'failed to help', or because it 'looked bad' and 'made their handicap too evident'.

People whose hearing problems were not being satisfactorily improved by hearing aids could have become a market for implants. But, as long as they could hear at all, such consumers were usually not prepared to risk surgery. In addition, they tended to mix frequently with profoundly deaf people and, thus, had an important influence on them as well as in the political arena.

Research was commissioned to assess the extent of the deaf phenomenon. It was estimated that approximately 500,000 *adults* worldwide were profoundly deaf, and that another 500,000 were severely deaf. Applying the rule of thumb for high-tech medical markets, it was assumed that the US accounted for roughly half of this amount.

Ordinary devices such as hearing aids were useless for the profoundly deaf, as the inner ear had become so damaged that surgical intervention was necessary. In ascertaining the real size of the profoundly deaf market, Cochlear took into account psychological and medical factors. Many people who became deaf early in life did not consider themselves 'sick' and, therefore, saw no need for surgery. People with heart problems had no choice; without surgery they could die. But, typically, deaf people would try to live with their deafness.

Many potential users were wary of the concept of an ear implantation, especially of having an electronic device inside the body. One piece of research showed that over 40% of potential users were against the idea of 'having wires in their head', 'were afraid of doctors and hospitals', or 'saw the procedure as far too risky to justify'.

Cochlear therefore estimated that only about 10% of the profoundly deaf, or about 50,000 patients worldwide, were possible implant candidates. Apart from this backlog, the data suggested that another 3,000 new cases occurred each year worldwide. In 1990 there were about 10,000 profoundly deaf *children* in the Western world, with approximately 1,200 new cases per year. As of that time, only 50 children had been recruited to the clinical trials in the US. These trials showed good results, particularly for the postlingually deaf and for children implanted very early in life. While deaf children had to go to special schools, those who had had the Cochlear implant could often attend normal schools, although teachers had to be briefed and trained.

Generally, deaf people tended to be less well off economically than those with normal hearing; Cochlear assumed that about 10% were able to fund the implant themselves. Widely dispersed geographically, there were deaf people in all age categories, although 25% of the profoundly deaf were over 65 years of age.

Decision-Making and Influences for Hearing Implants

The decision-making process for an ear implant could be complex, as there were many actors and influences well beyond just the end user. These included regulatory authorities, families, insurance companies, deaf associations and the media. Typically, patients would visit a doctor about a hearing problem. He would refer them to audiologists or ear-nose-and-throat (ENT) surgeons in hospital implant centers, where they would then be examined to see if they were suitable candidates for an implant operation.

The characteristics of patients and doctors differed in the US, Europe and Japan. American patients tended to be litigation prone and self-directed in their decisions. Although they were concerned about the implant's appearance, the prime consideration in their decison-making was whether and how much it would improve their earning potential. American specialists characteristically offered patients options rather than dictating what had to be done. European deaf patients were more influenced by the surgeon, were not as litigation minded, and the quality of life was more pivotal in their decision-making than were professional prospects. They were somewhat swayed by the look of the device, although less so than Americans. Since the main motive for Japanese patients was to cure the problem, they tended to do as their doctors told them.

To illustrate: an American doctor would typically say, 'You've got three options – do nothing, have it although it's not great cosmetically, or wait till there's something better on the market.' A European doctor's approach would have been more along the line, 'I know it looks awful, but it's good for you.' The typical Japanese patient would never have asked any questions.

Doctors in America tended to adopt new medical technologies before anyone else, and so, despite the stringency of the FDA, the US was always considered the most important market. In fact, it was taken for granted that, in order to succeed worldwide, a firm first had to become established there.

Of the 7,000 American ENT specialists, who were predominantly self-employed or worked for free enterprise hospitals, 200 fitted Cochlear devices in the implant centers of which 100 did so at least once a year. The doctor was strongly influenced by the need to make a profit, while the hospital hoped to at least break even. Audiologists, a profession unique to the United States, would diagnose hearing loss as well as fit hearing aids and speech processors. The doctor and audiologist worked closely with the patient before, during, and after the operation diagnosing, fine-tuning the system, counselling and training.

Private or government insurance covered most Americans, with 60 private health insurers providing coverage for about 75% of those insured; the government welfare programs, Medicare and Medicaid, insured the rest. These reimbursement schemes invariably fell a few thousand dollars short of the average $30,000 necessary for the product and procedure. It was then either left to the patient to find the money, or for the hospital to agree to carry the shortfall. Of the 200 US hospitals which purchased the product, about half funded the shortfall either for reasons of prestige or for furthering medical research.

Because of the changes which were anticipated as a result of 1992, regulatory medical bodies similar to the FDA, but less well funded, were expected to emerge in Europe. After six years of lobbying by Cochlear, the UK's Department of Health and Social Security decided in 1990 to fund 100 units per year for three years. With Sweden beginning in 1983 and Norway in 1986, Scandinavia sponsored about 20 units per year. Workers' disability insurance covered relevant cases in Switzerland. Germany, which accounted for 60 per cent of all European units sold, was the only country whose medical insurance system provided 100 per cent coverage to anyone who needed the implant. In the remaining European countries, implants were funded by research and charity institutions, and were motivated on a case by case basis.

Most European surgeons, typically affiliated with state run universities and hospitals, were not as profit oriented as the American doctors. Although held in high esteem, they were subject to 'hospital politics' and were more conservative and slower to adopt new innovations. The more adventurous, who had sufficient decision-making experience and were influential politically, tended to be in their sixties. Since audiology was not usually a separate specialization in Europe, all diagnosis and fitting was done by the surgeons themselves. Of the 2,500 European ENT specialists, 40 regularly implanted and fitted the device.

In Japan, surgeons also worked primarily at state run hospitals, which were often poorly funded. These hospitals lacked audiologists, and only a small number of surgeons specialized in ear surgery. Ear surgeons were usually university professors with high status but conservative in outlook and slow to adopt innovations. The more aggressive doctors tended to be in their sixties, but those with political influence were the 80-year-olds. As of mid-1990, eight surgeons had been involved in clinical trials in Japan.

Deaf peoples' associations were organized on state, national and worldwide levels and although membership was limited to 10,000–20,000, their influence was widespread. In certain cases, Germany for instance, families were part of the lobby for government support. Some associations or charities, such as the Royal National Institute for the Deaf in the UK, were continuously lobbying on behalf of the deaf to obtain more funding from the national health system.

Encouragement from families and friends of potential patients to seek help and undergo surgery depended largely on whether those families and friends were also hearing impaired and part of the strong 'non-hearing' communities which were growing worldwide.

The 'deaf pride' movement had become a powerful force in the '80s with various factions. Extremists went so far as to suggest that Cochlear was experimenting with deaf people's brains. Mainstream members emphasized that deaf people constituted an ethnic community with their own languages and culture. Many were opposed to any pressure or opportunity for individuals to hear. They claimed it was better to have perfect communication with sign language than imperfect communication with an implant which they said relegated them to the status of second-class citizens in the 'speaking' world. There were as many sign languages as languages and, because of increased mobility and the rapid internationalization of deaf associations, a move was on to develop a global version.

During the '80s, public awareness about deaf pride had grown. The film,

Children of a Lesser God had raised public consciousness on an emotional level because it dealt with the philosophic issue as to whether profoundly deaf people should *want* to change. At that time, there was also widespread media coverage of the Washington-based Gallaudet University exclusively for the deaf where students could follow a full university program in sign language. Public interest in this institution was enhanced when students protested over the nomination of a 'non-deaf' president, forcing him to resign.

The Cochlear Hearing Implant System

The Cochlear implant was named after the *cochlea*, a part of the inner ear about the size of a pea and shaped like a snail shell. *Cochlea*, in fact, is the Greek term for 'snail shell' which is what the product implant resembled. *(Refer to Exhibit 2 for a illustration of its technical characteristics.)*

People could become profoundly deaf either at birth or later in life due to injury or an illness such as bacterial meningitis or mumps. The inner ear has a multitude of sensory cells, or hair cells, each one connected to the hearing nerve which transmits sound in electrical messages to the brain. Profoundly deaf people lack or lose such sensory cells.

Hearing aids amplified sound. This instrument was only adequate for the 'hard of hearing' or, in some cases, the severely deaf. The Cochlear 'Bionic Ear' was for the profoundly deaf who could not hear at all. Micro-electronic engineering had been adapted to the latest research on hearing physiology to produce a high-tech system which consisted of five parts, all of which were necessary to enable the deaf person to hear:

- The *directional microphone* (fastened onto the ear) picked up sounds, converted them into electrical energy impulses which were sent to the speech processor;

- The *speech processor* (resembling a walkman and worn externally on a belt, shoulder pouch, or in a pocket) was a computer that selected the most important electrical impulses needed for hearing noises and words, coded them and sent them to the transmittor;

- The *transmitter* (placed behind the ear) relayed the coded noises and words through the skin to the receiver/stimulator in the implant;

- The *implant* itself (surgically placed in the bone behind the ear) consisted of a *receiver and electrodes*. The receiver, comprised of an integrated circuit with more than 1,000 transistors (similar to those

Exhibit 2 *Technical characteristics*

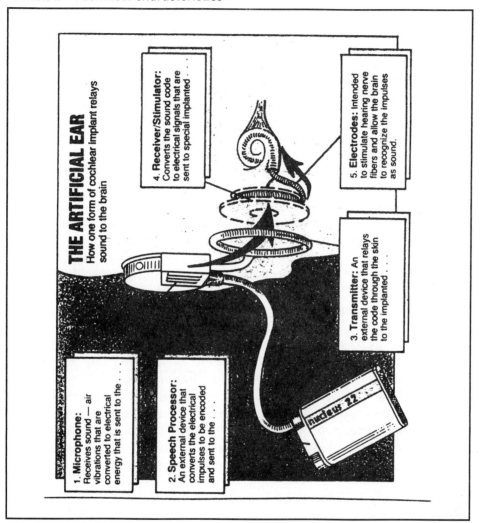

THE ARTIFICIAL EAR
How one form of cochlear implant relays sound to the brain

1. **Microphone:** Receives sound — air vibrations that are converted to electrical energy that is sent to the . . . .

2. **Speech Processor:** An external device that converts the electrical impulses to be encoded and sent to the . . . .

3. **Transmitter:** An external device that relays the code through the skin to the implanted . . . .

4. **Receiver/Stimulator:** Converts the sound code to electrical signals that are sent to special implanted . . . .

5. **Electrodes:** Intended to stimulate hearing nerve fibers and allow the brain to recognize the impulses as sound.

in a pacemaker), converted the codes into electrical signals and sent them to the electrodes. The electrodes, which substituted for the damaged sensory 'hair cells', electrically stimulated the hearing nerve fibres, and thus allowed individuals to hear a variety of high and low sound pitches which were subsequently transmitted to the brain to be deciphered.

Cochlear was the only company to have a 22-channel electrode. Unlike its earlier 1-channel unit, the multichannel device enabled more sounds to be heard and could be fine-tuned for a particular pitch and loudness by the surgeon, thereby catering to the individual hearing needs of each patient. But, no matter how much customizing was done, people who had become deaf could not hear in the same way as before the impairment. They would hear new sounds which had to be correlated with ones they had heard in pre-deaf years. This process was like learning to speak a foreign language, and it took, on average, three months of training and practice. For children, this process was even longer. It could take years for those who were born deaf to be able to hear and speak.

Despite Cochlear's technological superiority, it remained impossible to predict before a surgical operation how each individual patient would respond. Research showed that about 50% of patients who had the operation were eventually able to understand speech without lipreading, and could even use the telephone. The remaining 50% benefited as well, but to significantly varying degrees – from the worst cases, where only noises and warning signals were audible, to those who could follow speech only by lip reading. The result depended on each individual – the state of the ear as well as the brain's learning capacity – neither of which could be assessed at the outset.

All R&D in Australia was done by 25 people. R&D was grouped into three areas: implant technology, electronic engineering and mechanical design. Aware that many patients would be hesitant to undergo successive surgery because of improvements in technology, Cochlear's R&D team deliberately designed its first implant version in 1982 with much more capacity than the speech processor could then handle. The idea was to enable the patient's hearing ability to be improved at some future date, without having to undergo further surgery, by updating and modifying the speech processor.

Since then, most R&D efforts had gone into improving the speech processor, with rewarding results. In the first six months of 1990, the firm sold $4 million worth of upgrades and modifications to its existing customer base. Every new model or improvement of an existing model had to go through the FDA approval procedure. New product developments could not be heavily publicized because users would put off any buying decision when they anticipated a model change, which caused serious inventory problems.

All manufacturing was done in Sydney. Using a manual process with extensive computer testing, the 50 highly skilled and specially trained plant workers produced approximately 1,400 systems annually, but there was capacity for twice that amount. The components used were very specialized and tended to come from single-goods suppliers worldwide. A constant stock was kept to eliminate delays in the event of problems in the suppliers' market and in order to get bulk prices.

There were two main areas in Cochlear's factory: the section where the implant was made under 'clean room' procedures, and the non-environmentally controlled area where the speech processor 'externals' were made. For the implant, subassembled parts were first manufactured and then put together in small batches of 20–30 units. The entire cycle, which required using microscopes, would take at least three months. Discrete electrical components and custom integrated circuits were soldered onto circuit boards. The external parts of the system were made using standard assembly techniques similar to those used by any small volume, high-tech electronics equipment manufacturer. Staff turnover in the external area was very low whereas in the implant section it was high.

Improving reliability of the units and the performance of the system were key priorities. It required ongoing upgrading of the electrode manufacturing methods. Although the staff generated many ideas, 99% of them could not be used because of the difficulties of working with an item as small as .6mm in diameter.

Over the years, Cochlear looked at three other applications for its technology: implantable hearing aids, tinnitus, and functional electrical stimulation (FES). In 1986 it seemed that hearing aids had considerable synergy with its product. However, after having spent $1 million up to 1989, the company decided that the technology, marketing, manufacturing and profit margin formula were too different to warrant further investment. In 1989, Cochlear started work on the treatment of tinnitus ('ringing in the ears' syndrome), a condition experienced by 1 in 7 people. By mid-1990, half a million dollars had been spent. A large investment would have been necessary to perfect an FES device, an implant which electronically stimulated the nerves of paraplegics. Cochlear carried out some R&D, but decided, after losing a tender to supply the US department of Veterans Affairs, to give the FES only low level research support.

Overview of Cochlear's Competitive Position

The American multinational 3M had entered the market at approximately the same time as Cochlear, with a lower technology product that the company believed would yield a similar hearing benefit. As 3M's price was one-third lower than Cochlear's, 3M initially dominated the market. Once Cochlear entered, however, the US firm gradually lost market share and faded from the scene late in 1989.

Although there were five major players in the worldwide market, Cochlear was the only one with FDA approval. The others – Hochmair, Hortmann, Symbion, and Minimed – were all developing similar devices and intended to get the required approval. Because some European doctors protested that Cochlear was making too much money, one or two university medical schools in Europe, including the University College of London, developed their own low budget version of the implant. Although such hearing systems, distributed only through the universities' clinics, were only one-tenth the price of Cochlear's device, they were not regarded as sufficiently reliable to pose a serious competitive problem.

While Cochlear was confident, given its 3,500 satisfied patients worldwide and the FDA stamp, that it had a clear competitive advantage, the company constantly monitored the competitive strength of the main manufacturers, using four criteria: *1) organization, size and professionalism; 2) technology; 3) clinical benefit and effectiveness;* and *4) safety*.

Neither the Hochmairs, an Austrian team, nor Hortmann of Germany were considered serious opponents by Cochlear, given their lag in the important categories of clinical benefit, effectiveness and safety. However, the two American firms, Symbion and Minimed, were both perceived as potential threats to future sales.

Symbion, a firm associated with the University of Utah, was in the clinical trial stage. It had managed to produce a unit which, while using a much lower level of implant technology, nonetheless achieved the same hearing performance, and at the same price, as Cochlear's device. Symbion's accomplishment was due to putting considerably more effort into the speech processor than into the implant. A plug which connected the microphone headset to the implant by penetrating the skin created both an aesthetic and a safety disadvantage as the passageway could permit infection to enter the inner ear and the brain. It was considered a flexible product, however, because any kind of stimulation could be used whereas the Cochlear device only allowed radio wave transmission.

Affiliated with the well-known University of California at San Francisco medical school, Minimed began its research in 1966. Although its device had only 16 channels, Minimed's performance could potentially be as good as Cochlear's due to its capacity to better represent certain non-speech sounds. Because of problems with its micro-chip technology, the company had not yet been able to begin clinical trials, needed to receive FDA approval and medical coverage. There were rumours that the problem would soon be solved and by 1991 Minimed would be making clinical trials.

The company annually analyzed market share. With doctors eager for more players to enter the field, Cochlear had, in making its projections for

1990 and 1991, factored in the entry of Minimed and a growth in market share for Symbion. *(Refer to **Exhibit 3** for market shares from 1982–1989 and projections for 1990.)*

Cochlear's Marketing Strategy

Cochlear treated the ear implant market as a single one. The logic was that the medical profession and deaf associations were linked internationally through medical conferences and medical journals.

The product was identical worldwide. All units and promotional material clearly identified the Cochlear brand name and logo, and the 22-channel feature was used extensively to differentiate the product as the one with maximum clinical benefits.

Cochlear decided early on that it could not devote equal time and resources to both aesthethics and performance. Convinced that the latter would be the more important criterion for the market, the company decided to position itself as the most technologically sophisticated and clinically superior.

In early 1990, market research confirmed what top management had suspected: performance was more important than either price or appearance. This survey, which was intended to gain a better understanding of the needs and wants of the implant market, was conducted among 14 Cochlear implant patients, 11 audiologists, a surgeon and the director of an implant center in one of the US hospitals which fitted Cochlear devices. The results revealed that implant patients considered performance to be the most

Exhibit 3 *Market share and 1990 projections*

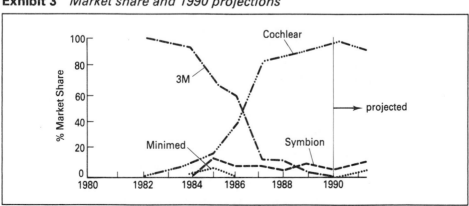

important factor. In fact, on a scale of 1–10, performance was ranked 8 out of 10, price 5, and appearance 3.

These people were extremely happy to be able to hear and, if given a choice, would have opted for an implant system that allowed them to hear speech, music, and environmental sounds over one where the external units were either cordless or worn behind the ear, but offered lower performance. Nevertheless, the patients did acknowledge that a segment of the deaf market would consider a Cochlear implant if a behind-the-ear system became available, and would probably accept a lower performance level to get a device so small and unobtrusive.

Cochlear had given some thought to the cosmetic appeal of its external units, particularly the speech processor. Initially, it had been made from plastic pipe, then from stainless steel and, in September 1989, a more contemporary design was developed using molded plastic.

For three months after surgery, patients had to return to the hospital or the doctor for training; check-ups were then repeated annually. The non-usage rate of all implant patients worldwide was 1%. For the very few patients who experienced a problem with their unit, there were doctors trained by Cochlear to 'troubleshoot'. If a unit proved faulty, it was sent back to the regional office for repair. While the implant was guaranteed for five years, it was expected to last a lifetime. The speech processor had an average breakdown time of three years, and each system had a three-year warranty. Hospitals had to maintain adequate supplies of spare units at all times to avoid any risk that the patient could be incapacitated due to a faulty product.

A premium price strategy was deliberately used and strictly maintained in order to highlight the Cochlear system's unique technology. The average $30,000 cost to patients included the Cochlear system as well as all hospital and surgical expenses. On average, the Cochlear device was priced at $17,000 for both adults and children, although it was slightly more in Europe and even higher in Japan. The figure was three times the price of the 3M model when it had been on the market. Symbion's price was equal to Cochlear's, and it was rumoured that Minimed would enter clinical trials at the same price level. Hochmair and Hortmann were priced in the middle range.

Cochlear distributed its products directly in three regions – Denver, Basel and Tokyo – each one headed by its own CEO reporting to the Sydney head office. The salespeople, clinically trained audiologists and engineers, called on doctors and hospitals. They were supported by a team of clinical experts who advised, counseled and handled any problems that arose, using clinical support centers in each region. These support centers would also work with patients who wanted an implant but were unsure how to handle the finances or apply for insurance. Every office also maintained a technical service team, reimbursement specialists, and 2–3 marketing people to organize conferences, handle PR and prepare brochures.

In the US, some private audiologists who had fitted and tested hearing devices would leave their own practices and, on a part commission basis to help cope with the workload, sell Cochlear implants. Some extra audiologists in hospitals were funded by Cochlear. In Europe, where the ENT surgeon was also the audiologist, the Basel-based European headquarters oversaw all sales except for the UK, Scandinavia and Israel, which were handled in London. Any direct selling by doctors would have been regarded as unethical in Europe. In Germany, Cochlear managed to persuade one of the largest hearing aid retailers to stock its cables and spare batteries.

Upgraded units became an important part of Cochlear's marketing activities. The $4 million in sales in 1990 was achieved by reaching users through doctors and offering a special reduction in price (from $6,000 to $4,000) if a decision were made by a particular date. The upgrade was introduced and launched at a promotional event hosted on a river boat. This event was followed by direct mail and by papers presented at conferences by doctors who had experienced improved performance during clinical trials. Most patients paid for their own new units in the US because the insurance companies refused to pay. In Europe, they were funded by the national health systems.

Publicity was aimed at patients and doctors. Initially, the novelty of the implant innovation made it relatively easy to get media attention and, on the whole, newspapers, radio, magazines and TV provided reasonable coverage, particularly of successful cases. Although no formal market research had been done, the Cochlear top team estimated that company awareness worldwide was 70–80% amongst ENT surgeons, and around 5% amongst potential users.

The company encouraged medical and scientific journal articles about its product and occasionally paid doctors' travel expenses when they delivered papers at conferences. The system was exhibited at major worldwide medical conferences, while local community forums and meetings with education departments and school authorities were routinely organized. Because it could be considered unethical to directly approach such supporting charities as the Rotary Club, Cochlear only provided information when needed.

Promotional material was distributed to doctors, hospitals, audiologists, and hearing aid retailers to enable them to respond to queries. Post-operative instructional booklets were provided for patients, and a newsletter was sent out from each sales office to doctors, to the existing patient base as well as to local family self-help events. Lectures were given to any deaf association on request, and papers were presented at conferences on deafness whenever possible. Inevitably, though, these activities engendered a certain amount of antagonism, such as walk-outs or other forms of protest from 'deaf pride' members in the audience.

———————

Mike Hirshorn continued talking. 'The FDA is on the verge of giving us the go ahead for children. That's a market worth another 10,000 units provided we do the job right. Parents will do anything to help their children, so I expect that market to be much easier and quicker to penetrate than it was for adults.'

He stood up and walked to the window watching the last rays of sunshine disappearing over the horizon. 'For a start, we could increase our salesforce. That way, we could break into new territories and increase the call rates with existing doctors.'

'What about the additional costs?' Brigette enquired.

'It's not a big deal,' Mike answered. 'Even if we doubled our salesforce worldwide, we would only have to sell 15% more units. The Sydney factory can easily handle the extra volumes.'

'We could, of course, use the capacity to make a cheaper second model instead,' Dennis Wheeler suddenly suggested. 'Maybe then we could get into some new countries like Turkey, Greece, the Middle East and Southeast Asia. Come to think of it, that could also push up our numbers in the States and maybe even in Europe.'

'That would ruin our image,' Brigette responded. 'If we want to keep our position, we have to stick to making the highest performance quality even if it means raising our price. Isn't there a section of the US market that could take a price hike, Dennis?'

'Yeah, maybe 10%, max 20% but of the privately insured market,' Dennis replied hesitantly. 'Don't forget, though, that this may be exactly what Symbion and Minimed are waiting for – to grab market share.'

Mike listened carefully. He knew that he would soon have to recommend to his board ways to maintain profitability despite sagging sales and more threatening competition. He agreed that Cochlear's future hope was its hearing technology. But, somehow the company had to get that technology used and appreciated . . .

SECTION 7

Promoting and Advertising Industrial Products

CASES

Leykam Mürztaler
Lussman-Shizuka Corp.

Leykam Mürztaler

This case was written by Professor H. Michael Hayes as a basis for class discussion rather than to illustrate either effective or ineffective handling of an administrative situation.

In February 1989, Dr. Gertrude Eder, Marketing Manager for Leykam Mürztaler AG, was reviewing a problem that had occupied her thoughts a great deal during the past few months. Although Leykam Mürztaler, like the paper industry in general, had been doing well in recent years, it was her opinion that it was time to think about ways to strengthen the company's ability to prosper as industry growth inevitably began slowing down. In particular, she was considering what recommendations to offer the Executive Board regarding the firm's branding strategy.

Leykam Mürztaler AG

The past few years had been good for the Leykam Mürztaler Group. Paralleling the industry's increased sales, the firm's total sales had risen from ASch4,842 million[1] in 1983 to ASch7,100 million in 1988, an increase of 47%. For Leykam Mürztaler AG, the principal operating component of the Group, 1988 revenues had reached ASch 6,300 million, an increase over 1986 of 41%, enhanced by the successful start-up of a new production line and by above average growth in demand for high-grade coated woodfree printing papers, the firm's main sales segment.

Leykam Mürztaler AG, together with its predecessor companies, had been a producer of paper for over 400 years. Headquartered in Gratkorn, Austria, the firm produced coated woodfree printing paper and newsprint, with integrated pulp production. Principal mills and offices were located at Gratkorn and Bruck, Austria. Export sales offices for coated woodfree paper were headquartered in Vienna.

In 1988, woodfree papers represented approximately 80% of sales, newsprint 13% and pulp 7%. Twenty-two percent of revenues came from Austria, 56% from Western Europe and 22% from exports to the rest of the world (including Eastern Europe). The highest share of exports was for coated woodfree papers at approximately 90%.

(Production volumes in 1987 and 1988 are shown in Exhibit 1.) The large increase in production of printing and writing paper in 1988 (to 340,900 tonnes) reflected successful selling of the output of the new coated woodfree paper machine at Gratkorn, with a capacity of 138,000 tonnes per year. The decline in pulp production reflected a change in product mix. External sales of pulp were declining as the company's pulp production was further integrated into the company's own paper production.

With the addition of the new production line, the company had become the European market leader in coated woodfree papers, with a market share of 8–10%. In December 1987 the Supervisory Board approved a project to establish a new production line at Bruck to produce mechanical coated printing papers (LWC) for magazines, catalogues and printed advertising materials. Planned capacity was 135,000 tonnes, to be put into operation at the end of 1989.

Exhibit 1   *Highlights of the development of the Leykam Mürztaler Group (Source: annual report)*

	1987	1988	%
Production (in tons)			
Printing and writing papers	272,900	340,900	+24.9
Newsprint (Bruck)	98,200	99,200	+ 1.0
Paper total	371,100	440,100	+18.6
Chemical pulp	209,500	204,500	− 2.4
Mechanical pulp	30,900	32,100	+ 3.9
Deink pulp	58,900	62,700	+ 6.4
Total sales (gross, in ASch mn)			
Leykam Mürztaler AG	5,234	6,300	+20.4
Export share	4,056	5,100	+25.7
Exports in %	78	81	−
Leykam Mürztaler Group	5,906	7,100	+20.2
Capital expenditure and Prepayments for fixed assets			
(in ASch mn)	1,418	1,500	+ 5.8
Cash flow (in ASch mn)	1,020	1,500	+47.1
Employees (excluding apprentices)			
as of 31 December	2,825	2,865	+ 1.4

Despite the increased level of investment, financial results were very good. In 1987, the last year for which complete financial details were available, profit was down slightly from the previous year *(see Exhibit 2)*, reflecting the greatly increased depreciation charges associated with the new paper machine and the decision to use the reducing-balance method of depreciation for it and some other equipment. Cash flow, however, was close to an all-time record, results were 'clearly better than originally forecast', and operating profits were near the top of the European woodfree paper producers, on a percent of sales basis. Preliminary indications were that financial results for 1988 would be still better.

The company marketed its coated products under its MAGNO series brand (e.g., MAGNOMATT, MAGNOPRINT, MAGNOMATT K) principally through wholly owned merchants in Austria and other merchants throughout Western Europe. In addition, it sold to other kinds of merchants in Austria as well as to some printers and publishers directly. Paper merchants were contacted by sales representatives in Vienna and Gratkorn, sales subsidiaries in Germany, Italy and France, and sales agents in other European countries. Some of its products were sold on a private brand basis to certain large merchants.

Although Leykam Mürztaler served paper markets on a worldwide basis, and planned to enter the LWC market, this case focuses on coated woodfree papers for printing applications in Western Europe.

Exhibit 2   *Financial results (*Source: *annual report)*

	1983	1984*	1985**	1986	1987
Total sales (gross, in AS m)	4,842	5,367	5,420	5,187	5,906
Export sales (AS m)	2,973	3,413	3,537	3,331	4,062
Export share of Leykam Mürztaler AG (%)	69	72	74	74	78
Capital investment (AS m)	313	253	444	2,461	1,518
Total depreciation (AS m)	374	344	337	476	1,064
thereof: reducing-balance depreciation (AS m)	–	–	–	125	674
Cash flow (AS m)	373	1,025	959	871	1,020
Profit for the year (AS m)	1	422	81	101	67
Personnel expenditure (AS m)	1,096	993	1,046	1,076	1,231
Number of employees (excluding apprentices) as of 31 December	2,918	2,424	2,364	2,578	2,825
Dividend and bonus (AS m)	–	54	81	101	67
(%)	–	4+4	4+8	4+8	8

  * excluding Niklasdorf Mill
** excluding Frohnierten Mill from 1 April 1985

The Pulp and Paper Industry in Western Europe[2]

Despite its maturity, the pulp and paper industry was undergoing major change. Characterized by high breakeven volumes, small fluctuations in demand could significantly impact profits, and there was some evidence that capacity was outgrowing demand. Despite the sophistication of paper-making technology, product differentiation was increasingly difficult to achieve. Some paper makers were integrating backwards to control the cost or assure the supply of pulp. Others were integrating forward, buying paper merchants in order to have better control of marketing. Still others were integrating horizontally to have a more complete product line.

Other changes were affecting the industry as well. Customers were being merged, acquired or reorganized, thus changing established purchasing patterns. Changes in advertising were impacting traditional usage patterns. Paper merchants were merging to gain economies of scale. Some were emphasizing private brands to reduce their dependence on paper makers. Markets were fragmenting as new, small businesses were forming at a record rate. Consumption patterns were changing. In Europe, consumption ranged from 233 kg per capita in Sweden to 60 in Portugal, but growth rates ranged from a high of 29.4 per cent in Greece to a low of 2.4 per cent in Denmark. There was some uncertainty about the implications of Europe's move toward a true common market in 1992, although trade barriers were not a significant factor in the industry.

Printing and Writing Paper

In the pulp and paper industry, the major and high growth segment was printing and writing papers. Both coated and uncoated papers were produced from mechanically or chemically processed pulp to form four broad categories: coated woodfree, mechanical coated[3], uncoated woodfree and mechanical uncoated. To be defined as coated, a paper had to have a surface coating of at least 5 grams per square meter (gsm).

Coated woodfree papers represented the highest quality category, in terms of printability, gloss, feel, ability to reproduce color and many other characteristics. Grades of coated woodfree papers were not precisely specified, but the industry had established further categories such as cast coated, art paper, standard and low coated. *(See **Exhibit 3** for categories and prices.)* The standard grade represented the bulk of sales. Within this category, however, there were many gradations – the amount of whiteness, brightness, stiffness and other characteristics. Leykam Mürztaler competed

Exhibit 3   *Prices per tonne (in $) of woodfree printing and writing papers in Western Europe (2nd quarter 1987 delivered)* (Source: *EKONO strategic study, September 1988)*

Grade	West Germany	UK	France	Netherlands
Cast coated, sheets	2,734	2,324	2,588	2,480
Art paper, sheets	1,897	1,660	1,837	1,736
Standard, sheets	1,283	1,212	1,235	1,166
Standard, reels	1,199	1,145	1,169	1,091
Low coated, sheets	1,172	1,130	1,136	1,066

Note: Cast coated paper was estimated to represent 5% of the coated woodfree market, Art paper 7–8%, Standard coated 70% and Low coated less than 20%. Within the standard coated category, actual transaction prices could vary as much as 25% as a function of quality and as much as 10% due to competitive or other factors.

principally at the high end of the standard grade, but was planning to enter the art paper segment also.

Coated woodfree was the smallest printing and writing paper segment (17.8 per cent of total consumption), but it was also the most dynamic, with an average growth rate of 8.4 per cent from 1980 to 1987. Expectations were that 1988 consumption would exceed three million tonnes.

Markets for Printing and Writing Paper

Principal markets for printing and writing paper were magazines (33 per cent), direct mail (17 per cent), brochures and general print advertising (15 per cent), copy paper (11%), other office paper (9%) and books (5%). For coated woodfree papers, it was estimated that advertising, direct and indirect, accounted for 85–90% of consumption[4].

On a country by country basis, there was significant variation in the mix of advertising expenditures, however. In the UK, for instance, the bulk of advertising expenditures went to newspapers and TV, whereas in Germany advertising expenditures were split somewhat evenly among newspapers, magazines, catalogues and direct mail[5]. Major uses for coated woodfree papers were direct mail, brochures, annual reports, etc. The dynamic growth of coated woodfree papers in recent years was largely fuelled by the rapid increases in 'non-classical' advertising. Changes in this mix could significantly affect country consumption patterns for coated woodfree papers.

Despite cost pressures and shifts in individual markets and end uses, coated woodfree papers were benefitting from demand for more and better four-color printing as advertisers sought ways to improve the impact of their messages.

The Printing Industry

The vast majority of orders for coated woodfree paper were placed by printers, either on the merchant or directly on the mill. In some instances, however, for very large orders, the order would be placed by either the printer or the publisher, depending on which seemed to have the strongest negotiating position with the supplier.

Selection of paper grade and manufacturer was a complex process that varied significantly according to end use, size of order, and sophistication of both the printer and the specifier or user. Almost without exception, the printer had the final say in the selection of paper make and could significantly influence the grade of paper as well. The specifier (ad agency) or user (advertiser, publisher, mail order house, etc.) influenced paper selection, particularly with respect to grade, and could also influence selection of make, subject to final agreement by the printer.

For the printer, key paper characteristics were printability and runability. Surface characteristics, whiteness and brightness were also important. Price was always important, especially when deciding between two suppliers with similar offerings or where paper costs represented a significant portion of the total cost of the printed product. Complaint handling, emergency assistance, speed and reliability of delivery were key service components. Sales representative knowledge was also important. Within limits, relative importance of decision criteria varied from one country to another. In Italy and the UK, for instance, price and quality tended to be equally important, whereas quality and service factors tended to predominate importance rankings in Switzerland. There was some favoritism given producers for patriotic reasons, but seldom at the expense of quality or price.

The user or specifier considered many of the same characteristics as the printer. Printability and delivery were usually at the top of the list, but the major concern was the paper's suitability for the particular advertising message, within the constraints of the overall advertising budget.

Despite the apparent similarity of products offered by different mills, there was substantial variation in runability, which could only be determined by actual trial. According to one printer:

> The final test is how well the paper prints on our presses. This is a matter of

'fit' between paper, ink and press characteristics. We find there are variations between papers that meet the same specifications, which can only be determined by actual trial. This is not cheap as a trial involves printing 3,000 sheets. Because the paper characteristics cannot be completely specified, we like the idea of a mill brand. One time we tested two merchant brands that we thought were different. Then we found out that the paper came from the same mill, so we really wasted our time on the second test.

The merchant's sales representative is important, but we don't need him to call all that frequently. We like to talk to him about trends or problems we're having, but when we need something quickly, we call the merchant.

Once we have selected a paper, it is critically important that its quality be consistent. Most suppliers are pretty good. Except for obvious flaws, however, we find they tend to want to blame problems on the ink or the press.

Over the past several years, the number of printers remained relatively constant, at about 15–20,000, with decreases from mergers and acquisitions offset by a growth in instant print outlets. In the last 10 years, the number of commercial print customers doubled to over 500,000, half of whom used instant print outlets.

As the number of small businesses and the use of desktop publishing continued to grow, it was suggested that within ten years traditional printers would perhaps only handle longer-run full color work. Monochrome and spot color work would be produced in customers' offices, with the paper buying decision being made by people with little knowledge about paper or printing.[6] In-plant printing, however, was not expected to have a significant impact on the coated woodfree market.

Paper Merchants

Printers and publishers were reached in two principal ways: direct sales from the mill and sales from the mill through merchants, either independent or mill-owned. Direct sales were more common for high volume products sold in reels, such as newsprint and LWC magazine paper. The pattern of distribution was influenced by characteristics of the transaction *(see **Exhibit 4**)* and the pattern varied significantly from one country to another *(see **Exhibit 5**)*. For coated woodfree papers it was estimated that 70–80 per cent of sales went through merchants.

As with all wholesalers, stocking to provide quick delivery in small quantities was a principal merchant function. Fragmentation of the fastest growing market segments (business and small printers) had decreased the average order size and increased demand for a wide choice of paper grades, making it more difficult for mills to directly access these customers.

Exhibit 4 *Transaction characteristics: a comparison of the roles of manufacturers and merchants* (Source: The European Printing and Writing Paper Industry, *1987*)

Characteristics	Manufacturer	Merchant
Order size (kg)	>1,500	200–500
Items carried	Small	2,500–5,000
Fixed costs	High	Low
Stock level (kg)	>2,000/item	500–1,750
Delivery	Often slow	24 hours
Service	None	Possible
Cash flow	Low	Low

Exhibit 5 *Market shares per distribution channel (%)* (Source: The European Printing and Writing Paper Industry, *1987*)

| Form of Distribution: | Country | | | |
	UK	France	Germany	Italy
Paper mills	48	50	59	80
Mill-owned merchants	52	50	–	20
Independent merchants	52	–	41	20

In warehousing, larger merchants had introduced expensive computer-controlled logistical systems, which reduced delivery times and the cost of preparing orders for delivery. Predictions were made that electronic interchange of information between merchants and their suppliers and larger customers would be the norm within the next few years. Merchants in the UK were spearheading an initiative to achieve industry standards for bar codes throughout Europe.

Changes in end user profiles and new customer needs had forced merchants to expand the scope of their activities and customer support functions. As a result, the merchants' role broadened to include a number of additional services, including technical advice on paper choice and broader printing problems.

Private branding, supported by advertising, had long been used by some merchants to differentiate their products and service. Some large merchants had also invested in testing apparatus, similar to that found in mills, to check conformance to specifications and to support their desire to become principals, with full responsibility for product performance.

Merchant margins varied with location, type of sale and nature of the transaction. For sales from stock, margins ranged from a low of 12 per cent in Italy and 15 per cent in Germany to 25 per cent in France and Switzerland. Margins reduced to about 5 per cent, or less, when a merchant acted as the intermediary solely for invoicing purposes[7]. *(A typical income statement for a paper merchant is shown in **Exhibit 6**.)*

Patterns of merchant ownership also varied from one country to another *(see **Exhibit 7**)*. In the UK, for example, Wiggins Teape, a paper producer established in 1780, became a merchant in 1960 when existing merchants resisted introducing carbonless copy paper in the market. The company opened a network of offices to stimulate demand and provide technical support for the product. Between 1969 and 1984, the company acquired control of several major merchants operating in the UK, France, Belgium, Italy and Finland. In 1984, sales of $480 million made Wiggins Teape the largest merchant in Europe.

On the other hand, Paper Union, one of the two largest merchants in Germany (turnover of $142 million and market share of 12 per cent in 1984), was an independent merchant. It was formed in the early 1960s, from three smaller merchants, in an attempt to reach the critical size of 100,000 tonnes

Exhibit 6 *Typical income statement: paper merchant (*Source: The European Printing and Writing Paper Industry, *1987)*

	(%)
Sales	100
Cost of goods sold	75
Contribution	25
Other costs	23
Net profit	2
Depreciation	.5
Cash flow	2.5

Exhibit 7 *Paper merchants: ownership and concentration per country* (Source: Paper Merchanting, the Viewpoint of Independent Merchants*)*

Country	merchants totaling 80% of country sales	Ownership
Sweden	2	mill-owned
Denmark	3	mostly mill-owned
Netherlands	5	mill-owned
Belgium	5	mill-owned
Switzerland	5	mostly mill-owned
Austria	2 (70%)	mill-owned
France	6	mill-owned
West Germany	7	all independent
UK	few big and	partly mill-owned
	many small ones	mostly independent

per year. Due to low margins in Germany, Paper Union had emphasized reducing operating costs and consistently fast delivery. Plans were being made, however, to introduce further services and advertising in an attempt to add value and increase customer awareness.

The move toward company-owned merchants was not without controversy. According to one independent merchant:

> We believe that independent merchants are very much in the best interest of paper mills. We're aware, of course, that many mills are integrating forward, buying merchants in order to maintain access to distribution. It is our view, however, that this will cause a number of problems. No one mill can supply all the products that a merchant must offer. Hence, even mill-owned merchants must maintain relations with a number of other mills, who will always want to supply their full range of products to the merchant, including those which compete with the parent mill. This will create serious tensions and frequently will put the merchant in the position of having to choose between corporate loyalty and offering the best package to the customer. The parent can, of course, impose restrictions on the merchant with respect to selling competing products, but the sales force would have serious problems with this.

> Our strong preference is for exclusive representation of a mill. This is particularly important where there are strong influencers, such as advertisers, to whom it is important for us to address considerable promotional effort. Also when we are an exclusive merchant, we provide the mill with extensive information on our sales, which allows the mill to do market analysis that both we and the mill find very valuable. We certainly would not provide this kind of information if the mill had intensive distribution. In a country like Switzerland, we can give the mill complete geographic and account coverage, so it's not clear to us why the mill needs more than one merchant. In our view, intensive distribution creates a situation where there is much more emphasis on price. While this first affects the merchant, it inevitably affects the mill as well.

> If we do sell for a mill that has intensive distribution, we prefer to sell it under our brand, although we identify the mill, in small print. This is somewhat an historical artifact, going back to the days when mills did not attempt to brand their products, but if we're going to compete for business with another merchant, selling for the same mill, we feel having our name on the product helps us differentiate ourselves from the competitor.

> At the same time, we should point out that we don't sell competing brands. There are about five quality grades within standard coated woodfree, and we handle two to three brands.

One industry expert predicted significant changes in distribution patterns[8].

> Looking to the future, it is predicted that there will be an increase in the number of paper grade classifications, moving from 4 just a few years ago to

20 or more. There will be an increasing number of different types of middlemen and distributors, and merchants will move into grades traditionally regarded as mill direct products (e.g., newsprint and mechanical grades) to bring these grades to the smaller customers.

Just as we have seen a technological revolution hit the traditional printing industry, we must now see a marketing revolution hit the traditional paper industry. Selection of the correct channel of distribution and the development of an active working relationship with that channel will be vital.

Competition in Coated Woodfree Papers

In varying degrees, Leykam Mürztaler encountered at least 10 major European firms in the markets it served in Europe. Some, like KNP and Zanders, competed principally in coated woodfree papers. Others, like Stora and Feldmühle, produced a wide range of products, from coated woodfree papers to tissue to newsprint.

There was considerable variation in competitive emphasis among producers. Zanders, for instance, generally regarded as the highest quality producer, mostly produced cast coated and premium art paper, competed only at the top end of the standard coated range and was relatively unusual in its extensive use of advertising. Hannover Papier was particularly strong in service, offering fast delivery. PWA Hallein, which had tended to emphasize price over quality, had recently improved its quality but was keeping prices low in an apparent effort to gain market share. Arjomari, the biggest French producer, owned the largest merchant chain in France and had recently purchased merchants in the UK and Southern Europe. It had recently entered the premium art paper segment, generally regarded as difficult to produce for. Burgo, a large Italian conglomerate, concentrated principally on the Italian market. *(See **Exhibit 8** for a report on the image of selected suppliers.)*

Rapid growth in the coated woodfree market had stimulated capacity additions by existing producers and was also stimulating conversion of facilities from uncoated to coated. Nordland of Germany, for instance, switched 100,000 tonnes of capacity from uncoated to coated by adding a coater in October 1988. Excellent in service, there was, however, some question about its ability to produce high quality.

Branding was a relatively new aspect of the industry. All the major producers had established brand names for major products or grades. To date, however, only Zanders had actively promoted its brand to the trade or to advertisers.

Exhibit 8   *Major mill reputation (Source: EKONO strategic study, September 1988)*

Company	Comments on Reputation
Zanders (Germany)	– Mercedes Benz in coated woodfrees – Excellent service – Strong promotion – Marketing activities have also been directed to advertising agencies, who can influence on choice of brand
Leykam Mürztaler	– Reliable supplier – Good service
Arjomari (France)	– Strong positions in France due to its own merchants
Condat (France)	– Good and stable quality
Feldmühle (Germany)	– Stable quality – Rapid deliveries and good stocking arrangements
KNP (Netherlands)	– Flexible supplier, also accepts small orders – Good service
PWA Hallein (Germany)	– Competes with price
Scheufelen (Germany)	– Good and stable quality – Reliable deliveries
Stora Kopparberg (Sweden)	– Reliable deliveries – Quality and service OK

Marketing at Leykam Mürztaler AG

Marketing activities at Leykam Mürztaler were divided between the Sales Director, Wolfgang Pfarl, and the Marketing Manager, Gertrude Eder. Pfarl, a member of the Executive Board, was responsible for pricing as well as all personal selling activities, both direct and through merchants. Eder was responsible for public relations, advertising and sales promotion, and marketing research. As a staff member, she reported to Dr. Siegfried Meysel, the Managing Director.

Coated Woodfree Products and Markets

In coated woodfree papers, Leykam Mürztaler offered a comprehensive product line of standard coated papers under the MAGNO brand, for both sheet and web offset printing. These were produced in a wide variety of basis weights, ranging from 80–300 grams per square meter depending on the particular application. The firm targeted the high quality end of the standard coated category by offering higher coat weights, better gloss and print gloss, and better printability.

Using Austria as its home market, Leykam Mürztaler focused its principal efforts on countries in Europe. The majority of sales revenues came, in roughly similar amounts, from Austria, Italy, France and the UK, with somewhat higher sales in Germany. Belgium, Holland, Switzerland and Spain were important but smaller markets.

The firm also sold in a number of other countries, including the United States. Penetration of the US market by the European paper industry had been assisted by the favorable exchange rates during the early 1980s. The firm's policy, however, was to maintain its position in different countries despite currency fluctuations. As Gertrude Eder explained:

> We believe our customers expect us to participate in their markets on a long-term basis and to be competitive with local conditions. This may cost us some profits in the short term, as when we maintained our position in the UK despite the weak pound, but now that the pound is strong again, this investment is paying off. If we had reduced our presence when the exchange rate was unfavorable, it would have been very difficult to regain our position.

Channels of Distribution

Over the years, Leykam Mürztaler had sold most of its output through merchants. To some degree the method of distribution was influenced by the country served as the firm tended to follow the predominant trade practice in each country. In Switzerland, Germany and the UK, all its business was done through merchants. In France, Italy and Austria, there was a mixed pattern of distribution, but with a strong merchant orientation.

Merchants were carefully selected, and the firm did business only with stocking merchants who competed on service rather than price. In some countries (e.g., Holland) it used exclusive distribution, but this was not the normal pattern. Gertrude Eder explained:

> As a large producer, we have a volume problem. In the larger countries, one merchant simply can't sell enough product for us, plus we believe it is risky to commit completely to one merchant.

Similarly, Wolfgang Pfarl commented:

> In Germany, for instance, we could go to one merchant only, but to get the volume of business we need would require going into direct business with some

non-stocking merchants, and that is something that neither we nor our stocking merchants want to happen.

To date, the trend toward mill ownership of merchants had not adversely affected the firm's ability to get good merchant representation. There was some concern, however, that with changing patterns of mill ownership, some merchants might be closed off to firms like Leykam Mürztaler in the future.

Service was also seen as a key to merchant relations. In this connection, the firm felt its computerized order system and new finishing facilities at the Gratkorn mill, highly automated, permitting flexibility in sheeting and packaging, and able to handle the total output of the new paper machine, provided great service capability and gave it a competitive advantage. As the mill superintendent put it:

> From a production standpoint, the ideal scenario is one in which we can run one grade of paper all year and ship it to customers in large reels. Reality is that meeting customer needs is critical, and I believe we have 'state-of-the-art competence' in our ability to meet a tremendous variety of customer requirements efficiently.

Pricing

Pricing practices in the paper industry had a strong commodity orientation and, for coated woodfree papers, industry prices tended to serve as the basis for arriving at transaction prices. *(See **Exhibit 3** for information on industry prices and paper grades.)* For sales to merchants, Leykam Mürztaler negotiated price lists, using the industry prices as a starting point, with final prices taking paper quality and other relevant factors into account. Price lists then remained in effect until there was a change in industry price levels. Routine orders were priced from the established price list. Large requirements, however, usually involved special negotiation.

According to one Leykam Mürztaler sales manager:

> We have some interesting discussions with our merchants about price. The customer knows we make a high quality product, so his principal interest is in getting it at the lowest possible price. In Europe there is no uniform classification of coated papers, as there is in the USA and Japan, so a standard approach is to try to get me to reclassify my product to a lower grade, and so a lower price. To some extent, though, my customer's preoccupation with price simply reflects price pressures he is experiencing from his customers. Still, it is frustrating because we believe we offer a lot more than just price and a good product. But I think we do a good job for the firm in getting the highest price possible.

Branding

In recent years, Leykam Mürztaler had followed the industry practice of branding its principal products. It did, however, supply products to certain merchants for private branding, a practice that was established when mill branding was not the norm. In 1988, some 30% of sales carried a merchant brand, largely reflecting the volume from Germany and the UK, where private branding was customary. Recently, however, the firm had started to identify most of its products by using a typical Leykam Mürztaler packaging, even for private labels.

Brands had been promoted primarily by the sales force, in direct contact with customers, using brochures and samples and by packaging. More recently, a series of superb visual messages was commissioned, using the theme, 'Dimensions in Paper', to suggest ways that high quality paper combined with printing could produce more effective communication. The script accompanying the visual messages was designed to appeal to both the advertisers, with emphasis on communication, and printers with emphasis on paper finish, touch, color, absorption, contrast and other key paper characteristics. On a limited basis, these messages had appeared in selected magazines and in brochures for customers.

There was general agreement within the firm that more emphasis needed to be placed on branding as a way to achieve product differentiation and convey the desired high quality image. There was less agreement on how much to spend promoting the brands or how to deal with merchants who were now buying Leykam Mürztaler products for sale under the merchants' labels. According to Gertrude Eder:

> Over the past few years we designed the corporate logo and corporate graphics and established blue, black and white as the colors for all corporate communication. We have worked hard to establish a consistent presentation of our corporate identity. Feedback from customers and the sales department indicates that this has helped improve our visibility and image. Nevertheless, we are currently spending considerably less than 1% of sales on advertising. Zanders, on the other hand, a firm of about our size, has been spending a lot of money on advertising for years and as a result has better visibility than we do, particularly with advertising agencies, as well as an enviable reputation for quality and service.
>
> I don't know what the right number is for us, but we will need to spend substantially more if we are to establish the kind of brand awareness and image we desire. I think that to have any significant impact would take a minimum of ASch3–4 million for classical advertising (i.e., advertising in trade publications, in various languages) and ASch8-10 million for promotions, including brochures, leaflets and trade fairs. In Western Europe we have to

advertise in at least four to five languages, and sometimes more. In addition, the nature of the ads varies. In private brand countries, our ads emphasize the company name and focus on the Dimensions in Paper theme as well as the company's experience and modern production facilities. In other countries we emphasize the MAGNO brand.

We are convinced that printers want to know what mill brand they are buying. Also, we believe that there is some subjectivity in selecting paper, particularly by the advertiser, and we want to convince the advertiser that his message will come across better on Leykam Mürztaler paper.

The decision on supplying Leykam Mürztaler products for private branding was even more complex. As Wolfgang Pfarl commented:

> I understand the position of the merchants who want to offer a private brand. The fact remains, however, that it is the mill that determines product characteristics and is responsible for meeting specifications. It is really a question of who is adding the value. In my view the merchant ought to emphasize those things which he controls, such as local stocks, good sales representation and service. Putting a merchant label on paper produced by Leykam Mürztaler misrepresents the value added picture. Don't get me wrong. Our firm strongly believes in merchants. In fact, we avoid direct business wherever there are strong stocking merchants. It's just that we think mills and merchants have distinct roles to play, and they should not be confused.
>
> Currently, we will still produce for a merchant's label, but we have started to insist that it also is identified as Leykam Mürztaler. The merchants aren't very happy about this, but we think it's the right thing to do.

Nevertheless, the situation with respect to existing merchants was difficult. As one of the senior sales managers said:

> We have been supplying some of our merchants with paper to be sold under a private label for a long time, and they have invested substantial sums of money in establishing their own brands. I completely support the company's position on this, but I don't know how we can get the practice to change. If we insist on supplying products only under our own brand, there are a lot of competitors who would, I think, be happy to step in and take over our position with some merchants. If we can't convince a merchant to switch over to our brand, we could lose a lot of business, in one or two instances as much as 6,000 tonnes. On the other hand, if we aren't uniform on this, we will not be able to really exploit the potential of developing our own brands.

In addition to questions about branding policy, it was not clear how to capitalize on increased brand preference, if indeed it were achieved. As Wolfgang Pfarl said:

We might want to think in terms of higher prices or increased share, or some combination. Exactly what we would do could vary from market to market.

Personal Selling

Contact with merchants and with large, directly served accounts in Europe was mainly made by the company's own sales force headquartered in Vienna, by sales representatives in subsidiary companies in Germany, Italy and France, and by sales agents in other markets (e.g., the UK). Direct sales representatives numbered 20. Including clerical staff, Leykam had some 60 individuals in its sales department, most of whom had direct contact with customers.

The major activity of the sales force was making direct calls on large customers and on merchants. In addition, sales representatives made occasional calls on a merchant's customers, generally accompanied by the merchant's sales representative. Objectives usually included negotiating long-term contracts, 'selling' the existing product line, new product introduction, and a review of customer requirements for products and service.

It was the firm's belief that its sales force was a major asset and that sales representatives could significantly influence relations with merchants. A major objective for all Leykam Mürztaler representatives was to do everything possible to develop close relations with assigned merchants. According to Wolfgang Pfarl:

> The average age of our sales force is between 35 and 40, and most of the individuals have spent their entire career in sales with Leykam Mürztaler. They are really committed to serve the customer, with on-time deliveries or any other aspect of our relationship, and the customer really respects their high level of service. In addition, they are good negotiators and represent Leykam effectively during contract negotiations. They do not need to be technical experts, but they make sure that our technical people provide technical information as required. Also, they monitor shipping performance, make presentations to merchants and may make joint customer calls with merchant sales representatives.

Mathias Radon, one of the Vienna-based sales managers, made the following comments:

> In total we call on about 100 merchants in Europe. I work with our sales offices in Italy, France and Belgium and handle 5 merchants personally in the UK, in cooperation with our representative there. I call on the merchants two to three

times a year and have extensive phone contact with our sales offices and representatives from Vienna.

In general, the customer wants to talk about quantity, price and service. We have conversations about private labelling. The new merchants would like us to give them private labels, but I think they know they can't get it. On the other hand, the ones to whom we are currently providing private labels don't want to give it up. The problem varies from country to country. In France, for instance, it's not such a big problem.

One of my objectives is to encourage more stock business versus indent (merchant orders for direct mill shipment to the customer). This means we have to give them better service and provide back-up stocks.

Some merchants handle mill brands that compete directly with Leykam Mürztaler, but most tend to do this under a private label.

From time to time we work to develop a new merchant, but generally we work on building long-lasting relationships with existing merchants. We encourage trips by merchant personnel to the mill. I will make short presentations to merchant sales representatives when I call on the merchant, but generally they are pretty knowledgeable about paper. We've tried contests and other incentives with merchants and are still thinking about it, but I'm not sure if that's what we should do.

From a quality standpoint, I try to stress whiteness, opacity, printability/runability and consistency. Lots of customers ask for lab figures, but I don't think you can rely just on lab reports. We have trial print runs every week by an independent printer to check our consistency. I think most printers feel the same way.

We tend to have lots of small problems rather than any one large problem. Branding, for instance, pricing, friction when we appoint a new merchant and country variations with regard to ways of doing business. I think branding will be important in all countries, but how we capitalize on it may have to vary.

After Sales Service

Problems in printing could arise due to a number of circumstances. There might be variations or flaws in the paper or in the ink. Presses could develop mechanical problems. Even changes in temperature and humidity could negatively affect printing quality. Because of the complexity of the printing process, the cause of a problem was not always clear, and reaching an equitable settlement could be difficult.

When problems did arise, the printer turned to the merchant or mill for technical advice and frequently wanted financial compensation for lost production. According to Wolfgang Pfarl:

When the printer encounters a production problem, it is important for us to be able to give him technical advice and work with him to solve the problem. Sometimes the sales representative can do this. More often, we have to involve one of our technical people from the mill. All too often, however, the printer is just looking for someone to compensate him financially, and we have to be very tough or we're likely to find ourselves paying for a lot of other people's mistakes.

Future Issues

Looking to the future, the firm was focusing its attention on managing 'through the business cycle'. As Wolfgang Pfarl put it:

Our real challenge is to strengthen our market position in Western Europe. Most of our coated woodfree paper goes into advertising. We have seen extraordinary growth in this market in the last few years, but we have to expect there will be a significant downturn in one or two years and that advertisers will then look intensely at their costs. In many cases this means the printer will suggest a lower cost grade as a substitute for coated woodfree. Our task is to differentiate MAGNO from the generic category and position it as 'a paper for all seasons', so to speak. In other words, we want our customers to think of MAGNO as the 'right' paper for high quality advertising, separately from coated woodfree.

In general, this means strengthening our corporate identity, being partners of the strongest merchants and encouraging our merchants to support the MAGNO brand.

In a similar vein, Gertrude Eder commented:

This is a business where the impact of the business cycle is made worse by the tendency of merchants to overstock in good times and destock in bad times. Our objective, I think, should be to position Leykam as the last mill the merchant or printer would think of cancelling in a downturn.

Notes

1. ASch12.48 = $1.00 in December 1988.
2. Western Europe included the countries in the European Community plus Finland, Norway, Sweden, Austria and Switzerland.
3. Designated LWC or MWC, depending on the weight, although the dividing line was not precise.

4.   ECC International, Limited, 1987.
5.   Papis Limited.
6.   By BIS Marketing Research Limited.
7.   The European Printing and Writing Paper Industry – 1987, IMEDE Case No GM 375.
8.   From a paper presented by BIS Marketing Research Limited.

Lussman-Shizuka Corp.

This case was prepared by Professor Dominique Turpin, with the assistance of Research Associate Joyce Miller, as a basis for class discussion rather than to illustrate either effective or ineffective handling of a business situation. Research for this case was made possible by a grant from Egon Zehnder.

It was 6:00 pm on June 22, 1991, and Rudolf Richter, President of Lussman-Shizuka Corp., could see several photographers and journalists representing Osaka's major newspapers gathered outside on the street 20 floors below. Richter sighed and glanced nervously at his secretary who was signaling him that yet another reporter was on the telephone wanting his view of the allegations recently made against the company. Four hours earlier, the Japanese authorities had arrested three of Richter's employees and accused them of bribing university professors to win orders of the company's products. In his entire 25-year career with Lussman Pharmaceuticals, Richter had never faced a more difficult situation.

Lussman in Japan

Located near Osaka, Lussman-Shizuka Corp. was a 50:50 joint venture between Lussman Pharmaceuticals based in Düsseldorf and Shizuka Corp., a Japanese chemical firm. Formed to produce and distribute anti-cancer drugs in Japan, the venture had operated since 1971 in what Richter called 'one of the toughest, most competitive markets in the world'. Richter had headed Lussman-Shizuka for the past six years and was the only foreigner working in the joint venture. Although he had begun learning Japanese, his ability to handle a business discussion was still limited. Consequently, most meetings were conducted in English. Two executives from Shizuka Corp.,

Hiroshi Shibuya and Yasumi Kato, served as vice presidents of Lussman-Shizuka and were involved in the daily operations of the joint venture. They both had a reasonably good command of English.

For many years, Japan had kept foreign products out of its national market with what Richter described as 'high tariffs and complex production and import procedures.' Through negotiations with the European Community, these trade barriers had gradually been dismantled, but importing goods into Japan was still cumbersome in Richter's view. Lussman Pharmaceuticals had entered the market by tying up with a leading Japanese company. The venture represented a rare success for a European company in Japan. Lussman-Shizuka sold quality products at competitive prices, serviced through a national distribution network. Technological leadership had given the venture its initial edge in the fight for market share. Currently, the company manufactured 10 per cent of its products in Japan and imported the remainder from a Lussman factory in Germany.

Over-the-counter drugs in Japan were primarily available through doctors rather than pharmacists. Japanese physicians typically charged low fees for clinic visits, relying on the sale of drugs for the bulk of their income. Doctors had a great deal of influence over their hospitals' buying decisions as well as the drug purchases of their former students now working in other medical institutions.

The Lussman-Shizuka Affair

Three weeks earlier, five doctors who worked at prominent university hospitals in Osaka had been arrested for accepting improper cash payments from Lussman-Shizuka. Two doctors, who had previously purchased Lussman products, had reportedly received $22,000 for entertainment expenses. Another was arrested for accepting $31,000 from Lussman-Shizuka for attending an academic conference in the United States. Two other professors in a major Japanese university were each accused of receiving $18,000 from Lussman-Shizuka, but prosecutors had not yet released their names. Shortly after this incident, the Ministry of Health, together with the Ministry of Education, advised all state university hospitals against purchasing drugs from Lussman-Shizuka for an unspecified period of time, a move that could have devastating consequences for Lussman's business in Japan.

Dr. Yutaka Hayashida, an Osaka physician, observed, 'Pharmaceutical companies commonly court doctors to buy their drugs because it is such a competitive market. Salesmen will do almost anything to get access to the most influencial practitioners. They'll give them presents, buy drinks, pay for trips, even help their kids get into the best universities.' Dr. Hayashida added that he had made a personal decision to turn down all such offers, although there was no hospital requirement to do so. He continued, 'Low-paid university professors and newly-established doctors are particularly vulnerable to such offers. The Lussman-Shizuka affair is just the tip of the iceberg. Most companies and most doctors do the same thing. In fact, much of the competitive bidding that does happen in hospitals is meaningless, because the doctors have decided in advance which drugs they want to buy and the specifications are set so that only those products will be accepted.'

The Reaction from Shizuka Corp.

Yasumi Kato, a director in the Japanese parent company who was also a vice president in the joint venture, offered his view of the situation:

> The fact that Lussman-Shizuka is an outsider makes the company especially vulnerable to exposure. Furthermore, in Japan, stability is very important. We brought attention to ourselves by marketing aggressively. Within less than a decade of its founding, Lussman-Shizuka moved to the top ranks in the industry in its particular specialty. Our share of the market did not come cheap. Where most Western companies in Japan will seek a small position and focus on maintaining high profits, Lussman-Shizuka wanted to be at the top in anti-cancer drugs, and the company matched Japanese discounts blow for blow. Now we are paying the price.

Richter knew that the venture's quick climb had created a lot of tension among the competitors. In fact, his Japanese partners had warned him of the danger of disrupting the market with an aggressive sales policy. Industry leaders had frequently complained that prices had fallen too low. Now, the venture's Japanese staff speculated that a competitor had leaked inflammatory information to the press. Richter was aware that scandals typically broke in the Japanese press after reporters were fed information aimed at undercutting foreigners who were seen to be undermining the status quo.

Why was Lussman-Shizuka singled out? According to Richter, 'In some respects, the company has been too honest. When investigators raided our office last week and demanded to see the company's accounts, we had only one set of books with a straightforward accounting of our activities. Many local companies have two sets of books or, at a minimum, they have couched the payments to doctors in vague terms, such as cooperative research. The reality in this industry in this country is that you are not a fully-fledged salesman until you have reached the point where a doctor will accept your gifts and agree to meet with you.'

Hiroshi Shibuya, a vice president in the joint venture, felt that what had gotten the company into difficulty was its effort to woo university professors. Investigators had told the press that Lussman-Shizuka had compiled a list of influencial doctors to be regularly targeted by its salesmen.

Where To Go Next

Richter had to decide how to proceed, and quickly. He could not help thinking that a scandal now would jeopardize his forthcoming retirement. His wife had already moved back to Bavaria, and Richter himself was scheduled to leave Japan permanently at the end of December. Now, the Japanese authorities had forbidden him to leave the country, and he could face a long trial if convicted.

While his Japanese partners tended to blame Richter openly for the consequences of aggressive selling, Richter felt they also shared some responsibility for the current situation. Although he knew that 'gift-giving' was a longstanding Japanese tradition and standard industry practice, Richter felt that the salespeople may have overdone it.

While Richter had been mulling over his alternatives, the crowd outside the office building had grown considerably. And, there were likely to be more waiting for him at his home, all with the same questions. Should he talk to the press and give his own version of the story, or should he try to avoid the media at all costs? Since Japanese doctors and the salespeople considered the alleged actions as acceptable industry practice, should he follow the advice of one of his managers to meet with the competition to work out some common actions? Should he also ask for assistance from his government, as one of his German business associates had suggested? Should he try to get help from his European headquarters?

Place / Promotion:
Sales and Distribution

CASES

Jac Jacobsen Industrier A/S
Grampro B.V.
Grasse Fragrances SA

Jac Jacobsen Industrier A/S: Acquiring A Competitor

This case was prepared by Professor Per V. Jenster and Research Associate Bethann Kassman as a basis for class discussion rather than to illustrate either effective or ineffective handling of a business situation.

On a rainy Monday in May 1990, Alv Inge Karlsen, chief executive officer of Jac Jacobsen Industrier (JJI) A/S of Oslo, Norway, looked around the meeting room at the group of managers from the firm's Luxo division. He had just introduced and welcomed his successor, Lars Harlem, and was about to announce the unexpected acquisition of Ledu, Luxo's fiercest competitor for the past 20 years.

The look of surprise on the faces of the country managers and functional executives quickly changed to satisfaction as they thought of the agonizing hours, tapped energy and scarce resources expended on this competitor in the European and US sectors. The managers were not slow to volunteer their comments: 'One down, and one to go!' 'No more bickering with distributors over margins vis-à-vis Ledu!' Others said, 'Why spend money buying Ledu when you could have given it to marketing and R&D; we could have beaten them in the market with better budgets!' 'What are our distributors going to say, how are we going to respond? How are we going to manage the channel conflict?'

Alv Karlsen and Lars Harlem exchanged glances as each thought about the issues of growth and control which the acquisition strategy raised. They had anticipated some of these reactions, but so many opinions was more than they had bargained for. Nevertheless, the Ledu organization had to be dealt with. Alv Karlsen leaned back in his chair and said, 'Gentlemen, these are all valid concerns. However, I would very much like to hear how you propose we deal with the international integration of Ledu and Luxo.'

History

Jac Jacobsen was founded in 1934 as a textile machinery company. Over the years, the focus of the company had changed to lighting, with all subsequent growth based on the phenomenal success of its Luxo Lamp.

The Luxo lamp, one of the world's more original designs, was a parabolic lamp with a flexible arm, developed by an Englishman. Mr. Jacobsen had found the lamp in a case of textile machinery. After receiving a manufacturing license to produce the Luxo lamp in Scandinavia, he subsequently redesigned it and gave it a new look.

The first Luxo lamps were produced and sold in Norway in 1937. During the war, the operation in Norway had to close. However, in 1939, a manufacturing company was established in Sweden. This company operated at full capacity during the war years and was highly profitable. When the war ended, the Swedish company represented a solid financial base for the international expansion in the years to come.

The company had started with a single product model. Over the years many new models were developed, all based on the original Luxo arm principle. Currently, the product portfolio included lamps for a number of applications for the office environment, health care sector, industrial segments, etc. By 1990, the original Luxo lamp accounted for no more than 1% of total sales.

When the patents for the original lamps expired in the late '60s, extensive copying took place throughout the world. Consequently, the company gradually upgraded its products and changed its strategy. It began producing asymmetric light for the high end of the modern office market – for premium offices and high profile locations where the quality of light was important. With the acquisition of Ledu in late 1990, that strategy was under evaluation.

In the USA, Jac followed a dynamic acquisition policy. Beginning in 1981, 11 companies in the lighting field were acquired over a seven year period. These acquisitions enabled the company to become the eighth largest producer of lighting in the US, and one of Norway's most internationally active manufacturing companies.

In 1989 the company was organized into three divisions, with two of them in lighting (these two divisions were Jac Jacobsen International A.S. Europe, and USA Lighting). The Group Holdings also included Jac Jacobsen Industries, Inc., USA, an American division, comprising the companies that had been acquired (in which Jac Jacobsen owned a 47.5% interest), and Jac Jacobsen Enterprises, Inc., Canada, a holding company which owned Luxo Lamp Ltd., Canada. *(Refer to **Exhibit 1** for further details* *of Group Holdings and **Exhibit 2** for the Consolidated Balance Sheet for December 1988 and 1989.)*

Exhibit 1 *(Source: annual report, 1989)*

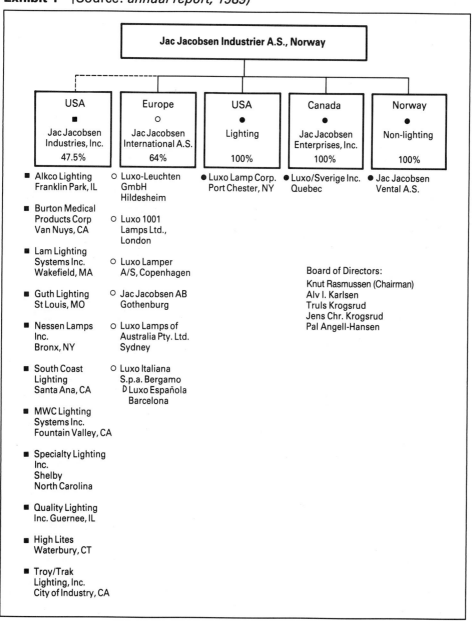

Exhibit 2 *Balance sheet*

Consolidated Balance Sheets December 31, 1989 and 1988*	NOK in thousands	
Assets	**1989**	**1988**
Current assets:		
Cash	80,477	27,879
Investments	82,461	30,084
Accounts and notes receivable	68,702	147,242
Inventory	68,096	188,238
Other short-term receivables	16,584	17,370
Total current assets	316,320	410,813
Investments in bonds and shares	18,567	7,715
Intangible assets	30,659	25,694
Machinery and equipment	24,574	88,794
Land and buildings	20,930	36,709
Total other assets	94,730	158,912
Total assets	411,050	569,725
Liabilities and Shareholders' Equity		
Current liabilities:		
Bank overdraft	24,966	19,370
Accounts payable	31,987	59,721
Accrued income taxes	11,932	17,387
Other current liabilities	38,322	58,786
Total current liabilities	107,207	155,264
Long term debt	34,159	157,473
Deferred taxes	4,292	9,493
Untaxed reserves	57,595	46,348
Minority interests	32,089	43,263
Stockholders equity:		
Share capital (3,000 shares of NOK 1000)	3,000	3,000
Other funds	172,708	154,884
Total stockholders' equity	175,708	157,884
Total liabilities and stockholders' equity	411,050	569,725

* These figures include all majority-owned companies.

International Growth

The first phase of Jac Jacobsen's internationalization process occurred in the late 1940s. The company located distributors and sold lamps in England and on the Continent. It was also during this period that the company made its first approach to enter the US market, but the results of these efforts were not impressive. The company realized that it had to get around the heavy trade barriers that existed at that time by establishing its own companies in the local markets. During the 1950s, therefore, new companies were established in Denmark, Germany, the US (New York) and Canada (Montreal), and a period of significant sales growth commenced.

In the mid-1960s, clear signs of what a company official termed 'volume disease' became apparent – rapid sales growth, high costs and deteriorating profits led to frequent and serious liquidity problems. When Alv Inge Karlsen was hired as managing director in 1964, he started to reorganize the company and build up the management control systems. Decision-making was centralized in Norway, where much of the production was also concentrated. Over the next five years, profitability improved significantly and, toward the end of the 1960s, the company appeared to be in good financial condition. These years, however, were a period with only modest sales growth because the focus was on planning and budgeting.

At the beginning of 1970, Norway found oil in the North Sea. Fear that this discovery would lead to higher labour costs and a strengthening of the Norwegian currency led Jac Jacobsen to a decision to contract out a major part of the production from Norway to subsidiaries in the US and Canada. (At that time, the US dollar had started to 'float', and the dollar/krone rate changed significantly over a short period of time.) Because Norway was not a member of the EEC, the company also found it necessary to establish a production unit within the EEC, thus a new plant was built in Northern Italy in 1971.

Along with the transfer of production outside Norway, the company saw the need to strengthen the organizations of the subsidiary companies. A number of new key local people were hired, most of them with a strong marketing background. Nearly all of these people were successful and, within a few years, the management – the old 'entrepreneurs' – in the various subsidiaries had been replaced. Again, reorganization took place. Decision-making that had been centralized in Norway was, to a high degree, delegated to frontline managers. The group was organized into divisions, and it became a profit centre where responsibilities were clearly defined and substantial profit-sharing possibilities were available to key employees. The parent company became, in effect, a holding company. Fast growth and solid profitability followed.

In the late 1970s, extensive numbers of counterfeit Luxo products made by Far East manufacturers began to flood the US market. Jac Jacobsen's high market share and premium price were particularly vulnerable to copying. In response to this threat, Jac Jacobsen decided to change the strategy of the US division. Instead of fighting the Far East competition, it was decided that the US division should enter new fields in the lighting market, while securing its growth through acquisitions. At the same time, the European division would concentrate all its efforts in traditional areas in order to balance this risk. When the first acquisition was made in 1981, Jac Jacobsen had one company in the US (Luxo Lamp Corporation) with sales of $15 million. By 1988 that one company had become a division comprising 12 companies with sales close to $100 million. At that time, almost 70% of the group's total sales were being generated by the US division.

The acquisition strategy in the US was a great success. However, continued diversified growth in the US would, management feared, tie up too many resources, thus preventing the company from making the most of even greater opportunities which were emerging in Europe. The company also realized that the technical expertise and knowledge gained through the US acquisitions achieved little added value for the European organization; the anticipated synergies did not occur because American companies were not able to meet the local requirements of European markets.

The company had originally planned to launch a public issue in the United States to raise funds needed for US operations. For various reasons, this approach proved impractical. Instead, it was decided to carry out extensive restructuring. The aim was to reduce the exposure in the United States and enhance the core business. Through this restructuring, the two original Luxo companies in the United States and Canada were 'bought back' by the parent company. The remaining companies (the acquired companies) became the objects of a Management Buy Out (MBO), in which a group of investors, headed by the American division's former management team, acquired a majority of the shares. These companies continued to operate under the name Jac Jacobsen Industries Inc. The parent company in Norway remained the largest shareholder, but its holdings were reduced to 47.5%.

Acquisition Strategy

The basic concept underlying the acquisition strategy in the US was to establish new business in other areas of the lighting market in order to compensate for the expected loss of market share within the traditional segments of the market, due to the heavy Far East competition. A detailed, long-term strategy for this new venture was developed including a set of criteria to evaluate potential acquisition candidates. These criteria identified the following:

1. Companies which were profitable in their own right;
2. Companies whose products were already commercial;
3. Companies which were niche players;
4. Small companies which were either in a complimentary area of lighting or with products that could expand Luxo's offerings.

The company also made it clear that it was not interested in 'turnaround projects' or 'bargain opportunities'.

The acquisition strategy was further enhanced by establishing a holding company (Jac Jacobsen Incorporated) in the US, which was used as a vehicle for identifying and acquiring suitable candidates. The company recognized the importance of separating the acquisition related tasks from those of the operating companies. A small professional staff was responsible for identifying and evaluating acquisition candidates, overseeing the 'due diligence' process, analyzing staff and organizational issues, and supervising external consultants brought in for specific analytical tasks. This was a costly process that included management reviews, and interviews with end users and distributors to determine the market perception of the potential acquisition candidate.

With few exceptions, Jac Jacobsen's strategy included assimilation of the acquired company. Following the purchase, a JJI team was sent to the new company to educate the staff about corporate philosophy, personnel and reporting requirements, financial accounting practices, and other steps necessary to ensure immediate alignment. At the same time, Jac Jacobsen tried to keep the original management team in place whenever possible, and to maintain the purchased company's identity and products.

Market Strategy: The Luxo Division in Europe

The Luxo companies were the market leaders in 'task lighting' for offices in major markets in Europe, and also a major supplier to the hospital/health care sector. Other competitors were not as broadly based within the product ranges or as internationally positioned as Jac Jacobsen. As the company entered the 1990s, its main focus was the modern office environment, especially lighting systems that interfaced with computers and ones that were energy efficient.

The marketing strategy for Europe called for quick market penetration by concentrating on the end user directly. The niche strategy of the 'modern office' was to be expanded by broadening product offerings with 'uplighters', both free-standing and wall-mounted. The industrial sector was receiving more emphasis than the health care sector, but both areas were being targeted as growth areas.

The hospital segment presented a challenge because the market was dominated by German suppliers; however, Jac Jacobsen produced for hospital wards, outpatient centres and physicians' offices, rather than specifically for the hospital industry.

Product Strategies: The Luxo Division in Europe

The stated product strategy emphasized 'international' products that looked the same and were sold throughout the Western industrial world. However, local market preferences differed among the major markets in Europe. Thus, the product development and marketing strategies of the production units in Norway and Italy continued to vary greatly.

In Northern Europe, Jac Jacobsen was the leading international supplier of ergonomic/asymmetric lighting. The trend toward ergonomic awareness was very strong in Sweden, and Jac Jacobsen believed Norway and Denmark would follow that trend in the early 1990s. Although the trend was expected to spread to Germany and England also, Luxo, as the leading supplier, intended to stimulate this market demand.

In Southern Europe, the preference was almost entirely for design and halogen lighting, which continued to be the driving force of Luxo Italiana. Its strategy was to expand the product range further into the lighting sector for projects and specifiers with indirect lighting systems.

These differences between Northern and Southern Europe led to difficulties in having uniform pricing, brochures, sales material, etc. Because of these dissimilarities, distribution was tailored to the needs of each market. Marketing and sales strategies also differed among markets and between the two Luxo product lines.

On the other hand, this 'dual' Luxo product strategy also created increased opportunities, as all major markets could be attacked with two different Luxo product lines, thus expanding the Luxo total business growth and market position.

European Trends

Total sales growth in Europe for 1987–1989 had been positively dominated by sales companies in Sweden and Germany, which respectively had sales increases of 20–25 per cent and 15–18 per cent per year. Sales projections indicated that both markets would continue to grow, with Germany identified as the market having the strongest real growth potential. Sales in Norway and Denmark had stagnated in the late 1980s, due to difficult national economic situations, but increased sales growth was expected through new product offerings in the early 1990s.

Australia and England, both new subsidiaries, were affected by recession-like economies that had high interest rates. Industry experts felt that England would bounce back in the early 1990s, but Australia would have to fight recession for a longer period of time.

Italy, Spain and France all experienced slow growth in 1989, and it was anticipated that 1990 would also be slow, but that growth could be expected through new product introductions in 1991.

Sales Organization

Luxo felt that a strong sales organization in major markets was its backbone. Thus, with the exception of Italy and Spain, where multi-company agents were used, most of the European market was served by Luxo's district salespeople. To compete in the project market, it became increasingly necessary to educate the sales personnel on a more technical level to enhance their communication with lighting consultants and architects. The 1991 budget added project salespeople to the sales organization to provide this knowledge on specific, new product introductions. *(Refer to **Exhibit 3** for details of the sales organization.)*

The European distribution channels used by the company varied greatly depending on the markets served, as summarized below *(refer also to **Exhibit 4**)*:

Norway	53.8% through wholesalers
Sweden	59.5% direct to office retail
Italy	56.0% direct to lighting retail
England	25.5% through medical supply houses
Germany	22.0% direct to end user

These local/national differences in distribution patterns had a strong influence on marketing strategies and tactics, which consequently differed from market to market. *(Please refer to **Exhibit 5**.)*

Major Competitors in Europe

The European lighting industry was very fragmented and, as Luxo Europe moved into new market segments, its competitors multiplied and became less well defined. In design and tube lighting, competitors were numerous and diffused, while the industrial market had few competitors. In the area of office lighting, the competition was consistent on a year-to-year basis. The economy market continually flourished with an infinite number of suppliers but with little real impact on Jac Jacobsen.

Exhibit 3 *Business plan 1991–93, Jac Jacobsen International (sales organization 1991 domestic market)*

	Sales Manager	District Salesmen	Project Salesmen	Order Receiv./ Inside Sales	Customer Records	Telemark	Total Empl.	Agents Single Company	Agents Multi Company
Norway	–	4	1	2½	–	–	7½	–	1
Sweden	1	5	1	4	–	–	11	–	–
Denmark	1	4	1	3½	–	–	9½	–	–
Germany	–	4	2	4	1	6	17	–	2
England	–	6	–	5	3	–	14	–	3
Italy	1	–	½	4	1	–	6½	2	22
France	–	3	–	2	–	–	5	–	1
Spain	–	2	–	3	–	–	5	–	12
Australia	1	2	–	2	–	–	5	–	–
Total	4	30	5½	30	5	6	80½	2	41

Exhibit 4 *Jac Jacobsen International business plan 1991–93 (distribution channels – % split)*

	N	S	DK	G	UK	I	ES	FR	AUS
Office Retail	17,5	59,5	42,0	39,0	7,9	21,3	27,9	20,0	10,0
Office Wholesale	27,7	–	–	–	18,5	–	–	10,0	38,0
Total Office	45,2	59,5	42,0	39,0	26,4	21,3	27,9	30,0	48,0
Lighting Retail	3,2	4,2	2,0	5,0	4,5	56,0	43,8	32,0	5,0
Lighting Wholesale	26,1	4,7	23,0	23,0	3,1	–	–	18,0	5,0
Total Lighting	29,3	8,9	25,0	28,0	7,6	56,0	43,8	50,0	10,0
Government	8,0	25,6	10,0	3,0	2,4	–	–	3,0	21,0
Medical	5,3	–	8,0	6,0	25,5	–	–	–	14,0
Industrial	–	–	–	–	4,7	–	–	–	6,0
Mass Merchand.	–	–	–	–	4,5	14,4	14,1	–	1,0
Direct (End-User)	10,5	4,4	8,0	22,0	19,4	7,8	14,2	8,0	–
Other	1,7	1,6	7,0	2,0	9,5	0,5	–	9,0	–
Total	100,0	100,0	100,0	100,0	100,0	100,0	100,0	100,0	100,0

Exhibit 5   *Jac Jacobsen International: total sales growth per market 1991–93, compared to last 3 years and estimate 1990 (Mill. Nok (1991 currency))*

Markets	A-87	A-88	A-89	EST-90	B-91	B-92	B-93
Norway	21.7	20.1	18.0	19.4	25.4	29.2	33.6
Denmark	31.0	30.0	31.3	32.7	34.6	40.6	47.5
Sweden	29.2	35.9	44.5	48.3	52.5	58.8	68.2
Germany	27.2	32.6	38.1	44.4	49.5	56.8	63.9
England	–	–	26.4	26.3	33.9	38.4	43.5
Australia	–	13.1	15.2	13.1	14.4	15.8	17.8
Italy	26.5	33.9	32.2	32.5	40.0	45.0	50.0
Spain	–	–	13.2	13.8	16.5	19.0	21.8
France	–	–	–	10.3	12.3	14.2	16.3
Sum Direct							
Luxo Sales Co.	135.6	165.6	218.9	240.5	279.1	317.3	362.6
Dir. Exp. USA/Canada	3.8	1.8	1.8	2.2	1.6	2.0	2.0
Dir. Exp. Norway	18.4	15.4	10.5	11.8	13.2	14.5	16.0
Dir. Exp. USA/Canada	3.1	4.4	3.0	1.5	1.5	2.0	2.0
Dir. Exp. Italy	27.6	35.2	20.0	26.1	24.8	23.7	30.0
Sum Dir. Exp.	52.9	56.8	35.3	41.6	41.1	44.2	50.0
Total Direct Sales	188.5	222.4	254.2	282.1	320.2	365.0	412.6
Increase	29.1	33.9	31.8	28.0	38.1	44.3	47.6
Increase %	18.3	18.0	14.3	11.0	13.5	14.0	13.0
Interco. Exp. Norway	38.0	51.8	70.1	67.6	80.9	91.4	103.3
Interco. Exp. Italy	13.1	16.1	24.5	33.7	31.0	28.7	30.0
Sum Interco.	51.1	67.9	94.6	101.3	111.9		133.3
Annual Cons. Sales							
Jac Jacobsen Inter.	189.0	229.2	255.4	280.3	318.4		

The task light market was divided into two standard categories: Consumer and Professional/Industrial task lighting. Consumer task lighting for private homes, was of little interest to Luxo, due to low prices and low margins. The exception was the high-priced design lighting from Luxo Italiana.

Of more interest to Luxo was Professional/Industrial task lighting for the work environment – for modern offices and industrial workplaces, particularly computer workstations, which required better quality ergonomic lighting.

In the modern office market segment, Ledu and Waldmann were the major competitors for ergonomic task lighting. In the interior design (task lighting) area, Luxo competed with Italian companies like Artimede, Targetti, PAF and Iguzzini. Most of the competitors had narrow geographical penetration of their product lines with large market share within their defined market segments.

In the indirect lighting systems area, Luxo competed with Ledu, Fagerhults, Concorde and Waldmann, in the tube systems area with Siemens, Philips, Staff, Erco and Hoffmeister. The Luxo introduction of the 'Cornice' and a new range of uplighters was designed to place Jac Jacobsen in a better position against these competitors. In this project market, competitive price and ability to fill technical specifications were of crucial importance.

In the 'industrial' market, Waldmann was the major competitor. Much of the strategy developed in the industrial area was designed to allow Jac Jacobsen to enter the market against Waldmann.

The 'medical' market was quite diffused; however, the dominant players were Hanau, Verre et Quartz, Dr. Mach and Fagerhults. *(Refer to* **Exhibit 6** *for a product/mix trend analysis.)*

In the 'medium to low price' market, Luxo competed with companies like Ledu, Lival, Massive and Fase. Lival had moved away from producing inexpensive task lighting towards a more comprehensive range including spot and track lighting. Both Massive and Fase had a wide range of products suitable for consumer segments. The latter two dominated the lower end category and had a firm grip in the department store market. There were also a number of smaller producers who sold primarily to department stores. Luxo's strategy was to de-emphasize this end of the market. However, the less costly products were the largest product group, in terms of volume, and provided products to use against competitors.

Research & Development

Jac Jacobsen saw a future in 'well-designed functional lighting'. To that end, it devoted 5–7% of the ex-factory budget to research and development, emphasizing electronic assembly and new products in the medical, office and industrial segments. Although R&D was originally focused totally in Norway, over time some research was delegated to the US and Italy. R&D in the recently acquired Ledu was to be coordinated to some extent with R&D in Luxo. Continual knowledge transfer amongst all divisions was a priority, although this was a difficult process because electrical standards differed from one country to another. 1992 was seen as a positive development in facilitating technical exchanges among divisions.

Jac Jacobsen's marketing strategy called for the development of new quality concepts in lighting and achieving a sustainable competitive advantage in the industry. In order to reach these objectives, R&D had to be strengthened and resources committed to assure success in the

Exhibit 6   *Jac Jacobsen International: business plan 1991–93, executive summary*

Chapter 2

GROWTH STRATEGIES 1991–93 / MAJOR PRODUCTS
FOR JAC JACOBSEN INTERNATIONAL CONSOLIDATED

PRODUCT-MIX TREND

Even if the product-mix varies greatly from market to market, we still have our *'LUXO-brand' product line* concentrated on two different product lines from our factories in Norway and Italy, with different product-mix concepts:

A.   *Luxo product-mix from Norway (units)*
     show the following sales trend from our Luxo sales companies (in total units):

Product Group	E–90	B–91	B–91	B–93	Growth % 93/90
Asy-lamps	91,400	98,000	107,800	116,800	+28
Magnifiers	49,600	52,600	56,200	60,200	+21
Industry	21,000	21,000	21,500	21,500	–
Medical	4,800	7,400	8,200	10,000	+107
Total Norway	166,800	179,000	193,700	208,000	+25

We plan a careful 'real' growth average of 25% in units for all products from Norway, including the stagnation of the old lamp FL–101, now classified as 'industrial product'.

B.   *Luxo product-mix from Italy (units)*

Product Group	E–90	B–91	B–91	B–93	Growth % 93/90
Economy lamps (incandescent)	222,000	215,200	222,500	230,900	+4
Economy (FL)/ T–80 / T–88	91,600	90,600	97,300	104,900	+15
Design lamps	19,200	21,500	23,600	24,800	+30
Total Lamps	333,000	327,300	343,400	360,600	+8
Total Systems (Via Lattea + Cornice)	17,400	23,200	26,600	28,900	+66
C. Uplighters from Italy and Norway	1,700	5,300	7,000	8,500	+408

development of new products. Additionally, R&D would concentrate on unique product development and bringing new products to market before the competition. Thus, it was critical to shorten the new product approval process in order to enter the market in a timely fashion.

To shorten the time frame between development and the market, Jac Jacobsen needed to reevaluate its production process. If the firm wanted to serve more than 10 different markets with 'international' or 'global' products, whether produced in Norway or Italy, restructuring was necessary. However, the factory in Norway continued to develop Scandinavian models based on ergonomic/asymmetric lighting technology and functional lighting needs, while the factory in Italy maintained development of high quality design products, basically for the Italian market. The production of 'global' products required that each factory make a more thorough evaluation of the demand for each type of lighting and have a greater sensitivity to the needs of the international marketplace. In order to meet the time factor demands of entering the market quickly, better market analysis communication in the early stages of development had to be achieved. In addition, the market research had to extend beyond the sales organizations and deeper into the markets in cooperation with the Luxo sales companies. To facilitate this process, an Italian-speaking engineer was hired for the R&D department in Norway and more funds were allocated for hiring outside competence when needed. A lighting expert, whose tasks were to educate the sales personnel and agents in general lighting concepts, and to increase technical information about lighting throughout the companies was also added to the staff.

Using outside designers was an accepted practice in Italy, coordinated by Luxo, Italiana. The Italian designs were highly innovative and consistently won a number of design awards, elevating Luxo's image.

Acquisition of Ledu

Ledu and Jac Jacobsen's history went back a long way. Not only had Ledu and Luxo been major competitors for 40 years, but the founder of Ledu had also previously been a general manager for Luxo's Swedish subsidiary. Although the European strategy was one of organic growth, Jac Jacobsen was very interested when Ledu became a potential acquisition candidate. It was felt that the JJI Group would be more strongly positioned in the international market segments of task lighting with a combined Ledu-Luxo ownership.

As perceived by Jac Jacobsen, Ledu's strengths were in its aggressive marketing and organizational flexibility. In 1990 Ledu's turnover was 148 million Norwegian krona. The company had a history of adjusting quickly to changing market conditions and was very strong in the French market where Luxo had limited presence. Moreover, Ledu had a firm hold on the residential lighting market and was believed to have a number of new products in the 'pipeline'. The R&D budget had been used innovatively and well to develop competitive lighting products in a variety of product lines. Ledu's weakness was seen as its sales and volume focus, at the expense of a profit orientation.

In September 1989, Mr. Hasse Larsson, Managing Director of Ledu International AB, initiated informal contact with Jac Jacobsen Industries, Inc. USA to explore the possibility of close collaboration between the two North American companies. Both companies had experienced a drop in US and Canadian profitability due to increased competition with small Far Eastern importers, and Ledu felt that its North American position would be enhanced by an alliance with Luxo. As the discussions progressed, the possibility of a worldwide merger between Jac Jacobsen and Ledu became realistic. Negotiations between the CEOs of the two companies were described as simple, open, honest and uncomplicated, thus providing a good starting point for future growth.

The purchase of Ledu was accomplished through a direct issue of shares to Saksinvest, an investment company which owned Ledu. Saksinvest retained a 15% share of Jac Jacobsen Industrier A/S, and one person from Saksinvest joined the board of Jac Jacobsen Industries. *(Refer to **Exhibit 7** for the Ledu International Group balance sheet.)*

Exhibit 7   *Ledu International Group: balance sheet (in Swedish krona)*

	Lin	Kong
Assets		
Cash and bank		3177
Acc. receivables, group		0
Acc. receivables, ext.		24395
Prep. costs and accr. inc.		1915
Tax receivables		0
Other short-t rec group		0
Other short-t rec ext		2064
Inventories		28790
Total current assets		60342
Blocked acc Swe c. bank		30
Shares in subsidiaries		0
Other shares		0
Long term rec grp		0
Long term rec ext		497
Brands, pat., leasehold		1
Development costs		1277
Goodwill		700
Machinery and equip.		4035
Buildings		0
Land and land improv.		0
Total fixed assets		6539
Total assets		66881

Ledu's Sales Organization

Ledu's sales organization was heavily dependent on distributors, while Luxo worked predominantly with salaried sales people. Ledu used distributors in 10 countries, with company sales teams only in Canada, Germany, Sweden, the UK and the US. *(Refer to **Exhibit 8** for details of the sales organization.)* The sales teams often sold through office supply buying groups or through wholesalers and catalogue houses. As the wholesalers and buying groups became multinational, Ledu was able to supply them from many locations throughout Europe. However, the role of distributors and sales teams was changing as the buying groups became more sophisticated. As an example, five years earlier, Germany had been served by one sales manager and 12 independent manufacturers' representatives, whereas currently the same structure was augmented by 15 salespeople to call on individual members of the buying group.

Exhibit 8 *Ledu's sales force*

Country	Organization
Australia	Distributor
Austria	Distributor
Belgium	Distributor
Canada	Represented by Luxo Canada
Denmark	Distributor
Finland	Distributor
France	Distributor
Germany	Own sales company 1 managing director, 1 sales manager, 2 customer service plus 15 agents
Holland	Distributor
Norway	Distributor
Spain	Distributor
Sweden	Own sales company 1 managing director, 4 salesmen, 2 customer service
Switzerland	Distributor
United Kingdom	Own sales company 1 managing director, 1 customer service
USA	Own sales company (JJI) 1 managing director, 1 sales manager, 2 customer service and a lot of reps.

Price compatibility among countries was also of concern as 1992 approached. Price variations of more than 5% created problems for the sales teams of both Luxo and Ledu, and was an issue which needed to be addressed quickly.

Ledu's Market

In the 1970s, Ledu's market focus had been in low- to medium-priced residential products. Survival required expansion beyond this market niche. Thus, beginning in the mid-1980s, Ledu gradually expanded into the mid-range industrial and office segments of lighting products. This expansion was later to create problems for Jac Jacobsen in that both companies were in similar channels of distribution with similar product ranges. In other areas, the companies were complimentary to each other. Ledu was strong in merchandising and in penetrating different markets from those of Luxo – such as warehouse clubs. Moreover, Ledu was strong in Southern Europe – particularly France – where fashion orientation was important, while Luxo was strong in Northern Europe – primarily in Scandinavia – where ergonomic lighting was important. *(Refer to **Exhibit 9** for the Ledu International Group sales.)* Many of Ledu's products were successfully manufactured in the Far East, whereas Luxo had had little positive experience in this region.

Exhibit 9   Ledu International Group: sales, 1989

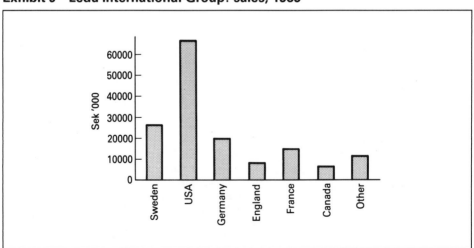

Ledu's Reaction to the Purchase

The initial discussions centered around a merger between the North American companies of Ledu and Luxo, a strategy which received the full support and enthusiasm of Ledu management. However, as the discussions expanded to focus on a worldwide merger, many Ledu executives experienced less positive feelings toward a Ledu acquisition by Jac Jacobsen Industries. There was concern that a worldwide merger would weaken Ledu's market position and that JJI management, which was unknown to Ledu's staff, would impose different work standards from the current ones.

As seen by Ledu, JJI's strengths were its well-developed product range in high end lighting and its strong management continuity. Unlike Ledu, which had experienced a succession of management changes over the years, JJI's weakness was perceived to be its inability to move quickly. Although not a major disadvantage previously, as the industry became more fashion oriented, an inability to move could quickly hamper market entry and penetration.

The strengths that Ledu would bring to JJI included a number of new, fashion-oriented products which were already in the 'pipeline' and the ability to move quickly through the new product development phase. Ledu's negatives included its lack of both profitability and management continuity. The strengths and weaknesses of both companies appeared to fit well together. Jac Jacobsen Industries could provide a secure financial position, a well-managed organization and knowledge of the lighting industry, while Ledu could bring quicker access to new products and markets.

———————

Alv Karlsen was pleased about the purchase of Ledu and the way it had been accomplished. He and Lars Harlem exchanged glances as they waited for suggestions from their managers.

Grampro B.V.

This case was prepared by Research Associate Bethann Kassman under the supervision of Professor Per V. Jenster as a basis for class discussion rather than to illustrate either effective or ineffective handling of a business situation.

On July 14, 1992, Mr. Dolf Zantinge, Managing Director of GRAMPRO B.V., a Dutch value added reseller of IBM equipment and tailored software applications, was discussing his business with a visitor as they were crossing the square in the small town of Houten in the Netherlands.

> We have grown into a highly sought after software development and systems integration firm over the past few years. Currently, we are working on several smaller assignments as well as four large projects, each of which could ruin the company if something went wrong. To amplify the nature of our dilemma, one large client approached me this week and asked if I personally could take the lead role in a 500-man-year project. Although it is flattering for our firm to be approached instead of much larger competitors, my role is to be the managing director of this firm, not a project manager, despite the size and desirability of this project. Therefore, our key task is to establish where and how our firm should grow, otherwise the commercial wind will take us in unforeseen directions and into dangerous waters.

The Solutions Business

In recent years, the computer industry had moved away from merely selling hardware ('boxes' in industry slang) with applied software, to selling solutions by integrating software, installation services, training, support and hardware.

Mainframe hardware tasks were being downsized to take advantage of cost efficiencies as well as to have the greater flexibility possible when larger hardware was combined with smaller cluster PCs and minicomputers. Because of increased pressures from traditional vendors, and new challenges from consulting firms and systems integration houses, the computer companies were eager to influence the customer's choice in hardware, software and services provided whenever an information technology solution was purchased. The ability to integrate information technologies within a business context was, therefore, the overriding concept pushing solution selling. As a result, the services market – with its emphasis on systems integration – was viewed as the most dynamic segment of the industry. The services component included understanding the business or engineering problem, conceptual formulation and translation of the problem into technical specifications, articulation of project components and team participants, project management, analysis, installation, maintenance, education, training and value added network services.

The systems integration market was a high growth, high risk environment which encompassed a great deal of complexity and uncertainty. The major systems delivery options became increasingly specialized as they moved towards total integrated solutions *(refer to Exhibit 1)*. At the same time, many companies were faced with fixing or replacing *ad hoc* and independent systems on aging mainframe computers. As the mainframes were downsized, eliminated or linked to smaller cluster computers, opportunities arose for any company with the flexibility to redesign system infrastructures and develop the complex applications required by the smaller machines. Serious players in the computer industry saw a need to integrate heterogeneous hardware configurations, develop customized products, manage subcontractors, budget and price correctly, oversee large projects, maintain unique systems and function in a non-information technological environment. They had to have the ability to take total responsibility for the business solution and its attendant risks.

All the large computer companies were either in or entering the solutions business. However, it was the newer systems houses that were forging ahead with advanced technology, techniques and powerful computer languages. The competition among the systems houses was becoming intense as the larger computer companies in Europe and the US – hindered by size, culture and bureaucracy – hurried to develop long-term relationships with the more innovative systems houses.

GRAMPRO's Role in the Industry

From its inception, GRAMPRO focused on providing technical solutions for

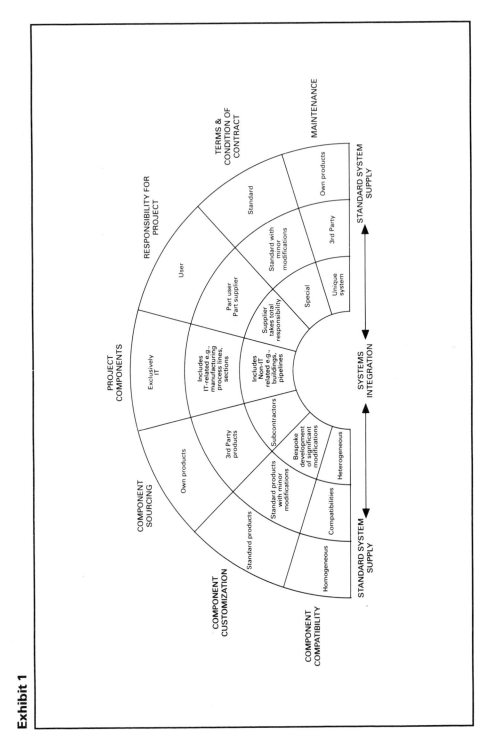

Exhibit 1

solving IT problems. The company was technically driven and was known in the Dutch market for its skills in systems integration and graphic environments, the development of specialized software and the application of knowledge engineering.

GRAMPRO operated at the intersection of a number of growth markets: the UNIX software application market, the market for relational-database management systems, and the market for knowledge-based systems. As such, it was a specialized market and a niche segment which satisfied needs for highly technical solution applications.

> UNIX was an operating system which, although used primarily in the scientific arena, was becoming more suitable for applied professional applications and office automation. The IBM RISC System/6000 used the UNIX system and IBM, interested in selling its RISC system, provided a market for UNIX.
>
> Relational databases provided the ability to process large amounts of data quickly, leaving the data easy to access by a variety of users. Flexible and transferable software that met high quality requirements was made possible through the use of a relational database. Most hardware suppliers were offering relational databases within their operating systems, providing an extra stimulus for their use and enhancing market growth.
>
> Knowledge-based engineering provided added value to the knowledge stored in a database by linking expert systems to existing applications. GRAMPRO designed and implemented complex databases and knowledge systems that were based on advanced knowledge engineering. Using this approach, rational decisions could be made by the computer.

By making the integration of these three areas the company's primary focus, GRAMPRO filled a gap in the technical, tool-oriented segment of the market. Selling itself on technical strengths rather than knowledge of specific businesses or industries, GRAMPRO used current technical assignments to become more user/application driven. Unlike other Dutch companies that sold only rule-based reasoning, GRAMPRO sold systems integration which built bridges between different technologies. *(Refer to Exhibit 2.)* Company equity was built through the continual acquisition of knowledge, investing in know-how and leveraging knowledge from past projects.

However, the market segment in which GRAMPRO operated was changing. In the technical area, new techniques were constantly being used to solve old problems and companies were hiring technical expertise to perform these solutions in-house. This left much of the increasingly complex solutions to companies like GRAMPRO. Additionally, the major main-frame manufacturers were developing hardware that incorporated a RISC system, and many were using a UNIX environment and knowledge-based

Exhibit 2

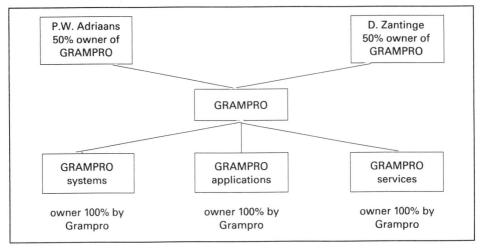

systems. The market challenges made it imperative for GRAMPRO to position itself for continued growth while maintaining its creative skills.

Background of the Company

GRAMPRO was started in January 1990 when Data Corp. merged with Software Intermediate. Data Corp., the holding company, had a turnover of G300 million and was the largest distributor of IBM hardware in Holland. The Data Corp., a division located in Utrecht, that specialized in the development of custom-made systems, was a primary competency center within the company, and was responsible for training and consulting on the software systems developed.

Software Intermediate was a small firm specializing in artificial intelligence and logic programming. Having a close contractual relationship with Data Corp. enabled it to provide expertise in the development of knowledge-based technology and draft technologies for relational systems as well as training. In 1989, two events occurred which influenced the formation of GRAMPRO: Data Corp. was taken over by National Systems Inc., a large PS2 dealer, and the software development, training and value added projects of Data Corp. and Software Intermediate were merged. Shortly thereafter, National Systems, Inc., wanting to concentrate on its core commercial activities in microcomputer sales, chose to withdraw from software development and value added projects. Dolf Zantinge, Manager of Data

Corp., and Pieter Adriaans, Manager of Software Intermediate, approached National Systems, Inc. with the idea of forming a separate company to manage the projects which National Systems, Inc. wished to relinquish. National Systems, Inc. Management agreed and, in late 1989, GRAMPRO was created by these two managers. However, National Systems, Inc. continued to provide a supportive environment for GRAMPRO.

In addition to assuming the risks associated with initial projects, National Systems, Inc. also provided GRAMPRO with space and infrastructure. This arrangement was advantageous to both companies. National Systems, Inc. was able to make the transition to its core hardware business, while assuring its customers that their software and service needs would be accommodated. GRAMPRO, meanwhile, was assured of having resources and guarantees during its start-up phase.

Organizational Structure

The ownership of GRAMPRO was limited to the two partners, Mr. Adriaans and Mr. Zantinge. The Board of the company was comprised of the two partners and an unofficial advisor. To reduce risk, all parts of the company were separately incorporated. *(Refer to Exhibit 3.)* A team of highly skilled specialists formed the core of the company. There were approximately 20 people being employed by mid-1992. The company was divided into three units which, although not operating independently, provided the basis for the scope of the services/products offered by GRAMPRO.

GRAMPRO Systems housed the hardware and standard applications division. As a value added remarketer of the IBM RISC System/6000, this division focused on selling the IBM RISC/6000 system, with its accompanying hardware primarily being used to provide solutions for specific problems. The RISC/6000 system was a UNIX system which could be used as a workstation as well as a heavy database. The hardware was used in conjunction with rational database systems and knowledge-based technology.

GRAMPRO Applications consisted of application development, the research department and project management. These areas concentrated on selling and supporting the products of third parties, along with selling IBM's computer language called Prolog, and developing standard applications. Designing standard applications was of strategic importance to the company. The applications had to use knowledge-based technology and/or relational databases, and they had to be within the scope of the hardware concept offered by GRAMPRO. The department also provided support for the software products sold.

Exhibit 3

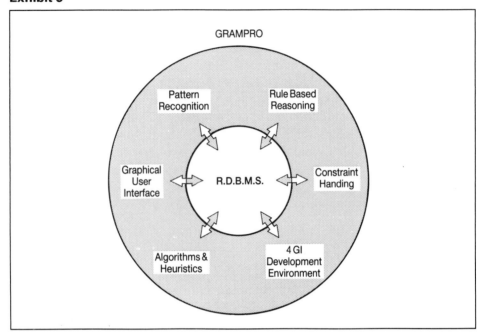

The Services division covered the areas of consulting and training. Consulting services were offered in drafting, and in developing relational and knowledge-based systems. Training courses were provided in cooperation with various organizations as well as entirely by GRAMPRO, and were directed to the areas of artificial intelligence, systems analysis, Prolog, UNIX, Oracle, etc.

The three operating divisions were formed to provide as much expertise as possible within the areas of the GRAMPRO organization. However, in practice, there was little distinction among the divisions, and staff members could operate freely throughout the overall environment of the company.

GRAMPRO's Relationship with IBM

GRAMPRO and IBM had a longstanding and complex relationship centered around the RISC System/6000, UNIX and Prolog. IBM needed professionals to support the IBM RISC System/6000 with software, value added resources and UNIX knowledge. GRAMPRO met that need and enhanced it when the company hired a UNIX expert. In addition, IBM was working intensively to develop applications for its knowledge-based technology. The language that IBM developed for use in the UNIX/RISC environment was called Prolog. GRAMPRO provided the support and training necessary to market this product.

While the initial relationships between GRAMPRO and IBM were being formalized, GRAMPRO was also attempting to determine the type of company it wished to become. There were three models being considered by management:

1. Being a dealer in hardware, which would provide limited added value;
2. Being consultants in technical applications in a largely industry/ business environment; or
3. Being a systems house which specialized in turnkey projects, developing software, selling specialized hardware and providing training.

Both Mr. Adriaans and Mr. Zantinge were interested in selling solutions and developing software, thus the idea of becoming a systems house that specialized in technical, turnkey projects appealed to both of them. They also favored the proposition of depending exclusively on IBM's UNIX version. Since GRAMPRO did not have a marketing or sales staff, it was felt that the firm needed IBM to help the company obtain projects. In addition, IBM allowed GRAMPRO to use its equipment for half a year. IBM offset the cost of advertising when GRAMPRO used the IBM logo in its ads, and provided access to IBM sales staff through seminars and training sessions. In return, GRAMPRO invested in new software development appropriate for the IBM environment, hired experts in Prolog and developed technical manuals for use with IBM and its customers. Under a separate agreement, GRAMPRO also became an official reseller of IBM equipment, an official PC dealer, a subcontractor for IBM on integration projects, the only authorized seller in Holland for Prolog as well as a provider of training and development courses, inside and outside IBM.

Grampro's Orientation and Philosophy

GRAMPRO embodied a philosophy which, although unique in certain areas, was much like that of other small systems houses established in Western Europe and America. As Mr. Zantinge stated, 'The company needs a few very bright people who play a strategic role.' To encourage this type of person to work at GRAMPRO, the company developed a casual, but dedicated, work environment that was augmented by a heavily technical culture. Like other technical systems houses, the management philosophy and style relied on a flat structure with no hierarchy and low overhead. Both partners were members of the team, and the team approach was emphasized. Value was placed on providing personal services to customers and much time was dedicated to maintaining informal relationships. Many customers were connected to the company by modems, and staff members were available by beeper to provide help during customer emergencies. A large part of a salesman's time was spent developing and maintaining an informal relationship with the varying levels of IBM staff who interacted with GRAMPRO staff or used GRAMPRO products.

The highly technical orientation provided the cultural background for the company. Keeping abreast of the newest developments in the scientific and technical fields was encouraged and, at least yearly, Mr. Adriaans presented a forward-looking paper at an academic seminar. GRAMPRO also had close ties with various universities in Holland, and the company sought out and interacted with professors and students pursuing new areas in relational databases and knowledge-based technologies. A few members of the staff came from academia and were experts in their fields of knowledge. In this setting, the greatest challenge was to provide openings for lower level staff to contribute positively to the growth of the company.

Financial Philosophy

The company's financial philosophy was unique in an age that was oriented towards accumulating stocks and assets. GRAMPRO issued no stock and had no plans to do so. The overall financial philosophy was to value only the true assets of the company, i.e., those ideas which could be converted to cash in a reasonable period of time. Thus, the working capital was not shown on any balance sheet; all depreciation was taken immediately and assets were purposely kept low. Fixed assets were leased to provide as much working capital as possible. *(Refer to Exhibits 4, 5, and 6.)* Although the banking community looked askance at the company's financial statement, this philosophy enabled GRAMPRO to be very clear about its own financial situation.

Market Strategy

GRAMPRO's overall marketing goal was to become one of the three major

Exhibit 4

Total Profit Turnover	2.542.344,82
Total Purchase	1.693.503,20
Operating Costs	
Costs Third Parties	9.978,00
Personal Costs	530.316,71
Depreciation	43.339,71
Housing Costs	49.805,08
Office Costs	47.297,33
Motor Costs	30.001,41
Consultancy and Auditor Costs	27.687,66
Sales Expenses	35.535,70
Interest and Financial Services	7.910,12
General Costs	53.066,15
Total Operating Costs	834.937,87
Special Fees and Commissions	−45.474,25
Nett Profit	59.378,00

Exhibit 5

Fixed Assets	
Immaterial fixed assets	5.833,33
Material fixed assets	219.064,46
Financial fixed assets	114.405,00
Total Fixed Assets	339.302,79
Liquid Assets	
Stocks	34.954,16
Debtors	387.875,96
Other claims	33.326,70
Cash	117.326,96
Total Liquid Assets	573.483,78
Equity	
Equity	−250.826,91
Provision	
Reservation	−52.000,00
Long Term Debts	
Long term debts	−173.511,32
Short Term Debts	
Creditors	−185.754,05
Taxes	−113.890,69
V.A.T.	−32.505,16
Misc. debts	−44.920,44
Total Short Term Debts	−377.070,34
Annual Balance	59.378,00

Exhibit 6

	1991	1990
Turnover	2.375	821
Cost Price	807	232
	1.568	589
Personal Costs	784	364
Depreciation	85	21
Other Expenses	422	181
Total Operating Costs	1.291	566
Trading Results	277	23
Financial profits and losses	−17	1
Tax	−98	−2
Nett Profit	162	22

scientific technical systems integration houses in Holland within the next four years. The company's short-term market strategy was based on increasing market share in the area of dedicated software applications in the field of knowledge-based systems and databases. To reach these objectives, an increasing volume of market share had to be attained yearly in order to control the market niche and prevent the competition from advancing up the learning curve.

GRAMPRO's strength was its ability to provide solutions across a variety of different technologies, something that most of its competitors were unable to do. Although there was strong competition within specific areas – such as graphical user interface, knowledge-based systems, relational databases, etc., competitors had not focused on forging links between areas. Thus, GRAMPRO held a fairly strong position in the marketplace.

Becoming known in the field was a necessary and important part of the overall marketing strategy. However, advertising had proven to be increasingly expensive, with unimpressive results. Therefore, Mr. Adriaans and Mr. Zantinge decided to limit all promotion to word of mouth, and to make an effort to expand their technical contacts to include administrative staff. In order to reach these objectives, they continued to give seminars, to increase their personal contacts, and to emphasize outstanding and thoughtful customer service. In addition, they also used a unique tactic. In the early stages of GRAMPRO's development, the partners had written a technical book which they subsequently used to enhance their credibility in the very competitive solutions environment. They later hired experts in highly technical areas who also published books about their specialties.

These books, although technical, provided an entrée to a number of companies by impressing the administrative people they wished to meet.

Risks Taken by GRAMPRO

From its inception, GRAMPRO displayed an amount of daring that was not only unusual, but also contributed very positively to its growth and position in the marketplace. The first risk taken by the partners was to approach National Systems, Inc. about taking over GRAMPRO's software applications and value added projects. Although this move could be viewed as – and was – a sequential step that benefitted both parties, GRAMPRO's resources at the time for carrying out projects were very limited in an area which demanded sophisticated tools. Having started out with a high degree of risk, GRAMPRO compounded it by undertaking subsequent projects with additional risk. Working on the edge of the known technical field for clients who expected projects completed within strict budget and time frames – and who tied renumeration and penalties to those conditions, kept GRAMPRO functioning at a very high level of tension.

The company continued to take high risks to enhance growth. In the technical areas where GRAMPRO operated, all projects offered a level of risk. In many instances, GRAMPRO mitigated the uncertain environment by hiring known experts from academic settings to cover strategic areas within the company. However, the projects the company sought in order to enhance its horizontal growth were increasingly complex and large. Each additional project required increasing levels of expertise and staff. In some ways, this situation was comparable to new companies that were rapidly expanding, but in GRAMPRO's case, the level of risk taken in each project was more intense because the company operated at the technical cutting edge of its environment and was constantly testing its limits. Being a technically driven company, still in the early stages of growth, with a dedicated and focused staff, enabled GRAMPRO to take risks which larger companies of a more mature nature would have found daunting. But, even GRAMPRO's days of risk taking were changing. As the company grew, projects were undertaken which required the partners to assume a greater percentage of personal financial guarantees to complete them. In the early stages of growth, risk taking was more acceptable because less was at stake. But, as the company became more mature, such risks had to be carefully weighed and the consequences analyzed more thoroughly.

Expanding the Project Base

By mid-1992, 70% of GRAMPRO's projects were originating from IBM customers or through IBM itself. Continued growth required a broadening of the applied application base of the company. To accomplish this goal, GRAMPRO actively tried to bid on new projects which utilized the knowledge acquired from past projects and which provided opportunities to expand into commercial environments where applications could be sold in duplicate or with minor changes. To that end, GRAMPRO bid on four large projects (described below). The common denominator of these four projects was to restructure the infrastructure of existing information systems and to downsize the computer hardware.

1. Blue Bird Airline had embarked on a restructuring effort to streamline its technical services organization and become more commercially driven. To accomplish this goal, Blue Bird Airline needed to develop an information system which merged its *ad hoc* and independent systems, while optimizing planning applications. The project involved 500 man years and, if awarded to GRAMPRO, required that GRAMPRO serve as the project manager as well as provide the technical experts. It was anticipated that the project would be awarded within the first two months of 1993.

2. International Airport was to undertake a very large expansion and modernization program in its quest to become the third largest airport in Europe by the turn of the century. International Airport intended to realize this growth by optimizing the operational systems and streamlining the passenger infrastructure. GRAMPRO's bid was to provide technical expertise for the project and to develop the optimization system. International Airport had proposed that GRAMPRO present a technical seminar to all potential project managers before the overall contract was awarded sometime in the fall of 1992. The project would comprise about 60 man years.

3. The Social Services department of the Netherlands was involved in decentralizing its hardware and rebuilding a system involving new applications as well as a new infrastructure. GRAMPRO was one of many companies bidding on this project, which in the fall of '92 was awarded to a competitor.

4. The Ministry of Education was interested in building an expert system for designing exams. GRAMPRO was the only bidder for this project; however, it was unclear whether the Ministry had the

resources necessary to begin the project. The project was to be awarded at the beginning of September 1992 and involved 6 man years.

Strategically, the Blue Bird Airline and International Airport projects were of great importance to GRAMPRO. Both projects gave GRAMPRO the opportunity to become technically responsible for a large publicly visible program. The award of any one of these four projects would stretch GRAMPRO's management capabilities, while receiving more than one project would require subcontracting the on-going assignments.

Options for Growth

As the company grew, some parts of the solutions industry became riskier. The projects were becoming very large and required personal financial guarantees. With large projects, there were long periods between payments, requiring financial creativity to fund the projects. Additional management expertise was needed to manage the different projects, and hiring project managers that fit into the company environment was a challenge. It was also becoming clear that maintaining the culture of the company and a creative team effort presented difficulties during a growth period.

Faced with these challenges, GRAMPRO realized that the changing financial status of the industry and GRAMPRO's own growth made it necessary to consider the advantages and disadvantages of seeking a joint venture or partner relationship.

Its options included the following:

1. Become a partner with a hardware vendor such as IBM or one of its competitors.
2. Stop selling hardware, where profitability was very limited (gross margins of 20%) and concentrate on systems applications only. This option allowed GRAMPRO to maintain its creative edge, but would probably force GRAMPRO to sever its relationship with IBM.
3. Establish a partnership/joint venture with IBM. This option was the most complex one available. With 70% of GRAMPRO's orders related to IBM, an ongoing relationship with IBM enabled GRAMPRO to continue its work in a rich learning environment. GRAMPRO would provide, in turn, the technical scientific environment that IBM needed to penetrate that aspect of the market, thus enabling IBM to have the flexibility necessary to

manage the new value added contracts that were becoming more prevalent in the industry. However, GRAMPRO was not totally comfortable with IBM's history regarding the management of new businesses. GRAMPRO was wary that it would lose its creative edge and control over projects. In addition, there was concern that GRAMPRO would be unable to maintain its personalized relationships with customers as well as its technical drive. Mr. Zantinge, aware that additional financial resources were needed for short and long-term growth, knew that he must seriously consider all the various options. He felt that IBM's history required that some ground rules be established before proceeding with any ongoing relationship.

GRAMPRO's success had resulted because of several factors: the high level of services provided and involvement with customers; the highly skilled creative staff; flat management and a talented staff who knew the industry both technically and commercially; the specialized management style of the partners which allowed staff to assume responsibility for their own work with little management oversight; and specialization as system integrators in turnkey projects – not to mention . . . a little bit of luck.

As the meeting with his visitor proceeded, Mr. Zantinge knew that he had only a limited time to decide the firm's future direction. Time was short. It meant that the analytical minds of his partner and himself would have to confront all the emotions they had invested . . . as well as a marketplace that would not wait.

Grasse Fragrances SA

This case was written by Professor Michael Hayes as a basis for class discussion rather than to illustrate either effective or ineffective handling of an administrative situation. All names, including the company name, have been disguised.

Grasse Fragrances, headquartered in Lyon, France, was the world's fourth largest producer of fragrances. Established in 1885, the company had grown from a small family-owned buiness, selling fragrances to local perfume manufacturers, to a multinational enterprise with subsidiaries and agents in over 100 countries.

For Marketing Director Jean-Pierre Volet, the last few years had been devoted to building a strong headquarters marketing organization. In February 1989, however, he was returning to France after an extensive tour of Grasse sales offices and factories, and a number of visits with key customers. As the Air France flight touched down in Lyon Airport, Jean-Pierre Volet was feeling very concerned about what he had learned on the trip. 'Our salesforce,' he thought, 'operates much as it did several years ago. If we're going to compete successfully in this new environment, we have to completely rethink our salesforce management practices.'

The Flavor and Fragrance Industry

Worldwide sales of essential oils, aroma chemicals, and fragrance and flavor compounds were estimated to be around $5.5 billion in 1988.

Five major firms accounted for something like 50 per cent of the industry's sales. The largest, International Flavors & Fragrances Inc. of New York, had 1988 sales of $839.5 million (up 76 per cent from 1984), of which fragrances accounted for 62 per cent. The company had plants in 21 countries, and non-US operations represented 70 per cent of sales and 78 per cent of operating profit.

Quest International, a wholly owned subsidiary of Unilever, was next in size with sales estimated at $700 million, closely followed by the Givaudan Group, a wholly-owned subsidiary of Hoffman-La Roche with sales of $536 million, and Grasse Fragrances with sales of $450 million. Firmenich, a closely held Swiss family firm, did not disclose results but 1987 sales were estimated at some $300 million.

Grasse produced only fragrances. Most major firms in the industry, however, produced both fragrances and flavors (i.e., flavor extracts and compounds mainly used in foods, beverages and pharmaceutical products). Generally, the products were similar. The major difference was that the flavorist had to match his or her creations with their natural counterparts, such as fruits, meats, or spices, as closely as possible. On the other hand, the perfumer had the flexibility to use his or her imagination to create new fragrances. Perfumery was closely associated with fashion, encompassed a wide variety of choice, and products had to be dermatologically safe. Development of flavors was more limited, and products were required to meet strict toxicological criteria because the products were ingested.

Markets for Fragrances

While the use of perfumes is as old as history, it was not until the 19th century, when major advances were made in organic chemistry, that the fragrance industry emerged as it is known today. Focusing first on perfumes, use of fragrances expanded into other applications. In recent years manufacturers of soap, detergents and other household products have significantly increased their purchases of fragrances and have represented the largest single consumption category. Depending on the application, the chemical complexity of a particular fragrance and the quantity produced, prices could range from less than FF40 per kilogram to over FF4,000.[1]

Despite its apparent maturity, the world market for fragrances was estimated to have grown at an average of 5–6% during the early 1980s, and some estimates indicated that sales growth could increase even further during the last half of the decade. New applications supported these estimates. Microwave foods, for instance, needed additional flavorings to replicate familiar tastes that would take time to develop in a conventional oven. In laundry detergents, a significant fragrance market, the popularity of liquids provided a new stimulus to fragrance sales, as liquid detergents needed more fragrance than powders to achieve the desired aroma. Similarly, laundry detergents designed to remove odors as well as dirt also stimulated sales, as they used more fragrance by volume.

The New Buying Behavior

Over time, buying behavior for fragrances, as well as markets, had changed significantly. Responsibility for the selection and purchase of fragrances became complex, particularly in large firms. R&D groups were expected to ensure the compatibility of the fragrance with the product under consideration. Marketing groups were responsible for choosing a fragrance that gave the product a competitive edge in the marketplace, and purchasing groups had to obtain competitive prices and provide good deliveries.

Use of briefs (the industry term for a fragrance specification and request for quotation) became common. Typically, a brief would identify the general characteristics of the fragrance, the required cost parameters as well as an extensive description of the company's product and its intended strategy in the marketplace. Occasionally, a fragrance producer would be sole sourced, generally for proprietary reasons. Usually, however, the customer would ask for at least two quotations, so competitive quotes were the norm.

Grasse Fragrances SA

Background

The company was founded in 1885 by Louis Piccard, a chemist who had studied at the University of Paris. He believed that progress in the field of organic chemistry could be used to develop a new industry – creating perfumes, as opposed to relying on nature. Using a small factory on the Siagne River near Grasse, the company soon became a successful supplier of fragrances to the leading perfume houses of Paris. Despite the interruptions of World Wars I and II, the company followed an early policy of international growth and diversification. Production and sales units were first established in Paris, Rome and Madrid. In the 1920s, company headquarters were moved to Paris. At that time, the company entered the American market, first establishing a sales office and then a small manufacturing facility. Acquisitions were made in England, and subsequently the company established subsidiaries in Germany, Brazil, Argentina and Italy.

Faced with increased competition and large capital requirements for R&D, plant expansion and new product launches, the Piccard family decided to become a public company in 1968. Jacques Piccard, oldest son of the founder, was elected president and the family remained active in the management of the company. Assisted by the infusion of capital, Grasse was able to further expand its business activities in Europe, the United States, Latin America and the Far East.

In 1988 total sales were $450,000,000, up some 60% from 1984; 40% of sales came from Europe, 30% from North America, 10% from Latin America, 5% from Africa/Middle East and 15% from Asia/Pacific. In recent years the company's position had strengthened somewhat in North America.

By the end of 1988, the company had sales organizations or agents in 100 countries, laboratories in 18 countries, compounding facilities in 14 countries, chemical production centers in 3 countries and research centers in 2 countries. Employment was 2,500, of whom some 1,250 were employed outside France.

Products

In 1988, the company's main product lines were in two categories:

- Perfumery products used for perfumes, eau de cologne, eau de toilette, hair lotion, cosmetics, soaps, detergents, other household and industrial products.
- Synthetics for perfume compounds and cosmetic specialities.

According to Jacques Piccard:

> From the production side, flavors and fragrances are similar, although the creative and marketing approaches are quite different. So far we have elected to specialize in just fragrances, but I think it's just a matter of time before we decide to get into flavors.

Following industry practice, Grasse divided its fragrances into four categories:

- Fine Fragrances
- Toiletries and Cosmetics
- Soaps and Detergents
- Household and Industrial

Marketing at Grasse

In 1980, Jean-Pierre Volet was appointed Marketing Director, after a successful stint as country manager for the Benelux countries. At the time, the headquarters marketing organization was relatively small. Its primary role was to make sure the salesforce had information on the company's products, send out samples of new perfumes that were developed in the labs, usually with little customer input, and handle special price or delivery requests. As Volet recalled:

> In the 1940s, 1950s and 1960s, most of our business was in fine fragrances, toiletries and cosmetics. Our customers tended to be small and focused on local markets. Our fragrance salesman would carry a suitcase of 5 gram samples, call on the customer, get an idea of what kind of fragrance the customer wanted and either leave a few samples for evaluation or actually write an order on the spot. It was a very personal kind of business. Buying decisions tended to be based on subjective impressions and the nature of the customer's relation with the salesman. Our headquarters marketing organization was designed to support that kind of selling and buying. Today, however, we deal with large multinational companies who are standardizing their products across countries, and even regions, and who are using very sophisticated marketing techniques to guide their use of fragrances. Detergents and other household products represent an increasing share of the market. When I came to headquarters, one of my important priorities was to structure a marketing organization which reflected this new environment.

*(The marketing organization in 1988 is shown in **Exhibit 1**.)* In addition to the normal administrative activities such as field sales support, pricing and budgeting, Volet had built a fragrance creation group and a product management group. More recently, he had established an international account management group.

The fragrance creation group served as a bridge between the basic lab work and customer requirements. It also ran the company's fragrance training center, used to train both its own salesforce and customer personnel in the application of fragrances. The product management group was organized in the four product categories. Product managers were expected to be knowledgeable about everything that was going on in their product category worldwide and to use their specialized knowledge to support field sales efforts as well as guide the creative people. It was Volet's plan that international account managers would coordinate sales efforts.

Field sales in France reported to Piccard through Raoul Salmon, who was also responsible for the activities of the company's agents, used in countries where it did not have subsidiaries or branches. In recent years, use of agents had declined, and the company expected the decline to continue.

Outside France, field sales were the responsibility of Grasse country managers. In smaller countries, country managers handled only sales, thus operating essentially as field sales managers. In other countries, where the

Exhibit 1   *Grasse Fragrances SA: partial organization chart*

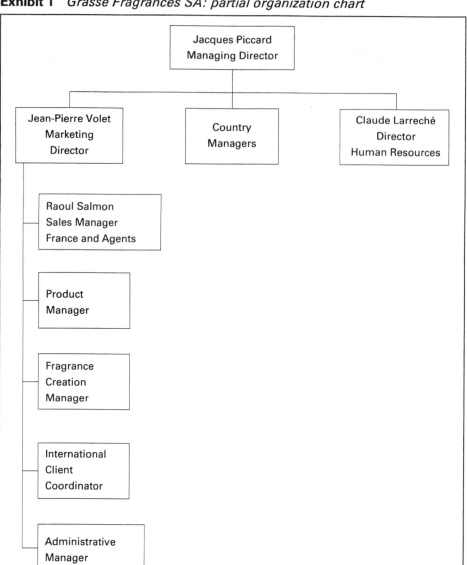

company had manufacturing or other non-selling operations, the norm was to have a field sales manager reporting to the country manager.

The company relied extensively on its field salesforce for promotional efforts, customer relations and order getting activities. There were, however, two very different kinds of selling situations. As Salmon described them:

There are still many customers, generally small-scale, who buy in the traditional way where the process is fairly simple. One salesperson is responsible for calling on all buying influencers in the customer's organization. Decisions tend to be based on subjective factors, and the sales representative's personal relations with the customer are critically important.

The other situation, which is growing, involves large and increasingly international customers. Not only do we see that people in R&D and marketing as well as in purchasing can influence the purchase decision, but these influencers may also be located in a number of different countries.

In either case, once the decision had been made to purchase a Grasse fragrance, the firm could generally count on repeat business, as long as the customer's product was successful in the marketplace.

On occasion, however, purchase decisions were revised, particularly if Grasse raised prices or if the customer's product came under strong competitive price pressure, thus requiring that a less expensive fragrance be considered.

The Quotation Procedure

For small orders, the quotation procedure was relatively simple. Popular fragrances had established prices in every country, and the salesforce was expected to sell at these prices.[2] In some instances, price concessions were made, but they required management approval and were discouraged.

For large orders, it was the norm to develop a new fragrance. Increasingly, customers would provide Grasse with extensive information on their intended product and its marketing strategy, including the country or countries where the product would be sold. To make sure the fragrance fit the customer's intended marketing and product strategy, Grasse was expected to do market research in a designated pilot country on several fragrances, sometimes combined with samples of the customer's product. According to Volet:

> Once we have found or developed what we think is the best fragrance, we submit our quotation. Then the customer will do his own market research, testing his product with our fragrance and with those of our competitors. Depending on the outcome of the market research, we may get the order at a price premium. Alternatively, we may lose it, even if we are the low bidder. If, on the other hand, the results of the market research indicate that no fragrance supplier has an edge then price, personal relationships or other factors will influence the award.

Because of the extensive requirements for development and testing, headquarters in Grasse was always involved in putting a quotation together, and close coordination was vital between headquarters and the branch or subsidiary. When buying influencers were located in more than one country, additional coordination of the sales effort was required to ensure that information obtained from the customer was shared and also to have a coherent account strategy.

Coordination of pricing was also growing in importance. Many large customers manufactured their products in more than one country and looked for a 'world' price rather than a country price. In these situations, country organizations were expected to take a corporate view of profits, sometimes at the expense of their own profit statements. The lead country (i.e., the country in which the purchasing decision would be made) had final responsibility for establishing the price. Increasingly, however, this price had to be approved in Paris.

Submitting quotations in this environment was both complex and expensive. According to Volet:

> Receiving a brief from a customer starts a complex process. We immediately alert all our salespeople who call on various purchasing influencers. Even though the brief contains lots of information on what the customer wants, we expect our sales people to provide us with some additional information.
>
> The next step is for our creative people to develop one or more fragrances which we believe will meet the customer's requirements. They are aided in this effort by our product managers who know what is going on with their products worldwide. If additional information is needed from the customer, our international account people will contact the appropriate sales people.
>
> After creating what we think is the right product or products, we may conduct our own market research in a country designated by the customer. This is usually done under the direction of our product manager, working closely with our market research people. Throughout this process, our salesforce is expected to stay in close touch with the customer to give us any changes in his thinking or any competitive feedback. Based on the results of this effort, we then submit our proposal which gives the customer the price, samples and as much product information as possible.
>
> With some customers, there is little further sales effort after they receive our quotation, and the buying decision is made 'behind closed doors'. In other instances, we may be asked to explain the results of our research or to discuss possible modifications in our product and, sometimes, in our price. Frequently we find that the customer is more concerned with our price policy (i.e., how firm the price is and for how long) than with the price quoted at the time of the brief.
>
> When you make this kind of effort, you obviously hate to lose the order. On the other hand, even if we lose, the investment made in development work and market research is likely to pay off in winning another brief, either with the original customer or with another customer.

International Accounts

In 1988 about 50 per cent of the firm's business came from some 40 international accounts. Looking to the future, it was expected that the number of international accounts would grow, and some estimated that by 1994 as much as 80 per cent of the firm's business would come from international accounts.

As of 1988, 18–20 international accounts were targeted for coordination by International Clients Coordinators (ICCs) in Paris. The principal responsibility of each ICC was to really know assigned customers on a worldwide basis and put that knowledge to use in coordinating work on a brief. The rest were followed in Paris, but coordination was a subsidiary responsibility. In either case, it was the view at headquarters that coordination was critical. As Volet described it:

> We rely extensively on account teams. European teams may meet as often as once a quarter. Worldwide teams are more likely to meet annually. For designated accounts, the ICC takes the lead role in organizing the meeting and, generally, coordinating sales efforts. For others, the Parent Client Executive (the sales representative in the country selling the customer component with the greatest buying influence) plays the lead role. In these situations, we hold the Parent Client Executive responsible for all the ICC's daily coordinating work with the customer. We also expect him to be proactive and already working on the next brief long before we get a formal request.
>
> Here in Paris, we prepare extensive worldwide 'bibles' on international accounts which are made available to all members of the team. We also prepare quarterly project reports for team members. Our next step will be to computerize as much of this as possible.

Sales Management Practices

In 1988, salesforce management practices were not standardized. Selection, compensation, training, organization, etc. were the responsibility of subsidiary management. Even so, a number of practices were similar.

Sales representatives tended to be compensated by a salary and bonus scheme. A typical minimum bonus was 1.5 month's salary, but could range up to 2.5 month's salary for excellent performance. The exact amount of the bonus was discretionary with sales management and could reward a number of factors.

Sales budgets were established from estimates made by sales representatives for direct orders (i.e., orders that would be placed by their assigned accounts). These estimates were developed from expectations of sales volume for fragrances currently being used by customers, in which case historical sales were the major basis for the estimate, and from estimates of sales of new fragrances. While historical sales of currently used fragrances were useful in predicting future sales, variations could occur. Sales activity of the customer's product was not totally predictable. In some instances, customers reopened a brief to competition, particularly where the customer was experiencing competitive cost pressures.

Predicting sales of new fragrances was even more difficult. Customers' plans were uncertain, and the nature of the buying process made it difficult to predict the odds of success on any given transaction. Grasse Fragrances, nevertheless, relied heavily on these estimates. The sum of the estimates was expected to add up to the company budget for the coming year. When this was not the case, sales managers were expected to review their estimates and adjust them appropriately.

The company had recently introduced, company-wide, its own version of management by objectives. Each sales representative was expected to develop a personal set of objectives for negotiation with his or her sales manager. Formal account planning, however, had not been established, although some subsidiaries were starting the practice.

Sales training had two components. Product knowledge tended to be the responsibility of headquarters, relying heavily on the fragrance training center. Selling skills, however, were principally the responsibility of the subsidiary companies.

Selection practices were the most variable. Some subsidiaries believed that company and product knowledge were key to selling success and so tended to look inside the company for individuals who had the requisite company and product knowledge and who expressed an interest in sales work. Others believed that demonstrated selling skills were key and so looked outside the company for individuals with good selling track records, preferably in related industries.

Sales Management Issues

A number of sale management practices were of concern, both in head-quarters and in the subsidiaries.

Influence Selling

Ensuring appropriate effort on all buying influencers was a major concern. According to Salmon:

Our sales representatives understand the importance of influence selling, but we have no formal way of recognizing their efforts. A number of our large accounts, for instance, have their marketing groups located in Paris, and they have lots of influence on the buying decision. If we win the brief, however, purchasing is likely to take place in Germany or Spain or Holland, and my sale representative will not get any sales credit.

In a similar vein, Juan Rodriguez, sales manager for a group of countries in Latin America, commented:

We have a large account that does lots of manufacturing and purchasing in Latin America but does its R&D work in the US. The customer's people in Latin America tell us that without strong support from R&D in the US, it is very difficult for them to buy our fragrances. The sales representative in New York is certainly aware of this, but his boss is measured on profit, which can only come from direct sales in the US, so he's not enthusiastic about his sales representative spending a lot of time on influence business.

In some instances, the nature of the buying process resulted in windfalls for some sales representatives. Commenting on this aspect, Salmon observed:

It can work the other way as well. Our Spanish subsidiary recently received an order for 40 tons of a fragrance, but the customer's decision to buy was totally influenced by sales representatives in Germany and Paris. Needless to say, our Spanish subsidiary was delighted, but the people in Germany and Paris were concerned as to how their efforts would be recognized and rewarded.

While there was general recognition that influence selling was vital, it was not clear how it could be adequately measured and rewarded. As Salmon pointed out:

In some instances (e.g., the order in Spain) we're pretty sure about the amount of influence exerted by those calling on marketing and R&D. In other instances, it is not at all clear. We have some situations where the sales representative honestly believes that his calls on, say, R&D are important but, in fact, they are not. At least not in our opinion. If we come up with the wrong scheme to measure influence, we could end up with a lot of wasted time and effort.

Incentive Compensation

Compensation practices were a matter of some concern. The salary component was established at a level designed to be competitive with similar sales jobs in each country. Annual raises had become the norm, with amounts based on performance, longevity and changes in responsibility. The bonus component was determined by the immediate manager, but there was concern that bonuses had become automatic. Still further, some held the view that the difference between 1.5 and 2.5 times the monthly salary was not very motivating, even if bonus awards were more performance driven.

Whether merited or not, sales representatives expected some level of bonus, and there was concern that any change could cause morale problems. At the same time, there was growing recognition of the increasing importance of team selling.

Overall responsibility for compensation practices was assigned to Claude Larreché, Director of Human Resources. According to Larreché:

> Some of our sales managers are interested in significantly increasing the incentive component of salesforce compensation. It has been my view, however, that large incentive payments to the salesforce could cause problems in other parts of our organization. Plus, there seems to be considerable variation in country practice with regard to incentive compensation. In the US, for instance, compensation schemes which combine a fixed or salary component and an incentive component, usually determined by sales relative to a quota, are common. To a lesser degree, we see some of this in Europe, and somewhat more in the south, but I'm not sure that we want to do something just because a lot of other companies are doing it.
>
> We're also thinking about some kind of team incentive or bonus. But, this raises questions about who should be considered part of the team and how a team bonus should be allocated. Should the team be just the sales representatives, or should we include the ICCs? And what about the customer service people without whom we wouldn't have a base of good performance to build on?
>
> Allocation is even more complicated. We're talking about teams comprised of people all around the world. I think it is only natural that the local manager will think his sales representative made the biggest contribution, which could result in long arguments. One possibility would be for the team itself to allocate a bonus pool, but I'm not sure how comfortable managers would be with such an approach.

Small Accounts

Despite the sales growth expected from international accounts, sales to smaller national accounts were expected to remain a significant part of the firm's revenues and, generally, had very attractive margins. According to one country sales manager:

> With the emphasis on international accounts, I'm concerned about how we handle our smaller single country accounts. Many of them still buy the way

they did 10 and 20 years ago, although today we can select from over 30,000 fragrances. Our international accounts will probably generate 80% of our business in the years to come, but the 20% we get from our smaller accounts is important and produces excellent profits for the company. But I'm not sure that the kind of selling skills we need to handle international accounts are appropriate for the smaller accounts. Personal and long-term relationships are tremendously important to these accounts.

Language

In the early 1980s, it had become apparent to Grasse management that French would not serve as the firm's common language. In most of its subsidiary countries, English was either the country language or the most likely second language. With considerable reluctance on the part of some French managers, it was decided that English would become the firm's official language. Personnel in the US and England, few of whom spoke a second language, welcomed the change. There were, however, a number of problems. As the Italian sales manager said:

> We understand the need for a common language when we bring in sale representatives from all over Europe or the world. And we understand that English is the 'most common' language in the countries where we do business. All of my people understand that they will have to speak English in international account sales meetings. What they don't like, however, is that the Brits and Americans tend to assume that they are smarter than the rest of us, simply because we can't express ourselves as fluently in English as they can. It's totally different when my people talk to someone from Latin America or some other country, where English is their second language, too.
>
> A related problem is the attitude that people from one country have towards those of another. This goes beyond language. Frequently, our people from Northern Europe or North America will stereotype those of us from Southern Europe or Latin America as disorganized or not business-like. My people, on the other hand, see the northerners as inflexible and unimaginative. To some extent, these views diminish after we get to know each other as individuals, but it takes time and there is always some underlying tension.

Language also influenced decisions on rotation of personnel. It was Volet's view that there should be movement between countries of sales managers and marketing personnel. Still further, he felt that sales representatives who aspired to promotion should also be willing to consider transfers to another country or to headquarters in Paris. As he pointed out, however:

> Customer personnel in most of our international accounts speak English.

Hence, there is a temptation to feel that English language competency is the only requirement when considering reassignment of sales personnel. In fact, if we were to transfer a sales representative who spoke only English to Germany, for instance, he would be received politely the first time, but from then on it would be difficult for him to get an appointment with the customer. It has been our experience that our customers want to do business in their own language, even if they speak English fluently.

An exception might be an international account whose parent is British and which transfers a lot of British personnel to another country. Even here, however, there will be lots of people in the organization for whom English is not a native tongue.

Therefore, we require that our sales people speak the language of the country and are comfortable with the country culture. Local people meet this requirement. The real issue is getting all, or most, of our people to be comfortable in more than one language and culture.

Sales Training

One of the most perplexing issues was what, if any, changes to make with regard to sales training. At headquarters there was considerable sentiment for standardization. As Volet put it:

> I really don't see much difference in selling from one country to another. Of course, personal relations may be more important in, say, Latin America or the Middle East than in Germany, but I think that as much as 80–85% of the selling job can be harmonized. In addition, it's my view that our international accounts expect us to have a standardized sales approach. Sales training, therefore, should be something we can do centrally in Paris.

This view was supported by those in human resources. According to Claude Larreché, Director of Human Resources:

> We no longer see ourselves as a collection of individual companies that remit profits to Paris and make technology transfers occasionally. Our view of the future is that we are a global company that must live in a world of global customers and markets. I think this means we must have a Grasse Fragrance culture that transcends national boundaries, including a common sales approach, i.e., this is the way Grasse approaches customers, regardless of where they are located. A key element in establishing such a culture is sales training here in Paris.

Others disagreed with this point of view, however. Perhaps the most vociferous was the US sales manager:

I understand what Jean-Pierre and Claude are saying, and I support the notion of a common company culture. The fact is, however, that selling is different in the US than in other parts of the world. Not long ago we transferred a promising sales representative from Sweden to our office in Chicago. His sales approach, which was right for Sweden, was very relaxed, and he had to make some major adjustments to fit the more formal and fast-paced approach in Chicago. I don't see how a sales training program in Paris can be of much help. Plus, the cost of sending people to Paris comes out of my budget, and this would really hit my country manager's profits.

In fact, I think we ought to have more flexibility with regard to all our sales management practices.

As Jean-Pierre Volet waited for his bag at the Paris Airport, he wondered how far he should go in making changes with regard to the salesforce. Whatever he did would be controversial, but he was convinced some changes were necessary.

Notes

1. $1.00 = approximately FF6.00 in 1988.
2. Subject to approval by marketing headquarters, each Grasse producing unit established a transfer price for products sold outside the country. Country prices were established, taking into account the country profit objectives and the local market conditions. Transfer prices were usually established for a year. Adjusting transfer prices for fluctuations in exchange rates was a matter of ongoing concern.

SECTION 9

Industrial Marketing Planning

CASES

Lafitte Oil (A)
Van Moppes-IDP Limited (A)

Lafitte Oil (A)

This case was written by Lawrence M. Rumble, Research Associate, under the supervision of Professor Christopher Gale. It is intended as a basis for classroom discussion, and not to illustrate effective or ineffective handling of an administrative situation.

On March 1, 1981, Robert Martin, 44, was named Strategic Marketing Manager of the Lafitte Oil Company. The position had been newly-created at the French-based multinational, and Martin given a specific mandate. His duties were:

> To formulate and prepare objectives and strategic marketing plans for Lafitte Oil worldwide taking into consideration:
> 1. The current and future strengths and weaknesses of the company worldwide;
> 2. The possible opportunities for the company; and
> 3. The possible threats from the environment and competition to the company
>
> to ensure the maximum utilization of the company's resources and the achievement of profit and marketing objectives.

Martin had been appointed to the post by Laffite's president, Claude Marbeau, who was concerned with the lack of strategic planning at Lafitte. Marbeau intended the formulation and implementation of a marketing planning system for the company to be a first step toward the development of an overall strategic planning function at Lafitte, one which would eventually include technical and manufacturing strategy planning as well. He conceived the need for such a system out of concern for the future of Laffite's current business activities. Martin, who had just arrived at headquarters from the company's Hong Kong office, and who had little previous experience in the field, was unsure how to begin.

Lafitte Oil

The Lafitte Oil Company was a manufacturer and marketer of lubricating oils, greases and brake fluids with head offices in Paris, France. With 1980 worldwide sales in excess of FF 4.5 billion (US$ 800 million) and profits of FF 340 million (US$ 60 million) it ranked well up on *Fortune*'s list of the top non-U.S. corporations. The company owned two refineries and 15 blending plants. At the retail level, Lafitte marketed over 2,000 separate products through subsidiary offices in 21 countries and had agency operations in 112 other territories around the world.

Though it was big, Lafitte's competition was bigger. Its competitors included seven of the top ten companies on the *Fortune 500* list.

Lafitte differed from the 'seven sisters' in that it did not control production at the well-head, not did it own any retail distribution facilities. The company purchased crude or refined oil in bulk, refined and/or blended it as the case demanded, introduced additives to come up with its own unique blends, and resold this to all sectors of the lubricants market. Its leading automotive oil, Lafitte Etoile, held as much as 26 per cent of the total automotive market in certain of its territories. Lafitte products were renowned for their quality and for being formulations representing the state-of-the-art in oil technology.

The Need for Marketing Planning

Like many major corporations, Lafitte traced its beginnings to the birth of the automobile. After the turn of the century, the need for lubricants for the internal combustion engines which powered this new mode of transportation provided the foundation for a growing industry in Europe and the US. The adaptation of engines for use in another new mode of transport – the airplane – provided a further demand for lubricants. As the number of automobiles steadily increased, so did the demand for lubricating oils. Since these inventions tended not to stay in one place for very long, oil companies found markets for their products were also becoming widely dispersed. As a result, though development of new and improved lubricating products was concentrated in the industrial centers of Europe and the US, where new and more sophisticated automobiles were being designed, oil companies found themselves expanding geographically on a market-by-market basis until their operations spanned the entire globe.

Since lubricants manufacturers literally followed in the path of the automobile there was no such thing as systematic market development in the early years. However, as the automobile became firmly entrenched, so oil companies found their markets began to mature. Claude Marbeau, Managing Director of Lafitte, used developments in the automotive lubricants business since World War II as an illustration of the changing marketplace for oil-based lubricants.

At the end of the war, he said, almost all automotive lubricating oils were mono-grades (to be used in a specified temperature range) because few vehicles went more than 1000 km without an oil change, an oil would be changed with the seasons. With the development of engines designed to operate for longer periods between servicing and oil changes, there was the need for oil which could withstand greater seasonal temperature fluctuations. Hence the development of multi-grades. Multi-grades soon took over a large segment of the automotive market, largely aided by altered distribution patterns. The growth of the do-it-yourself trend in the US and Europe, combined with the growth of 'self-service' gas stations, led supermarkets and automotive stores to begin selling lubricating oil. These outlets demanded an all-purpose oil to sell to the broadest possible spectrum of customers.

Multi-grades soon proliferated, and producers began competing on the basis of additives – anti-corrosion, detergent, and others. In the present market environment, multi-grade formulations differed more in the additives that competing blenders chose to introduce than in product quality.

However, with multi-grades in danger of becoming commodity products in the 1980s it was not clear what the future of automotive lubricants was to be. The proliferation of small cars with high-revving engines since the 1973 worldwide oil crisis, and subsequent tightening of government performance standards, plus pollution control requirements, made a move away from multi-grades back to new, improved mono-grades a possibility. On the other hand, there might equally be a continued drive toward development of a standard, all-purpose, all-weather oil, for the future. The development of technologically new lubrification products was yet another possibility. For the lubricants company, what had historically been fairly predictable market development was becoming increasingly difficult to forecast.

Added to this was concern about the plateauing of markets worldwide and the interest being shown by leading oil companies in the lubricants business. Some fully-integrated oil companies were already major competitors in European and Asian markets where they owned or controlled their own retail fuel distribution outlets. In the face of this increased competition, it was essential that blender-marketers such as Lafitte remain at the forefront of technological advance and maintain their high advertising and promotional profiles.

Added to such competitive threats was the further concern about future prospects for all oil products, given the finite nature of fossil fuels. It was conceivable that all 'oil companies' would have to redefine their spheres of activity by the end of the century. Those which survived and prospered, Marbeau believed, would be those which were most successful at predicting future trends and establishing longer term strategic marketing plans.

Lafitte Products and Markets

Lafitte products were divided into four main market categories: automotive, aviation, marine and industrial. The automotive sector was by far the largest, comprising 40% of sales volume and 48% of total corporate gross margin. Lafitte's multi-grade motor oil, Etoile, accounted for 55% of total automotive group sales, and 22% of total company sales. In addition to Etoile, the company marketed the Meteor multi-grade which comprised 20% of product group sales, and numerous mono-grade oil formulations. Automotive greases and brake fluids were also included in this product group.

The industrial product group was the most fragmented of Lafitte's product groupings, and included lubricants ranging from greases for heavy machinery to delicate oils for Swiss watch movements. Marine products dealt exclusively with the oils and greases used in marine applications, and the aviation sector, which was a minor part of Lafitte's business, dealt with aviation oils and greases. Sales and profits by market group are summarized below:

	Automative %	Industrial %	Marine %	Aviation %	TOTAL %
Unit Sales	40.2	39.4	15.1	5.3	100
Sales Revenue	49.9	34.3	11.1	4.7	100
Net Profit	56.5	30.4	8.5	4.6	100

The company had long been doing business in international markets, and some of its territories, e.g., the Far East, had been buying and using the company's products for over 60 years. (*Exhibit 1 provides the locations of Lafitte's facilities and subsidiaries around the world.*) As a general rule, products from all market groups were sold in all territories.

However, the proportion of the market held by certain products varied from territory to territory. For example in the automotive sector, the multi-grade motor oil Etoile was in great demand in temperate climates, whereas in tropical areas such as the Far East, mono-grade oils were much more

Exhibit 1   *Locations of Lafitte facilities worldwide*

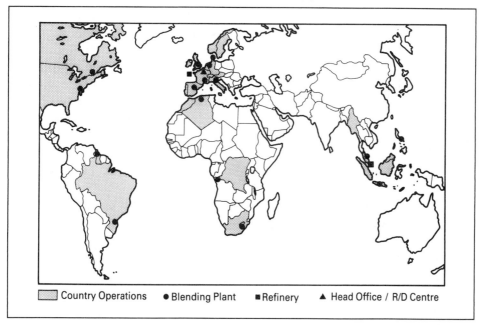

Country Operations   ● Blending Plant   ■ Refinery   ▲ Head Office / R/D Centre

appropriate. On the other hand, the lubricants marketed in the marine, industrial and aviation sectors were usually of similar type and formulation.

Problems at Lafitte

Marbeau's prime concern centered around product planning and development, and arose over fears about the future of Etoile, Lafitte's principal multi-grade and bestselling product. Should changes in automotive needs cause sales of this product to begin deteriorating, Lafitte had no innovative multi-grade formulation to replace it with. This was due to the fact that the company had no systematic way of predicting trends in the marketplace, and thus was unsure at this time of where to concentrate its development efforts. If the trend to monogrades materialized, Lafitte would be in the position of having no new formulations which represented significant advances to introduce in that market category either. A company which had traditionally been a market leader through technological advance, it was for the first time faced with the prospect of becoming a market follower.

Over and above this was the concern that there was no systematic marketing across territories of a great many items in Lafitte's existing product portfolio. A given product would be withdrawn from the market by the marketing department of one territory, while simultaneously being launched or relaunched with advertising and promotional support in another territory. To the degree that marketing efforts were not standardized, there could be no concerted marketing strategy on more than a country-by-country basis. Though this allowed for the tailoring of marketing plans to take account of conditions in individual geographic markets, it hindered the formulation and implementation of a company-wide marketing strategy, and made the assessment from the corporate perspective of the relative risks and potential returns of marketing existing and new products in existing and new markets almost impossible.

Marbeau explained: 'You can be an innovator in this business, but you don't necessarily make as much money as if you are a marketer. Where is Lafitte to put its emphasis – this we have to decide.'

Marbeau spoke about his fears in the following terms:

> In this company everybody is thinking tactically; nobody is thinking strategically. No one is looking at where we are going to be in five years – they only care about next year. Their five-year sales projections are merely extrapolations of the next year's projection. They project a ten per cent increase in sales volume, and they get only nine. Project that out five years and you've got to be concerned.
>
> I decided I had to take someone away from the day-to-day operation of this company and get them to start looking to the future. So I created the post of strategic marketing manager. I'm looking for that man to lay the foundations for future strategic thinking in this organization.

His choice of Robert Martin to fill a new post was based on his belief that only someone intimately connected with Lafitte's business could successfully develop a planning system as well as new marketing and product concepts, which would ensure Lafitte's growth and survival in years to come.

Robert Martin

When questioned about his new job, Martin stated:

> What I do in this job will be largely dependent upon my own view of what sort of business I personally think Lafitte ought to be in: whether I believe there are more opportunities in existing markets for us to expand, or whether I think we ought to be looking at new markets; whether or not we should be an innovator; whether I think electric cars and solar energy are coming in tomorrow; whether we should remain a lubricants company or become an

industrial company. As I see it, it's my job to shape the shell into which the future Lafitte organization will fall.

A fifteen-year veteran of Lafitte, Martin had first joined the company as a regional salesman in Alsace, where he spent five years on the road. Though highly successful, he could by 1971 see that the open-ended commission scheme that made the job so profitable was coming to an end, and requested to be moved into the Paris headquarters. His request was granted, and he that year became Lafitte's assistant automotive coordinator. In this position he devised an early consolidation scheme for automotive marketing plans, and was later promoted to automotive coordinator. In 1976, Martin went to Hong Kong to become marketing director for the Far East, and two years later was promoted to general manager of Far East operations. He devised and implemented a major marketing planning system while in the East, and expanded the area's marketing department so that it was the largest outside of France.

In late 1979, Martin knew he was under consideration for the newly-created post of strategic marketing manager. He recalled those days:

> I was called back from Hong Kong for interviews. It was to be between me and a candidate from outside the company. I really knew very little about marketing in an international sense, so when I arrived in Paris I went to FNAC (a well-known bookstore) and bought two books on international strategic marketing. I read these and had all the right basic concepts in my head when it came interview time.
>
> I was first interviewed by Claude, then one by one four of the senior directors came into the room. Each asked me the same questions, and I had to repeat the answers four times over. It became very tense after a while. Then after lunch Claude took me into a room, gave me a pencil and paper and told me to write down all the marketing and business activities you would consider in introducing a new product worldwide. The textbooks helped – I didn't miss much. And my experience as a line manager had taught me to consider logically all business activities which impinged upon marketing, including financial resources, manufacturing, raw materials, supply, and distribution. My answers were typed up and read by all of the directors, who elected to give me the job. I don't think I was any better than the other applicant, though. I think for top management it was in the final analysis a choice between the devil they knew and the devil they didn't.

Organization

Martin was one of six people reporting directly to Lafitte's commercial director *(see **Exhibit 2**)*. The commercial director was itself a new position

Exhibit 2 *Lafitte central organization*

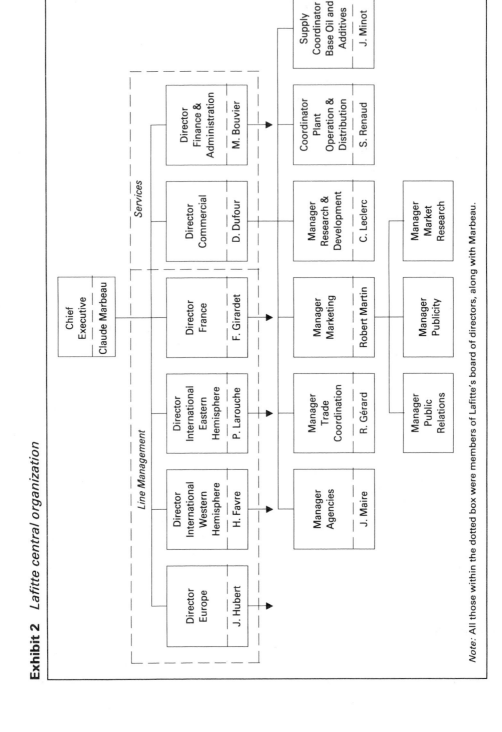

Note: All those within the dotted box were members of Lafitte's board of directors, along with Marbeau.

resulting from a corporate reorganization which had been undertaken by Marbeau, when he had become Managing Director in 1979. In a letter which accompanied distribution on the new organization chart, Marbeau stated:

> The commercial director is a new appointment. The intention of this appointment is that those services under his control will be coordinated and directed towards the needs of an integrated international company. While in no way restricting chief executives of operating companies from generating ideas in any field relating to our business, I will be looking to this division to coordinate the development of existing and new products with the development of existing and new markets, and thus provide our strategic plans for the medium to long term.
>
> The only top level in the organization, the commercial director was one of six reporting directly to Marbeau. Thus Lafitte was currently organized geographically and by support services rather than functionally or by product group *(Exhibit 2)*. As a result, Martin would be working from a staff position when trying to formulate and implement the new marketing planning system for the company's operating divisions.

Exhibit 3 presents the line reporting system down to the level of a single country operation. In undertaking his new job, Martin had under his direction the Lafitte publicity and public relations managers, a market researcher, and a secretary.

Present Reporting System

Marketing plans were presently submitted annually to the appropriate regional director at head office by the country managers of each of Lafitte's territories. Each was accompanied by a detailed financial plan. These two documents averaged 100 pages in length and together made up Lafitte's planning and control (P&C) reporting system. A territory plan would include a detailed one-year action plan plus a summary of expected sales and cash flows five years into the future. *Exhibit 4* presents the table of contents of a single territory marketing document.

Both the marketing and financial books were submitted to Paris in August *(see Exhibit 5 for Lafitte's annual planning calendar)*. Revisions or rewrites were completed as required over the next two months. Country managers were then called to head office in October and November to present their plans and for an annual yearly briefing. When the plans were accepted at head office, the figures they contained became the next year's budget.

Martin had several misgivings about the existing reporting system.

Exhibit 3   *Line responsibility within the Lafitte organization*

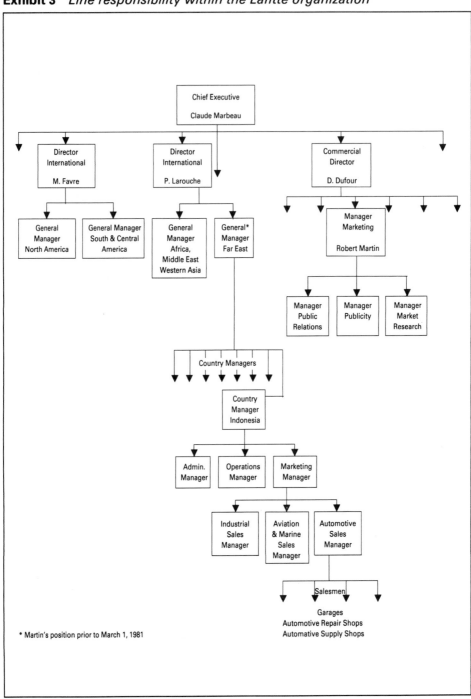

* Martin's position prior to March 1, 1981

Exhibit 4 *Contents of a country marketing plan: automative market*

ITALY

Marketing Plan – Automative – 1979–1980 and *Marketing Projections to 1984*

1.0 *Market Environment and Trends*
   1.1 Geographical
   1.2 Population
   1.3 Political
   1.4 Economic
   1.5 Other Facts

2.0 *1978 Results*
   2.1 Market and Sales Review and Appraisal

3.0 *Vehicle Population and Size of Automotive Lubricants Market 1974–1983*
   3.1 Public Roads
   3.2 Vehicle Population
   3.3 Size of Lubricants Market

4.0 *1979–1980 Forecast and Projections to 1984*

5.0 *1979–1980 Marketing Objectives and Long-Term Aims*
   5.1 Prime Objectives
   5.2 Secondary Objectives

6.0 *Marketing Strategy and Plans to Achieve Objectives – 1979–1980*
   6.1 Market Segmentation
   6.2 Assemblers (O.E.M.)
   6.3 Franchised Distributors/Dealers
   6.4 Non-Franchised Workshops
   6.5 Gasoline/Service Stations
   6.6 Motorcycle Outlets
   6.7 Spare Parts, Accessory, Speed, Hardware, Tire, and Battery Shops
   6.8 Oil Dealers
   6.9 Bus, Taxi, Truck Fleet operators
   6.10 Sales and Promotion Tactics, Investments
       – Existing Product Range
       – New Products
   6.11 Price Structure
   6.12 Packages
   6.13 Advertising
   6.14 Sales Promotion – Merchandising
   6.15 Sales Force

7.0 *Sensitivity Analysis*

8.0 *Alternatives to Preferred Plan*

Exhibit 5   *Lafitte oil planning timetable*

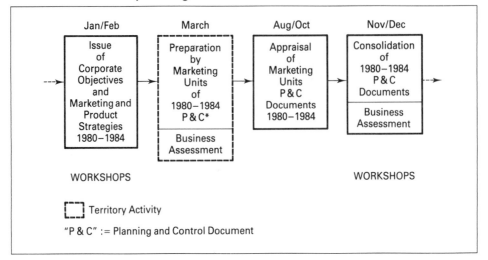

Principal among these was the fact that the descriptive nature of the marketing plans made the P&C system inadequate as an information-gathering tool. Plans from the various territories had no standard format, were uneven in the quality of information they rendered to head office, and there was no creative analysis being performed at the country level. Thus when information came in to Paris, head office could do little more than consolidate it, sending some reports back which did not provide an acceptable level of information or detail, and wait for them to be re-submitted.

Martin commented:

> Traditionally at Lafitte all our planning had come from the bottom. Projections come in from the territories, are OKed and then sent back to them as this year's objectives. This was great as long as territories were expanding, because everything would show an increase. But with the plateauing of markets worldwide, it has become necessary to change this.
>
> In addition, all our products have traditionally been developed here, at our Paris research center, and then adapted to foreign markets without sufficient control. So when sales projections come in from the territories we merely have to agree to them. Consolidated plans become next year's objectives. My task, as I perceive it, is to alter the planning system from one of bottom-up planning to one of top-down planning. The problem is how to go about it. You see, the top depends on information from the bottom.

With the present system Lafitte had no way of identifying either opportunities or real threats in its marketing environment. The system was tied to existing product classifications rather than any type of market demarcation points, so all plans and projections were being made on a product-by-product basis. Martin believed that this made it difficult to analyze the market in terms of future trends and to quantify market opportunities. However, he was also conscious of the fact that all Lafitte's trade structure, research and development was geared to product categories, and knew that any change in the reporting classification would have a major impact on departments throughout the organization. He would have to balance these conflicting considerations in designing a new planning document.

Because of the problems with information which came in from the territories there was little creative analysis being done at head office either. As a result, there was little strategic direction provided to the territories by those in Paris. Martin knew he would have to design a planning document which, once introduced, would enable those at head office to make strategic decisions which could be translated into directives which would not only be meaningful to the territories, but which would be actively embraced by them.

Political Considerations

The issue of how to implement change in a multi-tier, multi-product, multi-national organization such as Lafitte was also a major concern of Martin's. He was conscious of the fact that he would have to operate from a staff position in what was a newly-created division of the company. This meant he would have no direct authority to implement any marketing changes he devised, but rather would have to depend on line executives to do so. Since Lafitte was organized geographically and by support services rather than by product group or by function, he would have to decide whether his system should be devised so as to encompass the entire marketing operations of the company, or whether he should start with one geographic area, or one product group, and later expand the system market by market, or product group by product group. Whichever route he chose to take, he would be confronted by the problem of which level of the organization he should interface with.

The solution of this latter problem was largely dependent on the particular characteristics of Lafitte's own organization as diagrammed in *Exhibit 3*. The politics of the organization were unique in that the company had just gone through a major reorganization, and at the upper levels of management operating relationships were still uncertain and to some degree undefined. At the senior management level, directors were now members of the company's board of directors. This meant that any changes put forth by Martin would have to be approved by them. Reporting to some of the senior directors were the regional general managers, Martin's colleagues before he had taken up his new post. Martin believed that there was considerable solidarity and enthusiasm among this group, but was also cognizant of the fact that considerable power was vested in the hands of the country managers themselves, many of whom were well-entrenched in their positions. Certain of the country managers (e.g., in Germany) had high profits and were considered to be major opinion leaders of the company. The most powerful single group amongst these were the European country managers of Germany, Britain, Austria, Belgium, Holland and Italy, who, led by their senior directors, consulted together frequently on country strategies, partly for reasons of geographical need, and partly due to strong personal links built up between them in recent years.

Within the country operations themselves, Martin would have to deal directly with the country marketing managers. Though some of these were highly capable individuals, the level of expertise within this function was uneven, and Martin felt that, as a general statement, the marketing function at Lafitte was not highly developed. He believed that Lafitte was more of a 'sales' company than a 'marketing' company. To his knowledge, there was only one MBA in the entire worldwide organization.

Managers at the director, general manager, or country manager level at Lafitte were evaluated according to a strict system of accountability. Each had to meet financial, profit and growth objectives set for him by top management while staying within Lafitte's stated operating policy guidelines. Remuneration and promotion were tied to this system of performance evaluation, though the company did not use a bonus system. Martin stated that if a manager had not met his objectives or stayed within his guidelines when yearly results were submitted, an investigation was carried out by the Paris headquarters. If the manager failed to meet objectives for a second year, a thorough investigation was undertaken. If the poor performance continued for a third year, the manager was normally fired. Martin commented that one country manager had recently been fired after 20 years with the company because he refused to follow policy guidelines. Another had recently been fired for continued failure to meet profit objectives.

A Country Manager's View

In order to obtain a perspective from one of the territories, the casewriter travelled to Rome to interview Mr. Giorgio Perini, Lafitte's managing director for Italy, Mr. Perini had been with Lafitte for 20 years and had previously been managing director in Brazil. The interview took place in Mr. Perini's office, where he spoke candidly and frankly about relations with head office and the proposed planning system:

> The problem with dealing with head office is that it is just an enormous sponge – it soaks up information and gives nothing in return, or else the people there send us useless information back. The prevailing attitude is, 'It's no use writing to the center. It's not worth it, do it yourself.'
>
> There is also the problem of requests for information *from* the center. They are always asking for information they already have, and either don't know it or can't be bothered sifting through it.
>
> Let me give you a simple example. Last week I received a telex from head office requesting some basic market information to be compiled and sent within 24 hours. They already have this information at head office, so why do they ask it of me? And why within 24 hours? I sent them back a telex saying, 'I sent this information in May of this year *and* September of last year – go upstairs and look it up. I don't have time.'
>
> But it's always the same. Whenever we receive instructions from the center the reaction is negative – we give the man the figures he requests to justify his job. One has to be sensitive to the time it takes to compile all this information. People at headquarters are not; often they are simply shifting their work load onto us. Mind you, I think Lafitte is a worse offender than other companies in this regard. I keep reminding my managers of this.
>
> But now you tell me that there is to be a new marketing planning system. Good! What Robert (Martin) is saying is clearly needed in this company. But you must remember that his requests for new marketing information will not be the only requests we get from head office. They will be lost in the flood. If we go to all the work to compile statistics he asks for, will it be of any use to us or to the center? I don't think so. Are we then just creating more paper? We at this end fear that head office will not be able to handle the information we send them, or if they can, nothing will come of it, or not in the right order of priorities, or too late.
>
> Fortunately, Robert is an experienced manager with a track record, and not some unknown name at head office. Perhaps he can do something. But I think as a general statement, and I am not saying this is my attitude, I would say that managers in the territories prefer to have as little to do with head office as possible.

Alternatives

In his office at the Paris headquarters, Martin wondered where to begin. He repeated platitudes such as 'Fossil fuels are finite' and stared at the wall. Pointing to the shelf of P&C documents which lined it, he remarked to the casewriter: 'That shelf is three meters long. We don't have time to read all the material. And now I am faced with bringing in a new system.'

The most immediate issue was the problem of how to structure a manual for marketing planning – whether he ought to use existing product groupings or devise a new classification system which would make marketing departments begin to look critically at markets rather than products. If he did alter the system of reporting to the center, it would tax the resources of the territorial marketing staffs. Martin wished to have the territories involved hire a market analyst, and felt that devising a new system would encourage them to do so. However, he also was aware that it was the marketing managers in the territories to whom his manual would have to be sent – not the country managers. The country managers would in each instance be required to approve the hiring of a new staff member to cope with the implementation of a totally new planning system. How to approach this task was a difficult problem, especially in smaller territories where there were few staff, and the cost of an incremental salary could affect the year's results, for which the country managing director was responsible.

If Martin elected to maintain the old product classifications in his marketing planning manual, he would have to assure that the format of marketing reports highlighted the key market issues affecting each specific product classification, rather than the general descriptive format which the reports now followed. He had conceived the idea of drawing up standardized statistical and analytical market information forms and sending them out with a manual to be filled out and returned with that year's plan, However, the desirability of standardizing marketing plans was a hotly-debated issue among multinationals, and was not considered appropriate in all industries. Certainly a standardized format would not be equally applicable in all Lafitte's markets. In some markets in lesser developed territories such as Indonesia and the Middle East, market information was not readily available and statistics frequently unreliable. The units in these territories would thus be unable to match other territories in depth of reporting. Attempting to meet all the requirements of a standard report format could severely tax the resources of a marketing unit, especially in analyzing the highly-fragmented industrial product group. Martin was thus caught in the dilemma of how to elicit meaningful information from the territories without placing unrealistic demands upon them.

This problem was further compounded by the difficulty of getting information from the agency territories which were not staffed directly by

Lafitte. In some of these, such as Mexico or South Korea, Lafitte really had very little knowledge of the market.

Another issue centered around what analysis should be carried out at what level in the organization. Martin wanted to encourage more analysis at the country level, and had considered the idea of separating long-range strategic and short-term tactical plans, and having them prepared at different times of the year. He felt this would ensure that the strategic plan was developed independently, and would be more than just an extrapolation of the one-year marketing plan. This would mean altering Lafitte's planning calendar. It was also possible to have strategic and tactical plans prepared at different levels of the organization, something which was not done at present. These options were not mutually exclusive.

> The resolution of that problem is critical to the success of this job. There are many companies which have tried unsuccessfully to implement a marketing planning system. How am I to do this? How am I to approach managers? How am I to get my system accepted? Fortunately, I have the support of Claude [Marbeau] in this venture, but I myself have no authority over line managers.

On March 16 – barely two weeks after he has begun his new job – Martin was asked by Marbeau to give a talk on strategic marketing to Lafitte's country managers when they assembled at three Zone Conferences Marbeau had scheduled around the world for early April. These were another innovation of Marbeau's. Each conference would cover marketing, trade and technical issues which confronted Lafitte in the particular region, and would be chaired by Marbeau himself. The first would be held in New York in three weeks' time.

In considering Marbeau's invitation, Martin had to evaluate the costs and benefits of talking first to country managers rather than their superiors or the marketing managers he would have to interface with in his new job. If he did elect to address the country managers, he would have to decide on what the message of his talk would be, and how to establish his credibility in order to persuade them of the need for change. He was concerned about his ability to do this, since he knew very little about international marketing planning himself. It was with these considerations in mind that he turned his attention to the performance of his new job. (***Exhibit 6*** *contains some of Martin's notes.*)

Exhibit 6 *Excerpt from Martin's notes to himself on strategy*

- Read an article by Kotler* in Nov.–Dec. *HBR*. He draws an interesting distinction between 'sales' and 'marketing' companies. Divides them roughly as follows:

Sales Companies	*Marketing Companies*
a) Think in terms of sales volume rather than profits.	Think in terms of profit planning and plan sales volume around profits.
b) Think short-term rather than long-term.	Think in terms of future trends, threats and oppostunities.
c) Think in terms of individual customers rather than market-segment classes.	Think in terms of customer types and market-segment differences.
d) Think in terms of selling to customers rather than developing plans and strategies	Think in terms of creating good systems for market analysis, planning and control.

These concepts worth remembering.

---

* Article was 'From Sales Obsession to Marketing Effectiveness', by Philip Kotler. It appeared in the November–December, 1977, *Harvard Business Review*.

Van Moppes-IDP Limited (A)

This case was written by Professor H. Michael Hayes as a basis for class discussion rather than to illustrate either effective or ineffective handling of an administrative situation.

In November 1983, after a turbulent turnaround year, Ian W. Marsh, Managing Director of Van Moppes-IDP Limited (VMIDP), was considering the next steps needed to build on the past year's work and to position the firm for future growth and profitability. In particular, he was considering an offer by corporate staff to take advantage of PIMS (Profit Impact of Market Strategy), a program which, it was felt, might help in developing and implementing the firm's business strategy.

Background

Formed in 1981 by a merger between L.M. Van Moppes Limited and Impregnated Diamond Products Limited, the firm was a leader in ultra-hard technology products for cutting, grinding, sawing and drilling equipment for the engineering, glass processing and construction industries. Despite bright hopes for its prospects, the new company had not done well. Hard hit by a worldwide recession and a severe decline in diamond prices, the firm sustained severe losses in 1981 and 1982. When Ian Marsh was appointed Managing Director in November 1982, he had a clear sense that if the firm could not be turned around, its parent, Foseco Minsep, would seriously consider selling the business or shutting it down.

As a total stranger to the ultra-hard technology business, the first year was not an easy one for Marsh. In his first few weeks he was faced with a number of difficult personnel decisions in order to establish his own team, while at the same time making sure that key expertise was retained.

Simultaneously, he had to take immediate steps to stem the losses and to learn the business. Personally convinced that the business could be turned around, a key challenge for Marsh was to convince members of the organization that it could survive, if it did the right things.

By November 1983, the picture had brightened. Losses had been stemmed and the personnel situation had stabilized. Serious problems remained, however. According to Marsh:

> I was convinced that we were not focusing on the customer as we should and that we had serious product and service quality problems. The problem was how to get the organization more customer and quality oriented and how to ensure that this orientation got translated into appropriate action.

At this time, corporate staff informed Marsh that it had become a member of the Strategic Planning Institute (SPI) and that they would fund his use of the PIMS (Profit Impact of Market Strategy) data base and SPI consulting services if he decided on their use. Marsh knew, generally, that the PIMS data base represented the detailed experience of some 3,000 businesses and that many businesses had found this data base useful in their strategic planning. He was not sure, however, just how the data base or SPI consultants might be used to help VMIDP. He had heard that the concepts were quite sophisticated and that he and his staff would have to devote a lot of time to working with PIMS.

In evaluating the offer from corporate headquarters, he tried to weigh his need for help in formulating the right strategy for the business against the time he and his staff would have to commit, and the relative uncertainty about the benefits a PIMS study would provide.

The Ultra-Hard Technology (UHT) Industry

Major markets for diamond products were the aircraft, motor vehicle, glass processing, general engineering and civil engineering industries. In the manufacturing industries, few components were produced without involving the industrial diamond at some stage. In the aircraft industry, for instance, engine components such as rotor shafts, guide vanes and turbine blades were all precision ground, with grinding wheels formed by single point, multipoint or rotary type diamond dressers. With more carbon fibre, resin compacts and glass-filled materials, diamond type drills and diamond plated bandsaws were increasingly required. In the motor vehicle industry, engine components were precision ground, turned or bored with diamond tools. In the glass industry, spectacle lenses were production milled, and all kinds of flat glass was edged, bevelled or drilled using diamond wheels and tools. In the construction and mining industries, a wide variety of diamond impregnated drills and saws were used to cut or machine concrete, granite, marble or other rock formulations.

Historically, these markets had been served by a host of small specialized firms, making an extensive array of products, sold in relatively small volume. While some products could be standardized (e.g., saws for the construction industry), products for engineering businesses were sometimes actually designed for a specific machine tool in one customer's plant. Principal product categories were diamond tipped tools, diamond impregnated grinding wheels and devices, and diamond impregnated saws and drills.

Many firms were closely associated with, or grew out of, diamond merchants. In the early days of the industry, international expansion was the norm as diamond merchants looked for markets for the growing accumulation of industrial diamonds produced by diamond mining companies. In some instances only the sale of industrial diamonds was involved. In others, manufacturing operations were established. The product's high value to weight ratio facilitated participation in export markets. Specialized requirements, however, tended to emphasize local production and sales. Thus, the predominant pattern in recent years was to manufacture locally for local markets.

For many years the price of the final product was dominated by the diamond content. With a continuing rise in diamond prices, there was little emphasis on manufacturing economies. With the introduction of artificial diamonds, first by GE and then by DeBeers, and then a decline in natural diamond prices, industry economics were significantly changed. It appeared, however, that many firms had still not adapted to the new situation. While diamonds continued to be the principal element used for UHT cutting and grinding, silicon carbide was also being used, and cubic boron nitride (CBN) appeared to have great potential as a superabrasive material.

Van Moppes IDP Limited

VMIDP was an operating company of Foseco Minsep, an international specialty chemicals group manufacturing and selling a wide range of products and services, mainly to industrial customers, worldwide. Headquartered in Birmingham, England, Foseco Minsep had a 1987 profit on ordinary activities before tax of £35.2 million on a turnover of £515.1 million. The group was comprised of over 100 operating companies spread across 35 countries. Management control of these diverse operations was exercised by a Group Executive, with operating companies reporting through to members of the Executive on a predominantly regional basis *(See **Exhibit 1** for a listing of principal Group companies.)*

Foseco Minsep had three principal operating sectors: FOSECO, which supplied chemical products to the world's foundry and steel industries; Fosroc, which supplied chemical products for the building, construction, mining and tunneling industries; and Unicorn, with specialized expertise in hard materials technology for applications of natural and synthetic diamonds for industrial use, abrasive products and systems, as well as drilling systems and equipment for ground investigation and extraction.

Unicorn began to take its present form in the 1960s when two leading British abrasive manufacturers merged, the Universal Grinding Wheel Company Limited and English Abrasives Limited. Shortly afterward, they were joined by international diamond merchants and diamond tool manufacturers, L.M. Van Moppes & Sons Limited. Expansion continued and operations were developed in North and South America, Europe, Scandinavia and Japan. In 1980 Unicorn became part of Foseco Minsep. By 1989, Unicorn comprised three principal groups: Diamond Products[1]; Bonded Coated and Abrasives; and Electro-Minerals & Media.

L.M. Van Moppes & Sons Limited was founded by Louis Meyer Van Moppes in 1893, shortly after his arrival in London from Amsterdam. Founded principally as a diamond merchant, the firm moved gradually into manufacturing of diamond tipped tools. In 1950 its headquarters were established at Basingstoke, England. By 1970, when the firm was acquired by Unicorn, it had a worldwide network of sales offices and manufacturing activities.

Impregnated Diamond Products Limited (later IDP) began in Antwerp, Belgium, in 1932 when Peter Neven invented and patented a process for manufacturing an abrasive for the stone, optical and engineering industries. This process involved mixing crushed industrial diamonds with iron and other metal powders, heating the mixture to the sintering point and pressing. In the early part of World War II, the plant was 'spirited' to Gloucester where it played an important role in the war effort. In 1959 it was acquired by Universal Grinding Wheel, one of Unicorn's predecessors.

In May 1981 the UK diamond tools business of L.M. Van Moppes Limited was merged with IDP. Already, for a number of years, the two companies had been sharing marketing and sales resources and had jointly contributed to the funding of the R & D Laboratory at Gloucester. The relocation of another Unicorn company, which had shared the Gloucester manufacturing site with IDP, made space available in Gloucester for the diamond tools business, and the Basingstoke operation was shut down.

Exhibit 1 *Principal group companies (as of December 31, 1987)*

Country of incorporation	Principal operation	Group % equity interest	Country of incorporation	Principal operation	Group % equity interest
Argentina	Foseco Argentina SA	49*	South Africa	Foseco South Africa	
Australia	Foseco Pty Ltd	100		(Pty) Ltd	100
Austria	Giesserei-Dienst GmbH	75		Fosroc (Pty) Ltd	100
Belgium	*Belgian Tool Company NV*	*100*	South Korea	Foseco Korea Ltd	60
	Foseco SA	100	Spain	Foseco Española SA	50
Brazil	Fosbel Industria E			Fosroc SA	100
	Comercia Ltda	48	Sweden	Foseco AB	100
	Foseco Industrial E			*Svenska Unicorn AB*	*100*
	Comercial Ltda	95	Switzerland	Foseco AG	100
Canada	Foseco Canada Inc.	100		Foseco Holding AG	100
	The Gibson-Homans			Foseco Trading AG	100
	Company of Canada Ltd	100‡		*L.M. Van Moppes & Sons SA*	*100*
	Unicorn Abrasives of		Taiwan	Foseco Golden Gate Co Ltd	50
	Canada Ltd	100	United Kingdom	Abrasive Developments Ltd	100
Dubai	Foseco Minsep (UAE)			Celmac Ltd	100
	Private Ltd	70		Electro Furnace	
Egypt	Foseco SAE	60		Products Ltd	100
Finland	Foseco OY	100		English Abrasives Ltd	100
France	Foseco SA	99.9		Fosbel International Ltd	100
	Fosroc SA	100		Foseco (FS) Ltd	100
	Precidia SA	*100*		Foseco International Ltd	100†
Greece	Foseco Hellas SA	90		Foseco Minsep (UK) Ltd	100
Hong Kong	Foseco Industries Asia Ltd	100		Fospur Ltd	100
India	Carborundum Universal Ltd	22.5*		Fosroc CCD Ltd	100
	Fosroc Chemicals (India) Ltd	40*		Fosroc Ltd	100
	Greaves Foseco Ltd	50†		Fosroc International Ltd	100†
Irish Republic	Abrasives Ltd	100		*Holemasters Ltd*	*100*
	Ceimac (Ireland) Ltd	100		Midland Oil Refineries Ltd	100
	Fosroc (Eire) Ltd	100		Minerals Separation Ltd	100
Italy	Foseco SpA	100		Unicorn Industries plc	100†
	L.M. Van Moppes &			Universal Abrasives Ltd	100
	Sons SpA	*100*		Universal Grinding	
Japan	Fosbel Japan Ltd	51		Wheel Co Ltd	100
	Foseco Japan Ltd	92		*L.M. Van Moppes & Sons Ltd*	*100*
	Nippon Van Moppes Ltd	*100*		*Van Moppes IDP Ltd*	*100*
	Toyoda Van Moppes Ltd	*34**		H H Wardle (Metals) Ltd	50*‡
Malaysia	Foseco Minsep Malaysia		USA	Celtite Inc	60
	SDN BDH	100		Exomet Inc	100
Mexico	Exoternicos Monclova SA	80		Fosbel Inc	51
	Foseco SA de CV	100		Foscor Refractory Partners	50
Netherlands	Fosbel Europe BV	51		Foseco Inc	100
	Foseco Holding BV	100		Foseco Minsep Inc	100
	Foseco Minsep BV	100		The Gibson-Homans	
	Foseco Minsep Holding BV	100		Company	100‡
	Foseco Minsep			Preco Industries Ltd	100
	International BV	100		Unicorn Industries Inc	100
	Foseco Nederland BV	100	Venezuela	Fosven CA	49*
	HIM Chernie BV	100	West Germany	Foseco GmbH	100
New Zealand	Foseco Minsep (NZ) Ltd	100		Hermanns & Co GmbH	100
Philippines	Foseco Philippines Inc	100		*Indimant*	
Portugal	Foseco Portugal Produtos			*Industriediamanten GmbH*	*60*
	para Fundicao Lda	51		Dr Riedelbauch &	
Saudi Arabia	Fosam Co Ltd	50		Stoffregen GmbH	100
Singapore	Foseco Minsep			Steibe GmbH	100
	(Singapore) Pte Ltd	100	Zimbabwe	Foseco Zimbabwe (PVT) Ltd	100

Companies in italic are members of the Diamond Products Group.
† Shares held by Foseco Minsep plc.   ‡ Shares or business disposed of since 31 December 1987.
* Related company – total issued share capital as follows:
   Foseco Argentina SA (Argentina) *68,899,169 Nominative one vote shares of Australes 0.01 each*
   Carborundum Universal Ltd (India) *5,921,160 equity shares of Rs 10 each*
   Fosroc Chemicals (India) Ltd (India) *20,000 Ordinary shares of Rs 10 each*
   Toyoda Van Mappes Ltd. (Japan) *562,500 Ordinary shares of Yen 500 each*
   H H Wardle (Metals) Ltd. (UK)‡ *1,000 Ordinary shares of £1 each*
   Fosven CA (Venezuela) *5,000 Ordinary shares of Bolivars 1,000 each*

November 1983

As Ian Marsh recalled:

> When I came here in late 1982, it was clear we were facing serious problems. Losses in 1981 had been £1.5 million, on sales of around £5 million. Predictions for 1982 were not quite as bad, £0.7 million *(see **Exhibit 2** for the December 1982 profit and loss statement)*, but the situation was still very bleak.
>
> Foseco had bought Unicorn in 1980. When diamond prices dropped by half, it was discovered that much of the stock was redundant or very slow moving. Normal group accounting policies required writing off redundant inventory after a year, but an exception had been made for diamonds, on the premise that 'diamonds were forever'. It was clear that our policy had to change and, in 1981 and 1982, we took some large write-offs to reflect the realities of the situation. Much of this effort was led by John Cowley who, as acting managing director, was my predecessor. John also had started the process of analyzing products for their growth potential. He had another full-time job, however. There was a real limit on what he could do, and it was obvious that much more needed to be done.
>
> It was generally felt that the management team lacked credibility, both with the work force and the head office in Birmingham. Some of the products that had been transferred from Basingstoke turned out to be money losers, even though they had been making money at Basingstoke. We had serious productivity problems and morale was terrible. Although the predominant view was that there was no chance of turning the business around, there seemed to be little sense of urgency about the situation. The managing board was still having its customary gin and tonic every day at lunch.

Exhibit 2   *Financial results 1982 and 1983 (£000)*

	1982	1983
Total Sales	6,481.5	5,827.5
Cost of Sales	4,738.5	4,134.0
Gross Margin	1,743.0	1,693.5
Distribution	78.0	78.0
Royalties	21.0	36.0
Selling and Technical	1,249.5	946.5
Administration	411.5	484.5
Operating Profit	(117.0)	148.5
Interest (Receivable)/Payable	474.0	82.5
Non-Operating (Income)/Expense	99.0	295.5
Net Profit Before Tax	(690.0)	(229.5)
Factored Sales	1,812.0	1,659.0
Factored Materials	1,228.5	1,195.5

I knew I was going to have to take a number of actions which were going to inflict considerable pain. At the same time, I had to give everybody as much good news as possible, although there wasn't much good news to give.

My first step was to restructure my management team. I moved, or replaced, the directors for technical, sales and marketing, finance and production. We first focused our attention on the high scrap rates and low productivity. This resulted in a number of confrontations with the unions, but we made it clear to them that we had no choice. We didn't have time to figure out what the problems were with the Basingstoke products, so we closed one or two of them down and subcontracted their manufacture. We gave no wage increases the first year. In 1984 we tied the wage increase to agreements that gave us considerable more flexibility in work practices. We put much tighter controls on ordering material.

At the same time, we started a program of company briefings once a month, department by department. I felt it was critical for everyone in the organization to understand our situation and know what progress we were making. For instance, we made sure that everyone in the plant knew when we made a customer breakthrough. It was also important to get lower management levels to buy into what we were doing. Involving them in the communication process forced them to accept the 'responsibilities of management'. As soon as possible, we established a profit sharing scheme.

My view was that we needed to think of the turnaround in four stages. Stage one involved stemming the losses. Stage two involved consolidating, or trimming back. My goal for stage three was to achieve a 30 per cent return on capital employed (ROCE) and a 10 per cent return on sales (ROS). A real dilemma during these first three stages was how far could we go in cost cutting without hurting our ability to move into stage four – where I wanted to focus on growing the business. My basic assumption, however, was that we could preserve the core strengths of the business, so our real challenge was to devise an appropriate strategy and then organize ourselves to focus on doing the right things in the right way. If we were successful, I was convinced we could meet some aggressive sales and profit goals.

Products and Markets

The best way to organize the company was a complex question. As Table 1 shows, the firm served a variety of markets with a diverse product line.

Diamond products were also used in a wide array of other industries. Diamond wire dies, for instance, were used by lighting equipment manufacturers, and diamond knives were used by eye surgeons. Over time, WMIDP had developed products for these applications and a host of others.

Table 1 Principal Markets and Products

Markets	Products
Aircraft industry Automative industry	Dressers, drills, bandsaws, truers, turners, indenters, grinding wheels.
Glass industry	Grinding wheels, milling tools, diamond powder, smoothing pellets
Construction industry Mining industry	Segmental saws, core drill bits

When Marsh first joined VMIDP, the company was organized along functional lines. Although there was some sense of different markets, profits were calculated only for the total business. The salesforce tended to be organized along industry or market lines, but within the plant there was little or no industry or market focus. As Marsh put it:

> I had a feeling that we needed to reorganize the company, but I wasn't sure along what lines or how far to go. After all, we are a small organization and the idea of splitting still further seemed to have many problems.
>
> We had another problem. Although we didn't keep books that way, it was my view that some parts of the business were less profitable than others. I wasn't sure whether we should prune back those businesses that were unprofitable now or those which had less profit potential in the long run.
>
> Rotary truers, for instance, were going downhill fast. We had serious quality and productivity problems, and turnover had dropped to less than £200,000. Mining, by contrast (the firm's term for a group of products for which it acted principally as a reseller for products made by others), was doing well. Sales were holding steady, margins were good and, since we were buying and reselling, we didn't have any manufacturing problems. Our products for the stone and construction businesses and our general line of superabrasive products fell somewhere in between.
>
> If current profitability were the criterion, then it looked as though we should stay in mining, get out of rotary truers and try to turn stone and construction and superabrasives around. There was some thought that PIMS could help with this decision, but I wasn't sure. I had heard of PIMS but it sounded very theoretical, the kind of thing used in very large companies by strategic planners. Besides, my staff was really spread thin, and I wasn't at all sure that we could justify the time it might take to work with PIMS.

PIMS

The PIMS program originated at General Electric in the early 1960s. It was further developed at the Harvard Business School, in cooperation with the Marketing Sciences Institute, and is now housed at the Strategic Planning Institute (SPI), a not-for-profit business research and consulting organization located in Cambridge, Massachusetts. (See Appendix on p. 291 for a brief description of PIMS.)

Foseco became a corporate member of SPI in 1983. In January 1984, Keith Roberts, a senior consultant in the London office of SPI, met with C.W.N. Ward, Managing Director of Unicorn, and Peter Welch, Group Financial Director. At that meeting it was decided that VMIDP might represent an interesting opportunity for evaluating PIMS in a turnaround business situation. If Ian Marsh agreed, Keith would work with VMIDP but the costs would be borne by corporate headquarters[2].

As Keith Roberts recalled:

I called Ian and introduced myself. I told him a little about our meeting and about PIMS. I also told him that I felt the best way to proceed was for me to come to Gloucester and meet with him and some of his people. At that meeting, which I thought would take a day or two, we would make a fairly comprehensive presentation on PIMS, show him what kind of data we need and what kind of information we could provide about his business, after we had data on it entered in the computer. I suggested that he evaluate what he heard on the first day and then make a decision on whether or not to go further.

He agreed, and I met with him, Carol Spiller, then Marketing Director, Morris Edmonds, then Finance Director, and some of the technical people. I made a formal presentation that gave an overview of PIMS, with particular emphasis on its use as a framework for thinking about business units, performance measurement, investment intensity and marketing issues.

We then had a substantial discussion about his business and ways to reorganize. The guidelines for defining a business are reasonably straightforward – a well-defined external market, a clear-cut competitor, or set of competitors, control over all resources and so forth. Applying them is another matter. At first we got bogged down in trying to come up with good definitions, but finally we simplified it to High Tech (rotary truers), Stone and Construction, Mining and Me Too, a term we coined for their wide array of miscellaneous abrasives. Although some of their business came from abroad, we also decided to focus on just the UK market.

We then jumped right into a discussion of the PIMS concept of quality. I explained our view that it is the customer's judgment that defines quality, not the supplier's; that quality includes all the non-price attributes that count in the purchase decision; and that quality should be measured relative to competitors. Value then, or what the customer gets for his money, is a combination of relative quality and relative price. *(See Exhibit 3 for a graphical depiction of this relationship of relative price, relative quality and value.)* We then spent a lot of time trying to identify the key product and service related attributes for each of the four businesses and, finally, to assess how VMIDP stacked up against its major competitors. *(See Exhibit 4 for the form used to score competitive position.)*

At the end of the first day, it still was not clear to Marsh whether or not he should go ahead with PIMS. The normal PIMS data forms required information on some 160 variables, many of which would be difficult for VMIDF to obtain. Roberts had suggested that SPI could first do a so-called 'LIM analysis', which needs data on only 18 variables, but it was not clear how useful such an analysis would be.

According to Marsh:

> It had been a useful and interesting day. I was impressed by our discussion of how to define or organize our businesses and felt that the quality discussion was valuable. But I had some concerns about the additional staff time that would be required if we decided to go ahead. Many of the assumptions we made about our quality and our competitors needed further checking, much of the information PIMS wanted simply wasn't available or could only be estimated, and the financial information on the businesses as we had defined them was going to take considerable time to prepare.
>
> I was concerned that defining our market as just the UK could be misleading, given that some of our competitors had a much larger served

Exhibit 3   *Value map (5 generic price/quality positions)*
(Source: The PIMS principles)

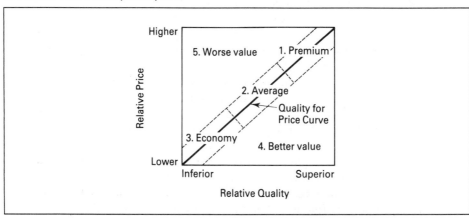

Exhibit 4   *Scoring our competitive position*

Business _____   Year _____

Customer Group (Name) _____   Importance (%) _____   Date _____

Quality (non-price) Attributes (Key Purchase Criteria)	Relative Importance to Customers (%)	Customer Rating					Our Business		
		Comp. A 0–10	Comp. B 0–10	Comp. C 0–10	Comp. D 0–10	Our Business 0–10	Super.	Equiv.	Infer.
Product-Related Attributes									
1									
2									
3									
5									
6									
Service-Related Attributes									
1									
2									
3									
4									
5									
6									
Totals	100%								

Market Share					
Price (relative to ours)					100
Direct Cost (relative to ours)					100
Technology (relative to ours)*					equal

*Ahead, equal, behind

Importance of quality vs. price in purchase decision

quality	
price	

100%

market. Also, as some of my staff said, PIMS focuses on what we are doing, not necessarily on what we should be doing. That is, it doesn't identify the key 'order getting' ingredients.

Finally, I really wondered what I would do if the PIMS analysis suggested a different set of conclusions from those I was leaning toward. For instance, Keith told me that one of the outputs of the report would be a comparison between actual ROI and PAR ROI (a PIMS concept that developed an expected ROI, based on the firm's strategic position). What if the businesses I thought we should stay in showed up poorly in the PIMS analysis?

Notes

1.   Companies in Exhibit 1 in italic were members of the Diamond Products Group.
2.   Cost of membership in SPI varied as a function of the firm's size. The membership fee covered the cost of assistance by the SPI staff to fill out the original set of data forms which comprehensively described the firm's business. Subsequent services were billed on a time and expense basis.

Appendix: PIMS (Profit Impact of Market Strategies)[1]

The PIMS research program was initiated in 1960 as an internal project at the General Electric Company (US). The basic concept was to examine a wide variety of businesses for the factors which explained, or predicted, superior operating performance. Using return-on-investment (ROI) as a measure of performance, regression models were constructed that 'explained' a substantial part of the variation in ROI. These models identified those factors that related most strongly to ROI and provided an indication of their relative role as explanatory variables.

Under the direction of Sidney Schoeffler, development of the models continued throughout the 1960s and early 1970s, first at GE and later at the Harvard Business School and the Marketing Science Institute. At that time the project was expanded to other corporations beyond GE. The Strategic Planning Institute, a non-profit corporation governed by its member companies, was formed to manage the PIMS program. As of 1987, around 450 corporations had contributed annual data, for periods ranging from 2 to 10 years, on some 3,000 product divisions or strategic business units.

PIMS Concepts

The fundamental concept underlying the PIMS approach to business analysis is that a business can learn from the experiences of strategy peers, as opposed to industry peers. That is, for instance, low market share companies in one industry can learn more about successful ways to compete from successful low market share companies in another industry than from analysis of a high market share company in one's own industry.

The architecture of the PIMS data base is built on two concepts: the business unit and its served market. Business units can be defined in a variety of ways. The PIMS definition is a division, product line, or other profit center of a company that:

- Produces and markets a well-defined set of related products and/or services;
- Serves a clearly defined set of customers, in a reasonably self-contained geographic area; and
- Competes with a well-defined set of competitors.

A firm's served market is a combination of customers for whom the product is suitable and to whom a marketing effort is made. Good identification of served market is important because:

- A business unit's market share is measured in relation to its served market.
- Market growth rates are measured or estimated for each unit's served market.

- The identity and market shares of leading competitors are determined by the scope of the served market.

- Assessments of the relative quality of a business unit's products and services are made in relation to competitors in the served market.

Factors that influence performance are generally grouped in three main categories:

- Those associated with the market environment (e.g., market growth rate, importance to end users, marketing expenditures, etc.);

- Those associated with competitive position (e.g., relative quality, market share, patent protection, etc.);

- Those associated with the capital and production structure (e.g., investment intensity, capacity utilization, vertical integration, etc.).

Twenty-two 'major' profit influences explain about 40 per cent of the difference in ROS and ROI among the PIMS businesses. A more complete model (the PAR ROI model) explains over 70 per cent.

The PIMS Data Base

Each participating company supplies more than 160 data items on various aspects of its strategic and financial position. Data that might make it possible to identify an individual company or business are disguised (by use of ratios, or multipliers) and elaborate precautions are taken to otherwise protect the confidentiality of information in the data base.

Many different industries, products, markets and geographic regions are represented in the PIMS data base. In 1985 some 90 per cent of the businesses were in manufacturing, vs 10% for service. About one-third produced consumer products, 20% produced capital goods, and the remainder were material suppliers. About two-thirds marketed their products/services in North America. The data base included about 400 businesses in the UK and Western Europe.

On average the data base tends to include the more mature, large and profitable businesses. Even so, there is great variation in performance and strategic situations. Average pre-tax ROI, for instance, has been around 21%, but ROI for individual businesses has ranged from −25% to +80%. Similarly, the data base contains start-up as well as mature businesses and also businesses well under $10,000,000 in sales.

PIMS Applications and Tools

According to PIMS, a successful strategic analysis of a business unit yields:

- A clear and precise definition of the business, its market, and its competitors;

- An understanding of the current strategic situation, including strengths and weaknesses relative to competitors, threats and opportunities;
- A program for getting the most out of the business in its current position, over the near term, consistent with:
    A specific strategy to be followed over the long term, to gain the maximum improvement in strategic position;
    Identification of tactics required to successfully implement the strategy, in enough detail to be easily translated into functional plans and budgets.

Major PIMS Tools include:

- *The PAR ROI Model*: Calculates the expected or 'normal' profitability for a business based on approximately 30 of its structural and operating characteristics;
- *Contribution Ratio Analysis*: Separates business profit-ability into Operating Effectiveness components and a Strategic Position component;
- *Operating PAR Models*: Determine expected or 'normal' levels of employee productivity, working capital, marketing, etc. based on various characteristics of the business and its market;
- *The Strategy Model*: Assesses the feasibility and expected financial results of major changes in the structural characteristics of a business, including the likely competitive dynamics of such changes (for example, growth in market share);
- *The Report on Look-alikes*: Focuses on structurally similar businesses in the data base to identify short-term opportunities and tactics for improving the performance or defending the current position of a business;
- *The Productivity Tracking System*: Identifies effects on profits of price/cost movements and changes in input/output relationships, providing normal or benchmark rates of change for each;
- *The Business Start-Up Model*: Gives an objective assessment of the marketing tactics and future prospects of start-up ventures, using a special data base of businesses in their first few years of operation;
- *Portfolio Models*: Examine diverse businesses within a portfolio to provide guidelines for resource allocation and tactical focus, in light of corporate constraints and priorities;
- *Limited Information Models (LIM)*: Permit analysis of competitors, acquisition candidates or associates, where data are not freely available;
- *PIMS OASIS data base*: Developed jointly with Hay Associates and the University of Michigan to study links between human resource issues, competitive strategy and business performance.

Note

1. This section draws heavily on a number of PIMS publications; and on Buzzell, Robert D. and Gale, Bradley T., *The PIMS Principles*, New York: The Free Press, 1987.

SECTION 10

Topical Cases

A.   Moving from Products to Services
SKF Bearings Series

B.   Organizing the Marketing Efforts: Solution Selling
IBM Branch Office: Irgendvoe, Austria

C.   Alliances and Strategic Customer Relationships
Digital Equipment Corporation International

D.   Technology Licencing
Potain S.A.

E.   Marketing–Manufacturing–Logistics Interfaces
Unichema

F.   Implementing Global Strategies
Logitech International SA

SKF Bearings Series: Market Orientation through Services
Restructuring the Before and After Market

This case was prepared by Professor Sandra Vandermerwe and Dr. Marika Taishoff as a basis for class discussion, rather than to illustrate either effective or ineffective handling of a management situation.

In the spring of 1987 Mauritz Sahlin, CEO of SKF, the world's largest bearing company, took a bold step. The time had come to do whatever was necessary to improve profitability and return on assets. He knew that his plan would require a complex reorganization of SKF with far-reaching consequences, but he had no other options.

Production had already been rationalized and was fully automated, leaving little room for real savings. The company could not pull back on R&D expenditures as they were essential to having technological prowess and quality standards. Cutting back on staff would upset the unions and provoke costly stoppages.

He was convinced that the only viable long-term solution was to change the strategic orientation of SKF from the production line to the market. Amidst great uncertainty and speculation, he called together the senior bearing managers from around the world to Saltsjobaden, Sweden, to announce his intention to split the company into three new areas.

> It is essential, he said, that we optimize by structuring around our market relationships instead of our manufacturing capacity. If we want to remain the industry leader in bearings, we must be prepared to give customers what they want rather than merely sell them what we make.

He knew that the traditional sluggish culture of the company had to be altered. Questions would have to be answered which were not yet part of the existing SKF vocabulary. He expected criticism, resistance and conflict among the divisions. Even confusion for a while. He was prepared to take the risks.

The Beginnings and Background

As in many industrial success stories, the formation of SKF happened by chance. At the turn of the century Sven Wingquist, a young Swedish maintenance engineer, was fed up with the poor quality of bearings, with frequent stoppages and replacements that were not only expensive but took weeks for suppliers to deliver. The frustrated Wingquist got his employer's blessing to begin work on a new bearing in 1905 and soon perfected a product that was more effective and longer lasting than competitors' models. By 1907 Svenska Kullager Fabriken (SKF), the new company set up to produce and market the technological innovation, was in business.

The ball bearing, a device which allows rotation around a shaft or axle with minimal friction, is an essential part of any motion dependent product, be it car, machine, truck, or train. As a result, high quality bearings soon became an indispensable item for all major industrial sectors, ranging from electrical and heavy industries to transportation. Over the next six decades, SKF grew in tandem with industrial growth and became the world leader in bearing technology and applications.

Up through the mid-60s, SKF was highly centralized; all aspects of the business such as logistics, global sales, application engineering and public relations were handled by the parent company in Göteborg. Five European plants produced a wide range of products geared to their own large local customer base. These regional units concentrated exclusively on the manufacturing process, particularly on maintaining cost effectiveness. Countries did not export to each other or operate internationally except rarely – when the initiative came from Göteborg.

The company's underlying drive was mass production and having high quality standards. In the words of one executive, 'Big was beautiful.' The plants were given significant capital budget allocations. Large economies of scale meant that huge quantities of bearings could be sold at competitive prices on the world market. Operations were integrated as much as possible both horizontally and vertically. A tools division was acquired in order to expand into the manufacture of engineering products and machine tools. Manufacturing machinery was designed in-house so that material flow systems and production techniques could be perfected and capacity increased.

R&D contributed greatly to SKF's strength. Since most bearings had an average life of five years, there was a continuous need to develop new products. About 200 people in the Netherlands were involved in product development and in improving the engineering and performance standards for the product lines. Input was received from the various plants where R&D had a close relationship. As a general rule, SKF preferred to overdesign its products to ensure that the needs and specifications of the plant managers were met.

The 70s and 80s: Japanese and European Competition

In the early 70s the Japanese, already strong in Asia, entered the European bearings market. As a result, SKF management was forced to cut costs further 'by whatever means' as well as begin exporting outside their traditional markets. To reach this goal while developing scale economies, production facilities were rationalized along the lines of the Japanese model, i.e., each factory became responsible for making and exporting a specific bearing type for world consumption.

The rise in oil prices in the early 80s, causing a drop in real wealth and in demand for capital goods and consumer durables, put additional pressure on margins. 'Production Concept 80', aimed at stimulating effective production, at cutting staff and underscoring the manufacturing process in company investment policy, was SKF's response to economic conditions as well as to competitive threats.

This concept, along with the continued emphasis on top quality standards, allowed SKF to remain the number 1 bearings producer. By the late 80s the company had 20% of the world bearings market share, nearly twice that of its closest competitor, Nippon Seiko of Japan. Another Japanese bearings producer, NTN, had 10%, followed by Germany's F.A.G. and Timken of the US with 8.5% each, and the Japanese firm Koyo with 6% of the world market.

Bearings producers were not the only competitors on the world scene. Automobile manufacturers, including Ford, Honda and Mercedes, through their spare parts divisions, were both competitors to and customers of SKF. This was also the case for some specific manufacturers of automobile parts, such as the UK's Quinton Hazel, which would typically purchase SKF bearings and sell them under its own brand name to distributors, thereby cutting into a segment of SKF's traditional customer base.

SKF's position had always been strongest in Europe and Latin America, with 35% and 30% of these markets respectively. In the US, SKF was in third position, with 12%. On average, Europe accounted for almost 60% of SKF's business, North America for 20%, Sweden 5% and the rest of the world 15%. Despite this comparatively strong market share, worldwide economic and industrial conditions continued to squeeze margins during the first half of the decade. This situation came to a head in 1985 when SKF's volume in the US, susceptible to economic changes and often indicative of what could happen in other regions, plunged 15%. The company was obliged to embark on a substantial restructuring program in the US.

1986: A Financial Ebb

By 1986, SKF had 48 factories in 13 countries operating at near or full capacity to produce two million bearings a day. SKF vigorously promoted its products through 35,000 local dealer and distributor (d/d) outlets worldwide, as well as a direct sales force of 600 throughout 130 countries. Dealers and distributors carried large stocks of limited range high turnover bearings for SKF, along with competitive bearings and complementary materials and tools.

When Sahlin took the helm as CEO in 1985, SKF was operating at the crest of what amounted to a roller bearing boom. Nevertheless, economic conditions and competitive pressure made it a buyers' market. Bottomline results began to turn flat at SKF that year, when sales slackened and margins narrowed. *(The financial profile for the years 1982 through 1986 are shown in Exhibit 1.)*

Segmenting the Bearings Market

With increasing competition, SKF found it more and more difficult to differentiate its product from the others. It had always applied one strategy and organization for all bearing customers. High quality products were sold in large quantities at competitive prices. Sahlin questioned this approach and, late in 1986, commissioned research to examine the bearings market in detail. He wanted to establish whether the market could be segmented along any natural split amongst the product lines according to specific customer needs.

Consumers were grouped into three categories:

Exhibit 1 *Financial Profile for 1982–1986 (*Source: *annual reports)*

In Skr (bn)	1982	1983	1984	1985	1986
Consolidated					
Net Sales	14.4	16.2	17.8	20.0	20.1
Operating Expenses	13.0	14.9	15.9	17.9	18.0
Income after Financial Income and Expense	.657	.604	1.3	1.4	1.5
Total Assets	18.8	18.6	21.8	22.0	22.8
Shareholder Equity	5.4	5.2	6.8	6.7	7.3
Return on Total Assets	8.0	7.4	9.8	9.5	9.3
Price per Share	29.2	42.0	43.0	75.0	84.0
Bearings: as % of Total Sales	80	82	80	76	77
as % of Total Profits	90	95	80	78	75

1. *Automotive OEM* (cars, trucks, electrical), with 32% of SKF bearings sales in Skr

2. *Machinery OEM* (heavy industry, railway, general machinery), with 27% of SKF bearings sales in Skr

3. *Aftermarket* (vehicles and industrial), with 41% of SKF bearings sales in Skr

Whereas bearings were regarded as vital components in the OEM market, in the aftermarket they were seen merely as spare parts. Large OEM sales were handled directly by the company's global sales arm. Contracts were substantial and steady. 'Large orders were signed and executed in a routine way.'

The aftermarket sales were made to distributors and dealers, who in turn served end users. Relationships were entirely different for these markets, as were the services demanded. Delivery requirements, lead times and quantities, along with type and range of bearings needed, also varied considerably.

There were more than twice as many OEM than aftermarket customers, although fewer in the vehicle business than in machinery. Automotive OEM customers were large and tended to operate centrally on a European, if not global scale. By contrast, machinery OEM users were smaller; their particular strengths tended to be in specific industries and geographic locations. Large OEM customers made up roughly 40% of the total SKF bearings sales in kronor. Lead times were stable and predictable, making forecasting straightforward. Profit margins were low in the OEM sector. The larger OEM customers, who often set their own prices on substantial, long-term contracts, were particularly cost conscious since 'every cent saved was money in the bank'. SKF was thus under constant competitive pressure to keep price increases at or below the inflation rate.

OEM customers were considered the glamorous end of the business, always given priority by the SKF factories. High volume production and sales standards set for the large OEM customers were applied throughout the rest of the organization. OEMs were not only allocated most of the new product funding, but also attracted SKF's best talent. Some of the reasons for this situation were:

- OEMs would typically deal with big name customers like Volkswagen or Ford, and would be involved in negotiations at a senior managerial level.

- Technical developments for OEMs were more challenging than for the aftermarket because they tended to be more complex and state-of-the-art.

- Orders for the OEM were larger, steady and more consistent, with lead times that made well-defined production schedules possible.

By contrast, the aftermarket tended to concentrate on single sale deals for motor dealers and factories. Although price was important, these clients, for whom speed, availability and assistance were essential, were prepared to pay more than the OEM customers. In fact, the higher prices in the aftermarket enabled SKF to do OEM business that otherwise may not have been justified. It had long been suspected that, despite being largely limited to single sales, the aftermarket was the most profitable part of the business. However, since operating results for all the markets were consolidated, this impression was never really confirmed.

The aftermarket was subdivided into two separate categories:

1. *The Industrial Aftermarket* (factory owners and plant managers), with 66% of SKF aftermarket sales in Skr

2. *The Vehicle Aftermarket* (fleet owners and repair shops), with 34% of SKF aftermarket sales in Skr

In their *industrial* aftermarket business, which contributed two thirds to the overall aftermarket sales, SKF had concentrated mainly on steel and paper mills. Mines and railways were also a part of this business. These customers had the same basic needs wherever they were geographically situated. The distributor network accounted for 80% of the sales.

For industrial users, the cost of the bearing was 'peanuts compared to the cost of standstill'. They sought to minimize downtime and maximize the recovery speed. Customers spent 75% of downtime locating the proper equipment and people, and only 25% on actually repairing the machine.

The lifetime of a bearing played a fundamental role in the success of these customer's production activities. Longevity was affected by: (1) the quality of the product, (2) how it was installed, (3) protecting the bearing from the environment, and (4) the quality of maintenance management at the factory. The last three factors depended on the users. Most bearings failed because of incorrect installation, inadequate or improper lubrication or environmental contamination.

The *vehicle* aftermarket accounted for one third of total aftermarket sales. Despite the fact that the automobile and truck sectors contributed 24% of SKF's OEM sales, the aftermarket had been relatively ignored. This neglect stemmed from the basic principle, 'if we made it, we sold it'. And since SKF made only a limited range of bearings compared to the great variety of autos, the aftermarket had never been considered a priority.

Dealers for automotive OEMs and independent distributors channeled spare parts through to the car and truck market. Because of the better service they were receiving, garage and fleet owners were increasingly shifting their business to the independents. Bearings comprised only 3–4% of distributor and retailer sales, compared to between 30% and 70% in the industrial aftermarket. The distance from the bearing manufacturer to the final user was much longer in the vehicle aftermarket, with the channel consisting of wholesalers, large retailers, and garages. Since cross referencing of bearing components was not consistent in the industry, it was difficult to ascertain which manufacturer's part was being replaced.

Vehicle dealers and repair shops wanted a bearing quickly because car owners expected vehicles back within a couple of hours. They also needed the right bearing for that particular vehicle. Replacing a bearing presented three problems for the bearing installer: (1) where to find the correct bearing, (2) how to mount and install it, and (3) how to obtain the various accessories to get the job done.

SKF had always regarded distributors as customers rather than as part of the channel to the end user. Bearings were sold *to* them instead of *through* them. Relationships with end users were left in the distributors' hands. Sales people loaded up the distributors' shelves and devised all sorts of deals to gain volume, even if items had to be taken back unsold. The distributor network gave Bearing Services the necessary local presence and coverage, and it was often more cost effective than using a direct salesforce to get the bearings to the customer. There was, however, no guaranteed preference for the SKF brand.

Splitting the Organization

Research showed that the market for bearings was far from homogeneous. This information confirmed Sahlin's instincts that different target segments had to have their own market strategies and organizations.

No one knew what to expect when Sahlin convened an urgent meeting in Saltsjobaden. As one manager described it, 'Phone calls had been made back and forth to try to find out what was going on and who had been invited. Most of us only found out the next day when it made *The Financial Times*.' At the meeting, Sahlin announced that, as of September 1, the bearings group would be officially reorganized into three new areas.

1. *Bearing Industries* would include all the manufacturing plants producing 'standard' bearings for OEM, both machinery and automotive. The selling would be done by its own salesforce in countries where SKF had factories, such as Germany, France, the UK, the US, Sweden, Brazil, Argentina, Mexico and Italy. In other countries such as Switzerland, Belgium and Holland, Bearing Services would do the selling.

2. *Bearing Services*, carved out of the global sales organization, would handle the entire vehicle and industrial aftermarket as well as some of the smaller OEM clients with whom the aftermarket distributors did business.

3. *Specialty Bearings* would handle products outside the standard line which needed highly specialized skills. This division would have its own factories and would utilize Bearing Industries' and Bearing Services' salesforce in most countries. Customers included the aerospace industry, medical equipment suppliers, large machine tool producers, and satellite manufacturers which required custom-designed products for highly specialized applications.

Each business area would have its own CEO and separate worldwide profit responsibility. Efforts would be made to keep these autonomous, thus minimizing the need for coordination. Sahlin believed the new structure would allow each business unit to be more flexible, to target and get close to its own customers, thereby commanding better margins. *(For the old and new group organization structures, see **Exhibit 2**.)*

The research confirmed Sahlin's earlier instincts that the aftermarket was indeed the profitable end of the business. He had long believed that this market had not been given enough attention but nothing had been done because it was not clear what to do and the financial significance of the aftermarket had never been established. Sahlin was convinced that the key to future profits and customer loyalty was in offering the aftermarket SKF knowhow and expertise. Bearing Services, he decided, would be a major focus for the company in the future.

Exhibit 2 *Old and new organizational structure*

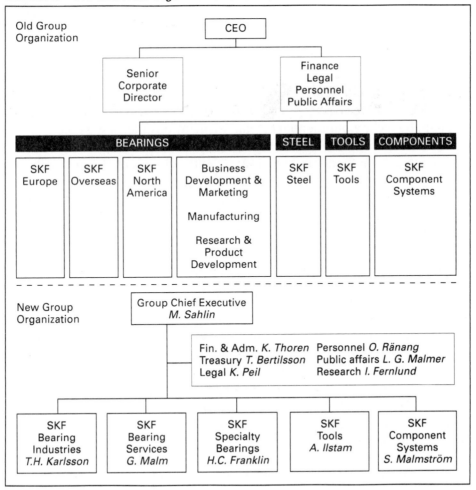

The sales management teams which had been dealing with the aftermarket had previously reported to the manufacturing companies. Now, in the newly formed Bearing Services, they were elevated to the same status as that of their former bosses. Sales and marketing directors in various countries became managing directors (MDs).

Transforming the Change Process

Previously, all changes at SKF had been very structured. Typically, before any decision could be made, numerous studies were undertaken and proposals scrutinized in order to minimize risk. A kind of 'bible' was then written stating exactly how the change would take place – what had to be done, by when and by whom. As little as possible was left to chance. Sales budgets, production budgets and action plans were put in place before the new process began.

It was clear to Sahlin that SKF not only had to become a market focussed company, but the process of change itself had to be transformed. Although the ultimate goal of improving profits was straightforward, exactly how it would evolve was not 100% clear. The company would have to learn by doing, by feeling out the market and being as flexible as possible.

One thing was obvious: the entire culture of the company needed a jolt. The manufacturing functions had always had the clout, but they would have to give up some of that power. The financial approach to the market would have to change as well. Marketing could no longer be considered an expense or cost centre, but would have to be handled like any other capital investment.

Sahlin knew it would be impossible to move the whole company at once. He expected Bearing Services to be a springboard to a new SKF market culture. Once they began making positive inroads into the market, he was convinced that the rest of the organization would follow. The goal was not to push for sudden and monumental changes but, rather, to let things take shape as they moved along. Small positive steps had to be taken to influence people and convince them about the new SKF way. He drafted a rough outline of how the organization would look and some guidelines for implementation. He wanted that the company's technical expertise be used to serve customers more fully, thus giving SKF a significant competitive edge. A new CEO would be appointed to each of the three areas and left to formulate his own plan.

Göran Malm, a sales and marketing specialist with a financial background, had been the European marketing and sales manager for SKF.

He had been Singapore area manager for less than a year when Sahlin called and asked him to head Bearing Services. Malm, who had been pushing for change at SKF for some time, had initiated and set up maintenance support centres in Sweden to provide services for the aftermarket there. He was, Sahlin believed, the ideal candidate for the job. At first Malm was reluctant: he'd only just begun to develop a network in Singapore. Sahlin remained adamant: 'I decide on the priorities, Göran,' came his voice late one night. 'I need you back here. You understand the aftermarket and what the customers want. Let me have your decision soon, Göran.'

Malm had smiled as he put down the phone. He knew the job would be tough, but he also knew he couldn't resist the offer to lead Bearing Services.

Some Reactions to the Restructuring

- Most aftermarket sales people liked the idea of the split; they would finally be elevated from the second class status to which they felt they had been relegated. As one marketing director expressed it, 'Suddenly we felt that we were as important as the guys in manufacturing. It was incredible. We knew then that Sahlin was serious about becoming customer oriented. There had been lots of jokes about the d/d club or, as some called it, the dinner/dance club. That's the way those of us in the aftermarket were seen – wining and dining customers without doing any real work. We were happy that at last someone was listening to us and we could concentrate on customers' needs.'

- Some of the more traditional administration, engineering and financial executives lacked enthusiasm. They couldn't quite see the point. 'It will simply add extra costs we don't want or need in our business' was the typical remark.

- Another reservation was whether or not to take the restructuring seriously. 'This is just another reorganization. We've had so many, how long will this one last?' was the refrain.

- Some thought that too many questions had been left unanswered and that the ultimate objectives were still too vague. It wasn't that they necessarily disagreed with the overall plan: they wanted more data and details so they could 'proceed in an orderly SKF fashion'.

- Others felt that such a novel approach would simply not be feasible in an institution as bureaucratic as SKF. The stringent reporting requirements to head office and rigid structural barriers were just some of the many obstacles which would have to be overcome. These executives were not convinced that the new structure could fit the managerial techniques and tools that they knew worked.

● The MDs who had previously controlled both sales and aftermarket did not all react positively when they heard Sahlin's reorganization plan. Some resented the sudden change in status of the people who had previously been working for them and who would be taking away a chunk of their business and their profits. 'Some executives tried to get around it by saying "yes", but then delayed implementation.'

When challenged about these concerns, Sahlin stated repeatedly that he understood the difficulties ahead, but was prepared to take whatever risks were necessary.

IBM Branch Office: Irgendvoe, Austria
Selling Solutions

This case was prepared by Professors Per Jenster, Werner Ketelhöhn and Research Associate Bethann Kassman, as a basis for class discussion rather than to illustrate either effective or ineffective handling of a business situation. Names, numbers and places have been disguised for confidential reasons.

Mr. André Bower, manager of the IBM Irgendvoe branch office, was reflecting on the conversation he just had finished with Markus Gall about an ongoing ASch420 million (US$35 million) systems integration project with the Austrian Bundesbahn (ABB). As André Bower looked out across the city of Irgendvoe, he shuddered when he thought about all the instances where this project could have gone wrong. Against all odds, until now Markus and his team seemed to have been able to avoid all the risks. 'If the branch is going to make money in the solutions business, and I am to survive without sleepless nights, I'd better develop a management process which manages the solution part of our business.'

IBM and the Drive Towards a Solution Business

During the period 1985–1987, IBM experienced a rapid deterioration of operating income from $11.2 billion to $7.7 billion worldwide. Although many factors contributed to this decline – particularly more competition from Japanese computer assemblers – IBM traced at least some of the results to the loss of its earlier privileged vendor position with many customers. Corporate customers increasingly understood computer technology, which allowed them to place greater demands on computer manufacturers. In addition, the customer base had changed. Much of IBM's success in the past had been attributed to its close ties with data processing managers. With the emergence of departmental computing and personal computers, data processing had become a commodity and was no longer an opportunity for competitive advantage.

Consequently, decisions about data processing investment were examined much more closely by managers, who were not necessarily in traditional data processing departments and who perhaps owed little allegiance to IBM. Their primary concern was to find a solution to a business need. As it became possible for hardware from different vendors to operate as a system, competition among manufacturers increased. IBM's response to this challenge was to refocus the company's strategy from a technology-driven to a customer-driven orientation. This shift from 'box' selling, as IBM insiders termed the sales strategy, to 'solution' selling meant more emphasis on software and services as well as greater flexibility in combining hardware, both IBM hardware and that of other vendors. Because of pressures from traditional vendors, and from new challengers in consulting services and systems integration houses, computer companies were eager to influence the customer's choice of hardware, software and services provided when an information technology solution was purchased. Ability to integrate technologies within a business context was, therefore, the overriding concept pushing solution selling. As a result, the services market, with its emphasis on systems integration, was viewed as the most dynamic segment of the industry. The services component included conceptual formulation, project management, programming, analysis, installation, maintenance, education and value added network services.

Within the framework of market-driven quality, IBM strove to be viewed by its customers as the premier solution provider. The firm recognized that it was no longer enough to be seen as the master of the data centre. The competitive computer vendor now had to be involved in how the customer operated his business. As John Akers, CEO of IBM, commented in a January 1989 interview with *Datamation* magazine: 'The more we get ourselves out of thinking about piece parts of computer systems and communications systems, and having people who really can add value in the customers' conference rooms, the better off we're going to be.' To this end, IBM Europe had decided to initiate this process by experimentally converting some of its 250 branch offices from revenue to profit centres.

The European Solutions Industry and Competitors

The systems integration market was a high growth, high risk environment which encompassed a great deal of complexity and uncertainty. The major

Exhibit 1

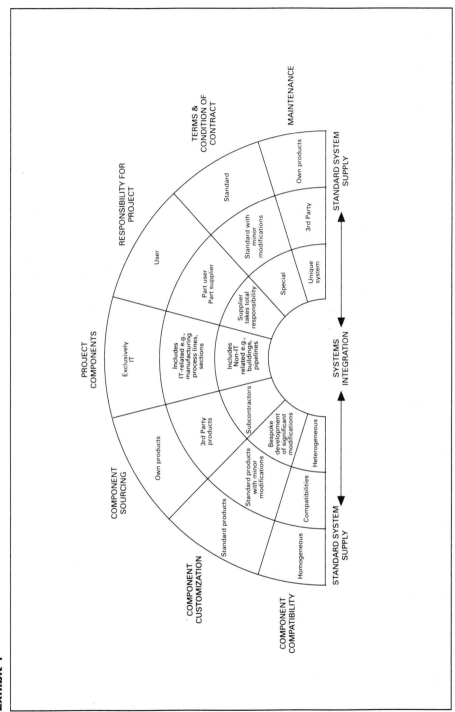

systems delivery options became increasingly specialized as they moved towards total integrated solutions *(as shown in Exhibit 1)*. Major players in the solutions industry had to have the ability to integrate heterogeneous hardware, develop customized products, manage subcontractors, maintain unique systems, and function in a non-information technological environment. In other words, they had to be able to take total responsibility for the business solution and its attendant risks.

The Western European Systems Integration market was worth $3.916 billion in 1990. *(Refer to Exhibit 2 for a review of the industrial sector breakdown)*. The leading players in this market were IBM, Siemens, Andersen Consulting and CGS. *(An indication of their relative strengths is shown in Exhibit 3.)* However, the market was extremely competitive with a number of companies actively pursuing greater market share in selected segments.

In a 1990 survey of eight countries (West Germany, France, Italy, Spain, United Kingdom, Belgium, Switzerland and Sweden), the United Kingdom and France were the largest European Systems Integration markets, each with a 27% share of the total West European market, followed by West Germany with a 19% share. Spain had the highest growth market and Switzerland the lowest.

IBM's competitive position varied in each of the countries surveyed. In West Germany, IBM had strong competition from Siemens, but was generally perceived as having good capability in all system integration areas except telecommunication skills. In France, CGS was seen as the strongest company, followed by Steria, Sema, Andersen Consulting and IBM. IBM was rated lower than its competitors in the areas of networking with partners, range of systems integration services, technical expertise, project management skills and multi-vendor skills. In the UK, Andersen Consulting, Sema and SD-Scion were ranked equally, followed by EDS and IBM. In Spain and Italy, Andersen Consulting outranked IBM. Italsiel was also strong in Italy, while CGS had a high rating in the Spanish market. In Switzerland, IBM was considerably stronger than its closest competitors, NCR and Andersen Consulting. In Sweden, Programator was ranked first, followed by Enator, CGS and IBM. In Belgium, Sema received the highest rating, with Trasys and IBM ranking second and third. In all markets, IBM's size and financial strength, transnational capability and product range were perceived as the company's strengths. Multi-vendor skills was considered to be its greatest weakness.

IBM Irgendvoe Branch Office

IBM Austria was divided into two divisions representing major industrial

Exhibit 2

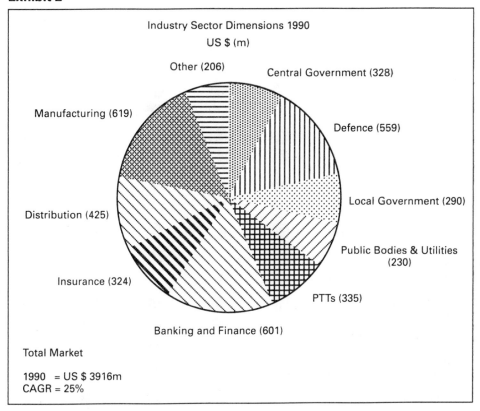

Industry Sector Dimensions 1990
US $ (m)

Other (206)
Central Government (328)
Manufacturing (619)
Defence (559)
Local Government (290)
Distribution (425)
Public Bodies & Utilities (230)
Insurance (324)
PTTs (335)
Banking and Finance (601)

Total Market

1990 = US $ 3916m
CAGR = 25%

sectors: the banking/services industries with offices in Wien, Innsbruck and Salzburg; and the government/public industries (mainly government and utilities) with offices in Wien, Irgendvoe, St. Pölten, Enns and Graz. The branch office in Irgendvoe reported to the Wien chief for the industry/public sector. *(Refer to **Exhibit 4** for details of the Irgendvoe branch office organization.)* The sales representatives and sales managers at the branch office were organized to focus on customers in a single industry. Thus, the industry segments in the public sector were served by four sales teams which were organized in the following manner:

1. The Federal government/defense team (1 manager, 7 sales staff and 4 technical staff);
2. The State university/State government team (1 manager and 3 sales staff);
3. The ABB (railroad) team (1 manager and 3 sales staff);
4. The PTT (telephone) team (1 manager and 3 sales staff).

Exhibit 3 *Systems integration: competitive positioning*

SUPPLIER	IBM	Other H/W Vendor (Siemens)	Leading Systems House (CGS)	Major Cons (Andersen)
Size and Financial Strength	●	●	●	●
SI Marketing	◌	◌	●	●
SI Track Record	●	●	●	●
Image in SI	◐	◐	●	●
Market Presence	●	◐	◐	◐
Partners Network	◌	◐	◌	◌
Transnational Capability	●	◐	◐	◐
Range of SI Services	◌	◐	◐	◐
Product Range	◐	◐	◑	◑
Technical Expertise	●	◐	●	●
Project Management Skills	◌	◌	◐	●
SI Terms & Conditions	◌	◌	◌	◌
Relationship Management	◐	◑	◐	◐
Multi-vendor Skills	○	◌	●	●
Telecommunications Skills	◌	◌	●	◌
Related Services (FM & MDNS)	●	○	○	○

Legend:

● Perceived to have good capability

◌ Perceived to have reasonable capability

○ Perceived to have weak capability

The industrial sector had one sales team consisting of 1 manager and 5 sales staff who were responsible for the manufacturing industry. The retail/ services team consisted of 1 manager and 5 sales staff responsible for the banking/services industry. These sales teams were composed entirely of salespeople and account managers.

All technical support was provided through systems engineering/

Exhibit 4 *Organization branch office Irgendvoe 1991 (tentative)*

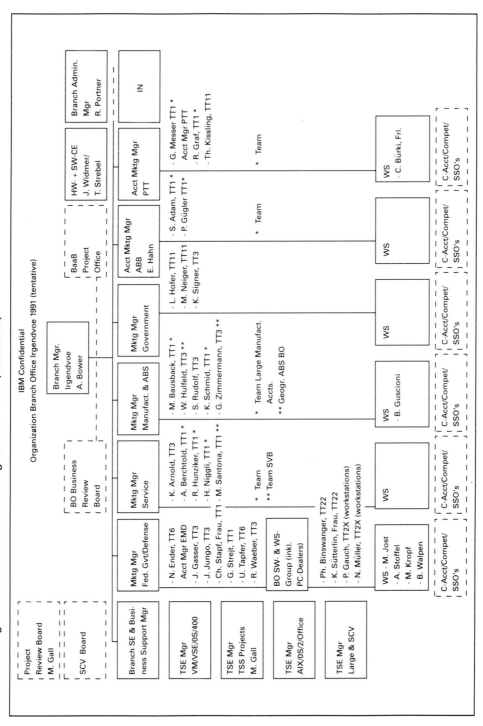

business support personnel. The technical support division was organized along the following lines:

1. Large systems (1 manager and 14 staff members);
2. Medium/mid-range systems (1 manager and 14 staff members);
3. UNIX/office systems (1 manager, 10 staff members and 2 student workers);
4. Systems integration/project organization (1 manager, 10 staff members and 3 student workers).

Of the technical support groups, it was the systems integration/project organization group which was responsible for project management and acted as consultants to the salesmen in proposing solutions for customers' problems.

Administration support was provided by staff members located in the Irgendvoe branch office who reported directly to Wien. The administrative department had 25 personnel, 24 of whom performed data entry functions in the management of order processing accounts and financial follow-up with customers.

The Irgendvoe office turnover in 1990 was ASch1,850 million ($154 million) of which 60% was in hardware and 40% in software and services. Revenue came from the following industrial sources:

	%
Federal government	25
State university	20
ABB	15
PTT	10
Manufacturing	10
Service	20

The Irgendvoe Branch Office as a Business

In 1989 IBM designated the Irgendvoe branch office as a business (BAB). This designation was initiated to empower the branch office with greater flexibility and an entrepreneurial spirit, as well as to look at bottom line profits. The advantages that a branch office had as a business included:

1. *Greater freedom to make business decisions quickly.* The BAB manager made decisions involving up to ASch125,000 ($10,500) vs. other branch managers whose decisions were limited to ASch25,000 ($2,100).

2. *Greater pricing flexibility*. The flexibility on price changes ranged from −2% to 3%.

Limitations in managing the office as a business were evident from the beginning. The tools needed to measure unit costs, as well as methodology for determining actual costs of solutions, were nonexistent. Although the BAB manager was supposed to meet profit targets, high fixed overhead costs assigned to the branch made it difficult. Also, there was mixed acceptance of the branch concept by various offices in Wien as well as at the Paris headquarters, creating problems for the BAB office staff. Compensation for the BAB staff was identical to that of the other branch offices, with the exception of a one-time financial award. Therefore, it was finding ways to simplify business and be more personally responsive to the customer that were the main motivating factors driving the BAB concept among the staff.

Solution Selling

Markus Gall, the manager of Systems Integration, defined solution selling as 'the selling of hardware, software and services', i.e., taking discrete pieces of technology and making them work together as a coherent entity for the customer. The sales object of solution selling was to solve the customer's problem with a turnkey solution including hardware specification, software adaptation and development, and service. When a customer contacted an account manager, salesperson or manager about a technical problem, the IBM salesperson defined the aspects of the problem with the client. Then the salesperson initiated discussions with the Systems Integration group, which had responsibility for overseeing the solution. Working with the sales team to define all aspects of the project, Systems Integration determined the project definition, assessed the skills and resources that existed in the branch office, and defined which resources were to be contracted to vendors in order to provide a complete solution to the customer's problem. The major success factor in solution selling was in the ability to define the project or problem correctly. The sales team maintained a lead position with the client, with Systems Integration providing technical skills and project oversight to keep the project on target.

A Systems Integration Contract

For over 1½ years, the Irgendvoe office had been working on a project for the ABB involving the maximization of the cargo scheduling service, as a precursor to a much larger scheduling system. In mid-January, Mr. Bower heard that the Irgendvoe office had completed the contract. From the records he had kept of all major contracts involving systems integration, Mr. Bower was able to review and reappraise the events that took place between March 13, 1989, when the office was first contacted by the ABB, and January 15, 1991, when the contract was completed.

March 13, 1989
The office received a call from Mr. Harris of the ABB regarding a project for which it was seeking bids. The ABB wanted to develop a system for updating, integrating and enhancing information regarding cargo scheduling. Mr. Hahn, account manager for the ABB, and Mr. Gohrin, one of the sales representatives assigned to the ABB, arranged a meeting with Mr. Harris on March 16.

March 16, 1989
Mr. Hahn and Mr. Gohrin called on Mr. Harris who informed them of the scope of the project. The ABB wanted to develop a cargo information system which coordinated regional/intercity traffic while minimizing waiting times and maximizing connections. The solution involved integrating currently-owned hardware with new hardware, combining multi-vendor hardware, networking among a large number of railway stations, and designing new software that was user friendly. The ABB also mentioned that there would be other parties bidding for the contract. Mr. Harris indicated that he would like an initial proposal within three months.

March 20, 1989
Mr. Hahn and Mr. Gohrin each reviewed the specifications over the weekend and realized that the project was complex. It involved combining technologies into a workable solution using specially developed software to run on a variety of IBM and other vendor hardware at a minimum of 114 sites. They contacted Mr. Gall and met with him to determine the scope of the project. It was agreed that during the proposal phase, Mr. Gohrin would serve as the proposal manager. A follow-up meeting was scheduled with Mr. Harris for March 30.

March 29, 1989
Mr. Gall and Mr. Gohrin reviewed the preliminary technical specifications. They also listed all the IBM hardware which the ABB was known to have purchased over the years, and put together a list of questions to review with Mr. Harris and his staff.

March 30, 1989

Mr. Gohrin met with Mr. Harris and his staff. The ABB gave him a very definitive list of the goals that the project should fulfill:

1. Development of a modern platform for cooperative processing
2. Central management for software and data
3. Automated distribution of software and data
4. Development platform
5. Production platform

Mr. Gohrin agreed to submit an initial proposal within the next two months.

March 31–April 19, 1989

Mr. Gohrin, Mr. Hahn and Mr. Gall reviewed the previous day's meeting and put together a list of critical elements which would become the focus of the proposal. They included a timetable, IGB platform, cargo information system (CIS), passenger information system (PRISMA), data centre management and migration, and office automation system. Mr. Gall began to define which people and skills were available in-house and what parts of the project would have to be subcontracted. As usual, the question of available systems engineers and programmers remained unresolved. During this phase, Mr. Gall emphasized the importance of determining a time schedule for allocating technical people to the marketing team, while still providing enough technical resources inhouse to support both the known and unknown projects that would be needing resources over the next year. Mr. Gall knew that his monthly meeting with marketing, on April 19, would be the only way he could determine the upcoming projects and their potential requirements.

Mr. Hahn, Mr. Gall and Mr. Gohrin also reviewed what parts of the project would have to be subcontracted and which subcontractors to contact.

April 19, 1989

Mr. Gall met with the marketing teams to determine the various projects in the pipeline. Using this information, he put together a Lotus spreadsheet to review the technical staff requirements needed over the next month and planned how he would manage all the projects involving systems integration. This spreadsheet provided a limited measure of comfort – in that all projects needing technical support could be handled; however, the need for developing better tools was evident.

April 5–April 20, 1989

Mr. Gohrin contacted and met with two potential software subcontractors, Softsystems and Syshouse. The traditional process for assessing the subcontractors was used – based mainly on previous experience with them, their ability to meet budget and timeline commitments as well as technical expertise. Since the office had no prior experience with either of these subcontractors, Mr. Gohrin's job in this case was not easy. Whichever subcontractor he selected would work on the initial proposal at no cost, in anticipation of working on the final project.

April 20–May 26, 1989

The marketing team for the ABB worked hard putting together an initial proposal. The date for submission was June 16, 1989. Mr. Gohrin selected Syshouse as the software subcontractor, but he ran into problems when defining the scope of the project with Syshouse. These problems were finally resolved on May 24, and the contract with the subcontractor was signed on May 26.

Through the proposal development phase, there were two full-time equivalents (FTE) staff people (1½ were from the sales team and ½ was from the technical area) assigned full time to proposal development. Once the contract was awarded, the project was anticipated to take 16 months to complete and would involve high level design with no performance commitments. However, there were some issues which highlighted potential problem areas. These issues included insufficient staffing and responsibilities within the ABB, insufficient information about competitors, delayed enhancements to OS/2 and possible shortage of temporary technical staff. Despite these problems, it was decided to proceed. The team estimated that the project effort would require 18,000 man hours from IBM and 10,000 man hours by the subcontractor.

June 16, 1989

The initial proposal was submitted on time. We also learned that Olivetti would be one of the competitors for the contract, but that its proposal would be less extensive than ours in that it would deal with the ticketing application only. The ABB announced that the initial contract would be awarded by July 12, 1989.

June 16–July 12, 1989

Mr. Gall continued to work on project preparation in the event the contract was awarded to the branch office. He formally assigned Mr. Bann to act as project manager. Mr. Bann had worked with Mr. Gohrin in developing the proposal, although that had been on a less formal basis. Mr. Gall and Mr. Bann began to put together a systems integration *plan* which described the entire project concept in detail and identified all the resources needed to complete the project. The systems integration plan was a crucial step as it defined our concept of the project. If our projected plan failed to meet the ABB's expectations, our chances of receiving the contract would be jeopardized. The systems integration plan would be completed as soon as our initial contract was accepted by the ABB.

During this same period, Mr. Gall also began to put together a PERT chart to determine activity costs and time lines required for monitoring activities. With no standard tools available to help him, this process was very tedious and involved much manual labour. All manpower reports were manual, knowledge on costs involved were not typically known or historically available to the branch office; all bills for various components of the different solutions were generated in the Wien office and sent to the branch office for follow-up.

July 12, 1989

Mr. Gohrin received a call from Mr. Harris with the unfortunate news that the ABB did not wish to use Syshouse, the subcontractor we had selected. We had not identified the subcontractor as a weak link in our initial plan and were surprised that the company was considered unacceptable. After a hurried meeting attended by myself, Mr. Gall, Mr. Bann, Mr. Hahn and Mr. Gohrin, we decided to approach two other subcontractors, SSD and Programmatic. To reduce our exposure, we developed a strategy which included involving the ABB in our final decision, having ongoing discussions together on the strengths and weaknesses of each of the vendors. We also requested and received a two month extension from the ABB.

July 14–September 1, 1989

Mr. Bann joined forces with Mr. Gohrin to find a replacement software vendor that would be more acceptable to the ABB. They met frequently with Mr. Harris and the ABB's management team to review each vendor's characteristics, assuring user involvement in the final decision. Through this process we were able to select SSD, a software vendor we knew would be acceptable to the ABB, although more expensive than our original choice, and also were able to resubmit our proposal ahead of the extended deadline.

September 27, 1989

We learned that we were awarded the contract to proceed with a project proposal for the ABB. A meeting was scheduled with Mr. Harris and his staff to review the conditions of the contract on October 2.

October 2, 1989

Mr. Bann and Mr. Gohrin attended the meeting with Mr. Harris. It was agreed that hardware and software changes would be addressed in planned amendments which were to be submitted after six months. Acceptance criteria, as defined by the ABB, were reviewed and appeared to be quite reasonable although we suspected that there might be some problems on standard terms and conditions. (Refer to *Exhibit 5 for details of the acceptance criteria.*) We submitted a tentative timetable for the project proposal, which was approved. It was agreed that detailed specifications would be submitted for approval during the first week of January 1990.

Two additional FTE technical staff were assigned to the project.

Exhibit 5

```
        ┌─────────────────────────────────────────────┐
        │   Acceptance Criteria                       │
        └─────────────────────────────────────────────┘


      – Defined in Austrian Government Standards
          – Deliverable Items per Phase
          – Delivery Date
          – Condition: Functional Demonstration


      – Test Approach
          – Unit Test by Developer
          – Joint System Tests (Test Environment)
          – Acceptance Test (Operational Environment)


      – Performance Requirements
          – 'Reasonable' Response Time


      – Availability Requirements
          – None


      – Warranty
          – 1 Year after Acceptance Test
```

October 5, 1989

Mr. Bann discovered that two of the committed staff assigned to work on the project were unavailable. After much scrambling, additional staff were taken off other projects and assignments were made to phase them into this project.

September 27–January 4, 1990

Mr. Gall finalized the systems integration plan with Mr. Gohrin and Mr. Bann. As project manager, Mr. Bann was responsible for managing the entire project.

Towards the middle of December, the project team realized that a hardware enhancement which IBM had promised for early January would not be available. This could have been a major problem, but this time we were prepared. We had made a preliminary backup plan for using available, but slightly less efficient, hardware which would enable us to remain on track. The contract with the ABB allowed for amendment submissions, and Mr. Gohrin quickly obtained an amendment to the contract enabling us to use the available hardware.

January 1990–June 29, 1990

Mr. Bann consistently identified potential problem areas where temporary employees with particular skills would be needed on certain dates required by the schedule. Since meeting the schedule depended on hiring qualified temporary employees, he made a concerted effort to find the right people and develop a pool of additional resources in case of emergencies.

Mr. Bann held weekly meetings with the IBM team and the subcontractor, SSD. Meetings with the ABB were held every two weeks or on request. These meetings helped Mr. Bann review what was being done and identified activities where additional resources might be needed. He also saw that the project team met weekly and regularly oversaw the work the subcontractor was doing.

Mr. Bann and Mr. Gall kept manual tallies of the hours spent on the project by the various staff members and on the hardware which was to be billed to the project. The few financial controls in place were 'hand made' by the project office.

During this period of time, the development platform and the production platform were successfully installed on schedule.

June 29–July 27, 1990

Mr. Bann had originally been concerned that the workstations used by the ABB would have to be replaced with updated models. As it became evident that this was the case, an amendment was submitted specifying the new type of workstations to be installed and the additional costs required for external resources to help with this phase of the project. Because we had worked to integrate all aspects of the project and had openly communicated with the ABB, the ABB had been part of the process all along. Therefore, the ABB realized that system efficiency required the new workstations, and we received timely approval to proceed with this change.

At the same time that this change was being processed through the system, Mr. Bann was working with the SSD to ensure that it was on target. At this point, there seemed to be little reason for concern. The results were good and the skill level of the programmers was excellent. However, the cost associated with management overhead was too high, a factor to be considered in other projects.

July 27–July 30, 1990

On July 27, Mr. Bann and Mr. Gall informed me that they had misjudged the complexity of the project and would have to assign three more FTE in order to conclude the project on schedule. When the back-up pool of temporary staff was tapped, two FTE staff were found, but they still needed another FTE. We quickly reviewed our options and realized that we would have to use in-house staff. Mr. Gall met with his project managers on July 30 and they identified two projects which could each loan half an FTE to complete the ABB project.

September 19, 1990

We learned that SSD would miss the October 12 deadline for testing the final phase of the software application. To date there had been no problems meeting deadlines, but one staff member assigned to test the software had become ill and was expected to be absent for an extended time. Mr. Bann and Mr. Gohrin met with the SSD people and developed an alternative schedule that would keep the hardware installation on target but delay the software testing. SSD was given an additional month to finish testing the software while we advanced our deadlines for integrating the workstations. The project looked as if it would still meet the scheduled deadline.

November 15, 1990

Mr. Bann presented an overview of the ABB project. The software was back on schedule and the hardware was in place. ABB staff were working with IBM staff at various sites to assure that the workstations were functioning properly and that the programs were working well. Additional testing and further training of staff still needed to be addressed.

November 29, 1990
Mr. Bann informed me that he was resigning because he had accepted a very desirable offer from Andersen Consulting Company. I was dismayed to learn that he was leaving; however, he assured me that he would stay until mid-February by which time the ABB project would be completed.

January 23, 1991
The project concluded a few weeks late but the ABB was satisfied. The milestones were reached on time, with only minor price modifications. In reviewing the project with the project management staff, we identified some areas which could have been handled differently. Many were concerned that assessing bottom line profitability was not yet possible as there was no way to measure the cost of each phase of the project and little historical data available.

'I am limited in my ability to assess system integration projects or their management since so many factors are outside my control,' Mr. Gall related. 'I guess we still have a long way to go before the branch office can successfully manage the solution part of the business, but we needed to start somewhere.'

Digital Equipment Corporation International:
Competing Through Cooperation

This case was prepared by Professors Per Jenster and Francis Bidault, and Research Fellow Thomas Cummings as a basis for class discussion rather than to illustrate either effective or ineffective handling of a business situation. Contributions from Michael Horner, Digital Europe, are gratefully acknowledged.

On the afternoon of February 19, 1986, David Stone, Vice-President of International Engineering and Strategic Resources for Digital Equipment Corporation International, sat in his Geneva office looking out across the Rhône valley. Eight months earlier, he had briefed senior officers at corporate headquarters in the US about an effort to try out a new customer relationship. It was supposed to be based on a collaborative software project between DEC (Digital Equipment Corporation) engineers and ITT Telecoms engineers located in four European countries. The DEC–ITT project was seen as an opportunity to try out a radically new approach to business partnerships in the information technology business. But how far could he let the 'experiment' run?

Rumours were coming in from the financial department and from the central engineering group at headquarters, as well as from different country managers and their account executives. Everyone seemed to have a different understanding of the DEC–ITT relationship. With income from the project not even coming close to matching costs, David Stone knew that he should reassess his original strategy.

He logged on to his electronic mail system, skipped the 38 new messages and accessed his E-mail archive to re-read the eight-month-old message from

DEC International's European Chairman which had been the catalyst leading to the 'cooperative activities' with ITT:

> To: D. Stone   July 15, 1985
> Fr: P. C. Falotti
> Status: Urgent
>
> David – news from the front . . . our courtship with ITT seems to have gotten off the track. Insider tells me that Apollo has a European (Brussels ITT) confirmation for 40 workstations. Don't know if ITT is looking for a counteroffer, but we need to act fast. We might be able to make something of our 'strategic relationship thinking' and link it to the recent work done by your Metaframe group. What can we do?

Background

Eight months earlier, Stone had asked a multi-functional team led by Michael Horner, part of the Metaframe 'think tank', to work with ITT on a partnership arrangement. Rather than simply sell hardware and software to ITT, Mike had assembled a team to build an engineering relationship. The team would rely on DEC's new workstation and computer assisted software engineering (CASE) technologies to transfer software development methodologies and project management know-how to ITT. Because of the potential partnership, some of the people involved believed that DEC had sold several million dollars worth of hardware. This rumour could neither be confirmed nor simply linked to this joint software engineering project. Nonetheless, David had committed some of his best people in the hope that a significant, long-term relationship with ITT would materialize, leading to major sales increases and useful new software tools. This activity had raised a lot of questions, both from inside the organization and from other customers with pressing needs.

Digital Equipment Corporation International (Europe)

Digital Equipment Corporation had established overseas sales and distribution in the late 60s which eventually had led to the founding of Digital Equipment Corporation International (Europe) as a wholly-owned operating company in 1979.

DEC Europe's mission was to import, develop, manufacture and market networked computing systems for customers in Europe. The first

Chairman and founder of Digital International was Jean-Claude Peter-schmitt, a polished European statesman and businessman from Switzerland. He contributed much of his time and energy to breaking down technical and economic barriers among the European States, and between the US and Europe. Peterschmitt believed that the computing industry was moving quickly from its US origins to an international computing and communications environment, and that Digital had a role to play, both as a vendor and as a developer of new technologies.

DEC Worldwide and European Sales and Personnel, 1978–85

	Worldwide		Europe (with % of Worldwide)			
Year	Sales ($)	People (000)	Sales ($)	%	People (000)	%
1985	6,686	89	1,945	29	18	20
1984	5,584	86	1,462	26	14	16
1983	4,272	73	1,074	25	11	15
1982	3,381	67	1,006	30	10	15
1981	3,198	63	935	29	10	16
1980	2,368	56	687	29	9	16
1979	1,804	44	486	27	7	16
1978	1,437	39	377	26	6	15

Wherever possible, Digital International had adopted a management structure similar to that of Digital US. The parent company had been a pioneer in organizational design and development. The company structure, known as the matrix, was built around key managers, who were responsible for core product groups. In Europe, there was a matrix between the core product groups and geographic regions. The core product groups were built on Digital's product and technology expertise, with country managers responsible for meeting regional quotas. A major addition to the matrix were the country managers, who had overall responsibility for coordinating Digital's business activities in and among different countries. *(Refer to Exhibit 1a.)*

Digital's structure worked well during its period of rapid growth in Europe, protecting its product base in two major market segments (engineering and scientific computing). At the same time, the strength of its product range insured strong growth in nearly all geographic segments. *(Refer to Exhibit 1b.)*

Product/Market Issues

Throughout the early 1980s, new competitors had reduced Digital's lead in scientific computing. In the high-end mainframe segment, IBM had recently

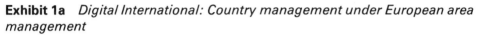

Exhibit 1a *Digital International: Country management under European area management*

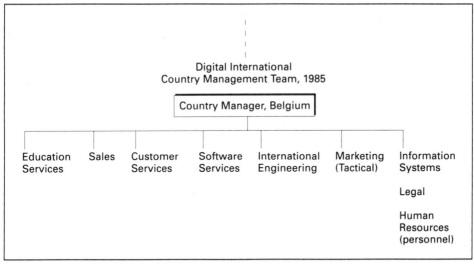

streamlined its products into four key product groups and was offering networking capabilities. In the low-end micro-computing segment, IBM had captured Apple's early lead by introducing the personal computer (PC and PC-AT) products in its traditionally strong business computing segments *(refer to Exhibit 2)*. DEC's strength had traditionally been in the mid-range mini-computer market, where it ranked second behind IBM. Competitors such as Sun Microsystems (founded in 1982) and Apollo were moving fast in a new segment – *Technical Workstations*. Digital realized the early possibilities of technical workstations and saw them as a way to incorporate new features and technological developments into high-performance, multi-task desktop computer configurations that would sell for less than £100,000 *(refer to Exhibit 3)*. Conflicting internal product development paths hindered Digital's ability to lead in this new segment. But, two bright lights were on the horizon: (1) the company's answer to the workstation market, the Microvax II and DEC's increasing share in the emerging software development and (2) computer assisted software engineering (CASE) markets.

In addition, the company was ready to announce a second generation VAX system, resulting from a three-year investment of over £2 billion in research and engineering. With the announcement of several new hardware, software and service products, Digital entered what industry experts called a new product transition phase. This meant that the new hardware and software products were not quite in sync with the existing orders for

Exhibit 1b   *Digital International: European area management team, 1985*

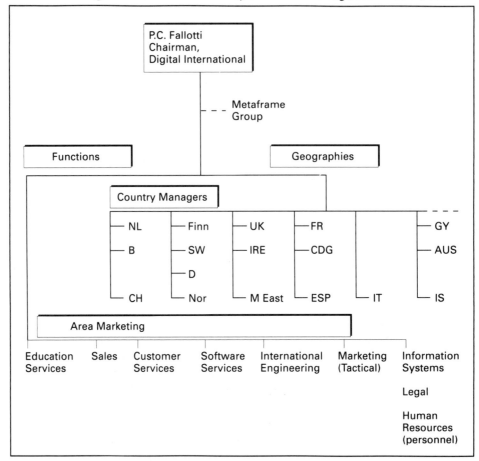

equipment. This factor was felt in the marketplace, offering further possibilities for competitor encroachment on Digital's traditional customers.

The Competitive Environment for Engineering Workstations

Workstations were one segment of the general computing market. Industry analysts often identified the other segments as mainframes, minicomputers, and personal or microcomputers. Minicomputer prices ranged from $30,000 to $100,000; workstations were from $15,000 to $60,000, and personal computers from $1,500 to $20,000.

The workstation market had emerged in the early 1980s with Apollo's

Exhibit 2 (Source: *DATA INFOCORP, Dec/ITT Indus. 1)*

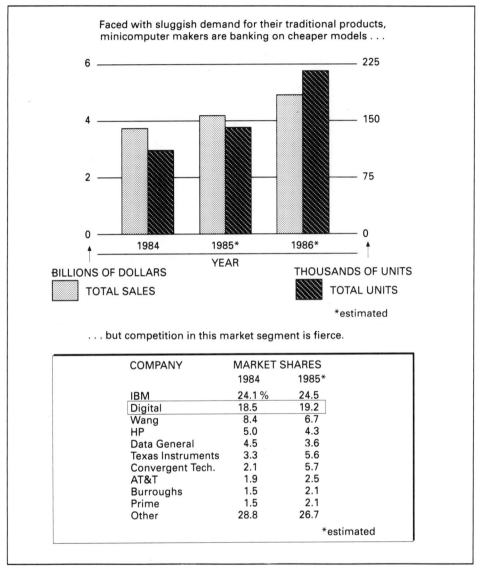

Faced with sluggish demand for their traditional products, minicomputer makers are banking on cheaper models . . .

BILLIONS OF DOLLARS

☐ TOTAL SALES

THOUSANDS OF UNITS

☐ TOTAL UNITS

*estimated

. . . but competition in this market segment is fierce.

COMPANY	MARKET SHARES	
	1984	1985*
IBM	24.1 %	24.5
Digital	18.5	19.2
Wang	8.4	6.7
HP	5.0	4.3
Data General	4.5	3.6
Texas Instruments	3.3	5.6
Convergent Tech.	2.1	5.7
AT&T	1.9	2.5
Burroughs	1.5	2.1
Prime	1.5	2.1
Other	28.8	26.7

*estimated

introduction of its technical workstation (1981). Sun Microsystems soon followed in February 1982 with the introduction of the Sun 1, a product that included a CPU printed circuit board, a video board, a power supply, and a high resolution monitor. Its typical customers were universities and sophisticated end users who followed technological developments. By 1984–85 the customer base broadened to include users in Fortune 1,000 companies.

Exhibit 3 *(Source: Datamation 1985)*

The Top 10 Companies in Minicomputers, 1984 & 85

Company	1985 Units	1984 Units	% Change
IBM	3,500	3,500	NC
Digital Equipment Corp	1,600	1,527	4.8
Hewlett-Packard	1,050	950	10.5
Wang Laboratories	870.9	970.5	−10.3
Data General Corp	799.7	840.0	−4.8
Prime Computer Inc.	563.7	479.1	17.7
Tandem Computers	533.1	477.1	11.7
Harris Corp	470.0	410.0	14.6
Fujitsu Ltd.	439.0	383.9	14.4
Nixdorf Computer	407.9	340.0	20.0

The Top 10 Companies in Microcomputers

Company	1985 Units	1984 Units	% Change
IBM	5,500	5,500	NC
Apple Computer Corp	1,603	1,747	−8.2
Olivetti	844.5	496.9	78.0
Tandy Corp	796.8	573.5	38.9
Sperry Corp	742.8	503.4	47.6
Commodore Int'l	600	1,000	−40.0
Compaq Computer	503.9	329.0	53.2
Hewlett-Packard	400	500	−20
Convergent Tech.	395.2	361.7	9.3
Zenith Electronics	352.0	249.0	41.4

Digital and Data General had both entered the market with proprietary CPUs in the workstation market, but it was still not clear whether the products would be accepted by users. Rumours of an IBM workstation were rampant, but had not yet materialized.

A key feature of the newly-defined workstation segment was rapid change. The life of a workstation design was short, 18 months at best, because the base technology of the workstation, the microprocessor, was continually improving in speed and performance.

Apollo Computer Corp. had a keen interest in redefining the market to include the new workstation segment. IBM had a virtual lock on the mainframe segment and, by then, 60% of the microcomputer market. The fuzzy middle ground included minicomputers, superminis and workstations, all with shifting price/performance characteristics. Domination of this segment was still undetermined, but workstations were taking the early lead.

It was still early in the game for engineering workstations, and sales would continue to hinge on both price performance specifications of the various machines, as well as software development. One way to push software development would be to form networked engineering partnerships.

Technological Innovation in Digital: The Role of Central Engineering

At the heart of Digital's technology development process was a high level group in the United States known as Central Engineering. This team, established by Kenneth Olsen, the founder of DEC, provided the platform for developing the base technologies of the company. Central Engineering relied on current technical developments in the field and feedback from the product marketing groups to decide on its portfolio of technologies. Once Central Engineering had agreed on a five-year technological trajectory for the company's products and services, the product groups were responsible for getting the base technologies into product/market areas.

David Stone saw, early on, that the Digital–ITT relationship would not easily fit into the technical development process and plans of Central Engineering. Under normal circumstances, it should fit into one of the product/market areas – *Software Services and Applications Services (SWAS)*. But the Digital–ITT relationship had both a market intent and software engineering mandate. It was working across Digital's product/market areas, trying to create its own expertise in software tool development for telecommunications companies.

Fortunately, David Stone could point to a history of joint technical development projects that his International Engineering Group had carried out in Europe. Differences in engineering approaches had given Digital Europe some leeway in its joint engineering approaches. The Engineering group of Digital Europe had written the company manual on university–industry partnerships. But university links were different from working with customer engineering groups. Sharing early knowledge with the customer in exchange for a clearer view of their current problems and future needs required a different management approach. David Stone knew that joint technical development and ITT would require having the project fit into one of the existing technical pipelines, but at the same time, called for a creative market/technology approach.

Forming Policies on Strategic Alliances in Europe

The period of 1984–1985 had been turbulent for the world computer industry. Market growth was beginning to slow down from a 25% average compound growth rate to a more docile 10–15% per annum. Industry experts spoke of two central issues: 'convergence of technologies' between computing and other industrial segments such as telecommunications *(refer to Exhibit 4)* and 'strategic alliances' that ranged from simple technology and market exchanges to industrial megadeals.

In Europe, Digital had received more than ten offers to form so-called strategic alliances *(refer to Exhibit 5)*. In the emerging spirit of European integration, Digital had even been approached about participating in Eureka, Esprit, and other joint technology development programs.

Digital Europe's top engineering people felt that the company was well positioned in an era of converging technologies. DEC had maintained its own proprietary hardware and software, and had migrated from scientific and engineering applications to a broader customer base. Digital had led the computer industry in several areas of its technical development. Ethernet networking software, an early product designed for networked computing systems, was one such technology. Digital engineers had also become experts at using their network technologies to carry out development projects simultaneously at several geographical locations.

Yet, partly because of Digital's proprietary technology path, a number of managers viewed strategic alliances as an overly complicated approach to business and technology development. Under Kenneth Olsen, Digital had become known as a 'go it alone' company. In the history of the company, Digital had made several acquisitions, but all were informal agreements and true joint ventures were a new development.

P. C. Falotti argued convincingly that Digital Europe would have to develop a systematic process for evaluating the offers of potential European partners, and that such a process would require a major shift in corporate values. David Stone had asked Michael Horner and Tony Setchell to form a low-key group that would build a framework for considering partnership proposals – one that would recommend how to act. The multi-disciplinary team, known as the 'Metaframe Group', took their mandate seriously. As Michael Horner often stated, 'We were working on an industry level, seeking industry solutions.' Over the next several months, they wrote a policy

Exhibit 4 *The convergence of computer and communications technologies: perspective of C&C Vision (courtesy of NEC Corporation, K. Kobayashi, 1985)*

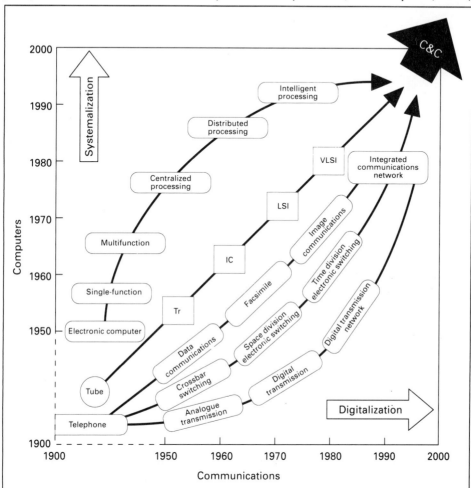

statement *(refer to **Exhibit 6**)* and carried out analysis that considered the following issues:

- partnership approaches
- future competition
- future technology trends
- market evolution
- how Digital provides solutions for customers

Exhibit 5 *Partnership approaches from European companies and national groups*

UK
BRITISH TELECOM
PLESSY

SCANDINAVIA/BENELUX
L.M. ERICSSON
TELEVERKET
PHILIPS

FRANCE
CGE-TELIC
THOMSON
MATRA

ITALY
OLIVETTI
FIAT
STET/ITALTEL

GERMANY
SIEMENS
NIXDORF
KIENZLE
BOSCH

PAN-EUROPEAN
ESPRIT
EC12 INTERCONNECT STANDARDS
NATIONAL GOVERNMENT SIGNALS IN UK, D, FR, ESP, SW

The group developed a visual mapping exercise that would juxtapose the competitive and technological positions of various companies across information technology industries. The mapping tool was also used to define Digital's strategic and technical position on the map, and suggest various possible partnering combinations *(refer to Metaframe, **Exhibits 7a and 7b**)*.

Potential partners were mapped according to the competitive positions in the information technology sectors. If a company looked promising, the Metaframe team would go to the next level of analysis and discussion. A detailed segmentation of a partners' core competences and geographic coverage revealed – through visual mapping – the degrees of overlap and points of convergence between Digital and virtually every other company that the team chose to map *(refer to **Exhibit 8**)*. These maps later proved useful before and during management discussions with potential partners.

Exhibit 6 *Statement of principles: the Metaframe group*

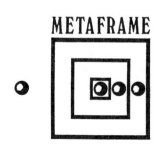

Statement of Principles:
the Metaframe Group

Vision of the Ideal – Metaframe Group, 8 April 1986

To become more productive, organizations must have a consistent philosophy of organization which empowers their employees to fulfill the company's mission. Below is Digital's vision of the ideal philosophy to achieve productivity (and high employee morale).

We believe in the dignity of the individual, the increase in his productivity which comes from associating freely with others in his organization accessing the information required by his job, and his obligation to provide information to others as he receives it. We want to help to increase the effectiveness of interpersonal communication. These beliefs lead to the peer-to-peer style of networking we produce, as well as to the management style we use: computer mediated information (notes, files . . .) is an appropriate implementation of this style. Interestingly, this style is applicable also to computers interfacing with machines; on the shop floor we could use the slogan "liberate the Robots" to identify the power which we can add to the manufacturing process when the parts of the process are appropriately connected.

We look forward to the evolution of the business world to the "one corporation" concept, in which the information flow between departments of two different companies is as easy as that between equivalent departments in the same company. This interaction would make clear that the primary long-term added value of a company is the processes which it has; if those processes are not clearly superior to those available externally, then the company should seriously consider using the external processes instead of its internal ones. This style of management would quickly lead to the distribution of processes to the place where they can be done best, just as distributed computing moves the computation to the place where it can be done best. Examples are just-in-time manufacturing which moves your inventory outside your company or external manufacturing which moves the whole process outside.

We define the mission of Digital as the production of quality information systems, products and services; where information systems are defined as "the way in which a company acquires, shares, integrates and uses data to fulfill its mission, optimize its productivity and competitiveness and plan its evolution."

The final stage of our relationship to other companies occurs when we take the risk of agreeing to do new things together as partners. Previous to this stage, we sell products, services, architectures and then processes which we already have. The partnership commitment is to make things both parties agree are necessary, but which were not previously part of the repertoire of either company.

We recognize that a major part of our perceived added value lies in the Digital Computing Environment (DCE), which allows high productivity in applications development, flexible restructuring of information flows to adapt to organization and mission changes, and enhanced capability for effective information management and exchange. We should therefore be developing programs to make the use of the DCE as attractive as possible to OEMs, software houses and internal company applications developers.

Exhibit 7a *Metaframe: mapping the competitive positions of possible partners (Source: B. Compaine, Understanding New Media, 1985)*

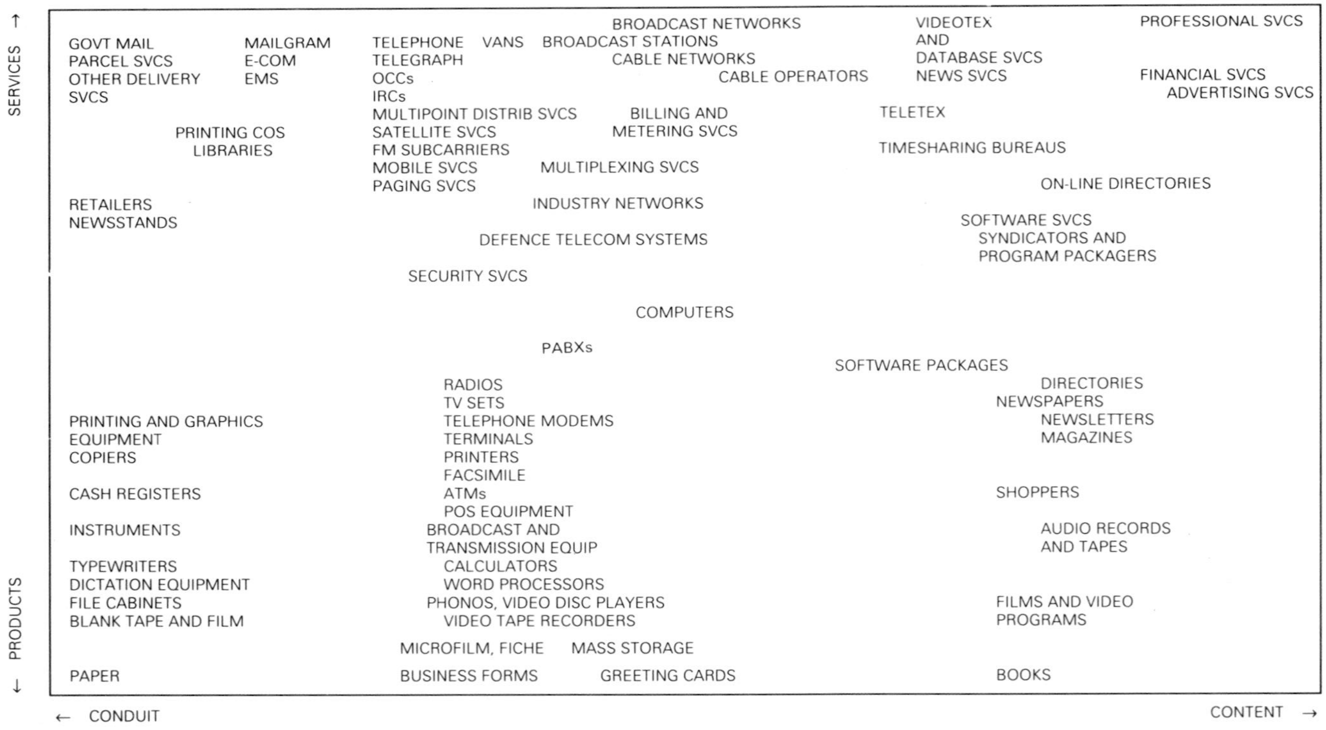

PROFESSIONAL SVCS

FINANCIAL SVCS
ADVERTISING SVCS

ON-LINE DIRECTORIES

SOFTWARE SVCS
SYNDICATORS AND
PROGRAM PACKAGERS

TIMESHARING BUREAUS

TELETEX

VIDEOTEX
AND
DATABASE SVCS
NEWS SVCS

DIRECTORIES
NEWSPAPERS
NEWSLETTERS
MAGAZINES

SOFTWARE PACKAGES

SHOPPERS

AUDIO RECORDS
AND TAPES

FILMS AND VIDEO
PROGRAMS

BOOKS

BROADCAST NETWORKS
BROADCAST STATIONS
CABLE NETWORKS
CABLE OPERATORS

BILLING AND
METERING SVCS

MULTIPLEXING SVCS

INDUSTRY NETWORKS

DEFENCE TELECOM SYSTEMS

COMPUTERS

PABXs

SECURITY SVCS

RADIOS
TV SETS
TELEPHONE MODEMS
TERMINALS
PRINTERS
FACSIMILE
POS EQUIPMENT
ATMs
BROADCAST AND
TRANSMISSION EQUIP
CALCULATORS
WORD PROCESSORS
PHONOS, VIDEO DISC PLAYERS
VIDEO TAPE RECORDERS

MICROFILM, FICHE   MASS STORAGE

BUSINESS FORMS   GREETING CARDS

TELEPHONE   VANS
TELEGRAPH
OCCs
IRCs
MULTIPOINT DISTRIB SVCS
SATELLITE SVCS
FM SUBCARRIERS
MOBILE SVCS
PAGING SVCS

MAILGRAM
E-COM
EMS

PRINTING COS
LIBRARIES

RETAILERS
NEWSSTANDS

PRINTING AND GRAPHICS
EQUIPMENT
COPIERS

CASH REGISTERS

INSTRUMENTS

TYPEWRITERS
DICTATION EQUIPMENT
FILE CABINETS
BLANK TAPE AND FILM

PAPER

GOVT MAIL
PARCEL SVCS
OTHER DELIVERY
SVCS

← CONDUIT

CONTENT →

← SERVICES

PRODUCTS →

ATM – Automated Teller Machine; E-COM – lectronic computer Originated Mail; EMS – Electronic Message Service; IRC – International Record Carrier; OCC – Other Common Carrier; PABX – Private Automatic Branch Exchange; POS – Point of Sale; VAN – Value Added Network

Exhibit 7b *Metaframe: mapping the competitive positions of possible partners (Source: B. Compain, Understanding New Media, 1985)*

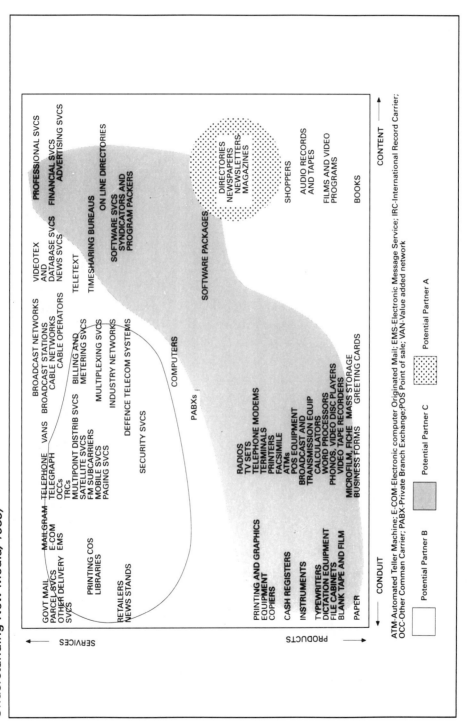

ATM-Automated Teller Machine; E-COM-Electronic computer Originated Mail; EMS-Electronic Message Service; IRC-International Record Carrier; OCC-Other Comman Carrier; PABX-Private Branch Exchange;POS Point of sale; VAN-Value added network

Exhibit 8 *Metaframe: detailed segmentation for partnering process*

GEOGRAPHIES		INDUSTRY SECTORS		CHANNELS	SERVICES	SYSTEMS	
NORTH AMERICA	M	AEROSPACE	D H I F S S C R E T E	AGENT	BROADCAST	ANALOGUE	T R S Y A R N A S T N E S M M I S S I O N
	Sales & Service	ELECTRONICS			NEWS	DIGITAL	
	S				MESSAGING	METERING	
	Research and Develop	AUTOMOTIVE				BILLING	
	R & D				DISTRIBUTION	EXTERNAL SERVICES	
		FOOD & BEVERAGE	P R O C E S S		LIBRARY	NATIONAL TRANSMISSION SYSTEMS	
EUROPE	M	CHEMICAL		DEALER	TIMESHARING	INTERNATIONAL TRANSMISSION SYSTEMS	
	S	PULP & PAPER	I N D U S T R I E S		CASE	TELEMETRY	
	R & D	OIL & GAS			SW PORTING	PROCESS CONTROL	
						BROADCAST NETWORK (TV, RADIO, CELLULAR)	
LATIN AMERICA	M	PHARMACEUTICAL		DISTRIBUTOR	PRODUCT TRACKING	DATA PROCESSING (MIS)	
		HEALTH CARE			EDUCATION	NETWORKS	
	S	EDUCATION			OPERATING COMPANY	TELECONFERENCING	
	R & D				FACILITY MANAGEMENT & MANAGED NETWORK	CAD/CAM	
		STATE & LOCAL GOVERNMENT		THIRD-PARTY		CIM	
ASIA AFRICA AUSTRALIA	M	BANKING	F I N A N C I A L		ENTERPRISE SERVICES	EFT	
					OFFICE BUSINESS CAPACITY DISASTER SECURITY SYSTEMS	POS & CREDIT CHECKING	
	S	INVESTMENTS	S E R V I C E S			EDI	
	R & D	INSURANCE		OEM	PLAN DESIGN IMPLEMENT MANAGE	INTEGRATED VOICE & DATA	
						FACTORY AUTOMATION	
JAPAN	M	PUBLISHING/PRINTING/ NEWSPAPER			FINANCIAL	OFFICE AUTOMATION	
						INTEGRATED SERVICES (RMM, DIAGNOSTICS)	
	S	BROADCAST/CABLE			MODELLING	PRINT SYSTEMS	
		TRANSPORTATION		PARTNERSHIP CMPs, SCMPs, DCMP	TRANSLATION	EDUCATION SYSTEMS (CBL, CAI)	
	R & D				IN PLANT PRINTING	CLINICAL MEDICAL SYSTEMS	
		WHOLESALE/ RETAIL DISTRIBUTION			RECORDS STORAGE	MODELLING & SIMULATION	
EASTERN EUROPE COMMUNIST WORLD	M	UTILITIES			CREATIVITY SERVICES	CALS	
	S	FEDERAL GOVERNMENT		DIRECT SALES FORCE	RESEARCH & DEVELOPMENT	FOURTH GENERATION LANGUAGES	
						EXPERT SYSTEMS	
	R & D	TELECOMMUNICATIONS			ENGINEERING SERVICES	SPECIAL SYSTEMS	

Exhibit 8 *Continued*

COMPOSITE PRODUCTS	BASIC PRODUCTS	COMPONENTS	ENABLING TECHNOLOGY
COPIERS	TRUNK LINES	PHYSICAL	COLOR IMAGE SCIENCE
FAX	FIBRE OPTICS (FDDI)		CHEMICAL
OCR	TELEPHONES		
IMAGE SCANNER	TRANSDUCERS	PLUMBING	OPTICAL
ATM & POS	MODEMS MULTIPLEXORS CONCENTRATORS	WIRING (INCLUDING BUSSES)	ELECTRO OPTICAL
WORKSTATIONS	LAN'S		ELECTRO PHOTOGRAPHY
TRUNK EXCHANGE	TRANSMISSION EQUIPMENT (ANALOGUE & DIGITAL)	POWER SUPPLIES	SILVER PHOTOGRAPHY
PICX (ELECTRONIC)			
DIRECTORY FUNCTIONS	TRANSMISSION MULTIPLEXORS		COATING
OPERATORS CONSOLE	TERMINALS	LENSES	MECHANICAL
SERVERS	PRINTERS		
	STORAGE	BOARDS	ELECTRICAL
GATEWAYS & IBM INTERCONNECT	CONSUMER GOODS, TV, RADIO, VCR, CALCULATORS, TYPEWRITERS, COMPUTERS	INJECTION MOULDING	ELECTRO-MECHANICAL
OPERATING SYSTEMS			
COMPILERS / S O F T W A R E	PROCESSORS		ELECTRONIC (DLECR, ETC)
INTERFACES	PC	FINAL ASSEMBLY & TEST	SILICON LSI
DB	TOOLS, HARDWARE, SOFTWARE		
GENERAL (SPREADSHEETS ETC) / A P P L I C A -	VOICE SWITCH (ANALOGUE & DIGITAL)		ARCHITECTURE
	DATA SWITCH (ANALOGUE & DIGITAL)	FINISHING	SIGNAL PROCESSING
OFFICE & TP / T I O N S	PAGING EQUIPMENT & MOBILE RADIO		
CAD/CAM	VIDEO EQUIPMENT	PACKAGING	DISPLAY-DEVICES
VOICE OUTPUT	INDUSTRIAL CAMERA		FABRICATION
DISCRETE SERVICES (FIELD SERVICE)	MARKING ENGINE	MATERIAL HANDLING	SOFTWARE
ROBOTICS	INSTRUMENTS & METERING		
TELETEX	ENCRYPTION & DATA COMPREHENSION		QUALITY & RELIABILITY
VIDEOTEX	SATELLITE EQUIPMENT	SOFTWARE	DEVELOPMENT
	OPERATING SYSTEMS		
VANS	SYSTEM LANGUAGE	TRANSPORT MECHANISM	KNOWLEDGE ACQUISITION PROCESS
VOICE RECOGNITION	UTILITIES		APPLIED RESEARCH
HOLOGRAPHY	FILM	MEDIA (DISKS, FLOPPIES, ETC)	PURE RESEARCH
IMAGE STORAGE AND RECOGNITION	DRUGS		

Segmentation and analysis was the first major step toward partner identification and opening discussions, but the Metaframe team also used the mapping to reveal a deeper understanding of Digital's own market and technological capabilities.

The Metaframe Group's work revealed that Digital's top management faced a difficult challenge: The company would have to sustain its current customer relationships, while developing new frameworks for identifying and building partnerships. Joint technology development and engineering with customers was highly recommended by the team. The Metaframe process also confirmed the value of visual presentation of communication tools. By overlaying the strategies of various companies, the group could surface critical issues before making choices about new technologies and business partnering. The Metaframe group remained an invisible task force until August 1985 when a request from ITT Europe provided David with an opportunity to take the group's abstract ideas and test them with a major customer of long standing.

ITT Corporation

ITT was a conglomerate multinational corporation that had grown enormously under the 23-year stewardship of Harold Geneen. In 1979 he stepped down as chairman of the board, having made more than 250 acquisitions and having built ITT into a vast confederation of companies comprised of 2,000 working units. During the same period, revenues had gone from $800 million to $22 billion, and earnings from $30 million to $560 million. The Geneen legacy was inherited by Rand Araskog on January 1, 1980. Unfortunately for Araskog, Geneen left behind a $5 billion debt accrued, in part, by his merger and acquisition activities. It was partly as a result of ITT's heavy debt burden and partly due to the restructuring of several ITT units, that ITT was targeted and subjected to hostile takeover bids during the early 1980s. Even *Fortune Magazine* took some stabs at ITT, calling it 'a museum of the investment and management ideas of the sixties'.

Araskog took a number of steps to reduce the size of ITT's corporate debt. Between 1980 and 1983, ITT sold 61 companies in order to generate proceeds of $1.3 billion. He streamlined the holding into five 'product' areas and four service areas.

Product Areas	Service Areas
Automotive Products	Insurance Operations
Electronic Components	Financial Services
Fluid Technology	Communications and
Defense and Space Technology	Information Services
Natural Resources	Hotels and Community
	Development

ITT Telecommunications was part of the communications and information services area, but relied on technical know-how, especially from the electronic components group.

ITT Telecommunications and the System 12

The telecommunications industry was rapidly shifting from analogue to digital switching systems, and virtually every major player wishing to compete in the global telecommunications business had reoriented their R&D strategies to move from electro-mechanical to digital switching technologies. Success in this technological shift had come at a price: an Arthur D. Little study estimated that, given the shortness of digital system technology lifecycle (5–8 years compared to 25–30 years for electro-mechanical systems), developers of new telecommunications switches would have to obtain 8% of the world market share in telecommunications switching equipment in order to break even on development costs. ITT engineers were also aware that 75% of digital switch development costs would be software, not hardware related *(refer to **Exhibits 9** and **10**)*.

ITT had embarked on its own ambitious development project in the late 1970s: the System 12. The company had developed its own technical protocols, including the CCITT development platform, a hardware architecture and software language intended to protect the company's investment, and establish a new telecommunications standard. The development project grew from the company's Connecticut laboratories to several key technology development sites in Europe.

From Digital's perspective, ITT was confronting one of the most demanding software development projects in the history of telecommunications – its System 12 (S-12). Over 2,500 software engineers in four European locations had been working on the project for seven years, and there was no end in sight (a print-out of the source code was said to fill two rail cars with paper).

Exhibit 9 *Telecommunications switch development: technology lifecycles*
(Source: *Ferdinand Kuznick, IMD lecturer*)

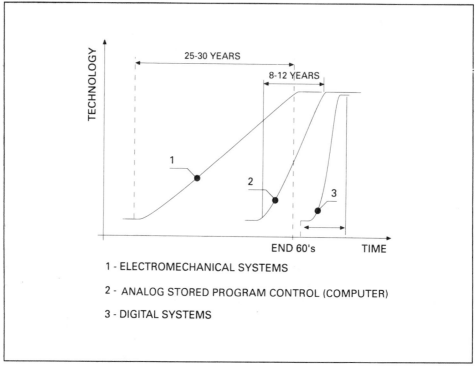

1 - ELECTROMECHANICAL SYSTEMS

2 - ANALOG STORED PROGRAM CONTROL (COMPUTER)

3 - DIGITAL SYSTEMS

The groups responsible for System 12 functional activities and engineering support were ITC Europe in Brussels and ESC in Harlow, UK, and for the development and manufacture of the S-12 were SEL in Stuttgart, Germany; BTM in Antwerp, Belgium; SESA in Spain; and FACE in Italy *(refer to Exhibit 11)*.

In the first phases of the S-12 project, it had been relatively easy to port software across programming languages and hardware configurations. As S-12 development grew in size and complexity, subtle changes became major events in which each engineering group had to consider the changes of another group before proceeding.

When different groups attempted to work with several million lines of code, modifications became inevitable, and engineers had to overcome bugs by inserting a 'patch'. One engineer noted, 'By the mid-eighties, we were putting new patches on top of old patches.' To remedy the situation, ITT hired Tony Kenny, an ex-IBM engineer. Tony had been keen to spread the risks of any major changes in ITT's software development procedures. His

Exhibit 10 *Telecommunications switch development: hardware vs software development costs* (Source: *Ferdinand Kuznick, IMD lecturer*)

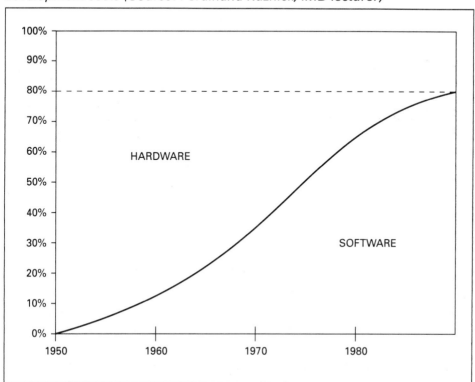

solution to the slowdown in the S-12 development project was to use Computer Aided Software Engineering (CASE) tools.

Various factors led to questioning the potential value of ITT's long-term switch development project. These included:

1. Lack of Support for Technological Development

In the race to develop telecommunications hardware, little thought had been given to developing software processes and tools for the ongoing modification of products and services. Two presumptions proved to be false: that computer companies could provide off-the-shelf software tools to system developers, and that the cost of software development would increase at a slower rate than hardware development costs.

2. Questionable Market Share for the System 12

The major world market for telephony, the United States, was shaken in

Exhibit 11

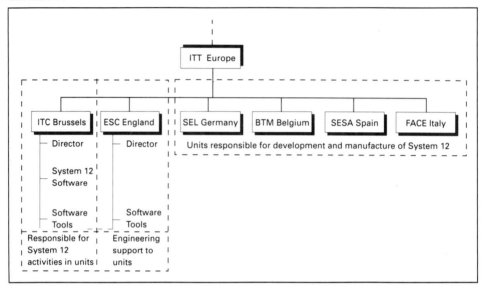

1983 by a consent decree which resulted in breaking up AT&T's regional telephone business into eight independent companies and splitting Bell Laboratories in two: AT&T Bell Labs and BellCorp. Despite the break-up, AT&T was moving fast in developing a digital switch and would be ensured a significant market share after its introduction. The AT&T break-up created eight new competitors on the world telecommunications scene. In October 1984, Rand Araskog noted that, given the cost of the project and the increasing number of competitors, 'there are doubts about the S-12's viability in the United States'.

3. ITT as a Potential Takeover Target
During the early 80s, ITT was the target of several hostile takeover attempts, each one proposing to split the company into several companies that would bring greater value for the shareholders. While Araskog succeeded in beating back each attempt, he was also required to dispose of several businesses.

The Request from BTMC and ITT (Europe)

In July 1985, the Belgian subsidiary of ITT (BTMC in Antwerp) sent a request for a tender to Digital's Belgian office *(refer to ITT Organization Chart, Exhibit 11)*. In simple terms, the offer focused on engineering workstations. Under normal circumstances, the Digital country manager would hear about the bid request in advance. But this tender offer puzzled him. Given Digital's long-standing customer relationship with ITT (dating back to Digital's first minicomputer purchase in 1968), the request had been hastily made, suggesting that BTMC was jumping at another new workstation offer. He was also aware of recent discussions about engineering workstations between Apollo Computer Corp. and ITT.

The country manager, being close to ITT headquarters in Brussels, had heard rumours of a 'strategic agreement' being forged between Kenneth Olsen and the ITT CEO, Rand Araskog, the chairman of ITT. Since the BTMC request referred to specific hardware, and because ITT was a strategic customer in several national markets, the country manager contacted David Stone in Digital's European headquarters. The ITT country manager decided to get clearer signals from senior management before proceeding.

Indeed, BTMC's request coincided with several ongoing discussions between ITT and Digital managers. Senior managers in two other ITT companies (ESC in Harlow, UK, and ITC Brussels, Belgium) had been talking with Digital about the development of software tools for the S-12. CASE tools were high on their list of needs. ITT's European headquarters (ITT Brussels) was at the centre of the various proposals to work with Digital.

It was the hardware request from BTMC (ITT Belgium) that led to Pier Carlo Falotti's E-mail message to David Stone. The country manager's hunches were correct. Over the previous several months, there had been several informal discussions between top level DEC and ITT personnel about hardware, software, and strategic collaboration. Digital's European Chairman Falotti knew that ITT was going through a strategic and technological transition. In the US, the company had successfully fought off several acquisition attempts by corporate raiders. In Europe, the System 12 telecommunications switch development project was taking significantly longer than expected. David remembered how thoroughly the Metaframe group had reviewed ITT's situation. He wondered, 'Was Digital courting a four-headed monster?'

By late summer and early autumn 1985, the trade journals were full of news about an overall computer industry slump. Kenneth Olsen had announced to shareholders: 'The marketplace is in turmoil. Much of the industry has been devastated in just the past two years.' The main hardware vendors IBM, Digital, Hewlett Packard, Apollo, Prime and Data General were repositioning their products and servies in the minicomputer segment. Digital's profit level was below that of one year earlier, yet it had outperformed most market analysts' expectations, thanks to cost controls and revenue growth, particularly in Europe. Apollo Computer, Inc. had reported an after-tax operating loss of $4 million and a $14.4 million inventory write-down, resulting in a net loss of $18.4 million. Prime Computer, Inc. posted a 7% profit increase in a 19% revenue gain that went from $165 million to $196 million. Data General Corp. saw its pretax earnings plunge 98% to $800,000. More than 60% of the companies had lower rates of return than in the previous quarters. Most experienced wide swings in stock prices, and a number of smaller competitors either merged, formed alliances or disappeared from the market.

Despite the overall industry downturn, there was growth in a few key segments, most notably, the emerging CAD-CAM and workstation markets. While some industry analysts pointed to the workstation as an exciting new development in computing, others downplayed its development, noting that workstations were only a reconfiguration of technologies from higher (mainframe) and lower (microcomputer) performing segments.

Apollo Computer Corporation was the founder of this segment and, along with Sun Microsystems, was one of the most aggressive marketers of engineering workstations. Their presence was only beginning to be felt in Europe. This firm had caught the eye of ITT's System 12 software development engineers.

DEC's Response to the ITT Tender Offer

David Stone had called Michael Horner, head of Engineering Strategy, to discuss ITT's tender offer to purchase workstations and related software products. David wanted to evaluate whether ITT might consider a joint technology development effort. He also saw it as a way to take the Metaframe Group's work into practice. Together, Michael Horner, the Metaframe Group and David Stone had reviewed ITT's proposed shopping list of hardware, software and support services. As David Stone had been aware of the high-level discussions between the two companies, he advised Michael Horner to coordinate a meeting with some of ITT's European managers before they responded with a bid. In the back of his mind he was intrigued by the complex software engineering problem facing ITT. If Digital could form a joint software engineering team that would help ITT solve its problems, there would be other customers facing similar challenges.

Horner coordinated the first meeting between ITT and Digital Europe management. The primary goal of the meeting, from Digital's perspective, was to explore how the two companies might consummate a broad agreement that would lead to joint technology development. Since the top management of both companies had called for a closer strategic relationship, David Stone's proposal would be to define the boundaries of a new strategic and technical relationship. Within a few days, a hardware sale had been delicately placed on the back burner, and strategic engineering groups had been assigned from both companies.

During the initial Digital–ITT meetings, two clear camps of managers emerged on the ITT side. Those who sought to purchase equipment and know-how from a computer vendor, and those who saw the opportunity to solve some larger software challenges through the newly created partnership. The ITT Engineers from ESC Harlow and SEL Stuttgart were particularly intrigued with a possible joint development effort. Michael Horner remembered the strong response from Gunter Endalee, the Chief Systems Engineer from SEL:

> Gunter was one of the brightest developers in ITT. He knew that the S-12 was a major undertaking, requiring multi-site engineering coordination. Except for announcing formal changes in software, he had given up trying to coordinate his efforts with the other ITT development groups in Europe. Digital's offer to review ITT's software development practices and propose new tools was an exciting possibility for Gunter. He never considered specific hardware and software to solve his problems. Digital had offered the conceptual breakthrough he sought.

Even after the Digital–ITT meetings in the autumn of 1985, ITT's BTMC division in Antwerp had continued to push for a range of computer hardware and software products that would help the company streamline and facilitate the S-12 software development process. In their eyes, a Digital–ITT agreement would not prevent a multi-vendor solution. The computer industry press had recently focused on two new developments in computing which were particularly promising for ITT engineers: the specialty engineering workstation, and computer-aided software design and engineering tools (CASE). The heart of ITT's tender offer had concentrated on these new tools.

Michael Horner organized Digital–ITT meetings for the top 20 ITT engineers and then for each major software engineering group in Europe. Digital showed how its software tools specialists in Valbonne, France, working with ITT engineers at several locations, could redesign ITT's software development approach. But with each successive discussion, Digital also learned about ITT's lack of a common strategy for the S-12 technology development. Key S-12 engineers at the different development and engineering sites had each been independently responsible for purchasing hardware and for S-12 development. Whole teams of ITT software engineers had developed separate components of the S-12 with different hardware and software standards. As one Digital engineer from Brussels, Etienne Bossard, put it:

> ITT is not a company. It is a confederation of companies. As a result, technical groups do not normally communicate across the confederation, which makes for chaos when they make changes.

Applying Metaframe to the Digital–ITT

The initial meetings with ITT went well. Digital and ITT engineers had agreed that a team would be assembled with the top echelons of ITT software engineers participating in introductory meetings.

Michael Horner became the European corporate sponsor of the Digital–ITT project for David Stone. Horner assembled an ITT Project Team that would implement discussions between ITT and the Metaframe Group. *(Refer to Exhibit 12.)* He brought in Bob Wyman from the US, one of Digital's leading software engineering experts. Bob Wyman had worked on Digital's most successful software development program to date: *All-in-One*. He also had an interest in extending his knowledge about Computer Aided Software Engineering (CASE) and saw the Digital–ITT project as a serious applied engineering challenge. Michael Horner and Bob Wyman agreed to meet the ITT's European managers and engineers to persuade them that DEC could assist ITT as it redefined its software development processes. From Michael's perspective, the first meetings with ITT engineers were successful. He recounted one meeting called to discuss hardware priorities.

> I simply began to describe how we went about developing software. I could see they were getting excited and wanted to hear more. For the next three hours, they questioned me about Digital's approach to software development. It was clear that I was describing a brave new world.

Over a two-month period in the autumn of 1985, Michael Horner and Bob Wyman travelled to all of ITT's S-12 development sites in Europe. As Michael observed:

> It was a process of getting buy-in from ITT's top management and then moving through the ranks. We targeted the first 20 people and prepared a road show. Each time, we made the following points:
>
> - Buying more equipment would not solve ITT's long-term S-12 problem.
> - DEC's knowledge of CASE tools and networked computing would be valuable if applied to telecommunications software development and,

Exhibit 12

Metaframe Group

David Stone, Chairman
Mike Horner, Technology Specialist
Tony Setchell, Telecommunications Strategist
Haskell Cehrs, Telecommunications Specialist
Lutz Reuter, Organizational Specialist
Eric Sublet, Contracts
Renato Rattore, Italy
Jean Paul Myeller, France
Peter Kohlhammer, Germany
Bill Strecker, Corporate Strategy USA
Skip Walter, Consultant (US based)

ITT Project Team

Mike Horner, Project Manager
Bob Wyman, Consultant
Patrick Scherrer, Software Engineer
Alex Taylor, Communications
Gerard Zarka, User Representative
Theo de Jongh, Project Manager Designate
Etienne Bossard, Technology Specialist
Specialist in Antwerp
Specialist in Harlow
Specialist in Stuttgart

---

since it was a generic problem, would serve the interests of both
companies.

- If ITT worked with Digital, it would be considered a privileged customer,
  and the S-12 engineers would be introduced to Digital's emerging
  technologies.

- As a result of a strategic agreement, Digital would provide equipment to
  key engineering sites and eventually assign a Digital engineer to work with
  the customer's engineers at each site.

Robert Wyman estimated that it would require around 8,000 man/years to
redefine and complete the software development for the S-12. This task had
to be managed among 2,500 engineers working in three to four parallel sites.
As Wyman put it:

> We had to network the sites and get them working together. But before ITT
> ever used CASE tools and workstations, we had to crash through the cultural
> and technical barriers.

Following the initial visits, the key sites were confirmed, and Digital began to establish network links between ITT sites: ESC Harlow, ITC Brussels, SEL Germany, and BTM Belgium. Digital, Valbonne, would serve as Digital's link to the network. Michael Horner had asked Gerard Zarka to find and configure the latest hardware and software, and to get it to several ITT European locations. Cost was not an initial consideration. Zarka was known throughout Digital Europe for his ability to get the latest equipment to the right place at the right time. He was also known less fondly by some country managers as someone who would jump the equipment delivery queue. Zarka described his efforts in Digital–ITT:

> I agreed wholeheartedly with the metaframe concept. ITT was asking for boxes. We refused. We focused on building their human/technical links through networked computing. Why? Because we knew that more machines were not going to make them more productive. Their problem had reached a too high level of complexity.
>
> The first step had been to build and demonstrate a network. We located some of Digital's state-of-the-art equipment: five Microvax 2-Q5 (fully loaded and networked) hardware configurations. They were the first ones shipped to Europe. The sales managers on the DEC side objected initially. We were shipping about $1.4 million of the latest technology to four countries, free of charge, and contributing who knows how many hours to the Metaframe cause. Since every country has its own budget in Digital, if a country sales person objected, we were stuck. In one case, two machines sat in customs for two months until the sales manager agreed to let us install the box at an ITT site.

The Digital Metaframe team realized that better coordination through a network was necessary for such a large and complex software development organization. Once the network was more or less in place, the teams had started to work on defining software tools that would integrate information, time and project management protocols based on Digital's early experience with CASE tools. All of the engineer-to-engineer discussions focused on streamlining the S-12 software development process.

The team had succeeded in 'championing' this approach at some of ITT's sites, but some ITT engineers and managers continued to drag their feet. They wondered if Digital were trying to take over their project and how a networked development approach would affect different sites. How would Digital react when ITT exposed its internal processes? Bob Wyman was the recognized technical 'champion' of the project at Digital, but attaining the role and status of project champion across companies remained inaccessible to him. Some ITT people had simply not accepted a genuine proposal coming from, in their eyes, an outsider (developers from other sites were also considered outsiders).

Michael Horner became increasingly convinced that the Digital–ITT relationship provided special opportunities for both companies. He convinced many people that his small group had developed a new approach to working with customers and business partners. Instead of focusing on 'getting the sale', they discussed how to solve ITT's long-term software development problems. The group had even coined the term 'representative target customer' to describe and define engineering specifications for a future set of customers who would have different price/performance requirements.

He viewed their work at ITT as a prototype for future engineering-to-engineering relationships. But as an active participant in the ITT process, he was becoming aware of the differences between the two engineering cultures. He had recently asked David for more time to see whether the model would work. David remembered Michael's emphatic words:

> Look, if we can get them to believe in what we do and in our approach, it is basically the same as an OEM sale. Inject the right people early on, inspire them, fund them, and wait a year for things to happen.

By the following February, eight months after members of the Metaframe group had been assigned to ITT, the project was adrift. The tools developed by Digital were not being integrated into the ITT development process at many of the sites – different sites continued to use their own software development techniques. The network was in place, but could not seem to overcome ITT's cultural barriers.

Digital's Central Engineering in the US was asking questions about the new software development project. From their perspective it had three problems. First, it was somewhat disconnected from Digital's Central Engineering strategy. Second, the development project itself involved a customer, requiring Digital to share proprietary software technologies and next generation hardware. And third, there were similar software tool developments going on in other parts of the company that had gotten approval from Central Engineering.

The partnership became increasingly complicated when the country management teams, who were closely linked to software services, started to hear about the project from their customers and field people. One manager contacted David Stone to find out why Digital's most advanced workstations were being shipped free of charge to ITT development labs, when his best customers were on a six-month waiting list for the same hardware.

Time for Action

David Stone had discussed the Digital–ITT relationship with his staff during the previous week, knowing that the product–market issues would have a bearing on what DEC could do with ITT. There was always a strong pull from headquarters in Maynard, Massachusetts, to keep technical developments and product/market segmentation close to home. Digital Europe's limited manufacturing capabilities reinforced this point. But at the same time, Digital Europe was doing comparatively well and had an expanding customer base. The country managers were generating a lot of business, and there were several advanced engineering projects and university–industry partnerships in the pipeline.

David Stone had still other reasons for being concerned about the Digital–ITT project. Very few customers had ever been in direct contact and worked together with people in Digital's engineering area. In addition, Digital's general management voiced a concern that Digital might be sharing its core technical competences with its partners. David Stone had had to build a strong case for developing a software engineering link with ITT Europe. Perhaps he would find new ways to justify the merits of the project.

David picked up the phone to call Michael Horner. Together they would decide how to proceed. As the dial tone sounded, he thought back to early 1985 when everyone was talking about alliances. He was surprised at how often he had been called to establish 'customer relationships'. Yet, ITT Telecom had some serious engineering challenges to overcome. As soon as David Stone heard Michael Horner pick up the telephone, he said: 'Michael, we'd better meet tomorrow at 8:30 to decide what to do about the Digital–ITT project.'

Potain S.A.

This case was based on teaching materials originally developed at the Lyon Graduate School of Business by Professors T. Atamer, Francis Bidault, Ham San Chap and Frank Zaeh. The English version of the case has been prepared by Research Associate Kimberly A. Bechler, under the supervision of Professor Francis Bidault, as a basis for class discussion rather than to illustrate either effective or ineffective handling of a business situation.

It was January 8, 1985 and Pierre Perrin, CEO of Potain SA, had just received a letter from MACHIMPEX (China International Machinery Import-Export Company) requesting a proposal for a 5-year licensing contract on Potain's FO23B crane. The Chinese wanted total know-how and know-why for crane design and manufacturing. *(Refer to MACHIMPEX letter in Exhibit 1.)*

Perrin asked his secretary to send a copy of this letter to the Export director and to the SEREX manager ('Service Assistance Technique Export') immediately. An urgent meeting had to be arranged to discuss the Chinese opportunity before putting together an offer, and to select Potain's delegation that would go to Peking to negotiate the licensing contract.

What did technology transfer mean to Potain and how should Potain handle it? Should Potain provide the Chinese with all its technology? What should the price be and what conditions should be made?

Market Trends

In 1979, 16,000 tower cranes (including both top-slewing and bottom-slewing or self-erecting cranes) were sold worldwide. Since then, the world market had weakened and continued to decline. In 1983, world sales were just

Exhibit 1

MACHIMPEX

POTAIN SA
18, rue Charbonnières
69130 ECULLY
FRANCE

Peking, December 28, 1984

SUBJECT: Request submission of an offer for the provision of know-how and know-why for the production of a top slewing crane by the Peking construction machine factory.

Gentlemen,

Following our visit to your factories and your 1984 visit to Peking, we would like to request that you submit an offer for the provision of know-how and know-why for a top slewing crane with a 20,000 lbs maximum load and 164-foot jib, which could be manufactured at our Peking factory.

The offer should include a description of the know-how and know-why concerning: crane design and calculation, specifications of raw materials, manufacturing, quality control, testing, as well as crane installation, maintenance and utilization. The price for the know-how and know-why, and a proposed payment schedule should be sent with the offer no later than February 1, 1985.

We would also like to invite you to come to Peking in April for final negotiations, after which, MACHIMPEX and the PRC Ministry of Urban Construction and Environmental Protection will choose the technology transfer partner; our goal is to start production as quickly as possible and according to the most advanced techniques.

Thank you in advance for your timely handling of this matter.

slightly over 9,000 units, and the first half of 1984 had led market followers to believe that the world market could fall below 7,000 units for the 1984–1985 fiscal year (March 1–February 28). The forecast for the 1985–1986 fiscal year offered little hope for improvement.

Potain's Situation

In one year, the number of employees at Potain SA had been reduced from 2,900 to 1,460. Heavily dependent on the crane market, Potain was near bankruptcy; a loss of FF 94 million on a turnover of FF 750 million had been estimated for the 1984–1985 fiscal year (these figures included the expenses and necessary financial arrangements incurred by layoffs). There was even a question about whether Potain's 1984–1985 forecasts for turnover would be achieved. In addition, the market decline was expected to continue for the next three years. *(Refer to **Exhibits 2–5** for financial information.)*

Exhibit 2

SITUATION FINANCIERE PREVISIONNELLE 1984-1985

(Fiscal Year: March 1 - February 28)

POTAIN: COMPTE DE RESULTAT PREVISIONNEL POUR L'EXERCICE 84-85
(en 1000FF)

C.A. Chiffre d'affaires	761 088
Autres produits d'exploitation	2 622
CONSOMMATION	500 150
VALEUR AJOUTEE	263 560
IMPOTS, TAXES, ASSIMILES	- 20 149
Charges de personnel	- 347 455
Subvention d'exploitation reçue	106
E B E Excédant brut d'Exploitation	- 103 938
Dotations d'exploitation	- 21 755
Autres charges	- 7 168
Autres produits	64 989

Exhibit 2 *Continued*

R.E. Résultat d'exploitation	-	67 872
RESULTAT FINANCIER	-	65 239
RESULTAT COURANT AVANT IMPOT	-	133 111
RESULTAT EXCEPTIONNEL		38 698
RESULTAT NET	-	94 413

<u>BILAN PREVISIONNEL SIMPLIFIE POUR L'EXCERCICE 1984-85</u>
(en 1000 F)

IMMOBILISATIONS (1)	187 000	CAPITAUX PROPRES (2)	42 000
STOCKS	241 000	PROVISIONS	46 000
CREANCES CLIENTS	211 000		
		DETTES (3)	604 000
AUTRES CREANCES	46 000		
DISPONIBILITES	7 000		
TOTAL	692 000	TOTAL	692 000

(1) dont: Immobilisations corporelles   130 000
           Immobilisations financières   55 500

(2) dont: Ecart de réévaluation   21 400
           Réserves   63 100
           Report à nouveau   -   105 270
           Résultat d'exercice   -   94 410
           Provisions réglementées   51 500

(3) dont DMLT
           Dettes à moyen et long terme   168 300
           Fournisseurs   151 000

Exhibit 3

Comptes de Pertes et Profits Comparés (en 1000 FFr) de POTAIN S.A.

	Au 2.29.1984	Au 2.28.1983	Au 2.28.1982	Au 2.28.1981
Perte d'exploitation	56509			
Participation salariés		2029		
Pertes sur exercises antérieurs	23450	8600	5868	1237
Pertes exceptionnelles	3995	9192	4761	9923
Dotations aux comptes de provisions hors exploitations ou exceptionnelles	68455	15939	17544	36203
Provisions pour impôts sur les Sociétés			16670	6033
Bénéfice net		4256	19043	6621
Total	152409	40016	63886	60017

	Au 2.29.1984	Au 2.28.1983	Au 2.28.1982	Au 2.28.1981
Bénéfice d'Exploitation		2121	28662	14375
Profits sur exercises antérieurs	17366	3910	3248	1778
Profits exceptionnels	7491	7242	8373	2983
Reprise sur provisions hors exploitation ou exceptionnelles	22279	26743	23603	40881
Perte nette	105272			
Total	152409	40016	63886	60017

Exhibit 4

Comptes d'Exploitation Comparés (en 1000 FFr) de POTAIN S.A.

DEBIT	Au 2.29.1984	Au 2.28.1983	Au 2.28.1982	Au 2.28.1981
Stocks au début de l'exercice	230356	221062	230140	217138
Dépréciation	33589	29827	29090	22474
	196767	191235	201050	194664
Achats	490699	449243	415529	447714
Frais de personnel	311295	268620	239995	223006
Impôts et taxes	17429	15064	13171	10959
Travaux,fournitures et services	134839	141622	135449	117087
Transport et déplacements	44416	47503	43261	34488
Frais divers de gestion	21942	24576	18728	16743
Frais financiers	43522	39318	37432	35160
Dotations aux comptes amortissements	23481	17665	15811	17573
Dotations aux comptes de provisions	17671	13486	16314	11279
Quote-part stés en particip	2			
Bénéfice d'exploitation		2121	28663	14375
Total	1302062	1210453	1165403	1123048

CREDIT	Au 2.29.1984	Au 2.28.1983	Au 2.28.1982	Au 2.28.1981
Stocks à la fin de l'exercise	316000	230356	221062	230140
Depreciation	42395	33589	29827	29090
	273606	196767	191235	201050
Ventes et produits	925008	951687	927391	876544
Subventions d'exploitation	283	27	56	47
Ristournes fournisseurs	964	3678	1858	2452
Produits accessoires	12819	12494	10565	17961
Produits financiers	17261	21446	17169	13010
Travaux faits par l'entreprise pour elle-même	5407	11035	6769	8151
Quote part résult. participation		40		
Perte d'exploitation	56509			
Travaux et charges non imputables à l'exploitation de l'exercise	10205	13279	10360	3833
Total	1302062	1210453	1165403	1123048

Exhibit 5

Bilans Comparés (en 1000 FFr) de POTAIN S.A.

ACTIF	Au 2.29.1984	Au 2.28.1983	Au 2.28.1982	Au 2.28.1981
Valeurs Immobilisées				
Frais d'établissement	69	94	184	137
Immobilisations	118191	123158	107358	113288
Autres valeurs immobilisées	115854	97382	100207	105328
Valeurs d'exploitation	273606	196767	191235	201050
Valeurs realisables à court terme ou disponibles	262686	277444	253907	211397
Resultats (Perte de l'exercice)	105272			
Total Actif	875678	694845	652891	631500

PASSIF	Au 2.29.1984	Au 2.28.1983	Au 2.28.1982	Au 2.28.1981
Capitaux Propres et Reserves	214632	214570	200414	189806
Subvention d'equipement	12	19	25	31
Provision pour pertes et charges	70457	24254	30631	37190
Dettes à long et moyen terme	127769	113212	77551	94302
Dettes à court terme	462808	338534	325227	303550
Resultats (Benefice de l'exercise)		4256	19043	6621
Total	875678	694845	652891	631500

Factory workers were worried about the rumors of bankruptcy, and some were already looking for other jobs. Perrin needed to take immediate action to put the company back on its feet, limiting the impact of a short-term problem on Potain's long-term future.

Competition

Potain's major competitors were: Liebherr and Peiner of Germany, and Edilgru, Alfa, and Cibin of Italy. The Dutch company, Kroll, was also a top challenger *(refer to Exhibit 6)*. Even though Italian manufacturers had the largest volume worldwide, with 4,430 cranes per year, these were mainly bottom-slewing cranes.

Most competitors were either already licensing or moving in that direction, and it was clear that if Potain did not go into China, another company would be sure to claim that market.

History

Potain was founded in 1928 in the small town of La Clayette in France's Sâone and Loire region by Faustin Potain, an iron craftsman. In the beginning, Potain manufactured building equipment such as cement mixers, scaffolding parts and small cranes. At present, the Potain Group essentially manufactured tower cranes for buildings and public works projects. Potain had tried to diversify but had remained heavily concentrated in tower crane manufacturing.

In 1985, with its corporate headquarters in Ecully, near Lyon, the Potain Group consisted of Potain SA (holding company), BPR (a former competitor purchased in 1977), Sologat (a crane rental subsidiary), Sambron (a lift-truck manufacturer purchased in 1983), Simma (an Italian crane manufacturer that had been 51 per cent controlled by Potain since 1972), Potain Iberica (a crane manufacturer and vendor in Spain) and sales subsidiaries in the US, West Germany and Switzerland.

Diversification Efforts

In the mid-1960s, the directors realized that Potain had become too specialized and started thinking about diversification. Potain formed an alliance with Poclain in 1968, creating Potain, Poclain Material (PPM) and

Exhibit 6

Crane Market 1984 (in units)

	Potain B*	Potain T*	BPR B	BPR T	Simma B	Simma T	Liebherr B	Liebherr T	Peiner B	Peiner T	Edilgru B	Edilgru T	Alfa B	Alfa T	Cibin B	Cibin T	Kroll B	Kroll T
Total Europe	467	148	95	49	76	115	718	125	94	40	192		100	42	500		69	10
E.E.C. Countries	358	102	87	18	76	115	567	87	77	33	150		100	42	500		36	4
COMECON		5																
Other Europe	109	41	8	31			151	38	17	7	42						33	6
Total Africa	91	31	35	9			25	19						3			1	15
Maghreb	80	10	26	3			12											
Other Africa	11	21	9	6	1		13	19						3			1	15
Middle East	23	11		4	1		5	18	1	5				2				
Far East	6	47		15			1	14	1	5				15			2	2
Total Asia	29	58		19	1		6	32	2					17			2	2
Oceania								1		40								
Total Americas	5	3	2	7				3		40							15	
North America	1	1		2				3									15	
Latin America	4	2	2	5														
World Total	592	240	132	84	77	115	749	180	96	120	192	192	100	62	500		87	27

*B = Bottom; T = Top. Bottom or top refers to whether the crane turns at the bottom (bottom-slewing) or top (top-slewing).

targeting the mobile crane market. Mobile cranes were self-propelled cranes with a single telescopic arm, which were often used to erect top-slewing tower cranes. However, this alliance had the effect of limiting Potain's activity rather than providing a vehicle for expansion; Potain could not sell mobile cranes with a load capacity of greater than 1,600 lbs (8 tons).

Potain had also tried to develop new products: tower cranes providing fast assembly and transport, mobile cranes travelling over any surface and lift-trucks. However, none of these products had a commercial success. Potain remained dependent on its original business of manufacturing tower cranes.

In 1977, under the pressure of the French Ministry of Industry, Potain agreed to take over BPR, a company combining three of its competitors – Richier, Boilot and Pingon – this move marked an end to its diversification efforts for the time being. In spite of the costs of Potain's aborted diversification efforts, Potain remained a strong company. At the end of the 1970s, Potain completely dominated the French market and shared the world leadership position with Germany's Liebherr, both companies enjoying a 30 per cent market share.

Finally, in 1980, after a long history of family control, Potain hired its first 'outsider' as CEO. Pierre Barrot believed that Potain's 'best diversification' was the tower crane and that further diversification should be limited in order to refocus the Group on its business and accelerate international growth. Due to a disagreement with the board on the best way to manage the crisis, Barrot left Potain in June 1984. He was succeeded by Perrin, a long-serving senior executive who had held various positions, mainly in technology, engineering and business development.

Crane Developments

In the early 1920s, the technology for cranes with liftable jibs was invented by the German firm, Wolff. The trolley-jib was developed in the early 1930s. The jib (or arm) that had always been attached to the top of the mast was now laid horizontally across it. Underneath the jib was a trolley car running on tracks which served to distribute the load with more precision than the liftable jib alone. Trolley-jib cranes enabled the load to be moved at any height, distance or direction by using four movements – hoisting, slewing, trolleying, and travelling or ground movement.

In 1935, Potain developed its first small crane with a liftable jib; gradually this technology was adopted by different manufacturers. Then in 1953, Potain introduced its first trolley-jib crane. Each one of the crane movements could be controlled by the crane operator by remote control either from his cabin or from the ground. These 'firsts' were followed by: in 1956, the development of a telescoping system – enabling tower cranes to self-erect automatically; in 1961, the launch of electrical mechanisms with variable speeds – enabling better control of crane movements and at the same time better precision in the 'delivery' of loads; and in 1969, Potain received the world record for its '982' crane weighing 250 metric tons.

Cranes were defined according to six characteristics:

- *the height under the hook* (vertical distance between the hook and the ground), the counterweights being at the extreme opposite end of the jib and the jib in its fully upright position);

- *free-standing height* (maximum height under the hook at which the crane could operate faced with bad weather conditions, without requiring auxiliary means for ensuring its stability;

- *the reach* (horizontal distance between the crane's point of rotation and the hook;

- *serviceable load* (weight of the load that could be suspended on the hook, this weight varying with the reach;

- *maximum load* (maximum serviceable load that the crane could lift; and

- *the load at the tip* (serviceable load that the crane could lift at its maximum reach.

However, the features the most commonly used to describe cranes were: free-standing height, maximum reach, maximum load and load at the tip. *(Refer to **Exhibits 7–9**.)*

In addition to cranes used in the construction industry, there were other types of cranes. Each type of crane exemplified a different technology as the usage determined the required features. For example, harbor cranes required less precision in lifting and rotating than building cranes as port 'loads' were not as fragile as prefabricated boards. However, harbor cranes required greater durability for heavier loads and uninterrupted handling. Other examples were: forest cranes requiring shorter jibs and counter-jibs, and offshore cranes requiring special tempering and steel casings.

Potain manufactured and sold two types of cranes: construction cranes and travelling cranes (for industrial applications). In the construction crane segment (or tower cranes), Potain's product range spanned the two main categories: top-slewing and bottom-slewing (self-erecting tower cranes). Top-slewing tower cranes rotated at the *top*, had free-standing heights of

Exhibit 7   *Topkit FO/23B (*Source: *Potain Company Materials)*

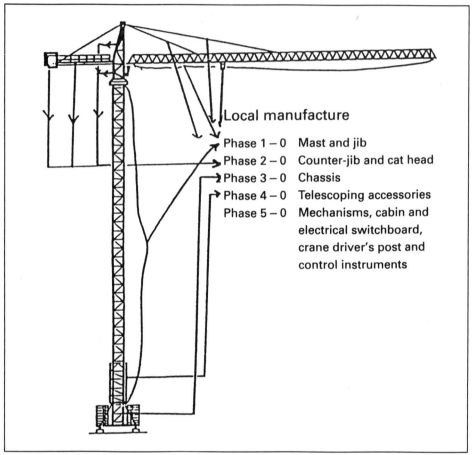

108–328 feet, reaches spanning 131–262 feet, and load capacities from 2,200 lbs at 131 feet to 44,000 lbs at 262 feet. Site applications included small, low and high-rise buildings, power plants, dams, and bridges.

    Potain's FO23B crane, for instance, was a top-slewing tower crane. Having a free-standing height of 202 feet, a reach of 164 feet, a maximum load of 20,000 lbs and load at the tip of 4,600 lbs, the FO23B was priced at FF 1,400,000 (which included Potain's 20 per cent margin on completed cranes). Adding the costs of transportation, customs and commissions, importing an FO23B would cost the Chinese FF 2,100,000.

    On the other hand, bottom-slewing or self-erecting tower cranes rotated at the *bottom*, had free-standing heights of 52–108 feet, reaches spanning

Exhibit 8 *Tower cranes (Source: Potain Company Materials)*

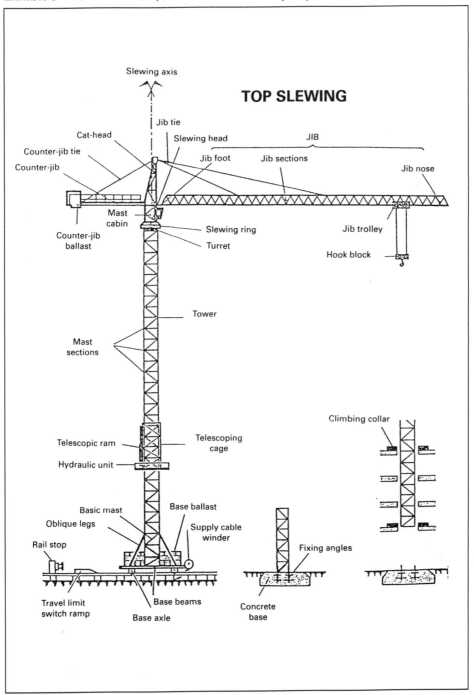

Exhibit 9   *Tower cranes* (Source: *Potain Company Materials)*

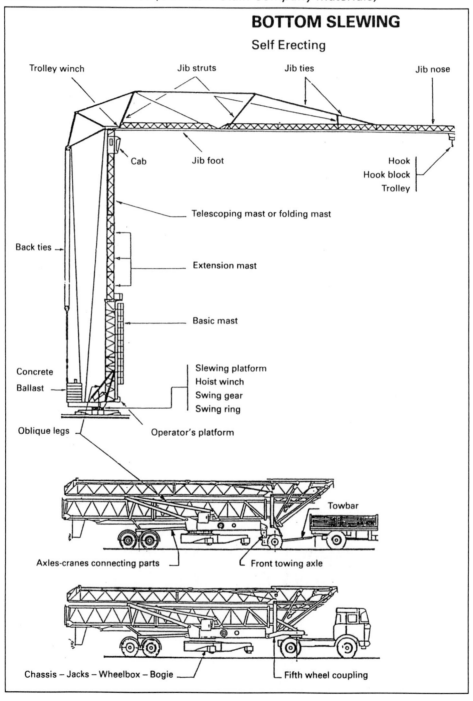

43–180 feet, and load capacities from 1,000 lbs at 40 feet to 4,400 lbs at 180 feet. Site applications included small- to medium-sized buildings (10 floors), individual houses, condominiums, small bridges and as auxiliary cranes on large projects such as dams or bridges.

Manufacturing

Cranes were not mass produced but, rather, parts were specially made to meet the various crane and usage requirements. The entire crane was manufactured by Potain except for the electric motor, which was purchased from another company, Leroy-Somer.

Potain's crane manufacturing took place in four factories: La Clayette, Montbrison, Charlieu and Moulins. These factories had diverse responsibilities. La Clayette was dedicated to the more technologically sophisticated components (such as electrical parts); Montbrison subcontracted mechanics and/or soldering to Charlieu and Moulins. Moulins and Charlieu were each responsible for a particular range of crane models. The distribution of work between these two factories was often problematic as the market growth for the two main product lines was very different.

Marketing

Over the past years, Potain had experienced sustained growth, which placed it in the uncontested leadership position in the French market with a market share of 85%. On a worldwide basis, Potain's share of the crane market had increased to roughly 20% of the bottom-slewing crane market, and to 40% of the top-slewing crane market. Potain's market presence was expanded and enhanced through its subsidiaries and licensees. For example, Potain was present in Italy via its 51% ownership interest in Simma (since 1972), which had a 35–40% share of the Italian crane market.

Potain did not have much information about its customer base as it sold mainly to dealers and seldom to end users. However, Potain's market share had continued to increase due to Potain's reputation for quality, service and industrial dominance. Potain placed a high priority on service, including training and technical assistance, and after-sales service.

The Potain Crane Institute was based at La Clayette and employed about a dozen people. Training covered areas such as crane assembly, maintenance and repair (especially electrical and electronic), and crane handling. Potain's after-sales service included preventive maintenance, crane renovation and repair. 25% of its after-sales activity was dedicated to the assembly and disassembly of top-slewing cranes; an activity which was not really profitable for Potain as there were many smaller firms offering this type of service at lower prices (FF 90–95 vs Potain's FF 120 per hour).

Internationalization

Export Sales and Subsidiaries

Potain 'internationalized' its business by emphasizing export sales, the development of subsidiaries and cultivation of licensees. Potain's International Business Organization was responsible for all of Potain's international operations: exports, subsidiaries and licenses.

Export sales were divided into three zones: Asia, America, and Europe/Africa. Potain had exported cranes since 1958 – first to Britain and the Commonwealth, then to Germany and Italy. In fact, exports were such a major portion of Potain's business that, in 1971, Potain received the 'Grand Prix de l'Oscar de l'Exportation'. For the 1983–1984 fiscal year, 70% of Potain's crane sales had been made outside France.

Potain had five foreign subsidiaries, four of which were located in the largest tower crane markets: Germany, Switzerland, Italy and Spain. The fifth one was located in the US which, although a minor market, was considered strategically important as all the major competitors (especially Germany) were there.

Licensing

Licensing Policy
Potain's licensing policy was developed during the 1970s in reaction to the slowdown in the major European markets. Licensing was seen as a means to reach remote or protected markets where it was almost impossible to import finished products. Typically, Potain looked for a licensee that would locally manufacture the heaviest and bulkiest parts of the crane. The most sophisticated parts would be imported by Potain and then assembled by the licensee.

To support this licensing policy, Potain developed a group of principles and tools composed of: a coherent international development strategy, capable technical support, a flexible business policy and precautions to manage the risk of creating potential competitors.

Until the present time, the precautions taken by Potain to protect itself against a licensee turning into a competitor included:

- not selling its latest technology, while at the same time being careful not to sell the license to products that were no longer part of its product line;

- requiring a minimum level of quality for products manufactured under license in order not to compromise its brand image;

- establishing a minimum of five years for the contract – reserving the provision of components, especially of mechanical parts which would always be manufactured in France;

- not giving the licensee exclusivity in areas considered outside the licensee's national territory, and to establish Potain's own sales network in these areas;

- and, in the event of a major long-term strategic position, considering a 'joint venture' which would enable Potain to control the licensee's activity by linking him as a partner.

Integration of Technology

The integration of Potain's technology for production was done in phases. For the proposed China deal, integration of the technology for manufacturing the FO23B crane would have five phases, with one phase integrated per year. During Phase I, the technology for the whole mast and jib would be integrated; Phase II included the technology for the counter-jib and cat head (or 'A' frame); Phase III comprised the technology for the crane chassis; Phase IV included telescoping accessories; and Phase V comprised the technology for the four mechanisms of hoisting, slewing, trolleying and travelling, plus the cabin with electrical switchboard, crane driver's post and control instruments. Phase V was usually not part of the 'technology transfer package'.

Serex

Potain was experienced in technology transfer, signing its first licensing contract in 1972 with South Africa. Recognizing the need for the formalization of its know-how and technology, Potain created its SEREX ('Service Assistance Technique Export') department also in 1972. Within the Potain organization, SEREX reported to the Industrial Director, while functionally working with the Export Sales organization.

Initially, SEREX only served to provide licensees with technical documentation adapted to each country. But, its general role had evolved to where SEREX was responsible for identifying potential licensing partners, and then for managing the transfer of technology and overseeing its local adaptation and implementation. Specifically, SEREX was: analyzing potential license candidates; defining the conditions for the integration of manufacturing by the licensee in coordination with the Export Sales organization; preparing the necessary documents and equipment for manufacturing; following up licensee orders for components, organizing training and technical assistance; and monitoring overseas licensee quality production.

Licensing Contracts

Potain's licensing contract with South Africa was followed by agreements with: Yugoslavia (1974), Iran (1974), Poland (1975), Venezuela (1976), Argentina (1976), South Korea (1978), Turkey (1979), Egypt (1980), Singapore (1980), Mexico (1981), Morocco (1981), and India (1983). These 13 licensing contracts were in various stages of activity, ranging in status from active to inactive.

Potain's partner in South Korea, for instance, was Hyundai, a company which produced two models of top-slewing cranes and one bottom-slewing crane. Until 1985, Hyundai had produced a total of 97 top-slewing and 11 bottom-slewing cranes; this licensing contract was slowly dying due to the incompatibility of the partners' objectives. In Singapore, as the market for new cranes had almost disappeared, Potain's licensing agreement was totally inactive. Therefore, the partner was moving towards Australia. The licensee, which had been a former agent in this marketplace, produced three different models of top-slewing cranes. Until 1985, this partner had produced a total of 80 cranes.

In contrast, Potain's licensing partnership in India was an example of a durable relationship. The licensee, a construction company, produced three models of top-slewing cranes and two models of bottom-slewing cranes. Up until 1985, 47 top-slewing and 59 bottom-slewing cranes had been produced.

China

The Marketplace

Potain had access to China through two channels: directly to China or indirectly via Hong Kong. Selling directly to China was Potain's weakest position; there were several sales agents with undefined territories and with little motivation to sell, and prices were not very competitive. However, Potain had a strong position in Hong Kong with almost 40% of the market.

In 1983, China's crane imports were FF 32 million, while in Singapore they were FF 79 million and in Hong Kong FF 20.5 million. In 1984, China's crane imports were only FF 12 million, where Hong Kong's were FF 39 million. However, 50–70% of Hong Kong's imports were then sold to China. Over the next three years, total direct imports of completed cranes were estimated at FF50–100 million.

History of Potain in China

Since Deng Xiao Ping's arrival to power in 1978, the operational word in China was 'modernization'. To achieve this objective, Chinese leaders expressed their desire to introduce equipment, advanced technology and management experience from developed countries. The construction industry was China's priority for modernization.

With the agreement of the Chinese and French governments, a mission to China was organized by French construction companies in 1979. Pierre Perrin, then deputy operational director, accompanied by the director of international development, led this mission for Potain. They were received by the Vice-minister responsible for technology transfer. The mission turned into a symposium on materials, and equipment for building and public works projects. At the time of this trip, Perrin understood that China was not interested in importing products, merely product technology. Despite a letter expressing an intent to cooperate sent by Perrin to the Vice-minister, no activity or further communication had followed this visit.

Then, in 1982, after three years of silence, MACHIMPEX sent a letter to Potain's International Business Organization requesting Potain to submit an offer for a licensing contract for the manufacture of construction cranes. MACHIMPEX invited Potain's technical experts to visit one of its factories in order to help them identify and define their technological needs. When two salesman arrived and were unable to answer MACHIMPEX's questions, the Chinese concluded that Potain was not serious about the proposition. Later, when one of Potain's engineers went to a construction site in Peking, he was invited to visit Peking's crane factory. As this engineer *was* able to answer all their technical questions, the Chinese had added Potain to their list of programmed visits for 1984 (which also included Liebherr and Peiner).

In January 1984, a Chinese delegation – composed of the Peking factory director and directors of research from the Institute of Technological Research for Mechanical and Electrical Construction – visited Potain; the delegation noted that Potain was well equipped to handle the transfer of its technology. However, the Chinese remained unsure about Potain's willingness to cooperate. Therefore, in March 1984, Perrin, Gendrault (Research Director), Liger (SEREX Manager) and a sales representative went to China. This visit lasted two weeks and ended with a 2-day cross-examination, during which the Chinese engineers asked over 150 pointed technical questions to establish Potain's level of expertise.

The letter that Perrin had just received was the first news since that visit.

The China Deal

MACHIMPEX was demanding the whole technology – '100 per cent integration' – for Potain's FO23B top-slewing crane. This 'licensing opportunity' represented a new situation for Potain; the Chinese wanted to produce everything, including the mechanisms, and wanted the 'know-why' for crane design which was a determining competitive advantage in the industry. In the past, Potain had only agreed to license Phases I-IV. Perrin also considered the opportunity cost; Potain's margin per crane was FF 280,000, but if Potain did not sell the technology, the market would be closed to Potain.

Looking at it from MACHIMPEX's perspective, Perrin thought about the costs incurred by China as a potential licensee. According to a SEREX study on China's production costs, China would save significantly on transportation and labor costs (direct production costs). Shipping and transportation costs for an FO23B crane would be FF 350,000 before the transfer of technology process began. Over the proposed 5-year contract period, these costs would vary according to the number of completed products versus components imported by China.

SEREX produced a forecast of the full cost of a FO23B in China *(refer to **Exhibits 10 & 11**)*. This forecast showed that the full cost of an FO23B would decrease from FF 2,100,000 before the transfer of technology to FF 383,000 when the licensee reached full integration. The final price to the end user would then be determined by a mark-up set by the Chinese Ministry of Industry. In similar industries, according to other Western companies that had done technology transfer in China, the mark-up was usually around 40% (i.e. margin of 28%), leaving almost no profit to the factory. The price of the FO23B crane in China would thereby be fixed by the Ministry in terms of a 'cost +' basis (full cost + margin), keeping the retail price at a minimum in order to make the product affordable to local construction companies; profit in China did not seem to have the same meaning as it did in France.

In preparation for his meeting with his colleagues, Perrin consulted a memorandum he had received from Antoine Colas, Export Director *(refer*

Exhibit 10   *Structure of Potain's production costs for FO23B*

Raw Materials (Steel)	18%
Components (Electrical Devices, ...)	12%
Factory Cost (Labor + Amortization = Factory Hourly Rate)	35%
General & Administrative	15%
Selling Costs	20%
Full Cost	**100%**
Margin = 20% (Markup = 25%)	25%
Total	**125%**
Ex-Factory Price of FO23B (before Tax)	1,400,000
Shipping & Forwarding	25%
Customs Duties	25%

to *Exhibit 12)*. Faced with an 'all or nothing' deal, Perrin thought about the complexity of the decision faced by Potain and the possible resulting long-term consequences.

Market Considerations in the Region

The world crane market basically included three zones: Europe (80%), the Far East and Asia (10–15%), and the Middle East (5–10%). The Far East and Asia, and the Middle East were the two markets expected to experience high growth in the future: the four 'dragons' – Japan, Korea, Singapore and Taiwan – were expected to exhaust their stock of cranes in 4–5 years; Indonesia, Malaysia and the Philippines were believed to be waiting to 'take off'; and Japan's construction companies were rapidly augmenting their technological expertise and developing a presence in foreign markets.

In addition, the Far East was potentially the second largest market after Europe for top-slewing cranes. With a potential market of 500 cranes, representing a turnover of roughly FF 200 million, China would possibly be the fifth largest market after West Germany, Italy, URSS, and France. China also had liberal technology transfer legislation *(refer to Exhibit 13)* as well as legislation providing cooperation and financial incentives for the development of 'Special Economic Zones'. *(Refer to Exhibit 14.)*

However, it was uncertain how long Deng's policy of openness would last, and Potain did run the risk of the Chinese becoming competitors in the fast growing markets of the Far East.

Exhibit 11 *Breakdown of the full cost of FO23B in China (in 1000 FFr) (Source: SEREX (disguised data))*

	Year 1	Year 2	Year 3	Year 4	Year 5	Before T.T.
1 Integration Phase (operational)	Phase I	Phases I–II	Phases I–III	Phases I–IV	Phases I–V	
2 Cost of components and parts shipped by Potain to China	739.2	616.0	459.2	380.8	0.0	1120
3 Margin	246.4	239.5	196.8	205.0	0.0	280
4 Price including margin (ex-factory before tax) = 2 + 3	986.5	855.5	656.0	585.8	0.0	1400.0
Shipping and forwarding per unit						
5 – Percent	51%	38%	21%	15%	0%	100%
6 – (1000 FFr)	178.5	133	73.5	52.5	0	350
7 Cost of imports per unit (before customs duties) = 4 + 6	1164.1	988.5	729.5	638.3	0	1750
Local costs of licensee (according to integration level)						
8 – Percent	34%	45%	59%	66%	0%	0%
9 – (1000 FFr)	130.2	172.3	225.9	252.8	383	0
10 China costs before customs duties	1294.3	1160.8	955.4	891.1	383	1750
11 Customs duties rate	15%	15%	15%	15%	0	25%
12 Customs duties (1000 FFr)	147.8	128.3	98.4	87.9	0.0	350.0
13 Full cost per unit in China (before tax) = 10 + 12	1442.1	1289.1	1053.8	979.0	383.0	2100.0
14 Price per unit in China (fixed by Ministry of Industry)						

Exhibit 12

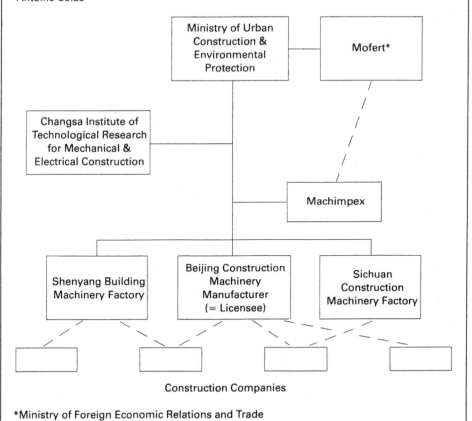

MEMORANDUM

TO: Pierre Perrin
            CEO, Potain SA

DATE: January 9, 1985

FROM: Antoine Colas
            Export Director

SUBJECT: Organizational relationships of the key 'players' in the licensing
            negotiations.

Mr. Perrin,
This memo is in response to your fax of January 8th. I thought it would be helpful in planning Potain's strategy to know who we will be dealing with and their respective relationships. The schema is outlined below.

Antoine Colas

Ministry of Urban Construction & Environmental Protection

Mofert*

Changsa Institute of Technological Research for Mechanical & Electrical Construction

Machimpex

Shenyang Building Machinery Factory

Beijing Construction Machinery Manufacturer (= Licensee)

Sichuan Construction Machinery Factory

Construction Companies

*Ministry of Foreign Economic Relations and Trade

Exhibit 13 *Chinese legislation on technology transfer (*Source: The Chinese Investment Guide, *3rd edition, Hong Kong 1985)*

Appendix 5C
LEGISLATION CHINOISE SUR TECHNOLOGY TRANSFER

Regulations of the People's Republic of China on the Administration of Technology Acquisition Contracts

Promulgated by the State Council on 24 May 1985

Article 1

These Regulations are formulated with a view to further expanding foreign economic and technical cooperation, upgrading the scientific and technical level of the country and promoting national economic growth.

Article 2

Importation of technology referred to in these Regulations means acquisition of technology through trade or economic and technical cooperation by any corporation, enterprise, organisation or individual within the territory of the People's Republic of China (hereinafter referred to as "the recipient") from any corporation, enterprise, organisation, or individual outside the territory of the People's Republic of China (hereinafter referred to as "the supplier"), including:

1 Assignment or licensing of patent or other industrial property rights;
2 Know-how provided in the form of drawings, technical data, technical specifications, etc. such as production processes, formulae, product designs, quality control and management skills.
3 Technical services.

Article 3

The technology to be imported must be advanced and appropriate and shall conform to at least one of the following requirements:

1 Capable of developing and producing new products;
2 Capable of improving quality and performance of products, reducing production cost and lowering consumption of energy or raw materials;
3 Favourable to the maximum utilisation of local resources;
4 Capable of expanding product export and increasing earnings of foreign currencies;
5 Favourable to environmental protection;

6 Favourable to production safety;
7 Favourable to the improvement of management;
8 Contributing to the advancement of scientific and technical levels.

Article 4

The recipient and the supplier shall conclude in written form a technology import contract (hereinafter referred to as "the contract"). An application for approval of the contract shall be submitted by the recipient, within thirty days from the date of conclusion, to the Ministry of Foreign Economic Relations and Trade of the People's Republic of China or any other agency authorised by the Ministry (hereinafter referred to as "the approving authority"). The approving authority shall approve or reject the contract within sixty days from the date of receipt. Contracts approved shall come into effect on the date of approval. Contracts on which the approving authority does not make a decision within the specified period of time shall be regarded as approved and shall come into effect automatically.

Article 5

The conclusion of technology import contracts must conform to the relevant provisions of the "Foreign Economic Contract Law" and other laws of the People's Republic of China. Both parties must specify in the contract the following items:

1 Contents, scope and essential description of the technology provided, and a list of patents and trade marks if they are involved;
2 Technical targets to be reached and time limit and measures for accomplishing the targets;
3 Remuneration, composition of remuneration and form of payment.

Article 6

The supplier shall ensure that it is the rightful owner of the technology provided and that the technology provided is complete, correct, effective and capable of accomplishing the technical targets specified in the contract.

Article 7

The recipient shall undertake the obligation to

Exhibit 13 *Continued*

keep confidential, in accordance with the scope and duration agreed upon by both parties, the technical secrets contained in the technology provided by the supplier, which have not been made public.

Article 8

The duration of the contract shall conform to the time needed by the recipient to assimilate the technology provided and, unless specially approved by the approving authority, shall not exceed ten years.

Article 9

The supplier shall not oblige the recipient to accept requirements which are unreasonably restrictive. Unless specially approved by the approving authority, a contract shall not include any of the following restrictive provisions:

1 Requiring the recipient to accept additional conditions which are not related to the technology to be imported, such as requiring the recipient to purchase unnecessary technology, technical services, raw materials, equipment and products;

2 Restricting the freedom of choice of the recipient to obtain raw materials, parts and components or equipment from other sources;

3 Restricting the development and improvement by the recipient of the imported technology;

4 Restricting the acquisition by the recipient of similar or competing technology from other sources;

5 Non-reciprocal terms of exchange by both parties of improvements to the imported technology;

6 Restricting the quantity, variety and sales price of products to be manufactured by the recipient with the imported technology;

7 Unreasonably restricting the sales channels and export markets of the recipient;

8 Forbidding use by the recipient of the imported technology after expiration of the contract;

9 Requiring the recipient to pay for or to undertake obligations for patents which are unused or no longer effective.

Article 10

In applying for approval of contracts, applicants shall submit the following documents:

1 Written application for approval of the contract;

2 Copy of the contract concluded by both parties and its Chinese translation;

3 Documents evidencing the legal status of the contracting parties.

Article 11

Application and approval of any revision and renewal of the contract shall be made in accordance with the provisions stipulated in Article 4 and Article 10 of these Regulations.

Article 12

The authority to interpret these Regulations and to formulate detailed rules for implementing these Regulations resides in the Ministry of Foreign Economic Relations and Trade of the People's Republic of China.

Article 13

These Regulations shall enter into force on the date of promulgation.

24.9 Procedures for examination and approval of technology import contracts

Approved by the State Council on 26 August 1985 and published by the Ministry of Foreign Economic Relations and Trade on 18 September 1985

Article 1

These procedures (hereinafter referred to as the "Procedures") are formulated in accordance with the provisions of the "Regulations of the People's Republic of China on the Administration of Technology Import Contracts".

Article 2

Technology import contracts hereunder listed must be submitted for governmental examination and approval in accordance with these Procedures regardless of country of origin, sources of funds and method of payment:

1 Contracts for transfer or licensing-in of industrial property rights and technical know-how;

2 Contracts for technical services, including that of feasibility studies or engineering designing entrusted to or in cooperation with foreign enterprises, that of provision of technical services through employing foreign geological exploration or engineering team(s), that of provision of technical services on technical renovation, technology or product design improvement, quality control and enterprise management, etc. but exclusive of

Exhibit 13 *Continued*

that for foreigners to be employed to work in Chinese enterprises;

3 Contracts for co-production which involves the transfer of industrial property rights and technical know-how or licensing, but exclusive of that for SKD or CKD operations, and processing with supplied materials or samples;

4 Contracts for the supply of complete sets of equipment such as plant, workshop or production lines, the aim of which is to transfer or licence-in industrial property rights and technical know-how as well as provision of technical services; and

5 Other contracts for the purchase of machinery, equipment or goods which involves the transfer of or licensing-in of industrial property rights and technical know-how as well as provision of technical services, but exclusive of those for the straightforward purchase or leasing of machinery and equipment, nor their after-sales provision of technical data, random operation manuals and maintenance instructions or maintenance service in general.

Article 3

For technical import contracts in which technology is acquired from foreign investors or other foreign parties in enterprises owned by foreign interests, and equity and contractual joint ventures that are established in the People's Republic of China, they must undergo the process of examination and approval according to these Procedures.

For contracts in which the industrial property rights or technical now-how concerned is entered as an equity share by foreign investors, they must undergo the process of examination and approval according to the provisions of the "Regulations for the Implementation of the Law of the People's Republic of China on Joint Ventures Using Chinese and Foreign Investment" and other relevant laws and/or administrative regulations.

Article 4

Technology import contracts are examined and approved respectively in the light of the following conditions:

1 Given existing norm stipulations, the contract for an above-norm project, the feasibility study report or equivalent document(s) of which are approved by the State Planning Commission is to be examined and approved by the Ministry of Foreign Economic Relations and Trade;

2 Given existing norm stipulations, the contract for a below-norm project, the feasibility study report or equivalent document(s) of which are approved by the responsible ministry or administration directly under the jurisdiction of the State Council is to be examined and approved by the Ministry of Foreign Economic Relations and Trade or the above-mentioned responsible ministry or administration entrusted by the Ministry of Foreign Economic Relations and Trade, which, however, is invested with the overall responsibility to issue the "Approval Certificate for the Technology Import Contract";

3 Given existing norm stipulations, the contract for a below-norm project for which the feasibility study report or the equivalent document(s) is approved by provincial, autonomous region or municipality government directly under the jurisdiction of the Central Government, special economic zones, coastal open cities and cities which come separately under national economic plans is to be examined and approved by the respective departments (commissions or bureaus) of the Ministry of Foreign Economic Relations and Trade. The contract or project for which the feasibility study report or equivalent document(s) is approved by city or county government is to be examined and approved by the respective departments (commissions or bureaus) of the Ministry of Foreign Economic Relations and Trade of provinces, autonomous regions and municipalities where the organs of the above-said cities or countries are located; and

4 Except those stipulated in item 2 of Article 3 of these Procedures, a technology import contract signed by a foreign-owned enterprise, equity joint venture or contractual joint venture of other foreign parties is to be examined and approved by the departments (commissions or bureaus) of provinces, autonomous regions, municipalities directly under the jurisdiction of the Central Government, special economic zones, coastal open cities and cities which come separately under the national economic plans where the above-said enterprises are registered.

Article 5

Application for examination and approval for a technology import contract mentioned in Article 4 must be submitted by the contract recipient to the

Exhibit 13 *Continued*

organs in charge within 30 days from the date of signature along with the documents as listed below:

1 Application;

2 Contract copy and its Chinese version; and

3 Certificate referring to the legal status of the contracting parties.

If the organs in charge consider it necessary, the applicant may be asked to submit other documents/data needed for the examination and approval of the contract.

Article 6

After receiving the application, the organs in charge must pay attention to the following points:

1 Whether the contents of the contract conform to that of the feasibility study report or the equivalent document(s) approved;

2 Whether the essential articles in the contract are as required;

3 Whether the property rights of the transferred technology and, where disputes arise over such property rights in the technology transfer, the obligations as well as the solutions thereof are explicitly and reasonably stipulated in the contract;

4 Whether there are reasonable stipulations in the contract for the technical level which should be achieved by the transferred technology, including the product quality guarantee, through the application of the said technology;

5 Whether the price and method of payment are reasonable;

6 Whether the stipulations in the contract for the contracting parties relating to their rights, responsibilities and obligations are definite, reciprocal and reasonable;

7 Whether any preferential taxation commitment is made in the contract without the consent of the Chinese Tax Authority;

8 Whether any provision is found in the contract violating the existing laws and regulations of China; and

9 Whether any provision is found in the contract that constitutes an encroachment of the sovereignty of China.

Article 7

The organ in charge must complete its contract examination and approval process within 60 days from the date of receipt of the application:

1 Once a contract is approved after examination, the organ in charge shall issue the "Approval Certificate for Technology Import Contract" printed and numbered by the Ministry of Foreign Economic Relations and Trade; and

2 If a contract is not approved after examination, the organ in charge shall put forth as soon as possible the reason thereof and request the recipient signatory party to hold renegotiations with the supplier of the technology and then grant the approval provided that the contract is amended accordingly.

To facilitate approval for the contract, the recipient negotiator may consult the organs in charge for the main contents or certain articles in the contract before or during the renegotiations or requests for pre-examination.

Article 8

After approval of the technology import contract by the government authorities concerned, all organs in charge shall submit a copy of the "Approval Certificate for Technology Import Contract" as well as the relevant data to the Ministry of Foreign Economic Relations and Trade for unified registration. The specific requirements for the data to be submitted shall be further notified by the Ministry of Foreign Economic Relations and Trade.

Article 9

The "Approval Certificate for Technology Import Contract" or a copy thereof must be presented when arranging for a bank guarantee, letter of credit, payment, settlement of exchange accounts, Customs clearance, payment of taxes or application for reduction or exemption of taxes or duties during the course of execution of the technology import contract; unless the said approval certificate is submitted, the bank, Customs and tax authorities are not entitled to process or handle the above request.

Article 10

Where substantive amendment or extension of the contract duration is made during the course of the execution of the technology import contract, reapplication for examination and approval shall be made according to the relevant stipulations of these Procedures.

Exhibit 13   *Continued*

Article 11	Article 12
The Ministry of Foreign Economic Relations and Trade shall be responsible for interpreting these Procedures.	These Procedures shall enter into force from tl date of promulgation.

Exhibit 14   *(Droit Chinois des Affaires, Meyer, Verva and Dupont, September–October 1987)*

Note on Tax Issues

China places great importance on the introduction of new technology and foreign investment in China. Foreign companies not residing in China and receiving Chinese revenues (including interest, dividends, licensing fees and royalties) will be taxed at the source at a rate of 20%.

However, the French–Chinese Convention provides for "tax sparing" so that a French company having done technology transfer in China can attribute a tax credit on its French revenues equal to 20% of the gross income earned.

The Meeting

It was January 11th, three days after Perrin had received the letter from MACHIMPEX. Pierre Perrin (CEO), Antoine Colas (Export Director), Bernard Liger (SEREX Manager), Philippe Gauguin (Director of Sales, Far East), and Paul André (Director of Operations) were assembled to discuss MACHIMPEX's letter and the implications for Potain. Perrin asked Liger to kick off the meeting by talking about SEREX's findings. The following discussion took place at the meeting.

Liger: The FO23B top-slewing crane is the crane model that we believe would best meet the Chinese's needs. The integration of Potain's technology for manufacturing this model would be done in five phases, or one phase per year. During this 5-year period, the percentage of production costs per unit remaining with Potain would be:

YR 1	YR 2	YR 3	YR 4	YR 5
66	55	41	34	0

This would leave Potain with a significant amount of exports to China. In addition, the weighted average margin (%) on sales to the licensee for each phase would be:

YR 1	YR 2	YR 3	YR 4	YR 5
25	28	30	35	0

This illustrates that mark-up margins on components increase as the components become more sophisticated.

Perrin: What if the Chinese decided to develop their own crane technology?

André: If we look at R&D costs in China, the estimated development cost for a crane like the FO23B would be roughly FF 2.6 million, including two elements, the crane structure at FF 1,635,000 and the mechanisms and control units at FF 1,050,000. But, this would take several years, four to five years at least.

Liger: Actually, R&D costs are not relevant since the Chinese have decided to buy technology from the 'outside' – either from Potain, Liebherr or Kroll (already producing in Hong Kong). The Chinese are in a hurry and they want the technology today! The idea would be to share the profits that would otherwise go into our competitors' pockets with our Chinese partners; that's the license's appeal. Especially as China has decided to manufacture cranes, China will do it with others if not with us. China is a country where we sold one crane in 1983 and six in 1984.

Gauguin: Yes, but China has only been importing cranes for the past two or three years. In 1984, we sold six of the 20 cranes imported. In fact, 50% of the cranes imported by Hong Kong are then sent to China, where we represent 42.5% of the market.

André: We also need to consider what will happen three to five years from now. Where will we be? Potain will not be selling them anything and they will take the Asian markets away from us.

Perrin: It's true that we must consider the risks in the long term. The transfer of technology to China cannot be contemplated without considering our own strategy in the Asian zone. However, let's also review the facts of China's current situation. China's objective is to produce 1,000 cranes per year. There already exist seven factories in China producing tower cranes with jibs of less than 98 feet in length. They have manufactured a few jibs longer than that, but these are not appropriate; this is why they seek to acquire Western technology. For the moment, they want to manufacture jibs 131–196 feet long with reliable materials. For these models, they have defined a need for 500 cranes per year, and they have estimated production at 500 cranes per year by the end of the third year of licensing. Looking at the construction activity in hotel and apartment complexes, it is my opinion that their needs will grow. In this type of situation, I believe, however, that the Chinese estimations will be cut in half; it would not be unrealistic to think that they will manufacture 25 cranes the first year, followed by 100 in the second, 150 in the third and then 250 in both the fourth and fifth years.

In relation to our strategy in Asia and according to what I saw in China during our visit to their factories, I think it will be a long time before they will be able to export cranes. Their needs are great, and it would be difficult to imagine them producing at a level above their needs. Given their technological level, I would agree with André's evaluation that it would take them four to five years to integrate the production of mechanical parts. Furthermore, I believe that they will have to increase their imports of cranes having jibs longer than 196 feet to complement the local production of the FO23B which has a jib of only 164 feet. By the way, Mr. Liger, what would be your best estimation of the transfer cost for the production of FO23B in the Chinese factory?

Liger: SEREX would need a budget of FF 2.5 million (with 1.5 million being spent in the first six months) to cover the transfer costs including: training of Chinese staff in France, provision of technical assistance, preparation of the technical documentation, provision of the specifications for equipment and plant layout, preparation and negotiation of the contract, hiring of consultants (lawyer and interpreter), supervision of the transfer, and monitoring of the license.

Perrin: And Mr. Colas, do you have any news about our competitor's bidding price?

Colas: In spite of Potain's intelligence effort, the export department has not been able to determine the price that the other crane manufacturers will be asking for a license. But, let me say that, looking at the developing market in South-East Asia, I think we should also seriously consider proposing a joint venture with the Chinese, in addition to a licensing contract. A joint venture would enable us to sell on the Asian market with competitive prices; we could economize on transportation and labor costs at least for the mast and jib. At the same time, we would establish a strong market position for the larger crane models.

Perrin: Yes, we should consider the possibility of a joint venture carefully. The 'Special Economic Zones' defined in South-East Asia have advantages which should not be overlooked. However, China's definition of these zones is a recent development. We should look at the operations already executed in formulating a conclusion. We will be better able to understand the movement of the South-East Asian markets after seeing the transparencies that Mr. Gauguin has prepared. *(Refer to Exhibit 15)*.

Gauguin: Planned construction in South-East Asia includes two nuclear generating stations, and several other energy stations and hotel complexes. It would therefore not be surprising if China imports 50–100 more powerful cranes than those manufactured under license. Of course, we must wait and see if China will have the money to finance these imports and whether its openness policy will continue.

I believe that we should see China as another opportunity for additional finished products sales. China has an immediate need for 25 model F023B cranes, and I think that Potain would certainly be chosen as the supplier if it would show its 'good citizenship' by agreeing to transfer technology. In addition, this is an opportunity for the Chinese to become familiar with Potain's products, and we could expect Potain to be in a good position to provide specialized cranes (high-rise tower cranes and special cranes for complex construction sites) which would generate further revenue in the future. For me, the license with China could enhance Potain's market position in the short term. Long term, if the Chinese do their own manufacturing, it is difficult to say what our position will be. However, a joint venture in a 'Special Economic Zone' could consolidate our position in the long term.

The group's concensus remained unclear; should Potain submit an offer for a licensing contract with MACHIMPEX? If yes, Perrin was still undecided about: the length of the contract, the use of Potain's brand name, export rights, what to include in the transfer of technology 'package' (old versus new technology), the price of the 'package', and the degree and form of Potain's involvement.

Exhibit 15   *Far East: market trends and Potain Group's market position*

Country	POTAIN SALES**				Market		Market Trends	
	1983 Units	1983 in 1000 Ffr	1984 Units	1984 in 1000 Ffr	1984 Units	1984 in 1000 Ffr	Short-Term 1986	Long-Term 1989
Singapore	20	10912	30	16705	43	22670	−	=
South Korea	46	47380	21	8844	35	29444	−	=
Thailand	6	6200	5	3429	18	11424	−	=
Indonesia	0		2	2451	8	7561	−	+
Malaysia	7	10550	7	6277	16	10001	−	+
Philippines	0		0	0	0	0	−	−
China*	3	6500	6	2630	20*	11834	+	=
Taiwan			2	2099	5	11983	=	=
Hong-Kong	10	11864	17	21883	40	38843	=	+
Australia			0	0	1	261	−	−
New Zealand			0	0	1	1299	=	=
Japan	0		0	0	0	0	=	+
Total Far East	92	93406	90	64318	187	145320	=	+
World Market	1845	935851	1316	659739	6178	1906543	=	=
F.E./W.M.	5.0%	10.0%	6.8%	9.7%	3.0%	7.6%		

*   Imports only.

**   Includes sales from Potain, its subsidiaries and licensees.

Unichema

*This case was prepared by Professors Per V. Jenster and Thomas E.
Vollmann as a basis for class discussion rather than to illustrate either
effective or ineffective handling of a business situation.*

On May 15, 1992, Mr. Jan Löwik, General Manager of Unichema B.V.,
Gouda, the Netherlands, was discussing operational strategy with his senior
management staff. The group was reviewing the importance of meeting
customer needs, the role of inventory control in meeting these demands, the
problem of changeover times and the constraints of the firm's asset base. The
following are excerpts from their conversation:

H.H. Ott, Commercial/Finance Manager:

My most recent analysis of the company's performance indicates some progress
in cost reduction. However, we are still not managing our assets as effectively
as we need to, and I cannot stress hard enough the pressures put on us in this
respect.

H.G. ten Barge, Manager of Logistics:

The new logistics system we have put in place is helping us in this respect. It
also enables us to talk directly with customers. This has helped us in producing
what customers need, but with some problems still remaining. Just last week
we had a situation which shouldn't have occurred. We were running product
number 1761 (a special product sold to a small number of customers) and asked
the salespeople to determine how much of this product customers needed over
the next few months. The response from sales was that 10 tons were needed,
so we made 10 tons and then cleaned the equipment and prepared a batch run
for another product. A few days later, a valued customer called to order 40
tons of 1761 ASAP. In order to meet his needs, we lost 2 days of production
due to changeovers with obvious cost consequences. We must find ways to
avoid these kinds of unpleasant surprises!

Mr. Griem, Sales Manager:

> I agree that we have to respond to our customers and anticipate their needs, but we will always face unpleasant surprises. We just need to be able to respond to these situations either by carrying more inventory or by being more flexible in manufacturing. Moreover, I am concerned that the direct contact which Logistics is developing with customers takes the sales department out of the loop. I believe that sales should be the primary customer contact in the company to ensure the ongoing relationship.

Jan Löwik studied each of his managers as he thought about the changing nature of the business. Responding to customer needs had to remain a top priority as did asset utilization, but balancing these issues with achievement of volume and good margins would clearly affect the way in which the entire organization functioned. Leaning back in his chair, he said:

> Gentlemen, these are all valid concerns. But, to complicate matters, some of our larger customers have an expressed interest in initiating aspects of Just-in-Time (JIT) in their businesses. They too recognize the need for a higher return on assets employed and see inventory reduction as a key means to this end. Our job is determining how best to meet this requirement . . . while, at the same time, achieving a higher return on *our* assets employed.

Unilever

In 1992, Unichema was a subsidiary of Unilever, one of the world's largest food and personal care companies. Total Unilever turnover in 1990 was $39.6 billion: 21% from detergents; 20% from margarines, dairy products and edible oils; 16% from food and drinks; 13% from frozen foods and ice cream; 12% from personal products; 8% from specialty chemicals and 10% from agribusiness and other operations. *(Refer to Exhibit 1 for a breakdown of turnover by operations and operating profits.)* Within specialty chemicals, the companies were National Starch, Quest International, Crosfield Chemical and Unichema International. *(Refer to Exhibit 2.)* The greater part of Unilever's business was in branded consumer goods primarily in the areas of foods, drinks, detergents and personal products.

Unichema International

Unichema International, with headquarters in Gouda, the Netherlands, produced over half a million tons of oleochemicals yearly for customers

Exhibit 1 *Unilever turnover and operating profit by operation*

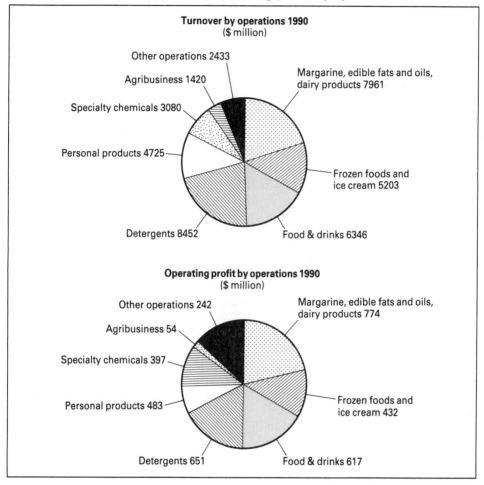

Turnover by operations 1990
($ million)

- Other operations 2433
- Agribusiness 1420
- Specialty chemicals 3080
- Personal products 4725
- Detergents 8452
- Margarine, edible fats and oils, dairy products 7961
- Frozen foods and ice cream 5203
- Food & drinks 6346

Operating profit by operations 1990
($ million)

- Other operations 242
- Agribusiness 54
- Specialty chemicals 397
- Personal products 483
- Detergents 651
- Margarine, edible fats and oils, dairy products 774
- Frozen foods and ice cream 432
- Food & drinks 617

Exhibit 2 *Unilever: specialty chemicals*

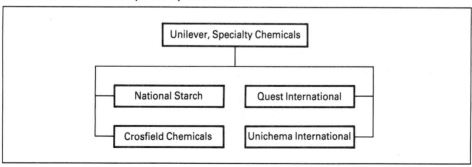

- Unilever, Specialty Chemicals
  - National Starch
  - Quest International
  - Crosfield Chemicals
  - Unichema International

worldwide. *(Refer to **Exhibit 3**.)* Oleochemicals were derived from natural biodegradable oils and fats from vegetable or animal sources. They were environmentally-friendly and very versatile products, which could be used in a number of diverse applications. Oleochemicals were the starting point for the production of distilled and fractioned fatty acids, stearine, oleine, glycerine and performance products like esters, amides, dimeric fatty acids and soap noodles. Esters, amongst many other applications, were the basic raw materials for biodegradable synthetic lubricants. The oleochemical products produced by Unichema had a large application area – in cosmetics, rubber, textiles, leather, paper and lubricants. *(Refer to **Exhibit 4** for a list of products.)* Unichema International produced these products in nine sites located on four continents. Unichema Chemie B.V. in Gouda was the largest of the production sites, employing approximately 450 people and hosting an additional 170 employees who reported to the corporate centre, also located on the site (development, marketing, etc.).

Exhibit 3   *Unichema production and sales (volume 000 tons)*

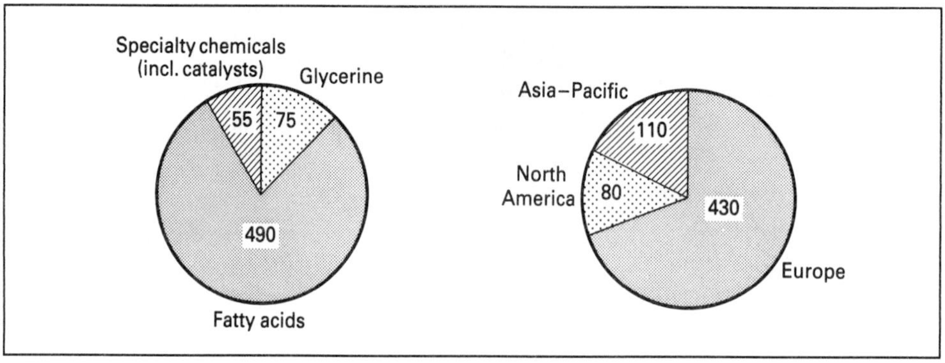

Exhibit 4   *Unichema products*

Unilever, Specialty Chemicals	Performance Products
● Glycerine	● Polymer Chemicals
● Catalysts	● Lubricants
● Fatty Acids	● Personal Care Ingredients
● Soap Noodles	

Unichema Chemie B.V.

The candle factory 'Gouda', established in 1858, used animal tallow for its stearines. This was the beginning of the activities on the site. After a merger with another candle factory in 1929, production of candles continued under the name of 'Gouda Apollo'. Gradually, from this base in tallow processing for the manufacture of candle wax and wool smoothing oil, a modern oleochemical process industry developed. In 1960, Unilever and the American company, Emery Industries, founded Unilever-Emery, with 'Gouda Apollo' becoming the centre of the joint venture. This venture subsequently developed several unique processes and products. In 1980, Unilever took over Emery's share and adopted its present name, Unichema Chemie B.V., 100 per cent owned by Unilever. Production of candles ceased in 1983; in 1992 the company produced over 200 industrial oleochemical products, which were sold throughout the world.

The Oleochemical Industry

The oleochemical industry was being affected by globalization and a concentration within the industry itself. Tightening legislation with regard to product liability, environmental issues and high operating fixed cost levels resulted in declining overall industry profitability. Pressure was also being exercised by over-capacity and imports of low-priced materials from Southeast Asian producers. *(Refer to **Exhibit 5** for a 5-year view of European prices.)*

Exhibit 5   *Fatty acid and glycerine prices, Europe (1985 = 100)*

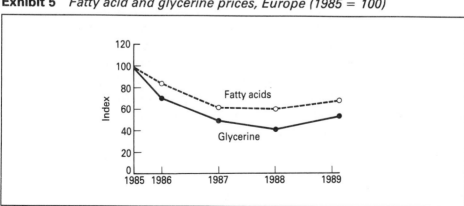

The European oleochemical industry produced more than one-third of all global oleochemical products in 1991. Large multinational groups were the leading producers in the industry, although there were still some small and highly specialized producers with a strong market niche. From a strategic point of view, the European industry was concentrating on a two-pronged approach. The first was to develop alliances with companies in Asia which had access to low-cost supplies of oleochemical raw materials. The second was to accelerate the degree of sophistication in developing new product derivatives and process technology, delivering total quality and service, and exploiting market desires for natural and biodegradable products. Future success was believed to depend on company flexibility and a strong technological base to optimize opportunities.

The Need for Efficiencies

Customer demands and market pressures were forcing the oleochemical industry participants to become more competitive and more responsive to customer requirements. Customers were demanding lower prices, shorter lead times on deliveries, precise timings for deliveries, better quality, and increased reliability over time. Oleochemical manufacturers increasingly found themselves in a position where they had to provide better response to customers, with lower prices, while maintaining and improving their own businesses.

Just-in-Time

The concept of Just-in-Time (JIT) was being adopted by more and more manufacturers to enhance efficiencies in their manufacturing environments. The ultimate objectives of JIT were zero inventory, zero lead time, zero failures, enhanced flow processes, flexible manufacturing and elimination of waste. Cost savings were achieved through reduction in the manufacturing cycle time, reduction in inventories, reduction in labor costs, reduction in space requirements, reduction in quality costs, reduction in transaction costs and reduction in material costs. JIT implementation affected all areas of manufacturing planning and control systems, as well as redefining manufacturing processes and how performance was evaluated.

Pressures on Unichema

All of these forces led the management of Unichema to a fundamental evaluation of how they were conducting their business. From a financial point of view, there was increasing pressure to maximize return on assets. The push to maximize profits, the narrowing of profit margins, increasing competition in the marketplace, and relatively flat sales necessitated that Unichema become more efficient. Analysis by the logistics and financial departments targeted material costs and investments in inventories as areas where *real* savings could be achieved. This targeting soon focused on areas in logistics planning and inventory control, where greater efficiencies could lead to cost savings. However, more than cost savings were required to achieve the desired financial return. After considerable analysis, Mr. Löwik and his management team became convinced that cost cutting could raise the return on assets by about 6–7%, but the goal was a 15% increase. This would only be possible with an improvement in market conditions. In other words, to reach the ultimate goal, cost cutting would not be sufficient. It was necessary to become more customer driven – to increase volume and/or provide new products and services to the customers. In determining how best to meet these new demands, Unichema realized that it was necessary to have a greater understanding of the customers' business needs, their product needs and their information needs.

Capacity Utilization

Unichema had invested significantly in new equipment over the last five years. The primary reason for the investments was to provide higher quality, more specialized products (with higher margins). Capital investments in the chemical industry typically were for large 'chunks' of capacity, considerably in excess of present market requirements. The expectation was that new business would be attracted before long, thus utilizing the capacity at higher levels.

This was clearly the situation at Unichema. Indeed, there was considerable pressure to, in fact, find the business to utilize the equipment and increase the return on the assets invested. Similarly, Unichema wanted to utilize its equipment as efficiently as possible in order to not only insure but maximize the return on assets. (***Exhibit 6*** *shows the operating results for four ester production units in 1991. As can be seen, the maximum operating time for each of the four plants is 8,736 hours. From this amount, public holidays (and startup hours after holidays) need to be deducted, as well as hours for which there are no customer orders [ester units 1 and 4]. The net result is then further reduced by various causes for lost capacity, both planned (standard) and actual. Logistical losses are the result of one piece of equipment*

Exhibit 6 *1991 Ester unit production*

	Ester Unit #1		Ester Unit #2		Ester Unit #3		Ester Unit #4	
	S	A	S	A	S	A	S	A
Max. Operating Time	8736	8736	8736	8736	8736	8736	8736	8736
Public Holidays	192	225	192	225	192	232	192	241
No Orders		1178		0		0		1413
Available Capacity	8544	7333	8544	8481	8544	8504	8544	7082
Factory Holidays	0	0	0	0	0	0	0	0
Planned Overhaul	0	24	336	868	336	729	281	310
Variety Changes	468	685	133	523	133	335	218	577
Breakdowns	126	1049	124	288	124	261	125	433
Logistical Losses	678	1163	683	684	682	907	678	641
Achieved Capacity	7272	4412	7269	6118	7269	6272	7242	5121
Variance (Standard − Actual)	**−2850**		**−1151**		**−997**		**−2121**	

in the ester production unit being idle while waiting for a batch of production to be completed in a previous or subsequent piece of equipment. The last row shows the overall variances [in hours] for each of the four ester units.)

Unichema's Response

Having determined that achieving efficiencies depended on the plant becoming more customer driven and less production driven, Unichema set out to identify areas where changes could be effected. In doing so, upper management consciously tried to support changes which drove a customer orientation within the company. The biggest change affected the areas of production, logistics, sales and customer service. Production – which had traditionally driven the company – became a secondary process, while logistics assumed a primary function. In real terms, this meant that the logistics department dealt directly with the customers and established a process whereby customer needs determined production runs. The process created a major shift in company priorities as well as in the functions of various departments.

Logistics, Production and Sales

In the new system, the logistics department assumed a coordinating role between the customer and production. Logistics served sales and production served logistics, which enabled customer needs to drive the manufacturing process. However, this change in orientation also forced a change in the traditional role of the salesforce. Sales had historically provided the major, and sometimes the only, contact between the customer and the company. Under the new system, logistics assumed the role of providing customer service on a day-to-day basis, interacting directly with customers to determine their specific needs and the exact timing of these needs. This information was essential if economies were to be obtained in the production cycle with minimal inventory levels. Knowing what products customers needed and the times at which they needed these products enabled production to schedule the most efficient production runs. This approach, in effect, created the heart of the new program.

Close order coupling of customer needs and production schedules were one cornerstone of Unichema's response. But it was not the only one. Many just-in-time fundamentals were also implemented. Attempts to reduce changeover times were another part of these efforts. In ester production, for example, there were four ester limits which were somewhat interchangeable. But ester 1, which had been recently built, had twice the capacity of each of the ester units 2, 3 and 4. One of the remaining units was dedicated to additives for edible products, and one other unit was being focused toward smaller lots and faster changeovers. It was believed that achieving high flexibility in this unit would allow the others to be run at maximum effectiveness.

Other aspects of a JIT philosophy were also being pursued. Total quality management was being adopted with a goal of zero mistakes, minimum variability and no 'surprises'. Formulations were being made more exact so that processing times could be better predicted. Workers were being cross-trained to be able to take on more job activities, particularly in a grouping (or cell) of equipment that produced a 'family' of products. Other changes in work practices combined activities formerly done by staff personnel – such as maintenance and quality inspection, with 'direct labor' activities.

After the new logistics process changed the role of the sales team – removing them from day-to-day customer service, it gave them an opportunity to concentrate on fostering partnerships and helping customers identify new product areas where Unichema could provide research and development as well as other kinds of support. One example of this kind of arrangement occurred with a customer who specialized in environmentally-friendly personal care products. Unichema and the customer developed a relationship where it was Unichema – with its extensive knowledge of oleochemicals – instead of the customer who provided the basic research and development. The customer's role was to determine what properties would be desirable in the products, rather than how to best achieve those properties. However, resistance to the partnership concept with logistics managing day-to-day interactions was strong in some parts of the sales department. One of the salespeople stated:

> Although I realize that customers want shorter and shorter delivery times, I believe that the sales team should manage day-to-day contact and maintain order responsibility with the customers. I do not like logistics assuming the lead role in this area. If I am going to establish a partnership with my customers, I cannot let someone else come between me and my customer.

Data Processing

Through JIT and logistics, changes at Unichema also depended on a more fully automated plant, enhanced technical processes, foolproof operations and an upgraded computer control system. This was seen as an ongoing effort. Many of the computer programs had to be changed and adapted to reflect those changes. The software was crucial for running production units efficiently – in order to more closely couple plant scheduling with actual customer needs – and for providing the data necessary to analyze and self-correct problems occurring on the production floor. Moreover, data was generated which tied into finance and pinpointed specific areas where cost savings might be achieved.

Personnel

Implementing Unichema's response created changes in the way people did their jobs as well as changes in the personnel department in terms of performance measures and job descriptions. Performance measures, which had traditionally been based on costs associated with producing the product, now had to place a value on better responsiveness to customer needs. Moreover, the old distinction between direct and indirect labor costs became less important in the new environment. At the same time, customer satisfaction measures came to be increasingly important in evaluating how successfully individuals and the company were performing. Personnel evaluation and career development needed to reflect these new directions, and performance measures had to be changed to correspond to the new priorities.

Job functions and roles also changed under the JIT system. Functions became more flexible. Enhancement of the computer system reduced dependence on the human element. The personnel manager stated:

> We need to focus more on quality and product predictability which will change the way we define specific jobs.

Partnerships

The initiation of better responses to customer requirements enabled the company to identify other areas where changes had to occur. In order to become more customer driven, Unichema had to consider all areas which made an impact on its ability to deliver the correct products to its customers in a timely fashion. As an example, one area where Unichema had to excel was in shipping the products exactly as the customer wished. The products had to arrive on time, in good condition, and the drivers had to be able to take the products through customs in a number of different countries. Since Unichema contracted with haulers, one way to ensure that the best tariffs were obtained and the best service delivered was to form partnerships with a select number of haulers. This enabled Unichema to establish a mutual relationship where both partners focused on the customer. Unichema began to evaluate trucker complaints on a yearly basis, and to monitor and set standards of cleanliness in the trucks being used. Based on these measures, Unichema was able to improve shipping performance to customers.

Unichema was even more interested in forming partnerships with certain customers. By knowing precisely how each customer was using its products, Unichema could tailor the products (solutions) to individual customer problems more effectively. Moreover, these partnerships allowed Unichema to understand which product features/parameters were most critical to particular customers.

Unichema also worked to establish partnerships with suppliers so that joint problem-solving could be achieved. These partnerships included sharing information on production schedules, anticipated needs, critical parameters and problems at Unichema that might be jointly addressed.

The partnership program allowed Unichema to serve customer needs better as well as establish efficiencies in costs and in the production cycle. Working with a limited number of customers, suppliers, vendors and haulers enabled Unichema to develop better production schedules, integrate with actual customer needs and coordinate logistics. Dealing directly with customers so as to fully understand their needs and problems in product, packaging, delivery, and service areas allowed Unichema to produce more products to order instead of stocking them in anticipation of order, thus saving time, inventory holding costs, and enhancing the production cycle.

The importance of fully understanding customer needs involved truly knowing how the customer used the product. Mr Löwik gave an example:

> A long-standing customer had been receiving regular shipments of a product in a color which required special and costly production runs. One day a production run resulted in the product being produced in an off-spec color. Due to time constraints and customer time demands, the product was sent to the customer. However, I became concerned and decided to visit the customer to apologize for the off-spec product color. I discovered that the customer used this particular product in a waste water treatment plant and was totally unconcerned about its color. Had the customer's business been better understood in the first place, the product could have been made in a regular production run, saving changeover time and money.

In an effort to further strengthen its relationship with customers, Unichema developed a 'Partnership Evaluation Program'. This program involved development of a booklet for each customer in which specific needs and requirements were defined. The sales team then used the booklet with customers to further develop joint problem-solving. The booklet was part of the company-wide quality drive directed towards providing improved service and products for customers.

ABC Analysis

Unichema recently developed an 'ABC analysis' of its customers and products. ABC or 'Pareto analysis' was based on the idea that a minority of the customers typically comprised a majority of the sales.[1]

The ABC analysis for Unichema customers found that, in 1992, the firm had approximately 250 customers. Of these, the top 50 (20%) accounted for more than 80% of sales. Purchases of the next 50 customers amounted to an additional 15%, while the remaining 150 customers accounted for only 5% of the annual sales. Unichema was attempting to form partnerships with the first 50 ('A') customers, providing special services and actively trying to promote joint problem-solving. (**Exhibit 7** shows a 10% sample of the 250 Unichema customers.)

The ABC analysis for *products* found that Unichema produced 61 major products: 16 of these accounted for 80% of the total sales in 1991. Another 11 accounted for the next 15%, while the remaining 34 products comprised the last 5% of sales. (**Exhibit 8** provides an abbreviated version of

Exhibit 7 *Sample ABC analysis of customers (10% sample)*

Customer Class A	1992 Total Purchases (Guilders)
Customer #	
1	3548
2	1072
3	513
4	320
5	216
Customer Class B	
Customer #	
6	115
7	91
8	75
9	55
10	42
Customer Class C	
Customer #	
11	31
12	26
13	20
14	14
15	9
16	6
17	5
18	3
19	2
20	1
21	1
22	1
23	0
24	0
25	0

Unichema's product ABC analysis. As shown, the 1992 sales [in tons] are not completely consistent with the earlier ABC classification – e.g. product 6, an 'A' product, was not purchased in 1992.)

Exhibit 8 *ABC analysis of products*

'A' Products	Customer Class Buying	1992 tons
1	A, B	2890
2	A. C	867
3	A, B, C	1686
4	A	1572
5	A, C	406
6	A, B	0
7	A	1256
8	A	1080
9	A, B, C	821
10	A	1161
11	A	789
12	A, B	629
13	A	287
14	A, C	357
15	A, B, C	408
16	A	272
'B' Products		
17	A, C	394
18	A, C	238
19	A	297
20	A	255
21	A	204
22	A	340
23	A, C	17
24	A	129
25	A, B	294
26	A	17
27	A, C	141
'C' Products		
28	C	212
29	A, B	102
30	A, C	68
31	A, C	54
32	A, B	43
33	A	0
34	A, C	177
35	A	54
36	C	1836
37	C	26
38	C	680
39	B	9
40	B, C	17
41	A	9
42	A, C	0
43	A	340
44	A, C	0

Exhibit 8 *Continued*

'A' Products	Customer Class Buying	1992 tons
45	C	0
46	C	0
47	A, C	17
48	A, B	0
49	A, B	2
50	B	0
51	C	0
52	C	0
53	C	0
54	C	0
55	B, C	0
56	C	0
57	C	0
58	C	0
59	C	0
60	C	0
61	C	0

Future Challenges

Market Demands

Unichema, like many companies throughout the world, was faced with increasing competition, shrinking markets, global customers and changing technology. These forces pushed the management to reevaluate the way in which the company was being run both internally and externally. Although strides had been made in understanding the customer, it was evident that further understanding of customers' businesses was necessary. This would necessitate greater involvement of the technical staff with customers, further complicating the roles of the sales team and the technical personnel. With changes occurring in customer businesses as well, Unichema also had to be responsive to changing product needs and prepared to provide increasing research and development support for customers. Cost pressures and stagnant markets put pressure on Unichema's customers which, in turn, affected Unichema.

Internal Response

As customers demanded totally reliable products delivered on time,

Unichema was faced with continuous improvement of technology, better evaluation of the fit between products and markets, elimination of all mistakes, and a quicker response based on techniques such as reduced changeover times. At the same time, Logistics (and production scheduling) were faced with the challenge of utilizing equipment as effectively as possible in order to maximize the return on assets. All of these issues required new solutions. However, better software programs were leading to better problem definitions and the development of improved solutions. Automated data collation in the factory was being tied to financial numbers that could pinpoint problem areas to be targeted for cost savings. In addition, logistics was now the lead contact with customers, undertaking sales activities that encompassed more than just typical order taking. The underlying objective was to become very knowledgeable in helping customers define *their* needs and how Unichema could meet them more effectively.

Partnership Development

As noted earlier, partnerships were increasingly important in providing a network for meeting customer requirements. Establishing exclusive relationships with customers, suppliers, vendors, etc., led to a further redefinition of personnel functions within the company. But, these relationships were expensive in terms of employee time and effort. Specific people needed to be deployed to specific customer partnerships. Unichema wanted to achieve a good return from these partnership efforts. With exclusive relationships, the role of the sales team in particular underwent a transformation. The traditional role of order taking and problem identification became institutionalized within other divisions, such as logistics. Unichema wanted to target its sales efforts for maximum effectiveness. Attracting new customers became increasingly difficult in an environment where many of the large competitors had already established partnership relationships. Unichema needed to find ways to overcome these hurdles – while, at the same time, making them even greater for their competitors.

Unichema sought to establish its own partnerships in a timely fashion, to develop unique partnership features that customers would find attractive and to make those partnerships ever more impervious to competitive actions.

Jan Löwik was pleased with the progress made to date and wanted to build on this base of accomplishments. His first thoughts for the group were:

I think we have been doing a great job and we should all be proud of our accomplishments. But now is not the time to sit back and relax. We need to redouble our efforts and link the various individual efforts in ways that will achieve even greater synergies. Let me hear your views on how to accomplish this goal.

Notes

1   The concept was widely applied:

- *In quality management, a few defects account for the majority of the scrap.*
- *A minute percentage of a university's alumni donate the vast proportion of alumni gifts.*
- *20% of the beer drinkers consume more than 80% of the beer in many countries.*

Logitech International SA

*This case was prepared by Professor Vijay K. Jolly and Research
Associate Kimberly A. Bechler, as a basis for class discussion rather than
to illustrate either effective or ineffective handling of a business situation.
 The authors wish to acknowledge the generous cooperation and
assistance given to them by a number of managers at Logitech
International SA in the preparation of this case, especially the Chairman,
Mr. Daniel Borel.*

'I don't know where I'm going, but I'm on my way,' stated a poster that used to hang in the offices of the people who created Logitech SA – one of Switzerland's most successful start-up companies of the 1980s. Founded in 1981, it had rapidly grown so that by 1990 it had a sales turnover of SF 205 million and employed 1,450 people on three continents. While the academic community had been debating the characteristics and merits of global strategies throughout the decade, Logitech was already actually confronting them. In general, these strategies tended to be discussed in the context of large established multinational companies, seldom with start-ups. Logitech, however, had succeeded in assuming many of the essential features of such companies.

Although the poster had long since disappeared, the spring of 1991 made people remember that cheerful self-mocking message. It was time to take stock in preparation for the decade ahead; while some things had obviously been done well, others could have been handled differently. One issue was the company's international strategy. Was, for instance, the pattern of investment and trade that had evolved appropriate for the new challenges ahead? How global was Logitech? What changes were necessary in its organization to become a more effective competitor internationally? These questions assumed an even greater importance because the company's business scope had begun to change. Best known as a leading mouse company, it had started to position itself as a supplier of a broad range of desktop tools for personal computers.

The Beginning

Logitech had been incorporated in two locations almost from the start – as Logitech S.A. in Apples, Switzerland, in 1981 and as Logitech Inc., in Palo Alto, California, in 1982. This dual incorporation occurred because of the nature and domicile of the main founders – one Swiss (Daniel Borel) and two Italians (Pierluigi Zappacosta and Giacomo Marini).

Borel and Zappacosta had met while studying computer science at Stanford University in 1976. After graduation, Borel returned to Switzerland, but Zappacosta stayed behind in California. The two, however, shared a common interest in personal computers and soon started to work together on developing a generalized wordprocessing system for desktop publishing. Bobst Graphic, a Swiss typesetting company, supported their work over a three-year period. However, just as the system was up and running, Bobst Graphic was sold, leaving the two of them empty-handed with a staff of ten.

In order to continue what they had started, Borel and Zappacosta teamed up with Giacomo Marini, who had just opened his own software consulting company in Ivrea, Italy, after a career with IBM and Olivetti. The three became the principal shareholders in the new company, Logitech SA; a few others, like Jean-Luc Mazzone, a former collaborator at Bobst Graphic, also joined the company as shareholders.

On the organizational side, Borel looked after marketing and the office in Switzerland, while Zappacosta managed the US operation, where Marini joined him. By the end of 1982, there were 6 employees working in Switzerland and 12 in the company's Palo Alto office.

In line with the work Borel, Zappacosta and Marini had been doing, Logitech too started out as a software consulting company. Based on its expertise in word processing and desktop publishing systems, it won – among others – a $2 million development contract with Ricoh. Logitech was to analyze and design a graphics workstation into which the latter's peripheral products could be integrated. Most of the work on this contract was performed in Logitech's US office. Meanwhile, recognizing the need for a good software environment for such applications, Logitech approached Professor Wirth of the ETH in Zurich. Known as the 'father of *Pascal*', he had recently developed a new high level language called *Modula*-2, which was particularly suited to desktop publishing systems. With Professor Wirth's cooperation, Logitech gradually developed special capabilities in this new language.

From Software to the Mouse

It was the interest in *Modula-2* and the Ricoh contract that eventually led the founders of Logitech to think about the mouse.

Starting already in the 1950s, a range of pointing devices had been developed to facilitate interaction with computers. These included *light pens, keyboard cursor keys, cursor disks, touch screens, touch pads, trackballs, joysticks* and the *mouse*.

The world's first mouse was developed by Doug Engelbart at the Stanford Research Institute (SRI) in 1964 as part of a program researching screen selection techniques. The term 'mouse' originated with the device created by Engelbart; its shape – a round-edged wooden box with a cable – resembled a mouse. It consisted of two wheels placed perpendicular to one another; when rolled forward, one wheel rotated freely while the other dragged along without turning. When rolled at an angle, each wheel turned in direct proportion to the extent of horizontal or vertical motion. The wheels functioned as a potentiometer – similar to the volume dial on a home stereo – sending different voltage levels as they turned, which were then translated into digital signals for the computer. Although the wheels were big and noisy, and the resolution they provided inadequate for most purposes, the device worked and Engelbart was issued a patent on it in 1970.

The Engelbart mouse was picked up by Xerox PARC and further developed by one of its staff, Jack Hawley. Licensing the basic wheel system from SRI, Jack Hawley replaced the potentiometers with a digital encoding system in 1972. Then, in 1975, Xerox commissioned Hawley to improve a mouse developed by another Xerox employee, Williard Opocensky, which used ball-bearings instead of wheels. This mouse became the first commercial mouse, establishing the standard for mechanical mice.

Professor Wirth, had seen this Hawley mouse when on sabbatical at Xerox PARC in 1976. It had been used with the famous Xerox *Alto*, the first screen-based graphics machine with WYSIWYG (What You See Is What You Get) capability. Returning to Switzerland, he persuaded an acquaintance, Professor Nicoud of the Ecole Polytechnique Fédérale de Lausanne (EPFL), to develop the device further for possible use on a workstation he was designing based on *Modula-2*.

The mouse that Professor Nicoud developed in Lausanne in 1978 was an opto-mechanical one, in which wheel motion was detected by opto-electronic components. He was also the first to use a floating ball concept in place of wheels. Not only was this mouse design technically superior, but it also became a familiar and popular feature when Apple introduced it with its *Lisa* computer in 1982.

In parallel with the development of opto-mechanical mice, some people had begun work on pure optical mice as well. These optical mice required specially designed pads to communicate movement to the cursor. Instead of balls they used LEDs (Light-Emitting Diodes) to reflect position. (*Refer to* **Exhibit 1** *which compares the four different technologies.*)

Compared to other pointing devices, the mouse quickly became the preferred computer interface. Typically, early users tended to be engineers, using the mouse for computer-aided design and manufacturing. All three major technologies – mechanical, opto-mechanical and optical – had their own following in the beginning, with the opto-mechanical concept eventually dominating.

Logitech as a Value-Added Distributor of Mice

After Professor Nicoud had developed his opto-mechanical mouse, he contacted a small company, Depraz S.A., near Lausanne, Switzerland, to arrange for a regular supply. These mice were sold mainly to universities and laboratories.

While working on the Ricoh job, Logitech observed these developments close up and became convinced that mice could easily become a popular tool in creating a user-friendly interface with computers. Indeed, Logitech saw the mouse as a new business opportunity rather than a mere development tool.

'We were a small group of people with a great dream,' Borel said about this opportunity. 'From the beginning, we dreamt of the day when Logitech would grow beyond its role as a consultant for other companies and would be established in the world market with a recognized name, providing fun and innovative products.'

As more people began to inquire about the device – particularly through the ARPANET (Advanced Research Projects Agency Network), Logitech approached Depraz in August 1982, obtained worldwide distribution rights to Professor Nicoud's *Series 4* mouse and began selling it under the Logitech name.

The relationship with Depraz, however, left much to be desired. Being a small company, it was unable to meet the quality standards that Logitech deemed essential for the product. Soon after the introduction of the *Series 4* mouse, Professor Nicoud, therefore, started work on its successor, the *Series 5* mouse, using the market feedback Logitech could provide. This new model was turned over to a larger Swiss company, Câblerie de Cortaillod, for manufacture.

Exhibit 1

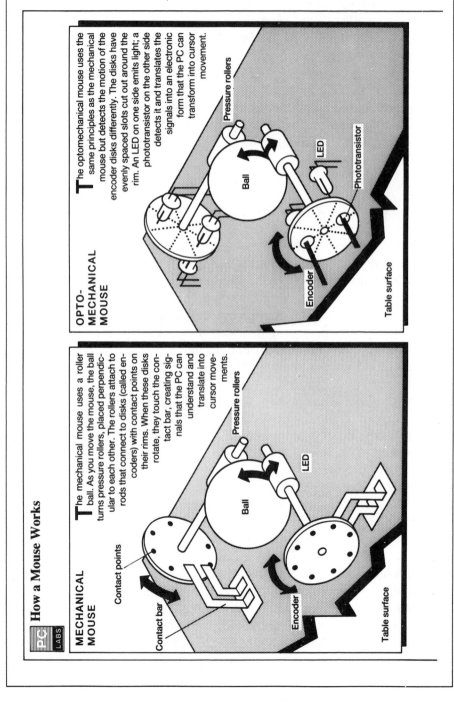

How a Mouse Works

MECHANICAL MOUSE

The mechanical mouse uses a roller ball. As you move the mouse, the ball turns pressure rollers, placed perpendicular to each other. The rollers attach to rods that connect to disks (called encoders) with contact points on their rims. When these disks rotate, they touch the contact bar, creating signals that the PC can understand and translate into cursor movements.

Contact points
Contact bar
Pressure rollers
Ball
LED
Encoder
Table surface

OPTO-MECHANICAL MOUSE

The optomechanical mouse uses the same principles as the mechanical mouse but detects the motion of the encoder disks differently. The disks have evenly spaced slots cut out around the rim. An LED on one side emits light; a phototransistor on the other side detects it and translates the signals into an electronic form that the PC can transform into cursor movement.

Pressure rollers
Ball
LED
Phototransistor
Encoder
Table surface

Exhibit 1   *Continued*

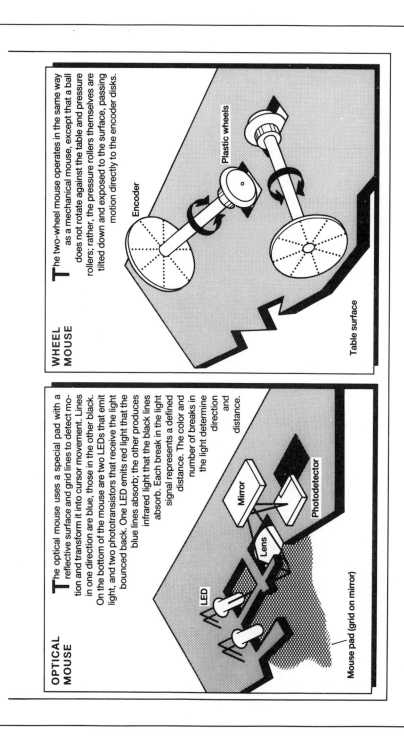

OPTICAL MOUSE

The optical mouse uses a special pad with a reflective surface and grid lines to detect motion and transform it into cursor movement. Lines in one direction are blue, those in the other black. On the bottom of the mouse are two LEDs that emit light, and two phototransistors that receive the light bounced back. One LED emits red light that the blue lines absorb; the other produces infrared light that the black lines absorb. Each break in the light signal represents a defined distance. The color and number of breaks in the light determine direction and distance.

Mouse pad (grid on mirror)

LED

Lens

Mirror

Photodetector

WHEEL MOUSE

The two-wheel mouse operates in the same way as a mechanical mouse, except that a ball does not rotate against the table and pressure rollers; rather, the pressure rollers themselves are tilted down and exposed to the surface, passing motion directly to the encoder disks.

Encoder

Plastic wheels

Table surface

Unfortunately, the experience with Câblerie de Cortaillod was no better. After nine months, when the company was not making the large sales promised by Logitech, Cortaillod became reluctant to invest further in the product's manufacture. Costs were high, too.

Buying Rights to the Mouse

In October 1983, realizing that it either had to control everything or get out of the mouse business, Logitech bought the rights to the *Series 5* opto-mechanical mouse from Cortaillod for about SF 1 million – a combination of cash and a commitment to buy a certain number of mice at a high fixed price.

When Logitech acquired these rights, it had had no prior experience in volume hardware manufacturing. The device was still used mainly by universities and laboratories, with a worldwide market of barely 15–20,000 units in 1983.

The Early Competition

Although the personal computer industry was starting to take off, it was not clear which pointing devices would benefit most and to what extent. Furthermore, Logitech was neither first nor alone in the market.

Among the companies already in the mouse business in 1982 were: Mouse Systems Corp. (MSC) with its optical mouse; and Mouse House, founded by Jack Hawley himself, which made a mechanical mouse. MSC was strong in the retail segment, while Mouse House mainly pursued the OEM market. Both subcontracted out the manufacture of their mice to other companies. MSC, for example, first used a Silicon Valley company for its manufacturing and, then later, used a company in Singapore.

In 1983, Microsoft was the next one to enter the market. Using the mouse as a complement to its application software business, the company soon built up a strong position in the retail segment. It, too, subcontracted the manufacture of its mouse – to Alps of Japan. Apple Computers had also developed its own mouse. In addition, two other companies were getting ready to enter – KYE, a Taiwanese company that made PC housings, and Mitsumi, a Japanese company. Both were adopting Logitech's opto-mechanical technology.

Growing the Business Internationally

The Swiss Base

After taking over the manufacturing rights from Cortaillod, Logitech built a small 'factory' in Apples near Lausanne in 1983, concentrating both its hardware and software development there. Since the mouse design evolved rapidly in response to market feedback and developments in technology, manufacturing was kept light and flexible. The total capacity installed was around 25,000 units per year.

Logitech also immediately set about improving Professor Nicoud's mouse. Among the early achievements of its R&D were: the development of a cordless mouse; a patented, lightweight ball cage system which, in addition to improving resolution, was easier to manufacture and handle; and the use of data signals to power a mouse, thus eliminating the need for a separate power cable.

Although the development and manufacture of the mouse was based in Switzerland, the main market was in the US. Therefore, promoting the business was handled by the company's Palo Alto office.

Hewlett-Packard OEM Contract

It was the early market development in the US that led to Logitech's first major breakthrough. Hewlett-Packard, also based in Palo Alto, was looking for a mouse in 1983 and became interested in Logitech's product. But, H-P wanted a high quality, reasonably priced product made to its specifications. Therefore, from the summer of 1983 until May 1984, H-P helped Logitech not only redesign the mouse for its proprietary use, but also provided instruction and training on mechanics, manufacturing and quality. In order to supply the OEM contract placed by H-P in 1984, Logitech decided to set up its own manufacturing facility in California.

The US Site

Until this time, there had been the inevitable debate inside Logitech about whether or not to become a manufacturing company. The H-P contract, in fact, resolved the debate. As Zappacosta recalled, 'We basically needed to manufacture in order to have a chance with the OEM market; if we had been selling to the retail market instead, we probably would never have said "Oh, how beautiful – manufacturing", because people who sell to retail always feel that a little bit of marketing wizardry can take you a long way.' Borel then went on to explain why the company had established manufacturing in the US, 'OEMs want you to be nearby, they want to be able to inspect.'

California gradually became Logitech's main production facility, although mice continued to be developed and built (in smaller quantities) in Switzerland. The 'H-P mouse', furthermore, was followed by other mice designed for AT&T and Olivetti. By the summer of 1985, Logitech had about 10 large OEM accounts. The manufacturing capacity installed to support them was about 300,000 pieces/year.

From OEMs to Retail

A couple of years after the OEM contract with H-P, which had turned Logitech into a manufacturing company, Logitech's founders decided to gamble on the retail market while pursuing other OEM customers. This effort was first launched in the US in early 1986 with the introduction of the *Logimouse C7*.

'However,' Zappacosta recalled, 'although the *C7* was an excellent product, probably the best available at that time, we had no retail presence. Also, using the traditional channels to access the retail market meant going through distributors, convincing them to take the product, and hoping they would do a good job in reaching dealers. It also meant that significant advertising support would have to come from Logitech, which we could hardly afford.'

In order to bypass the traditional channel for accessing the retail market for mice, advertisements for a $99 mouse were placed in trade publications like *PC Magazine* and *Byte*, together with coupons that people could send in to buy directly from the company. (***Exhibit 2** shows one of the early advertisements used.*)

With Microsoft, whose leading brand was selling at $179, this $99 price not only attracted great interest but turned Logitech into a pioneer in buying such products by mail order. Given the fact that production volume was still small, it was also a viable method.

The success of this direct selling effort later facilitated Logitech's entry into the retail market by the more traditional distributorship route. As more customers began to inquire about Logitech's products, dealers and then distributors were eager to carry them.

Exhibit 2

Taiwan – the Second Non-Swiss Site

Parallel to pursuing the retail market in the US, Logitech continued to search for other OEM customers as a means to grow the business.

Apple and IBM were the OEM accounts most sought after by the company. Both sourced from Alps, a large Japanese manufacturer of electronic components, which had also become the exclusive supplier to Microsoft.

The fact that it was much smaller and relatively inexperienced compared to Alps did not deter Logitech's managers. To acquire the Apple business, however, Logitech had to be able to produce at high volume and at a low cost, as well as offer a better-designed mouse.

Although still not sure about the Apple account, Logitech started to look for an additional manufacturing base and eventually selected Taiwan. With luck, and the help of a good lawyer, the company was accepted in the Science-based Industrial Park in Hsinchu for an affordable 'entrance fee' in 1986. 'It was rather like hang-gliding, you jump and you hope the wind will be there,' Borel described the prematureness of this investment. Then, Apple demanded terms that were more challenging than Logitech had expected. 'We took the business at a price we could not meet, but sometimes you have to force yourself to reach certain goals,' Zappacosta explained.

Cost had been influential in choosing Taiwan, but there were also other reasons for the choice – a well-developed supply base for parts, qualified people and a rapidly expanding local computer industry. In fact, direct labor accounted for only 7 per cent of the cost of Logitech's mouse.

Starting with a mere $200,000 investment, the Taiwanese factory soon surpassed Logitech's US facility as a manufacturing base. After the Apple contract, other OEM contracts also started being served from Taiwan, increasing the total capacity to 10 million pieces/year. Finally, in late 1988, the company also obtained an important contract with IBM, after offering a highly competitive price.

Europe and the Irish Site

At the time the Taiwanese factory was being built, in mid-1986, 75 per cent of Logitech's sales came from the US – mainly from OEM customers.

The company's first major breakthrough in Europe happened early on. Soon after winning an OEM contract with AT&T in the US, Logitech succeeded in gaining a similar contract with Olivetti in Europe in 1985, which was supplied by the Swiss facility. One reason Logitech won this contract was that it was already qualified as a supplier for AT&T, which had a recently made alliance with Olivetti at that time.

The European retail market took more time to develop. The problem had to do with the nature of the market and the way Logitech positioned itself. The US was one big market which could be reached through a handful of publications. There was also a well-developed home use market which, being price sensitive, was especially attracted by Logitech's low-price positioning.

'Europe,' according to Borel, 'was completely different, and we learned through a number of mistakes. The main market in Europe was corporate, which tended to be brand rather than price sensitive. It instinctively preferred to buy IBM and Microsoft. Users, moreover, were engineers and production people. Each country's market profile, use pattern, and distribution channels were also different.'

Realizing that the 'mail order' strategy was unsuitable in Europe, Logitech approached distributors. Compared to the US, where there was a trend towards no-fringe low-cost mass outlets, European distributors preferred high margins rather than market share. Logitech wanted them to price its mouse at SF 199 against Microsoft's SF 600, in order to repeat what it had done in the US. The distributors, however, insisted on a SF 300–350 price, which they felt was competitive enough. 'Unfortunately,' Borel recalled with some bitterness, 'the Taiwanese did to us what we had done to Microsoft in the US. They got in at a DM 99 price, catching us in a higher price position than we intended. In a few years we lost a lot of the market to them and, when we reacted strongly in 1988, it was rather late. Now, we are trying to regain the position we could have had all along.'

With a strong commitment to developing both the retail and OEM segments, Logitech started to look for a manufacturing site in Europe and opened its fourth manufacturing plant in Cork, Ireland, in the fall of 1988 – barely 18 months after starting up in Taiwan.

Locating in Ireland brought Logitech closer to its major European customers. Apple, for example, was located in Ireland as well, while Apollo, IBM and Compaq had their facilities nearby in Scotland. As Borel put it, 'We could not have developed OEMs like Apple Europe and IBM Europe, and we would have had a problem delivering to Olivetti; OEMs expected to receive delivery from inside Europe. Retail-wise, too, we wouldn't have been able to serve the market in French, Italian, German and Spanish without a European site.'

The choice of Ireland was influenced by a number of other factors. Apart from being an EEC member, it offered investment subsidies, low tax rates (10 per cent), a skilled and motivated labor force at a reasonable cost and, compared to Switzerland, no problem with work permits. When the Irish plant came on stream with a capacity of 1–1.5 million pieces/year – comparable to the US level at that time – all manufacturing in Switzerland ceased.

The Japanese and East Asian Market

The retail market in Japan and the Far East was even more difficult. For a long time, the Japanese market for PCs had been dominated by NEC, which supported its own input devices. There was no Japanese software running a mouse, and the PC market as a whole had taken longer to emerge. When Logitech entered the Japanese retail segment through a small distributor in 1988, it was soon in a stagnating situation.

In other countries, the main market was for OEM products. The retail segment was small and, especially in Hong Kong and Singapore, re-exports occurred frequently. While developing whatever retail potential there was, Logitech was worried that such re-exports might mean losing some control over its worldwide marketing policy.

The net result was that Logitech's market coverage began to trail somewhat behind its manufacturing base. While it fairly quickly established a global manufacturing infrastructure, most of its revenues came from the US. (*Exhibit 3 shows the growth the growth in Logitech's sales and its distribution by principal segment.*)

Exhibit 3   *(Source: Logitech SA)*

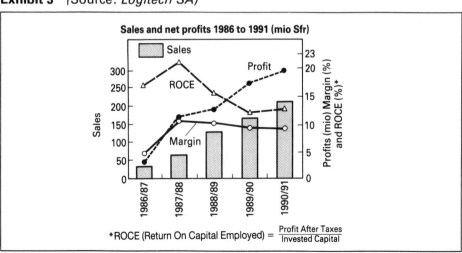

Exhibit 3 *Continued*

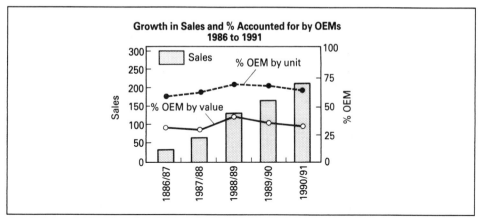

Growth in Sales and % Accounted for by OEMs
1986 to 1991

Managing Its Infrastructure

The international spread of Logitech's investments eventually raised the issue of assigning roles to the various sites and, within them, to each of the functions.

The Trend until 1987

Until 1987, when Switzerland, the US and Taiwan were the main sites, the trend was towards functional specialization. Switzerland, where Logitech's Chairman, Daniel Borel, resided, and from where most of the early financing was raised, naturally became the locus of the finance function. After successfully adapting and improving Professor Nicoud's *Series 5* mouse, the Swiss site also became the center for hardware development for mice. The fact that some manufacturing took place there as well facilitated design and prototyping in one location. Finally, given its location, Switzerland took on the responsibility for developing European sales.

California, where Logitech's software expertise had been located from the beginning, became the center for software development. Since the US was Logitech's principal market and Zappacosta was based there, this facility also took the lead in worldwide marketing coordination.

Taiwan, in addition to becoming the main manufacturing site, first took on some manufacturing engineering roles, then some mechanics development and procurement of certain components. The last two roles had to do with the local supply base.

The Evolving Network

The picture started to become more complex when the Irish plant came on stream in 1988 and each of the three 'regions' began to grow in size. Practical considerations and the way Logitech had become an international company started to make these units more and more self-contained.

In manufacturing, both the US and Ireland started to develop capabilities in engineering alongside Taiwan. To some extent, this was aided by the new CAD/CAE technologies that diminished the advantages of using Taiwan for prototyping and tooling.

It was natural that the marketing function should become the most regionalized, especially when the European market grew in importance. Rather than rely on product management and marketing support from the US, another group was created in Switzerland. Although not the initial intent, Taiwan too gradually started to assume some marketing responsibility for the Far East. It succeeded in introducing a Chinese version desktop publishing software package for its regional market and, more recently, had taken the lead in establishing a new venture in Shanghai to develop software for mainland China.

To support its marketing effort, the company decided to establish a number of regional and national sales companies over time, which were also grouped under the three regional centers.

R&D and Engineering – employing 170 people out of a workforce of 1,450 – also became dispersed. Roughly 80% of the R&D and Engineering resources were devoted to new retail products, the rest being allocated to supporting OEM product development. Four principal areas of expertise were covered – optics, electronics, mechanical engineering and software.

Inevitably, each site developed its own support and administrative functions too. Switzerland continued to act as the locus of the finance function – even more so, in fact, as Logitech went public there in June 1988. However, the three units – Europe, USA and Taiwan – each had their own finance function, and managed their own investment and performance control systems. They were also responsible for their own human resource management. *(Exhibit 4 shows the way the company's infrastructure evolved and Exhibit 5 the growth in headcount by function and region.)*

Costs and Benefits of the Infrastructure

While a network of 3–4 full-function units – plus a number of sales companies – did carry a cost penalty, Logitech also saw the advantages this situation provided.

Exhibit 4

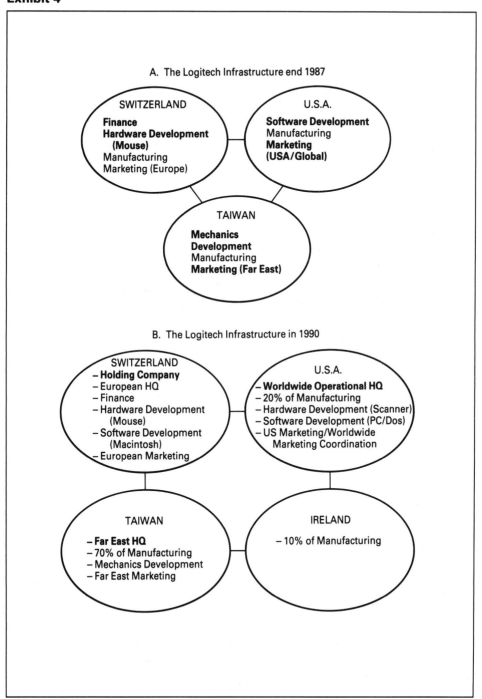

A. The Logitech Infrastructure end 1987

SWITZERLAND

Finance
Hardware Development
(Mouse)
Manufacturing
Marketing (Europe)

U.S.A.

Software Development
Manufacturing
Marketing
(USA/Global)

TAIWAN

Mechanics
Development
Manufacturing
Marketing (Far East)

B. The Logitech Infrastructure in 1990

SWITZERLAND
– **Holding Company**
– European HQ
– Finance
– Hardware Development
   (Mouse)
– Software Development
   (Macintosh)
– European Marketing

U.S.A.
– **Worldwide Operational HQ**
– 20% of Manufacturing
– Hardware Development (Scanner)
– Software Development (PC/Dos)
– US Marketing/Worldwide
   Marketing Coordination

TAIWAN
– **Far East HQ**
– 70% of Manufacturing
– Mechanics Development
– Far East Marketing

IRELAND
– 10% of Manufacturing

Exhibit 5   *(Source: Logitech SA)*

Growth in Headcount (Permanent and Temporary) by Location (March 31 of each year)

	1982	1983	1986	1988	1990	1991
Switzerland*	2	10	40	82	110**	123
USA*	5	20	87	228	378	456
Ireland					75	153
Taiwan*				141	400	712
Sales Offices	3	3		12	17	26
	10	33	127	463	980	1470

** Includes country sales offices
** Closed production in Switzerland, moved to Ireland

Logitech Companies
Headcount by Functional Area (for period ending 31/03/91)

Functional Area	Far East	N America	Europe	Total
	Perm	Perm	Perm	Perm
Administration	32	61	47	140
Sales	10	60	50	120
Marketing	4	47	29	80
R&D/Engineering	42	83	45	170
Manufacturing – Direct	487	126	80	693
– Indirect	58	30	23	111
– Staff	82	49	25	156
Total	715	456	299	1,470

Logitech International SA
Distribution of R & D and Engineering Personnel
by Location and Discipline (March 31, 1991)

Discipline	Europe	N. America	Far East	
1. Software	11	21	9	
2. Electronics Engineering	13	17	11	
3. Optics	1	1	0	
4. Mechanical Engineering	2	14	7	
5. Other (Mfg., Eng., QA, product				
management)	8	30	15	
Totals	45	83	42	170

All production facilities shared a common manufacturing process *(refer to **Exhibit 6a**)*. A typical line included 25 stations, was 25–40 meters long, and had a throughput time of about 20 minutes. Each line had a capacity of about 1,800 mice/day and could handle multiple models. Compared to the US and Ireland, where three lines were installed, Taiwan had 16 identical lines.

Exhibit 6a *Steps in the manufacturing process for mouse*

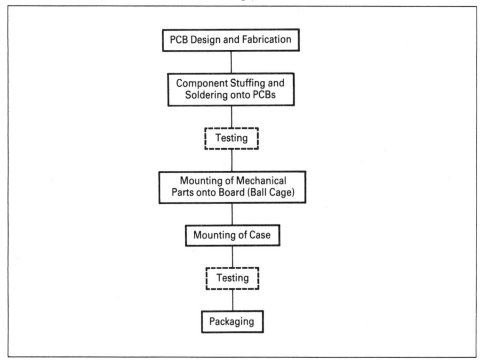

Borel summed up his assessment of the manufacturing function:

> The trick is to deliver fast, but without tying up your inventory with anything
> specific before it is necessary. It is really a trade-off between . . . 'What do I
> do if I get an order of 500 tomorrow morning that needs delivery within 24
> hours?' and 'How fast should I be ready?'. So the complexity is high in Ireland
> where one has to deliver in several languages. In the US, you have one mouse
> and one documentation language that is the same all over the US. There, you
> can prepare yourself, you can build inventory ahead of time – that is, in the
> summertime for the Christmas season. In Europe, you cannot do that to the
> same extent.

Sourcing from plants was initially on an *ad hoc* basis. Gradually, the
criterion when selecting sites for sourcing became total acquisition costs –
not just the cost of the product but the cost of shipping, duties and flexibility,
i.e., the ability to deal with changes in customer orders. If Ireland or the US
could manufacture at Taiwan's cost plus roughly 10%, then the company
would prefer to manufacture for local markets.

Being present in three regions had a procurement advantage, too. Since the material content in the mouse represented around 70% of the cost, procurement was always an important function at Logitech. With the bulk of the components being sourced in the Far East *(refer to Exhibit 6b)*, the Taiwanese factory had a key role in qualifying and dealing with suppliers for the entire group. Each facility was, however, free to do its own sourcing.

In marketing, too, there were certain benefits. For example, no one was exactly sure about Logitech's 'nationality'. In fact, a Taiwanese journalist once asked the General Manager of Logitech-Ireland why a Taiwanese company had chosen to locate in Ireland as a way to penetrate the European market!

It was this 'localness' that also helped the Taiwanese unit win an OEM contract with IBM Asia. Y.S. Fu, the Head of Logitech Taiwan, and Jim Ho, one of Fu's colleagues, found someone in IBM's Taipei International Procurement Office (IPO) they knew and, after doing some design work together, got the Taiwanese unit of Logitech approved as a worldwide supplier for IBM's PS/2 and PS/1 personal computer models – a very satisfying achievement for them.

Exhibit 6b *Logitech International SA: material procurement for mouse products*

Major commodities[1]	Procured from			
	Taiwan	Japan	USA/SA	Europe
Plastic raw material	X	X	X	X
Plastic injection	X		X	X
Diecasting and machining	X		X	X
Stamping	X			
Cable/connectors	X			
PCB (under 6 layers)	X			
Passive components	X			
Semiconductors	X	X	X	X
% Distribution by area[2]	69%	13%	11%	7%

1. Representing 75% of total material inputs for mice.
2. By value. The 69% procured in Taiwan represents 60% from Taiwan itself and 9% from the rest of the Far East excluding Japan.

The Worldwide Mouse Market

From a slow start in 1982, the worldwide market for mice expanded rapidly to reach approximately $500 million by 1990.

The mouse itself was a fairly standard product. As Zappacosta described it, 'We believe strongly that most of the world has similar requirements. Certainly in our market – computers – it's hard to imagine why a European user should need a mouse that is different. In fact, the reason we stopped using a power supply was that it was one element we had to adapt for Europe, Asia and the US. We wanted one product.'

Even so, there were a number of ways to segment the mouse market: by product, channels, buyer groups and even by geography.

Product

In terms of positioning, mice could be roughly placed in three categories – upper-end, middle and low-end products. In 1991, the manufacturers' list prices ranged from around $100 for upper-end products to $6–10 for the cheapest, with corresponding retail prices anywhere from 20–100% higher. Microsoft was well established as the 'leading brand', commanding a premium price at the retail level, partly because of the parent company's reputation and the perception 'that the safest way to run Microsoft software is by using a Microsoft mouse'. MSC, which dominated the optical mouse business, had long been considered the 'Rolls-Royce' of the industry. It gained this reputation in part because of being the major supplier to workstation manufacturers such as SUN Microsystem and Silicon Graphics. Over time, however, MSC had become a marginal player in the industry overall and was bought by KYE in 1990.

Logitech, which entered in the middle, gradually covered the entire range. In 1988 it launched a low-end product under a new brand name called *Dexxa* whose retail price was in the $18–30 range. This competed against KYE's *Genius* brand and against several other Far East Asian manufacturer's products. Later, in order to compete directly with Microsoft and MSC, Logitech launched the *Series 9* in January 1989, followed by the *Mouseman* (corded and cordless) models. At this time, Logitech also introduced its *Logimouse Pilot* (known as *First Mouse* in the US) for first-time users, to strengthen its position in the low to middle end of the product spectrum. *(**Exhibit 7a** summarizes Logitech's product introductions; **Exhibit 7b** illustrates positioning changes of various companies over time both in the US and Europe; **Exhibit 7c** pictures some of Logitech's major products.)*

Channels and Buyer Groups

The two main channels for distributing mice were OEMs and retail. There

Exhibit 7a   *Logitech International SA: history of product introductions*

Products	1982/83	1984	1985	1986	1987	1988	1989	1990	1991
1. Mouse									
a) Upper-end							Series 9	MouseMan	MouseMan Cordless
							TrackMan Trackball		Trackman Portable
b) Middle	Series 5		Series 7		High Res. Mouse			Logimouse Pilot	
c) Low-end						Dexxa-I		Dexxa-II	Dexxa-III
2. Software									
a) Development tools	Modula 2 Compiler	Modula 2 Cross Dev. System		: Modula 2 Windowing : Modula 2 Translator		Modula 2 os/2			
b) Applications				: Logi Cadd : Logi Paint	Paintshow		Finesse	Catchword	
3. Other Products for 'Computer Cockpit'						Scan Man Optical scanner		ScanMan 256	ScanMan 32

Exhibit 7b   *Competitive positioning in the retail mouse market*

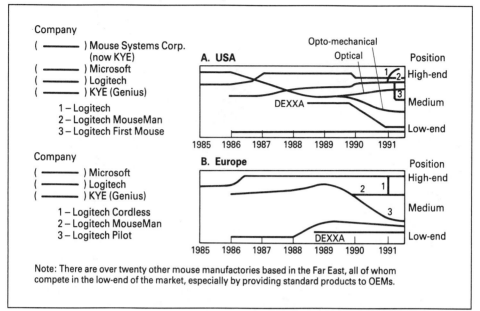

Note: There are over twenty other mouse manufactories based in the Far East, all of whom compete in the low-end of the market, especially by providing standard products to OEMs.

were two main sub-segments within the OEM group – customized and non-customized. In the former, the mouse was either jointly developed by a mouse manufacturer and an OEM – for example, the Logitech/Apple project for the latter's high-end product – or was fully specified by the OEM, with a mouse company acting mainly in a subcontracted manufacturing role. In the non-customized segment, the mouse was typically designed and built by a mouse company and supplied off-the-shelf to OEMs. Logitech was mainly active in high-end products for both customized and non-customized versions, especially the former *(as shown in **Exhibit 8a**)*.

Both in the US and in Europe, there were four main sub-segments within the retail market – home, education, corporate and small business. *(**Exhibit 8b** summarizes the main characteristics of these four sub-segments in Europe.)* The US profile was comparable, with an additional 'government' sub-segment that had its own buying process and criteria. Logitech served all of these retail segments.

Geography

The behavior of each of these segments in the retail market varied somewhat

Exhibit 7c

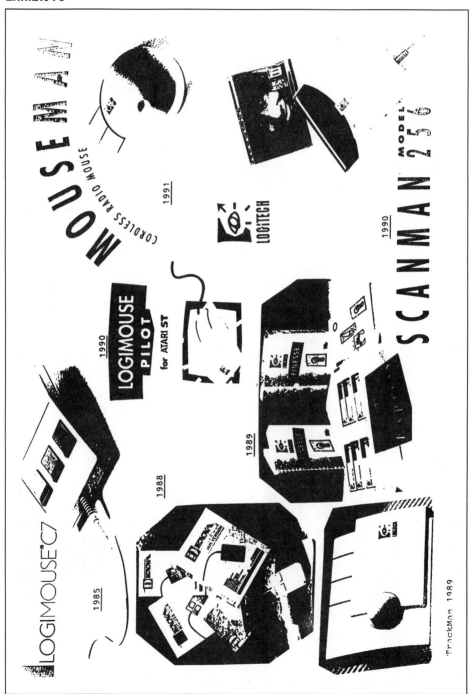

Exhibit 8a   *Logitech International SA: Sub-segments within the OEM market*

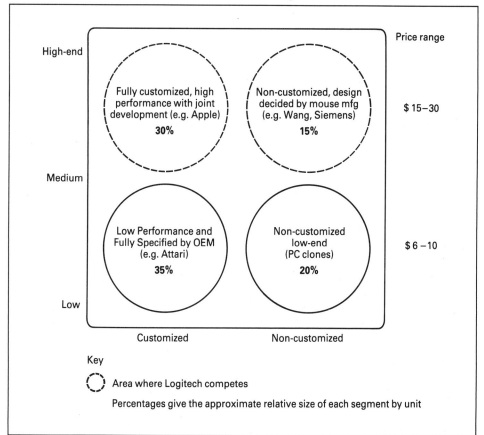

from country to country. There were, moreover, some distinct differences between the US and Europe. The US was a large market, with a few nationwide distributors (such as Softsell and Ingram), and retail chains (such as Egghead Software and Businessland) that had a close relationship to suppliers. The European market was more fragmented, although the UK was starting to approach the US in some regards. The relationship between manufacturers and distributors/retailers was also weaker; whereas, for instance, service tended to be the manufacturer's responsibility in the US, European retailers considered service to be a value-added feature which justified asking a higher price.

The retail or 'street' price differences between the US and Europe reflected these market characteristics. While the street price was 20–60%

Exhibit 8b *Profile of the major sub-segments in the European retail market*

Profile	Home	Education	Corporate	Business
1. *Personal Computers* % of total market	23	10	33	33
By Type IBM PC Compatible	48	80	94	89
Apple Non-		11	6	6
Compatible	52	9		5
Distribution	– Consumer Electronics – Computer Stores – Dept Stores – Specialized 'School' Dealers	– Direct from Manufacturer – Specialized Dealers	– Specialized Dealers – VARs	– Computer Stores – VARs – Catalogue
2. *Mice* Who	– Adults (20–55) for education/ business and entertainment – Children	– Teachers (25–55) – Educational purchasing units	Central purchasing unit (MIS)	Individual users (25–55)
Values	– prices (1) – ease use/ install (2) – aesthetics (3) nat'l versions (4) – SW bundle (5) – accessories (6) – quality (7)	– price (1) – quality (2) – nat'l versions (3) – compatibility (4) – support (5)	– compatibility (1) – ease use/install (2) – quality (3) – price (4) – support (5) – aesthetics (6)	
Channel	Retail: CE, Dept, computer stores	Specialized dealers	Specialized dealers	Store front, catalogues, VARs, computer stores
Platform	52% non compatibles	PC & Apple	IBM compatibles	IBM compatibles

higher than the distributor's list price in the US, it was 50–100% higher in Europe depending on the country and channel.

Logitech and its Competitors

In the OEM segment, Logitech's main worldwide competitor was Alps of Japan, a $3 billion company that was Microsoft's exclusive supplier. It had recently announced a collaboration with Lunar Design of Palo Alto, California, to design new 2- and 3-button mice to sell to OEMs, and was targeting Thailand and Malaysia as sites for new production facilities. In 1990, Logitech had 35% of the OEM market compared to Alps' 43%. Mitsumi, the other major player, had a share of approximately 10%. An all-round electronic parts maker, Mistumi was a leading manufacturer of OEM keyboards sold to makers of portable computers. It too was opening new plants in the Philippines, Thailand and in Mallow, Ireland. Two or three other companies accounted for the remainder of this segment, including KYE/MSC.

The leader in the retail segment was Microsoft, with a 39% share; Logitech was next with a 27% share, followed by KYE with 23% *(refer to Exhibit 9)*. In Europe, control of the retail segment varied from one country to another. Logitech was clearly the dominant player in Switzerland; in France, Microsoft was in the lead; in Germany, while Microsoft held the 'corporate' market, several Taiwanese companies had established a strong position in the 'home' market; in the UK, Amstrad sold its low-end microcomputers with its own mouse sourced on an OEM basis. Overall, however, KYE had the largest market share in terms of units (28%) followed by Microsoft (23%), Logitech (20%) and IBM (9%). The remainder was accounted for by some 20 other companies.

Except for KYE/MSC Logitech was the only company competing in both the OEM and retail segments. It made over 20 different mice models in a variety of configurations.

In addition to offering technically superior and customized products, Logitech also emphasized the service dimension in its business. Service was defined differently for the OEM and retail segments. For the OEM market, service meant designing to customer specifications, having one person from Logitech deal with a particular OEM account on a dedicated basis, and meeting delivery targets in a flexible manner. In the retail market, service included a 30-day money back guarantee and access to a technical support group.

In contrast, Microsoft was successful with just one shape and colour at the upper end. It also continued to source its products outside, mainly from Alps. The several Taiwanese and Far East Asian companies did their own manufacturing but competed with standard products too at the low end. Although active in Europe they did not manufacture there. Most had one product, one manual with different languages and one box.

In response, Borel stated, 'We too could manufacture everything in Taiwan and sell in Europe. But then, Logitech would have the complexity of a bigger Taiwan, a longer lead time and a greater overhead. It is easier to manage two companies with 500 people each than one company with 1,000.'

Exhibit 9 *Worldwide market shares in the mouse business (by units)* (Source: *Logitech SA*)

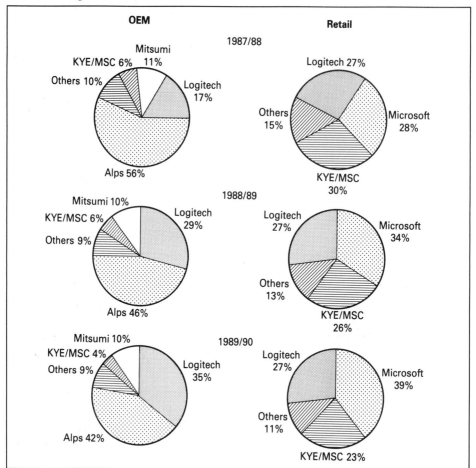

Logitech: Organization

The people who founded Logitech in 1981 really had two aims – to participate in the fast-growing personal computer industry by providing software and hardware products; and to create an organization that would span the world imbued with their own sense of excitement, aggressive opportunity seeking, and flexibility. The word 'flexible', in fact, pervaded every aspect of the company. Words such as 'flat structure', 'open-door policy', 'team work', 'employee participation', 'networks of small groups' became the building blocks of the organization.

Among the founders, Giacomo Marini was the only person who had previously worked for large international companies (IBM and Olivetti). Being the Chief Operating Officer, he felt the need for a more formal structure and had been instrumental in designing whatever structure the company did have in 1989/90. Neither Borel nor Zappacosta felt any urgency in this regard. 'Zappacosta is our visionary, our long-term thinker who wants to make sure the business is on the right track,' Borel explained. In turn, one of his colleagues described Borel with a different compliment: 'Borel is for action yesterday, he is a doer.'

Between 1984 and 1988, Logitech's managers were far too busy working on many different projects; there was no time to think about a formal structure. Business was booming and, after the Taiwan facility was underway, there was the Irish factory to set up. Being practical, the three founders just assigned themselves different roles and got the job done. With his interest in sales and manufacturing, Borel assumed the role of Vice President of Manufacturing for the entire Group in 1986. *(Refer to **Exhibit 10** for the organization chart of the US company in 1986.)* Marini, who became interested in R&D and materials, took charge of operations while Zappacosta concentrated on marketing. Together, they started to coordinate all the functions of the Group and shared responsibility for business development. The culture, organizational processes and policies they had established made a more formal structure at all levels seem unnecessary during that time period.

During this time, the structure could best be described as 'confederal'. As Hank Morgan, who joined Logitech in 1989 from Wyse Technology, put it, 'There was nobody clearly in charge. You had a number of different people who shared the power. And the roles evolved. The people running the US organization did not feel they should tell Switzerland what to do, even though they were collectively the principal shareholders. The hierarchy was very, very fuzzy.'

The Structure in 1990

In order to cope with the larger and more complex infrastructure that evolved, Logitech made some organizational changes in April 1990. The main purpose was to bring together the geographic units and the functions of the company on a more global basis than previously. On April 26, 1990, an internal memorandum from Daniel Borel announcing these changes stated:

Exhibit 10 *Logitech Inc. (USA): organization structure (summer 1986)*

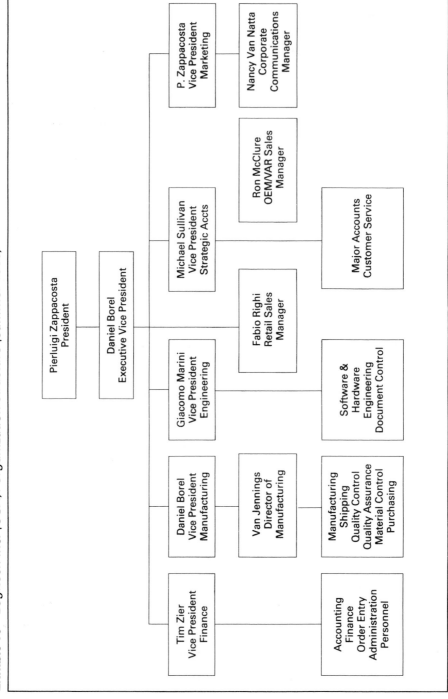

The success, the growth and the maturity of the Logitech Group worldwide requires a new, more cohesive international management structure. We believe that the new organization structure will allow [us] to best compete in the worldwide market [by] making the most of being a truly internationally minded company. This structure will allow us to think globally and act locally. It will give us the flexibility to adapt to change and market evolution. It will support entrepreneurial spirit, creativity and technological innovation, which are key for our long-term success.

One feature of the new organization was the creation of an 'Office of the President'. Although the three founders had performed this role informally, the new structure formalized its existence and clarified reporting relationships at the Group level. A small corporate staff team was also created to assist this 'Office' in planning, control and communication activities.

With Daniel Borel as Chairman, taking care of special projects and acting as Group coordinator, the Office of the President consisted of Zappacosta, President and CEO of the Group, and Marini, Executive Vice President and Chief Operating Officer. All geographical areas and worldwide functions would report to this 'Office', with direct reporting to Marini. Moreover, this 'Office', in addition to Group level management responsibility, had direct management responsibility for the US site and its corresponding geographic area. (*Exhibit 11a provides an organization chart of the new structure.*)

In terms of their respective roles, Zappacosta would concentrate on the activities of setting directions, making the synthesis of strategies, identifying and setting corporate goals'. Marini would 'concentrate on translating corporate directions and goals into operating plans, initiating and controlling their execution, and exercising the day-to-day management process with the operating managers'. To symbolize their joint role, Zappacosta and Marini moved their offices (in the US) next to each other, whereas previously they had been at opposite ends of the building.

To assist and complement the Chairman and the Office of the President in top level management activities of the Group, the Executive Management Committee (formed in 1989) was expanded in April 1990 to include – apart from the three founders – Morgan (Chief Operating Officer, Europe), Fu (Senior Vice President & General Manager, Far East), and Mazzone (Vice President Strategic Marketing for the Group, but based in Europe).

The main organizational units, however, continued to be the areas. Logitech retained its traditional policy of giving local management at each site full profit and loss responsibility.

For cohesiveness at a global level, some executives were, however,

Exhibit 11a *Logitech International: organization structure (April 1990)*

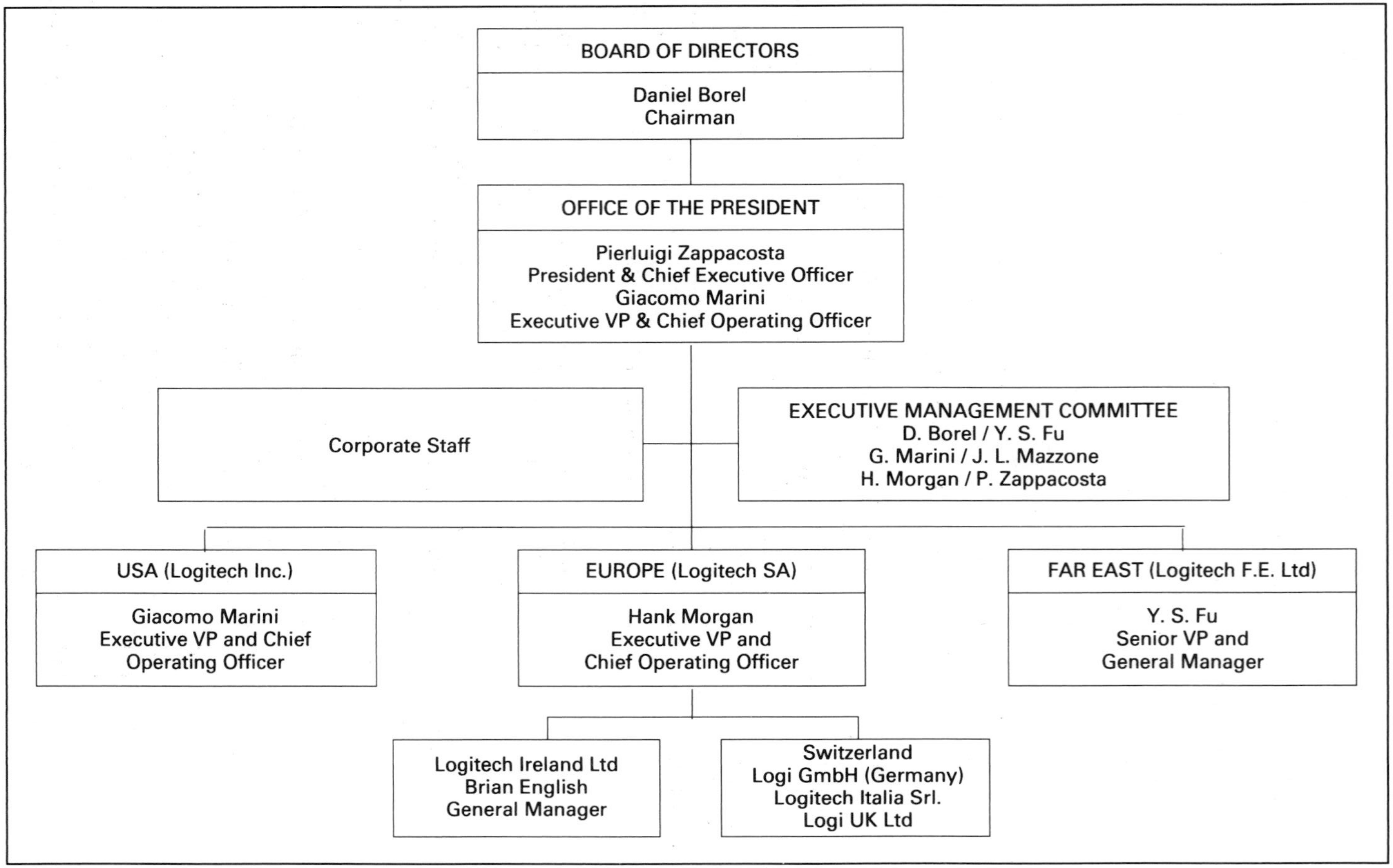

BOARD OF DIRECTORS

Daniel Borel
Chairman

OFFICE OF THE PRESIDENT

Pierluigi Zappacosta
President & Chief Executive Officer
Giacomo Marini
Executive VP & Chief Operating Officer

EXECUTIVE MANAGEMENT COMMITTEE
D. Borel / Y. S. Fu
G. Marini / J. L. Mazzone
H. Morgan / P. Zappacosta

Corporate Staff

USA (Logitech Inc.)

Giacomo Marini
Executive VP and Chief
Operating Officer

EUROPE (Logitech SA)

Hank Morgan
Executive VP and
Chief Operating Officer

FAR EAST (Logitech F.E. Ltd)

Y. S. Fu
Senior VP and
General Manager

Logitech Ireland Ltd
Brian English
General Manager

Switzerland
Logi GmbH (Germany)
Logitech Italia Srl.
Logi UK Ltd

given worldwide mandates for certain functions. The worldwide functional manager was not really expected to direct operations; rather, he would coordinate and provide team leadership for the particular function, working closely with site managers responsible for their function at the local level. The latter had a dotted line reporting to the worldwide functional manager and direct reporting to the site chief executive or general manager. In most cases, the worldwide functional manager resided in the US, but this was not a requirement.

Functional managers with worldwide responsibility and their locations were: Morgan (Finance and Administration, Switzerland); D'Ettore (Human Resources, USA); Righi (Sales, USA); Van Natta (Corporate Communications, USA); Mills (Quality, USA); Marini (Engineering, USA); and Zappacosta (Marketing, USA). Both Marini and Zappacosta were 'acting' heads of their functions, until someone else was appointed.[1] *(**Exhibit 11b** shows the allocation of worldwide functional responsibility and **Exhibit 11c** the structure of the US company.)*

Logitech's Values and Culture

'We work in one place, the globe.' This simple phrase stated the business spirit and the cosmopolitan attitude at Logitech – the basis of its founders' beliefs from the beginning. The composition of the Executive Management Committee – Borel (Swiss), Fu (Chinese), Marini (Italian), Mazzone (Swiss), Morgan (American), and Zappacosta (Italian) – not only tangibly expressed the company's philosophy, but guaranteed that different geographic and cultural perspectives would inevitably be advocated within Logitech.

Coupled with its cosmopolitan make-up, Logitech's management reflected youthfulness, daring and a spirit of adventure, a combination frequently found in high-tech start-ups with excellent results. At Logitech in 1991, the emphasis was on small groups that met 'horizontally' for particular issues and projects; direct contact between senior management and employees was promoted; employees were urged to be more involved in running Logitech; and, the one thing to be abhorred was formal policies. As the head of administration, Bavaud stated, 'We don't want a police state at Logitech.'

Logitech's basic values consisted of a belief in people, trust, caring for the feelings of others and the ability of everyone to do what is right. The metaphor often used to describe the organization was 'a family that has bridged national differences'.

Exhibit 11b *Logitech International: Group level functions (April 1990)*

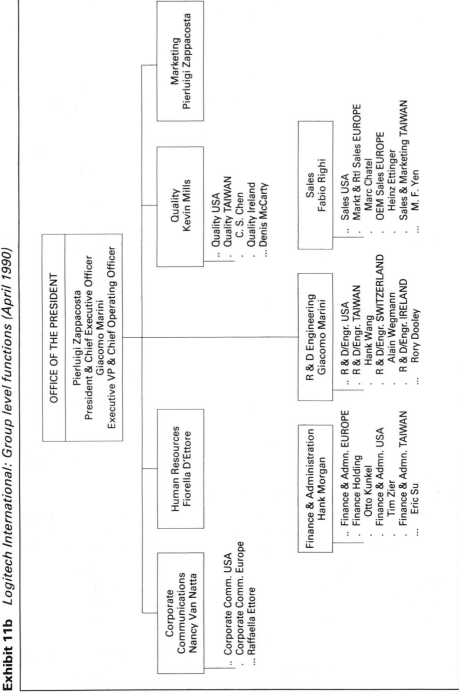

Exhibit 11c *Logitech Inc. (USA): Corporate headquarters organization structure (April 1990)*

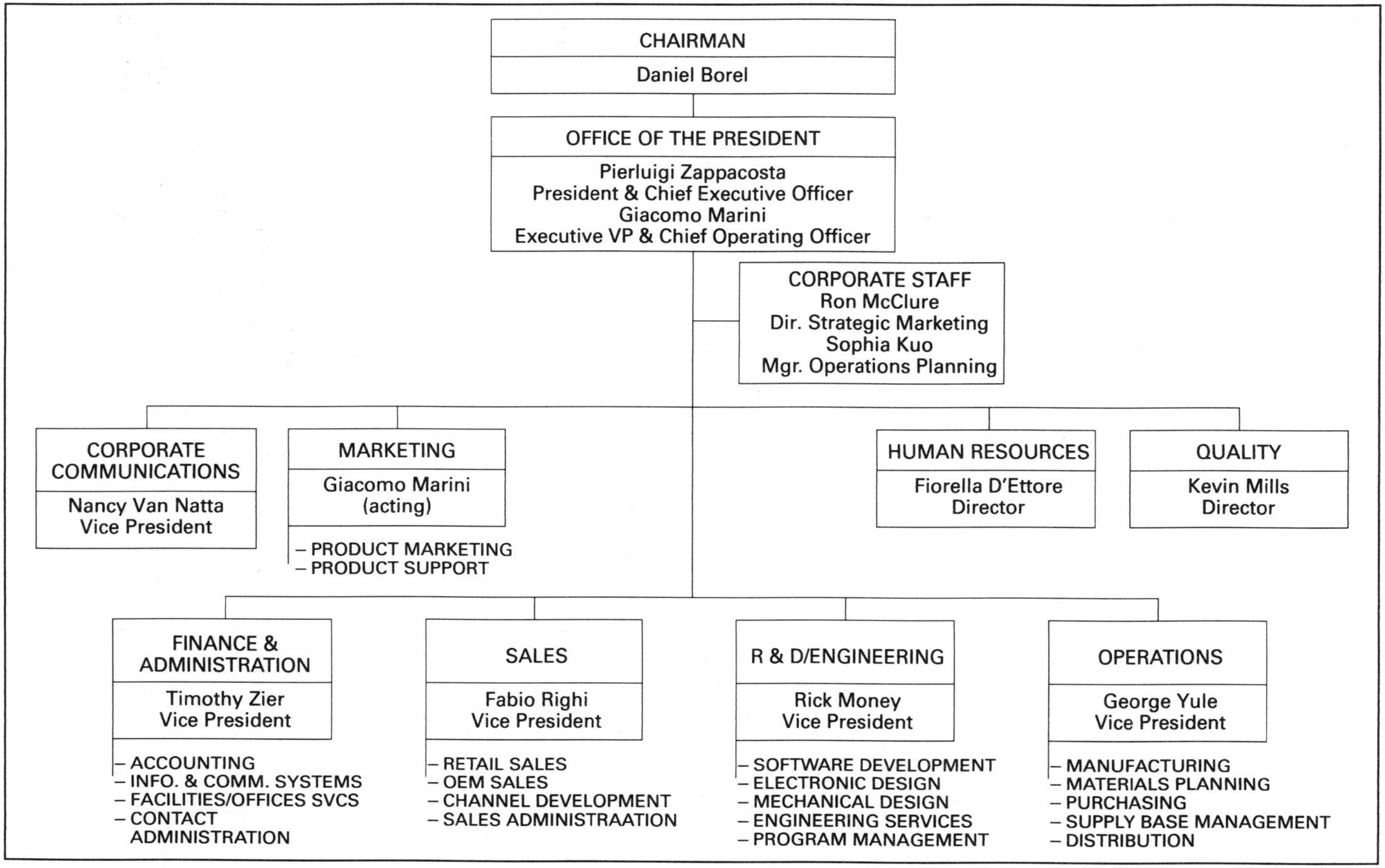

CHAIRMAN
Daniel Borel

OFFICE OF THE PRESIDENT
Pierluigi Zappacosta
President & Chief Executive Officer
Giacomo Marini
Executive VP & Chief Operating Officer

CORPORATE STAFF
Ron McClure
Dir. Strategic Marketing
Sophia Kuo
Mgr. Operations Planning

QUALITY
Kevin Mills
Director

HUMAN RESOURCES
Fiorella D'Ettore
Director

OPERATIONS
George Yule
Vice President
– MANUFACTURING
– MATERIALS PLANNING
– PURCHASING
– SUPPLY BASE MANAGEMENT
– DISTRIBUTION

R & D/ENGINEERING
Rick Money
Vice President
– SOFTWARE DEVELOPMENT
– ELECTRONIC DESIGN
– MECHANICAL DESIGN
– ENGINEERING SERVICES
– PROGRAM MANAGEMENT

SALES
Fabio Righi
Vice President
– RETAIL SALES
– OEM SALES
– CHANNEL DEVELOPMENT
– SALES ADMINISTRAATION

MARKETING
Giacomo Marini
(acting)
– PRODUCT MARKETING
– PRODUCT SUPPORT

CORPORATE COMMUNICATIONS
Nancy Van Natta
Vice President

FINANCE & ADMINISTRATION
Timothy Zier
Vice President
– ACCOUNTING
– INFO. & COMM. SYSTEMS
– FACILITIES/OFFICES SVCS
– CONTACT
ADMINISTRATION

Organizational Processes

Despite giving freedom to individuals and groups to pursue their tasks in a creative and responsible manner, no effort was spared to establish links throughout the company.

Communication was one of the important tools used. The electronic mail system, installed in 1982 the same day that Logitech had two locations, was continuously expanded. As Morgan put it, 'We send and receive messages or copies of messages from all over the world every day. So we tend to know very quickly what is going on.' *Logi News*, an internal newsletter, and formal meetings were other ways of keeping people involved.

Setting overall direction took place at two levels – the Executive Committee and the functions. The Executive Committee met every two months, with the discussions going on for a long time, sometimes over two days. A lot of things would be talked about. Decisions were not always made, but direction nevertheless evolved at these meetings. The decisions that were taken then were communicated and discussed throughout the organization via monthly company meetings at each site.

At the operational level, functional heads from each site met approximately once a year in order to coordinate policies and practices worldwide. Depending on the function, there would be frequent telephone and electronic mail exchanges as well.

In addition to these functional meetings and exchanges, a number of cross-functional, inter-site teams were created. The main ones were *project teams* built around the introduction of new products, taking projects from initial development to mass production. *(Exhibit 12 reproduces the membership of a recently constituted project led by the US organization.)* In 1991, there were some 20 *project teams* with about half led by the US and the remainder by other sites. Marini had coordinated the work done by these teams in the past, but they became the responsibility of the head of engineering, Rick Money, with the organizational restructuring.

The other main area where multi-functional, multi-site teams were used was in *product management*. These teams worked to launch new products on the market which also included making competitor assessments, preparing translations and manuals, and designing and placing advertisements. In 1991 *product management* teams were being coordinated by Fabio Righi, Vice President, Sales and Marketing.

Exhibit 12   *Logitech International SA: composition of a recent project team for developing and manufacturing a new product (number of individuals from each function in parentheses if more than one)*

---

1. *USA*
Product Marketing (3)
Mechanical Engineering (2)
Cost & Reliability Engineering (3)

Electrical Engineering
Software Engineering
Product QA
Technical Publications (3)

Technical Support
Supply Base Management
Quality Assurance
Materials Planning
Production Engineer
Test Engineer

2. *Logitech Switzerland*
Product Marketing
Product Management
Project Planning

3. *Logitech Taiwan*
Product Engineering
Project Planning

4. *Logitech Ireland*
Product Engineering
Project Planning

Policies

Prior to June 1988, when Logitech went public, there were occasional attempts to consolidate the worldwide operations, but they resembled 'exercises' to ascertain what the total entity might look like. A worldwide budget was, in fact, put together for the first time in 1988, enabling Logitech finally to compare 'actual' with 'budgeted'.

It was seldom exactly clear where Logitech's HQ was located although the US unit gradually started to assume that role. This, according to Marini, resulted from the fact that the Silicon Valley played an important role as a lead market, as well as providing Logitech with credibility. The managers anyhow believed that 'headquarters' should provide a 'service' rather than a 'control' function, and should not have the power that most companies normally gave to headquarters.

Each site also had its own policies with no formal 'central' coordination. One policy area shared by all the company's locations was human resource management. Although acknowledging local practices and legal requirements, Logitech tended to hire people who would fit into its culture. Potential employees were expected to be flexible, internationally minded and good team workers. Due to this careful selection process, Logitech had a very low turnover rate, a particularly remarkable achievement given its location in the Silicon Valley.

The company also encouraged transfers between sites. It hoped, thereby, to increase inter-cultural awareness within the company, decrease friction between sites and increase employee identification with Logitech International, rather than with a particular unit.

Challenges for the 1990s

The overall market for pointing devices, especially mice, was continuing to grow rapidly. Even so, just as with many other new 'high-tech' industries, fast growth and a rapid rate of new product introduction could not prevent the mouse from becoming a 'commodity'.

Recognizing the dangers of being a 'single product' company Logitech had already begun to broaden its offerings. In addition to maintaining its software business and introducing new products based on *Modula-2* and desktop publishing applications it successfully introduced a hand-held optical scanner in 1988. The latter was first bought from Omron, a Japanese company, on an OEM basis. In order to differentiate and add value to this product, Logitech developed its own interface protocols. Later, as the product gained acceptance, it worked on improving and manufacturing it in-house. By 1990, the company was gaining 75 per cent of its total revenue from mice, 15 per cent from the scanner and 10 per cent from various software products.

The natural question was whether the approach taken until 1990 was sufficient to sustain profitable growth for the company in future. Apart from deciding on the nature of the business, the company needed to reassess its international infrastructure. On the latter, Borel remarked, 'Being international can sometimes be a liability. The goal is to turn it into an asset. But, the ones who will never make it an asset had better stop right away!'

As for the debate on organization, while some managers were satisfied with the structure announced in April 1990, others wanted to see greater clarity in the reporting relationships. Who, for example, should functional heads really report to, especially when they carried global responsibilities for their function? They would also like to see more effective team *processes* without, however, creating a bureaucratic organization. The engineering function had already set up a 7-man 'Engineering Services Group' to oversee quality assurance, alpha and beta testing, cost and reliability, and documentation control. Working in matrix, their role was to make sure the 50 or so project teams worked according to adequate standards, especially since that was what OEMs wanted. Similarly, Marini had previously coordinated procurement and operations through inter-site teams, but the company then in 1991 decided to create two new posts – Director for Strategic Procurement and Operations Planning Manager. *(Exhibit 13 summarizes their job descriptions.)*

Exhibit 13   *Logitech Inc.*

> ### Job Descriptions for New Appointments in Operations
>
> #### Director, Strategic Procurement
>
> As Strategic Procurement Director, you will work closely with the Chief Operating Officer in the formulation and implementation of procurement strategies for LOGITECH manufacturing worldwide. Your major responsibilities will include; manufacturing,communicating and maintaining the international procurement policies, working with a global team to implement strategies, providing directives and recommendations to the worldwide procurement groups, identifying areas where multiple sources will be needed, defining strategic commodities and project needs, maintaining a database of strategic commodities, vendors and relevant data, and preparing reports and analyses.
>
> #### Operations Planning Manager
>
> Reporting directly to the C.O.O., you will be involved in the formulation and implementation of worldwide operations planning and strategy for new products, manufacturing and distribution. Your job responsibilities will include: developing global manufacturing strategies, allocating manufacturing tasks to worldwide facilities, establishing performance measurements and monitoring the results, analyzing worldwide shipments and forecasts, reviewing operation reports, and preparing site reviews.

Regarding the *project* and *product management* teams, there were two issues: how to make them smaller and less cumbersome; and how to maintain accountability and responsibility at the functional manager level for the tasks being accomplished.

Some people at Logitech felt undisguised nostalgia for the informal networking character of the company's earlier organization. With all the information technology at Logitech's command, they asked: 'Why not simply continue as a modern distributed network structure, especially since so many management experts write about its virtues?' Even Borel admitted, 'Why can't we operate as fast as we did when we were 20 employees?'

A more general issue was how to preserve Logitech's ability to act as a global company. Although the three founders were the main locus for a global view, they also realized that the company had become too large and complex for them to play this role exclusively. If changing Logitech's organization structure could be a way to meet this challenge, what sort of configuration would be most appropriate?

If Logitech stayed with its present *area* organization – with separate structures for Europe, the Far East and the US – it would still be able to focus on different segments (e.g., Taiwan could handle all OEM business), but would lose important synergies in product development and production planning. How, moreover, would business functions be governed and on what basis would competitors be identified?

Another option was to organize by *product technology* – mice and trackman (both sharing pointing device technology), scanning devices, application software, etc. Alternatively, it could organize along *product/ market segments*, such as pointing devices and application software for scanning devices. The latter approach would, at least, maintain the link between hardware and software which groupings along '*products*' might lose.

Making a choice was not expected to be easy. As Y.S. Fu, the General Manager of Logitech Taiwan, explained, 'We try to be locally present, this is both our strategy and our strength; we deal with local customers as local people; when IBM's Taiwanese International Procurement Office (IPO) talk to us, they feel they are talking to an independent company; we can make all the decisions, provide all the support; we don't have limitations from Switzerland or the USA which is different from other foreign companies.' A counter argument was found, however, in Borel's example of the way the company worked: 'When Logitech Europe launched its Pilot Mouse (for first-time users) in order to combat the Taiwanese, the US did not think an introduction was warranted in that region since there was already a strong presence at the low end. Eventually, the product was introduced at a later date.'

Exhibit 14 *Logitech International SA: selected consolidated financial data*

(In '000 – except *) Full Year ending	Swiss Fr. 3/31/89	Swiss Fr. 3/31/90	Swiss Fr. 3/31/91	US $ 3/31/91
Consolidated Revenues	124,111	179,786	205,871	154,907
Net Income after tax	11,207	14,161	16,872	12,695
% of Revenues	9.03%	7.88%	8.20%	8.20%
Cash Flow	14,290	17,450	23,287	17,095
% of Revenues	11.51%	9.71%	11.31%	11.04%
Earnings per Bearer Share*	76	96	114	86.07
Dividend per Bearer Share*	12	16	20	13.71
Engineering, Research & Development				
Expenses	8,397	13,710	17,999	13,543
% of Revenues	6.77%	7.63%	8.74%	8.74%
Number of personnel*	731	980	1,470	1,470
	3/31/89	3/31/90	3/31/91	3/31/91
Current Assets	75,527	107,859	128,782	88,343
Property, Plant & Equipment Gross	22,422	30,571	51,287	35,182
less Accumulated Depreciation	(5,223)	(8,511)	(14,926)	(10,239)
Property, Plant & Equipment Net	17,199	22,060	36,361	24,943
Other Non-Current Assets	1,184	3,926	5,599	3,841
Goodwill	13,094	11,193	9,294	6,376
Total Assets	*107,004*	*145,038*	*180,036*	*123,503*
Current Liabilities	36,776	32,212	54,217	37,192
Long Term Debt & Deferred Taxes	10,541	43,489	46,109	31,631
Stockholders' Equity	59,687	69,337	79,710	54,680
Total Liabilities & Stockholders' Equity	*107,004*	*145,038*	*180,036*	*123,503*

Attention also needed to be focused on some *functions*. One such area was procurement. Compared to the current practice of letting each site procure on its own behalf, the idea was to centralize purchasing in order to gain better overall terms for Logitech. By creating several International Procurement Offices (IPOs) – like at IBM, where staff would be paid a commission on what they could source locally, the hope was to diminish the present dependence on the Far East for components. This would also introduce some competition in the procurement function itself. What would the effect of these IPOs be on Logitech's structure? 'You have an IPO in Taiwan – does he report to the local manufacturing site or does he report to a worldwide sourcing organization?' Borel asked.

Finally, another question relating to organizational dimension was whether, and to what extent, the company should begin to set up divisions. Its initial software engineering business had been spun off into a new company – MULTISCOPE, Inc., but so far, Logitech had gone no further toward creating *divisions*.

Note

1.   Recently, a Vice President for Engineering, Rick Money, was appointed to this position, and Fabio Righi took on the marketing role as Vice President, Sales and Marketing.